FLANNERY O'CONNOR AND ROBERT GIROUX

Flannery O'Connor

and

Robert Giroux

A Publishing Partnership

PATRICK SAMWAY, S.J.

University of Notre Dame Press
Notre Dame, Indiana

University of Notre Dame Press
Notre Dame, Indiana 46556
undpress.nd.edu

Library of Congress Cataloging-in-Publication Data

Names: Samway, Patrick H., author.
Title: Flannery O'Connor and Robert Giroux :
a publishing partnership / Patrick Samway, S.J.
Description: Notre Dame, Indiana : University of Notre Dame Press, [2018] |
Includes bibliographical references and index. |
Identifiers: LCCN 2018008582 (print) | LCCN 2018008712 (ebook) |
ISBN 9780268103118 (pdf) | ISBN 9780268103125 (epub) |
ISBN 9780268103095 (hardcover : alk. paper) |
ISBN 0268103097 (hardcover : alk. paper)
Subjects: LCSH: O'Connor, Flannery. | Giroux, Robert. |
Authors, American—20th century—Biography. |
Book editors—United States—Biography. |
Authors and publishers—United States—20th century—Biography.
Classification: LCC PS3565.C57 (ebook) |
LCC PS3565.C57 Z855   2018 (print) |
DDC 813/.54 [B]—dc23
LC record available at https://lccn.loc.gov/2018008582

∞ *This paper meets the requirements of ANSI/NISO Z39.48-1992*
(Permanence of Paper)

In memory of a wonderful friend,

ROBERT GIROUX

(1914–2008)

CONTENTS

NOTES ON THE TEXT

During the twenty-plus years that I knew Robert Giroux, he sometimes repeated informally the same anecdotes about his authors, and thus I did not provide a specific date for each of the hundreds of times we met. I taped an interview with him in 1997 on a two-hour plane ride from New York to New Orleans, during which he related much of his personal life. In addition, Jonathan Montaldo videotaped Giroux for sixteen hours over a period of several months a few years before Giroux's death. Both of our interviews are housed in the Robert Giroux Collection in the Special Collections Room, Monroe Library, Loyola University, New Orleans.

I acknowledge that some of the observations and quotes by Giroux concerning T. S. Eliot, J. D. Salinger, and Robert Lowell's mother, to cite but three examples, can be found in George Plimpton's interview with Giroux ("Robert Giroux: The Art of Publishing III"). I also acknowledge using material from the biographies of Flannery O'Connor written by Jean Cash and Brad Gooch, as well as Sally Fitzgerald's chronology in Flannery O'Connor's *Collected Works*. Some of my comments about O'Connor's *A Prayer Journal* were previously published in my review of that journal in the *Flannery O'Connor Review*. Some of the material in this book concerning O'Connor and theology appeared in a talk I delivered, "Jesuit Influence in the Life and Works of Flannery O'Connor," and also in my essay "Toward Discerning How Flannery O'Connor's Fiction Can Be Considered 'Roman Catholic.'" In addition, some information about Giroux's final months at Harcourt, Brace can be found in my essay "Tracing a Literary & Epistolary Relationship: Eudora Welty and Her Editor, Robert Giroux" and in my introduction to *The Letters of Robert Giroux and Thomas Merton*.

I am most grateful to the following people for their gracious encouragement in writing this book: In the United States, Louise Florencourt; Robert Giroux; Charles Reilly; Mr. and Mrs. Hugh James McKenna; the Jesuit communities at Saint Joseph's University and Saint Peter's University; JoAlyson Parker, Peter Norberg, and my colleagues in the English Department at Saint Joseph's University; my most capable and steadfast agent Albert LaFarge; Mark Bosco, S.J.; Ben Camardi; Art Carpenter; Gary Ciuba; John Desmond; Joseph Feeney, S.J.; Victoria Fox; Marshall Bruce Gentry; Roberta Rodriquez Gilmor; Cynthia T. Harris; Harriet and Michael Leahy; Helen Menendez; Judith Millman and Robert Miss; Susan and Rex Mixon, William Monroe; Kathleen Healey Mulvehill; Eanan Nagle; Trish Nugent; and Dominic Roberti. In France, la famille Michel Gresset, la Communauté des Sœurs de Jésus au Temple à Vernon, and Ben et Nadine Forkner.

I am likewise grateful for permission from Maria Fitzgerald to publish from the letters of Robert and Sally Fitzgerald; Charles R. Lindley, M.D., to publish from the letters of Denver Lindley; Alison McCallum to publish from the letters of John McCallum; Sheila B. Riordan to publish from the letters of Mavis McIntosh; and Percy "Pete" Wood to publish from the letters of Caroline Gordon. The Estate of Robert Giroux has given permission to publish Robert Giroux's letters to Flannery O'Connor as found in his personal files, in the files of Farrar, Straus & Giroux in the New York Public Library, and in the Harcourt, Brace archives. The Mary Flannery O'Connor Charitable Trust (© Flannery O'Connor, renewed by Regina Cline O'Connor) has given permission to publish an excerpt from Flannery O'Connor's essay "The Writer and the Graduate School" and her letters to Robert Giroux as found in his personal files, in the files of Farrar, Straus & Giroux in the New York Public Library, and in the Harcourt, Brace archives, as well as from Flannery O'Connor's letters to Elizabeth Bishop, William Jovanovich, Maryat Lee, Elizabeth McKee, John McCallum, and George White, as found in various repositories and indicated as such in the endnotes. The repositories for the unpublished letters are cited in the endnotes. In some cases, copies of letters can be found in two or more repositories; in all such cases, I have cited only one repository.

For citations and material taken from O'Connor's published letters not found in the endnotes, I have relied on letters in two books: *The Habit of Being: Letters of Flannery O'Connor* and O'Connor's *Collected Works*. It should be noted that some of the letters in the latter volume did not appear in *The Habit of Being*. For those who wish to consult the larger context of these published letters, I indicate the recipient and the date or time period of each letter, since I did not want to burden the reader with an enormous amount of bibliographical citations. In a very few cases, I have made silent corrections to O'Connor's use of punctuation.

Reprinted by permission of Farrar, Straus & Giroux, LLC: Excerpts from "Revelation" and from "Introduction" by Robert Giroux from *The Complete Stories*, by Flannery O'Connor. Copyright © 1971 by the Estate of Mary Flannery O'Connor. Excerpts from "Introduction" by Robert Giroux from *Everything That Rises Must Converge*, by Flannery O'Connor. Copyright © 1965 by the Estate of Mary Flannery O'Connor. Copyright renewed 1993 by Regina O'Connor. Excerpts from *The Habit of Being: Letters of Flannery O'Connor*, edited by Sally Fitzgerald. Copyright © 1979 by Regina O'Connor. Excerpts from "Introduction" by Flannery O'Connor from *A Memoir of Mary Ann*, by the Dominican Nuns of Our Lady of Perpetual Help Home. "Introduction" copyright © 1961 by Flannery O'Connor. Copyright renewed 1989 by Regina O'Connor. Excerpts from *Mystery and Manners*, by Flannery O'Connor, edited by Sally and Robert Fitzgerald. Copyright © 1969 by the Estate of Mary Flannery O'Connor. Excerpts from *A Prayer Journal*, by Flannery O'Connor. Copyright © 2013 by Mary Flannery O'Connor Charitable Trust. Excerpts from *Wise Blood*, by Flannery O'Connor. Copyright © 1962 by Flannery O'Connor. Copyright renewed 1990 by Regina O'Connor. "Man and Wife" from *Collected Poems*, by Robert Lowell. Copyright © 2003 by Harriet Lowell and Sheridan Lowell. Excerpts from *Letters of Robert Lowell*, by Robert Lowell, edited by Saskia Hamilton. Copyright © 2005 by Harriet Lowell and Sheridan Lowell.

AT   Allen Tate
BU   W. L. Lyons Brown Library, Bellarmine University, Louisville, KY
CC   Catharine Carver
CG   Caroline Gordon
CW   Flannery O'Connor. *Collected Works.* Edited by Sally Fitzgerald.
DL   Denver Lindley
DU   David M. Rubenstein Rare Book and Manuscript Library, Duke University, Durham, NC
EB   Elizabeth Bishop
EL   Erik Langkjaer
EM   Elizabeth McKee
EU   Stuart A. Rose Manuscript, Archives, and Rare Book Library, Emory University, Atlanta, GA
FOC   Flannery O'Connor
FS&C   Farrar, Straus & Cudahy
FS&G   Farrar, Straus & Giroux
GC   Library and Instructional Technology Center, Georgia College, Milledgeville, GA
HB   *The Habit of Being: Letters of Flannery O'Connor.* Edited by Sally Fitzgerald.
HBA   Harcourt, Brace's Archives
HU   Modern Books and Manuscripts Collection, Houghton Library, Harvard University, Cambridge, MA
JB   John Berryman
JM   Jacques Maritain

JMC	John McCallum
MEC	Maurice-Edgar Coindreau
MM	Mavis McIntosh
MandM	*Mystery and Manners*
NYPL	FS&G Papers, Manuscripts and Archives Division, New York Public Library
PH	Paul Horgan
PS	Patrick Samway, S.J.
PU	Rare Books and Special Collections, Firestone Library, Princeton University, Princeton, NJ
RF	Robert Fitzgerald
RG	Robert Giroux
RGF	Robert Giroux's Files
RL	Robert Lowell
SF	Sally Fitzgerald
TM	Thomas Merton, O.C.S.O.
TSE	T. S. Eliot
UL	unpublished letter
UNC	Walker Percy Collection, Wilson Library, University of North Carolina at Chapel Hill, NC
VC	Catherine Pelton Durrell '25 Archives and Special Collections Library, Vassar College, Poughkeepsie, NY
WP	Walker Percy

Introduction

She could put everything about a character into a single look, everything she had and knew into a single story. . . . For her, people were complete in their radical weakness, their necessarily human incompleteness. Each story was complete, sentence by sentence. And each sentence was a hard, straight, altogether complete version of her subject.
—Alfred Kazin about Flannery O'Connor,
New York Times Book Review, November 28, 1971

Giroux is a great man of letters, a great editor, and a great publisher.
—Charles Scribner Jr.,
in his 1990 memoir *In the Company of Writers*

Robert Giroux, former editor in chief of Harcourt, Brace & Company and former editor in chief and chairman of the editorial board of Farrar, Straus & Giroux, was Flannery O'Connor's devoted friend and admirer. Though not her sole editor, he edited her three books published during her lifetime, as well as the collection she completed just before she died. While O'Connor had a fine rapport with her two other editors at Harcourt, Brace, Catharine DeFrance Carver and Denver Lindley, who successively replaced Giroux after he resigned from the firm in the spring of 1955, they never took credit for editing any of her published books. This does not mean, however, that she did not enjoy their friendship or respectfully consider the critical comments they made about her work—

just the contrary, especially in the case of Carver, whose literary judgments never failed to impress O'Connor.

O'Connor reserved her greatest accolade for Robert Giroux— sometimes referring to him casually as "Old Giroux" and an "old friend"—whom she considered not only a "very nice person" but "the best" of her three editors.[1] It was on the basis of this judgment that she wrote to Giroux on April 17, 1958, immediately after Lindley resigned from Harcourt, Brace, to inform him that she felt comfortable returning to him, this time as her editor at Farrar, Straus & Cudahy. She was "properly back where she started from," and Giroux remained her editor until her death on August 3, 1964, and even, it should be emphasized, after her death. In retrospect, this series of editors had a dramatic impact not only on the manner in which O'Connor approached her fiction, but also perhaps on the actual number of her stories—and novels—simply because Carver and Lindley did not orchestrate and move forward the publication of her fiction in book form. Most likely they felt pressure, as Giroux certainly did, from several Harcourt, Brace senior officials to focus more on compiling academic textbooks and less on promoting and publishing imaginative literature. Carver, unfortunately, did not write about her appreciation of O'Connor's fiction, but Lindley did in his letter of reference as part of O'Connor's application in 1955 for a Guggenheim Fellowship:

> From her first published story, Flannery O'Connor has shown remarkable technical skill in writing and a strong individual point of view. Her recognition by the critics was a little slow in coming, perhaps because of her bizarre and sometimes gruesome themes. With her last volume of short stories, however—*A Good Man Is Hard to Find*—the experts tried to outbid one another in praising her. Her first novel *Wise Blood*, which we published in 1952, though not a popular success, aroused interest out of proportion to its actual sales. . . . Miss O'Connor is a very serious and determined writer. She does not produce rapidly, but the result is always both technically excellent and emotionally affective. A Fellowship would enable her to devote all her time to creative work and would, I believe, thus make a real contribution to American writing.[2]

Though his comments about O'Connor's technical skills and gruesome themes have merit, if explained in more detail and with contextual examples from her fiction, Lindley omitted mentioning O'Connor's religious sensibilities and her focus on the relationship between human and divine mystery. Due to his Roman Catholic background and close editorial work with a variety of religious writers, Giroux perceived instinctively what O'Connor was doing. In addition, he believed that a crucial part of the success of any talented fiction writer was to publish regularly at strategic intervals. In early March 1949, O'Connor, just about to turn twenty-four, looked forward to meeting Giroux as her prospective editor because he might open wider the door to her future as a creative writer. Pleasant, affable, totally professional, and always searching for new authors, Giroux, approximately eleven years older than O'Connor, had clearly established himself as a rising star in the publishing world and had an uncanny ability to recognize talented individuals. When the noted poet Robert Lowell, who wanted to advance O'Connor's career as a published author, brought her to see his editor at Harcourt, Brace, O'Connor could not have been more pleased. Giroux considered Lowell to be not only a dear friend and someone whose literary judgment he valued, but among the best poets of his generation.

When O'Connor and Lowell entered Giroux's office at 381 Madison Avenue, near Forty-Sixth Street in midtown Manhattan, Giroux was immediately taken by this young woman, as he mentioned in his introduction to O'Connor's *Complete Stories*: "Behind her soft-spoken speech, clear-eyed gaze and shy manner, I sensed a tremendous strength. This was the rarest kind of young writer, one who was prepared to work her utmost and knew exactly what she must do with her talent."[3] O'Connor had already signed an option with another publisher for her novel in progress, part of her award for taking first prize in the Rinehart-Iowa Fiction Contest while at the Iowa Writers' Workshop. In talking with the young O'Connor, Giroux grew in his appreciation of this talented, original author, who was carving out new terrain in her fiction. One could all too easily cite some possible distant precedents, such as the Georgia humorist Joel Chandler Harris, notable in his depiction of poor, white Reconstruction farmers in *Free Joe, and Other Georgian Sketches*, or Grace King, whose *The Pleasant Ways of St. Médard* portrays life in post–Civil War New Orleans on both sides of the color line, but these comparisons simply miss the target. If anything, O'Connor's writing reflected the imaginatively restrained quality of Nathaniel Hawthorne's *Twice-Told Tales*, as well as the serious intensity of Herman Melville's *Moby-Dick* (though clearly her stories and novels are shorter, more fluid and direct, without Melville's lengthy detours and side maneuvers). But most of all, Diane Arbus's photographs, which invite considerations about the seemingly eccentric, marginalized, decentered, grotesquely ordinary, and bizarrely conventional among us, capture a palpable feeling that one can find in O'Connor's fiction.[4] "There's a quality of legend about freaks," Arbus wrote, "like a person in a fairy tale who stops you and demands that you answer a riddle. Most people go through life dreading they'll have a traumatic experience. Freaks were born with their trauma. They've already passed their test in life."[5] Whether photographing *Hermaphrodite and a dog in a carnival trailer, Md.* or *Tattooed man at a carnival, Md.*, Arbus, as Susan Sontag (another of Giroux's authors) notes with great perspicacity in her book *On Photography*, gives a privileged glimpse into the lives of her characters, constantly revealing their unusual form of interconnectedness.[6] Arbus's photographs re-present the mystery that is here now and will remain in the future. In a similar manner, O'Connor, distrustful of artificial posing, sentimentality, and hypocrisy, is not a voyeur, but allows us to witness characters during select moments in their lives that may be decisive ones. O'Connor hoped that her matter-of-fact depiction of sometimes shocking, painful, and embarrassing situations could change the perceptions of her readers. Her interest in Protestant preachers of any ilk, whom she does not patronize or mock, reinforces her acute desire to probe the fullness of God's mysteriously inexhaustible word / Word for each human being.

Right from the beginning, the literary relationship and personal friendship of O'Connor and Giroux took on a character of its own and thereafter never remained static. It changed in subtle and unpredictable ways as their lives intersected at various times in configurations that could never have been predicted, particularly due to Giroux's decision to leave Harcourt, Brace and to O'Connor's debilitating illness, caused by disseminated lupus erythematosus, a chronic inflammatory disease, as well as the exhaustion resulting from typing and retyping her fiction and essays. In late June 1960, when O'Connor felt great stress on a number of fronts, she wanted to make sure that none of this affected in the least her relationship with Giroux: "I don't know how the rumor could have originated that I am dissatisfied with my publisher," she wrote to Elizabeth McKee, "because it certainly isn't true. . . . If Giroux has got the notion I am dissatisfied, please tell him there is nothing to it."

Toward the end of her life, as O'Connor became more and more incapacitated, Giroux's 1961 laconic and positive reply to her request to have a book published by Farrar, Straus & Cudahy about the short life of Mary Ann Long, who suffered from a large cancerous tumor on her face in addition to having had one eye removed, showed the tremendous confidence he had in O'Connor's judgment: "I read the story, with a few misgivings which somehow are not important."[7] Neither Carver nor Lindley, I believe, would have risked accepting this book about a girl who died so tragically, but Giroux, calling on years of experience with a vast array of authors, a good number of whom were Catholic and had written books not unlike what O'Connor was proposing, appreciated and valued the literary and theological significance of each work she submitted to him for publication. O'Connor, who wrote the introduction to the book, was overjoyed by Giroux's response, and in February 1961 she considered getting this book published a "genuine miracle"—not a phrase she would use offhandedly. In a more unguarded moment, O'Connor wrote of the book, "It's very badly written but should be published and Giroux had the good sense to see it."[8] Only years of respect and trust could have brought such an author and such an editor together in mutual accord. It should be mentioned, too, that after O'Connor's death, her mother served as the executrix of the Estate of Mary Flannery O'Connor and Robert Fitzgerald as O'Connor's literary executor, and after Fitzgerald's death in January 1985, Giroux served for a while in this capacity.[9]

The lives of O'Connor and Giroux cannot be set out synoptically in clear, parallel fashion because their age differences, family backgrounds, educations, personal and professional interests, travels, friendships, obligations, and differing longevity do not allow facile coordination. Yet the gaps in time and place—those generational spaces that separated these two individuals—become highly relevant and add a specific tone and texture to their particular relationship, opening up connections that might not always have verifiable certitude, but go from the sense of the possible, to that of the probable, to that which approximates the real. While facts can ground biographical perspectives, they sometimes fail to capture the imagination that demands interpretive interspaces. It is possible in hindsight to make certain connections that most likely were intuited but rarely articulated by either O'Connor or Giroux, but which nevertheless permitted these two individuals to form a bond that withstood unforeseen setbacks and changes. Giroux, for example, did not know the complete story behind the Rinehart-Iowa Fiction Contest until after O'Connor's death; only then could he fill in the pieces and reconfigure in his mind what O'Connor was going through when they first met.[10]

When friends of Gertrude Stein first saw the portrait of her done in 1906 by Picasso, for which Stein had at least eighty sittings, they turned to the famous artist and, not liking Stein's heavy-lidded, masklike face, said, "Gertrude doesn't look anything like that." To this Picasso coyly replied, "Oh, but she will."[11] In like manner, when O'Connor preferred that her 1953 self-portrait be used for the cover of her first collection of stories, she wrote to Giroux in January 1955 that it would "do justice to the subject for some time to come."[12] Curiously, when she painted it, after suffering from a particularly acute siege of lupus, she did not look at herself in the mirror or at the pheasant cock, for she knew what both looked like. Such is the power of portrait artists (and writers of critical books and essays that contain biographical information, as well as writers of biographies) to create enduring personal images that are distinctive and, if successful, compelling.

This book intends to bring into focus two quite disparate lives, those of a Southern female fiction writer and her Northern male editor, and the impact they had on each other. O'Connor's relationships with her two interim editors, as well as her two literary agents and a host of writers and intellectuals mainly connected with Princeton University, among other institutions of higher learning, need to be added to this equation, so that the emerging sequential patterns have an acceptable degree of coherency. To a great extent, the tone and texture of the letters of these six individuals, but principally between O'Connor and Giroux, allow us to get a close-up glimpse of the way they communicated with one another and especially the way in which O'Connor wrote and revised her fiction. One of Giroux's greatest gifts to O'Connor was to allow her complete freedom to make changes in galleys and page proofs right up to the moment of publication. Their correspondence, the nature of which could not be predicted in advance, came in time and over time. Many of the letters included here have never been published before; citing them, at times in their entirety, gives readers an added sense not only of how these individuals related to one another, but also of the letters' contextual importance.

Since no critical book to date has focused in depth on the history of O'Connor's writing career, with particular attention to the interrelated development of her stories and novels as detailed in her extensive correspondence, it has not been possible to appreciate what she did and how she did it from this perspective. The letters that O'Connor and Giroux exchanged provide the greatest insight into their relationship, first when Giroux was at Harcourt, Brace and then at Farrar, Straus & Cudahy, which became Farrar, Straus & Giroux soon after O'Connor's death.[13] In light of this, I have relied heavily on these letters, not omitting the correspondence with her two other editors and two agents, as a way of giving a faithful framework to what transpired on an ongoing basis. I believe this primary biographical data contributes significantly to the presentation and evaluation of their relationship. Furthermore, I have been fortunate to know personally some of the people who knew O'Connor and the value of her published works, particularly Robert Giroux, Maurice-Edgar Coindreau, Paul Horgan, Walker Percy, and Eudora Welty, as well as Giroux's close friend Eileen Simpson, who introduced me to the importance of O'Connor's Princeton-based friends and admirers, all of whom Simpson knew, especially Robert Lowell.[14] Moreover, William Lynch, S.J., who knew Giroux, had an extensive correspondence with Allen Tate, and influenced O'Connor more than anyone else concerning the relationship of theology and literature, was one of my theology professors.[15]

When O'Connor and Giroux first met, each could deal only with unstructured impressions and try to withhold superficial judgments about the other, since they were strangers with quite different backgrounds. O'Connor was born in Savannah, Georgia, on March 25, 1925, but her move as a young adolescent to Milledgeville, a small city southeast of Atlanta, shaped her personality in essential ways and stayed with her until the end of her days. Giroux's happiest memories, the ones to which he often returned, were rooted not so much in early life in his native Jersey City, New Jersey, but rather during his college days and, after his time in the navy, his early work experience.

In spite of the effects of the Great Depression on her modest Southern family, O'Connor coped fairly well as an only child, no doubt because she had an extended family network. (Her mother had a total of fifteen sisters, brothers, half-sisters, and half-brothers.) Born a Catholic, she attended Catholic grade schools, developed a deep personal spirituality, and continued to grow in her faith, mainly through personal prayer, sacramental life, and reading books and articles on medieval Scholasticism. She lived most of her life in central Georgia, which remained racially divided and had relatively few Catholics, though both sides of her family prided themselves on their long-standing Irish Catholic roots. After her father's death in 1941 from lupus, O'Connor experienced a dispiriting, unarticulated void in her life. When she was diagnosed with the same disease in early 1951, her mother, Regina, out of extreme maternal concern, no doubt revealing deep-seated trepidation, kept the diagnosis of this disease from her until she learned about it in June 1952. Neither Regina, with whom she lived almost her entire life, nor any male companion ever helped O'Connor to develop her potential for intimacy. "He died when I was fifteen," she wrote about her father in mid-July 1956 to her close friend Betty Hester (designated as "A" in the posthumous letter collection *The Habit of Being*), "and I really only knew him by a kind of instinct."

O'Connor's nurturing instincts became most apparent in the chickens, ducks, and geese—and eventually peafowl—that she raised. She made clothes for her pet duck in Margaret Abercrombie's high school home economics class and later designed for herself a signature emblem shaped like a bird.[16] Her childhood friend Nell Ann Summers distinctly recalls being invited to see young O'Connor's backyard menagerie: "bantam hens dressed in striped trousers and white piqué jackets; chickens with sunflower bonnets and starched aprons; peacocks in their natural glory fanned out forming a backdrop; little houses for her barnyard birds; street signs for the fowl that walked the formal paths of the garden."[17] As a teenager, O'Connor also owned one hundred and fifty miniature glass and china fowl. Thus her creative imagination, rooted in her native surroundings, manifested itself at an early age. Her delightfully informative essay "The King of the Birds" shows her adult attachment to peafowl, while her 1953 poem "The Peacock Roosts" reveals a more controlled, Romantic appreciation for this bird:

The clown-faced peacock
Dragging sixty suns
Barely looks west where
The single one
Goes down in fire.

Bluer than moon-side sky
The trigger head

Circles and backs.
The folded forest squats and flies.
The ancient design is raised.

Gripped oak cannot be moved.
This bird looks down
And settles, ready.
Now the leaves can start the wind
That combs these suns

Hung all night in the gold-green silk wood
Or blown straight back until
The single one
Mounting the grey light
Will see the flying forest
Leave the tree and run.[18]

Furthermore, in her story "The Displaced Person" a peacock is magnificently transformed into a symbol of Christ's Transfiguration just as an elderly woman is given the opportunity to reflect on the deeper significance of her Christian faith. But most of all, O'Connor's sustained effort to write three novels, two collections of short stories, essays, book reviews, and talks—as well as a prizewinning posthumous volume of letters and a spiritual journal—reveals extraordinary talent and dedication, which continue to be appreciated in the United States and throughout the world.

O'Connor's friends and close acquaints, beginning for the most part during her graduate school days, never doubted her writing talent, and yet her illness caused her to adjust constantly to realities beyond her control. Most notably, she was confined for all practical purposes to "Andalusia," a two-story house and farmlands set amid 544 acres of rolling red-clay hills and stands of pine trees four miles outside Milledgeville, from shortly after her twenty-sixth birthday to her death at age thirty-nine. O'Connor's particular medical situation charged her creative energies; her limited environment at Andalusia—restrictive but supportive—allowed her imaginatively to touch the bass strings of her existence on this earth. Surprisingly, in June 1957 she gave an unabashedly honest and upbeat perspective about returning as an adult to Milledgeville to her friend Maryat Lee, who had indicated that she, too, would like to move to the South: "You get no condolences from me. This is a Return I have faced and when I faced it I was roped and tied and resigned the way it is necessary to be resigned to death, and largely because I thought it would be the end of my creation, any writing, and any WORK from me. And as I told you by the fence, it was only the *beginning*" (emphasis mine). Lee, who harbored negative feelings about the pretentious attitudes of many Southerners, first met O'Connor at Christmastime 1956, and according to Lee they corresponded thereafter at least twice monthly on average. During their first encounter, O'Connor told her new friend in a flat, honest tone that she had lupus. So upsetting was this news that Lee leaned against a nearby fence for balance. As they looked at each other, these two women realized that they had not so much a kinship as a type of undefinable knowledge that had special significance for each.[19] O'Connor knew the value of direct personal communication that opened up moments of authentic human revelation.

O'Connor is forever identified with Milledgeville, which had by 1957 approximately 1,200 inhabitants and was noted then mainly for four institutions: Georgia State College for Women, Georgia State Training School for Boys (a reformatory), Georgia Military College, and Central State Hospital for the mentally ill, the latter a source of considerable speculation about the origin of some of her characters. Like Henry David Thoreau accurately surveying the width and depth of Walden Pond or William Faulkner mentally delineating and populating Yoknapatawpha County, O'Connor had to discover the breadth and scope of what would always be dearest to her. Once, as a participant in the literary festival at South Carolina's Converse College in April 1962 with Eudora Welty, Cleanth Brooks, and Andrew Lytle, she heard Welty read her famous essay "Place in Fiction," which she found "very beautifully written," reinforcing her own feeling that, in addition to having a good ear, a writer of Southern fiction needs to look at life locally for a check on reality:

> I think the sense of place is as essential to good and honest writing as a logical mind; surely they are somewhere related. It is by knowing where you stand that you grow able to judge where you are. Place absorbs our earliest notice and attention, it bestows on us our original awareness; and our critical powers spring up from the study of it and the growth of experience inside it. It perseveres in bringing us back to earth when we fly too high. It never really stops informing us, for

it is forever astir, alive, changing, reflecting, like the mind of man itself. One place comprehended can make us understand other places better. Sense of place gives equilibrium; extended, it is sense of direction too. Carried off we might be in spirit, and should be, when we are reading or writing something good; but it is the sense of place going with us still that is the ball of golden thread to carry us there and back and in every sense of the word to bring us home.[20]

In her fiction, O'Connor depicted both the local and the universal—or, more precisely, the transcendental—before returning home imaginatively to begin again. Her "improbable combination of religious faith and eccentricity," as novelist John Hawkes put it, "accounts in large part for the way in which 'unknown territory' and 'actuality' are held in severe balance of her work."[21] Not a reclusive Southern version of the Belle of Amherst, she knew the value of reaching out to others not only through the written word but also by giving more than sixty readings and talks at various colleges and universities while living at Andalusia.[22] Over the years, but especially after editing *Everything That Rises Must Converge* and reading her marvelous letters in *The Habit of Being*, Giroux came to realize O'Connor's overwhelming dedication to her craft and how tenacious and indefatigable she actually was.

If O'Connor's locale had a distinctive down-home character to it, Robert Giroux's was much more diverse and cosmopolitan. Descended from relatively obscure French Canadian immigrant stock, he was born in working-class Jersey City on April 8, 1914, the youngest after four siblings: Arnold, Lester, Estelle, and Josephine. His Canadian-born father, Arthur Joseph, worked for a while in the silk industry, while his mother, Katherine Regina Lyons Giroux, a grade-school teacher of Irish descent, took care of the household. Friends and relatives seem to agree that the Giroux family never rose above the ordinary, a key factor that impelled Robert to excel in whatever he did, first at Saint Aloysius School in Jersey City, then as a scholarship student at the Jesuit-run Regis High School in New York, and finally at Columbia College. In late June 1932, he received the first Nicholas Murray Butler Scholarship sponsored by the Columbia University Alumni Club of Hudson County, New Jersey, after achieving the best grades in a triple test in which fifty graduates of county high schools competed. During the second part of the test, an interview, Giroux and two others proved equal. A subsequent four-hour intelligence test proved decisive for Giroux. With this partial scholarship in hand (a typical semester cost him less than $200), he anticipated entering Columbia's Pulitzer School of Journalism but then abandoned it to take the regular courses in Columbia College.

Much to his dismay, his father had stopped working by that time and withdrew more and more from involvement with his family.[23] As a result, family activities were kept to a minimum and Giroux grew progressively ill at ease inviting classmates to his house. Like O'Connor, he dealt with the problem of a missing father at a critical age in his life. While at Columbia, however, he became more expansive and developed a deep and lasting friendship with Mark Van Doren, one of his professors, and with two classmates, John Berryman and Thomas Merton, whose books he went on to edit.

As an editor who worked his entire life in New York—rising to become an editor in chief at Harcourt, Brace and eventually taking the same position at a firm that bore his name, Farrar, Straus & Giroux—he achieved a great awareness of the complexity and plurality of an overwhelmingly large metropolitan city—something he thoroughly relished. Giroux possessed an invaluable knowledge of the works of his authors, as well as sensitivity to the problems that both he and they faced in seeing their books through the press. While O'Connor considered New York "totally unsuitable to grow up in," she entertained the idea of moving there in April 1949, at least until her money ran out.[24] Giroux treated each of his authors as individuals and worked with them on a one-to-one basis, aware of each writer's literary genotype and, at the same time, of the larger, interconnected human patterns that inevitably develop within the publishing world. When he started as an editor in the early forties, book publishing in America enjoyed a different character from today's global industry, with its foreign and domestic mega-mergers, acquisitions editors who never edit, and inflated literary super-agents. He thought in terms of the *formation*, rather than the formal education, of an editor, as exemplified in the editorial careers of Edward Garnett, who launched Joseph Conrad, D. H. Lawrence, and John Galsworthy in England, or Maxwell Perkins, who published F. Scott Fitzgerald, Ernest Hemingway, and Thomas Wolfe at Scribner's. Giroux commented archly on the great difference between an acquiring editor, a line editor, and what he considered the work of a genuine editor:

The truth is that editing lines is not necessarily the same as editing a book. A book is a much more complicated entity, the relation and portions of its parts, and its total impact could escape even a conscientious editor exclusively intent on vetting the book line by line. Perhaps that is why so many books today seem not to have been edited at all. The traditional function of the editor as the author's close collaborator from manuscript to printed book, and through all the aftermath, has too often been neglected, with deplorable consequences, in the current atmosphere of heightened commercial pressures and a largely acquisitive publishing posture. Editors used to be known by their authors; now some of them are known by their restaurants.[25]

A good editor, for Giroux, has judgment, taste, and most of all empathy and the capacity "not only to perceive what the author's aims are, but to help in achieving their realization to the fullest extent." This later point, absolutely central to Giroux's philosophy as an editor, served as the basis of many discussions we had together over the years.

By looking at the way Giroux dealt with his fellow editors and authors, one can get a better sense of the way he gradually developed his editorial philosophy, particularly when the publishing winds shifted and he had to adjust his tack, moving forward with each project, seeing it to completion, knowing that he was an important part of the process. Editors were and are under a lot of pressure; there is always a contest to receive famous awards. Giroux knew that his authors' books had to make money, and he gradually learned, once he could sign book contracts himself, that he needed at times to take risks. He likewise knew the direction he wanted to take, but how to get there, given the numerous manuscripts on his desk at any one time, was not always apparent. He often said that editorial and sales meetings gave him a definite awareness of the practical side of publishing. Above all, he had to make sure that he retained his humanity and did not let his growing success and visibility govern his behavior. He had to be grounded in all sorts of ways, so that when he spoke—especially to his authors—he said good, true, and efficacious words.

While some biographical sketches of Giroux exist, no formal, in-depth biography of him has been attempted. I first made his acquaintance in the mid-1980s, during a weekend in Charlottesville, Virginia, where we both were houseguests of one of his authors, Mary Lee Settle. I grew to know and admire him over the years, not as a father figure, but simply as my editor, mentor, and friend. Conversation always flowed naturally between us. From 1999 to 2001, while I held a visiting professorship at Saint Peter's College in Jersey City, we had dinner together a couple of times a month. I regularly visited him during his final years, when he resided in Seabrook Village, a few miles inland from Asbury Park on the Jersey shore. With enthusiasm and tact, he was never hesitant about discussing the authors he knew and the works he edited. His deep chuckle still resonates in my ears as I recall him recounting some wonderfully humorous incidents in his life.

Since Giroux edited a collection I assembled of Walker Percy's essays and talks, entitled *Signposts in a Strange Land*, as well as my biography *Walker Percy: A Life*, I have a firsthand appreciation for the ways in which he integrated his professional and personal life. As he mentioned to me, his role in editing O'Connor's works was fairly simple and straightforward. In the case of *Wise Blood*, he knew that criticism from O'Connor's faculty and mentors at the Iowa Writers' Workshop, in addition to the critical advice of Caroline Gordon and Robert Fitzgerald, had given the novel the structure it needed to allow the fullness and depth of the story to reveal itself. Most of O'Connor's stories had been published before they were collected into book form, so he felt no particular need to make suggestions on how to recast them. From personal experience, I know that he read every word of a text, used a red pencil to suggest corrections, and then attentively reread subsequent versions. He was most concerned about the overall content and structure of a work. After one of Giroux's authors, who had received some adverse criticism from him about novel in progress, called me to share some built-up anxiety and frustration, I mentioned this to Giroux. He said to me honestly and without equivocation, "I read the novel and felt that certain sections needed to be altered. My ultimate role as an editor is to help all my authors write their very best." I considered this last sentence his personal, sustaining mantra. Though he might question his own judgment from time to time, he knew that his overall experience served him in good stead.

When O'Connor first met Giroux, she could not have imagined the impact that meeting would have on her life, nor of some of the incalculably fluid dynamics already at play. At that moment, the lives of these individuals, as well as certain of their friends and acquaintances, flowed into one another, creating an unanticipated multilevel *confluence* whose swirling vortices move forward, creating receding eddies or new currents of one sort or another—a powerful image used by Welty in *The Optimist's Daughter*. In this novel, as Laurel McKelva dreams about traveling with her fiancé, Phil Hand, from Chicago to Mount Salus, Mississippi, to be married in a Presbyterian church, she senses the interconnectedness of all that surrounds her: "All they could see was sky, water, birds, light, and confluence. It was the whole morning world. And they themselves were a part of the confluence."[26]

Critical essays and books about O'Connor that contain biographical information and the two biographies about her written by Jean Cash and Brad Gooch, as well as the letters in *The Habit of Being*, can serve as the basis for explaining the specific elements or facets of her life. If the resulting biographical creation authentically unites these elements, the result is recognized as the subject re-presented not as a living clone, a creature revivified through genetic manipulation, but as a three-dimensional, intelligent and intelligible individual who has depth and coherence. In short, this verbal re-presentation is analogous to giving birth to someone who then grows and develops before the reader's eyes. Yet it is often assumed—naïvely, in my opinion—that the reader, having finished a biography, sees the subject exactly as the biographer does; rather, the reader must analyze and decode the sign systems, re-inscribing mentally what he or she has read. Critical essays and books containing biographical information about O'Connor constantly force us to consider the basic intersecting dimensions of her life. Yet a problem remains throughout this process: to what extent can O'Connor critics and biographers raise hypotheses and suggest possibilities without distorting their viable ongoing model? Still and all, a biographer or critic can discover an amalgam of elements that reveals the multifaceted nature of the person under consideration.

One crucial factor in evaluating and interpreting biographical information about both O'Connor and Giroux is to consider whether a particular biographer had personal knowledge of the subject and the subject's family, friends, and acquaintances, as did Sally Fitzgerald, whose biography of O'Connor, most likely partially written before her death, has not been published. Giroux, who would have edited the book, told me in the spring of 1997 that he never read a page of it, though he had hoped to see it published in 1986.[27] In much the same way, an authorized O'Connor biography, tentatively entitled *"Stalking Joy": The Life and Times of Flannery O'Connor*, which William Sessions was writing before his death in August 2016, will, if and when published, undoubtedly change our views of O'Connor. As a former Regents Professor of English at Georgia State University and a friend of both O'Connor and Betty Hester, Sessions had access to material not previously available to other O'Connor scholars. Fitzgerald and Sessions had a distinct advantage in that they could test the accuracy of their views against the mimetic pull of O'Connor's mannerisms and voice, and of those times when they enjoyed her company. While such knowledge does not guarantee a successful biography, it does add authenticity of a degree very close to that known by members of the family, at least at the level of reportage.

Biographers are not hesitant about discussing this crucial issue. Joseph Blotner, author of two biographies of William Faulkner and my mentor in graduate school, has written specifically about his recollections of Faulkner dating from 1953, though he readily admitted in three essays, "Did You See Him Plain?," "The Sources of William Faulkner's Genius," and "William Faulkner: Life and Art," that Faulkner was too varied for a single image and, at the same time, too strong to fail to leave behind a powerful image. "To be with him alone," Blotner writes, "to talk with him alone, was to learn a new mode of communication. He felt no need whatever to engage in talk just for the sake of talk. He was a master of avoidance. Even the most gregarious of us experience moments when he simply does not want to talk with the friendly stranger in the elevator who though wordless is pregnant with some well-meant and trivial conversational gambit. It was as though Faulkner by a subtle act of will or legerdemain compressed his ectoplasm and retreated within himself." While writing his biographies, Blotner retained a powerful image of his subject: "Many times, nearby or at a distance, most of us see in one figure almost a double of another that we know. This has never happened to me in all the years since I first saw William Faulkner."[28] Perhaps the same could be said by those who knew O'Connor, and in doing so they would underscore that which made her inimitable, though she would be among the first not to invite any type of comparison between herself and Faulkner.[29] In the final analysis, literary critics know that biographical portraits of noted writers and their editors and friends will never be finished. These portraits change as more dimensions of the subjects' lives are brought forward and put into appropriate literary and human perspectives, as a way of paying more apt, discerning, and fitting homage.

Over the centuries, portrait artists have used profile views, full-face views, three-quarter views, and other techniques to depict their subjects in various poses in order to help us comprehend what they see. John Keats takes a different, more ekphrastic approach in his "Ode on a Grecian Urn," a poem favored by Faulkner, in rendering two phases of ancient Greek life that have perennial significance: an amorous young couple on one side of the urn and some type of solemn procession on the other. Since it is impossible to see both sides of the urn at the same time, we are invited by Keats to ask questions about the two scenes as we rotate the urn slowly, gaining a sense of the relationships between infatuated youth and rituals of sacrifice and death. Both highlight enigmatic notions of beauty and truth. In similar fashion, we are invited to study O'Connor's intense passion for writing fiction while living with a deadly disease in order to appreciate the fullness of who she was and what she so ably accomplished during her lifetime.

CHAPTER ONE

The March 2, 1949, Visit

When Robert Lowell brought Flannery O'Connor into Robert Giroux's office on March 2, 1949, he carried with him years of experiences and situations that had certain unarticulated resonances or reverberations but were nevertheless quite real, if not always evident. As Giroux told me, he first met Lowell and his wife, Jean Stafford, in October 1941, when both were working at the publishing firm of Sheed & Ward in New York. He was interested to learn that Stafford had worked at the *Southern Review* and was now writing *Boston Adventure*, which she submitted in early 1942 to Harcourt, Brace. When Giroux, manuscript in hand, later boarded a train on his way to see some friends in Connecticut, he was so absorbed in reading the novel that he missed his stop. "It is surely one of the greatest experiences than an editor or indeed any reader can have," he told me, "to lose oneself in a book so completely that the world and time itself momentarily disappear."

O'Connor met the dashingly handsome, chain-smoking, thirty-year-old "Cal" Lowell in October 1947 at a dinner party in Iowa City, where she was pursuing graduate studies. They met again in early November 1948, after Lowell had divorced Stafford, when he arrived to take up residence in the West House at Yaddo, the bucolic writers' colony in Saratoga Springs, New York. Just north of Albany, Saratoga tended to attract wealthy summer visitors, many of whom stayed at the Grand Union Hotel or the Gideon Putnam during August to attend the horse races.

Drinking the terrible-tasting, sulfuric mineral water and indulging themselves by taking the town's famous mud baths, they could renew themselves physically and mentally before returning to the humdrum of their daily lives. O'Connor had arrived in June 1948 for an initial stay of two months and was subsequently invited to return in mid-September and remain through the end of the year; in fact, her invitation was again extended through March and possibly beyond. Lowell had held a previous summer residency at Yaddo in 1947, spending a good deal of his time translating Jean Racine's *Phèdre*.

The relationships of O'Connor, Giroux, Lowell, T. S. Eliot, and Ezra Pound serve as but one example of the unexpected—albeit peripheral—Weltyesque confluences in the lives of these five individuals. From October 1947 to October 1948 Lowell served as the sixth Consultant in Poetry at the Library of Congress, a post he held not without some heated controversy, revealing the depths of his passion for poetry as well as his assertive and sometimes belligerent nature. (In 1943 Lowell spent five months in a federal prison in Danbury, Connecticut, because of his stance as a conscientious objector during World War II.) In February 1947, he had run into considerable opposition when promoting Ezra Pound for the 1948 Bollingen Prize, awarded by the Fellows of the Library of Congress in American Letters, for the publication of the *Pisan Cantos*, especially from poet and former Harvard professor Robert Hillyer. Yet his efforts proved successful, particularly his support of three noted poets: W. H. Auden, Allen Tate (another Fellow in American Letters), and Eliot. John Berryman, prompted by Tate, wrote a letter of protest in support of Pound, signed by eighty-four interested parties, which appeared in the *Nation*. It should be noted that in November 1948, not long before bringing O'Connor to Giroux's office, Lowell attended a soirée in Princeton during which he caught up with Tate (the subject of four of his poems) and Eliot.[1] Perhaps taken with his own renown as a poet, Lowell soon began to address his letters to Eliot a bit maladroitly as "Uncle Tom."

Also in November 1948, Giroux visited Eliot, then sixty years old, at Princeton, where he was a fellow at the Institute for Advanced Study working on his play *The Cocktail Party*. It was also a chance for Eliot to meet some old friends, such as Jacques Maritain, and to make the acquaintance of Eileen Simpson, Berryman's wife, who wrote *Poets in Their Youth: A Memoir*, a detailed account of her life among some of America's most important literary figures.[2] Eliot's workroom at the Institute was one of the classrooms, where Giroux once found him diagramming the frequency of the appearances of the characters in his play in each of its three acts, using letters from each character's names. His writing resembled a mathematical equation, as Giroux told me. "Have you noticed the sign, *DO NOT ERASE?*," Eliot asked Giroux.[3] "That's because Albert Einstein occasionally uses this blackboard for excursions into the fourth dimension. I wonder what he'll think of my equations." (By naming one of his characters Sir Henry Harcourt-Reilly, Eliot tipped his hat to Giroux [Harcourt] and Charles Reilly, Giroux's close friend and companion.) After Eliot had been informed that he had won the Nobel Prize and Giroux accompanied him to Idlewild Airport for his flight to Europe, a reporter asked him if the prize was given for a specific work. Eliot replied, "I believe it's given for the entire corpus." The reporter then asked, "When did you write that?" Eliot always thought *The Entire Corpus* might make a good title for a murder mystery.

In an emblematic and rather bizarre way, Pound had an impact on those in Giroux's office that March morning. After moving to Italy in 1924, he embraced Benito Mussolini's fascism and made, to the chagrin of some of his friends and followers, hundreds of radio broadcasts against the U.S. government and particularly Jews. He was arrested for treason by the American forces in 1945, transported to the United States, and eventually incarcerated for twelve years in Saint Elizabeths Hospital, a psychiatric institution in Washington, DC. Considered mentally unstable with a condition that warranted long-term, psychiatric treatment, he nevertheless continued writing, focusing especially on his translation of Sophocles' *Women of Trachis* and *Elektra*.

Lowell had been attracted to Pound's poetry ever since he first wrote to him in May 1936 as a nineteen-year-old freshman at Harvard.[4] O'Connor met Pound's son Omar, a sophomore at Hamilton College (his father's alma mater), when he visited Lowell at Yaddo in 1948. Later she inquired about Omar in a letter to Lowell, since she had met a physician who knew Mr. and Mrs. Pound and liked them both.[5] Giroux had first encountered Eliot in the spring of 1946 and was impressed by the dedication of his poem "The Waste Land" "To Ezra Pound, *il miglior fabbro.*" He was most anxious to meet the controversial poet, which he and Lowell did in September 1948.[6] Pound had been influential in the publication in *Poetry* magazine of Eliot's "The Love Song of J. Alfred Prufrock," so

Eliot on occasion visited his old friend in Washington. (Berryman, who visited Pound with Lowell, would publish an in-depth introduction to Pound's poetry in the April 1949 issue of the *Partisan Review*. Robert Fitzgerald, an important person in O'Connor's life, had visited Pound in Italy in 1932 and later sent him a draft of his translation of Homer's *The Odyssey*.)[7]

In talking to Giroux at Saint Elizabeths, Pound mocked Giroux's colleagues Frank Morley and Eugene Reynal, for he had little tolerance for such established editors. After Pound made reference to "Weinstein Kircheberg" (in German *church* and *hill*), it took Giroux a minute or so to figure out that Pound was referring to Winston Churchill.[8] Given that Giroux, then a former naval officer, had personally witnessed the devastating aftermath at Pearl Harbor and had spent stressful months of his life at sea, participating in six major engagements against the Japanese military, he left the short visit vehemently opposed to those who sentimentalized Pound or made excuses for his pro-Axis broadcasts and anti-Semitic tirades. Giroux last saw Pound at a memorial ceremony for Eliot: he wrote to Berryman, "I've just got back from London. The services for the Old Possum [Eliot] at Westminster Abbey were marvelous, and everyone turned out. The most impressive presence was that of Ezra Pound, white-bearded and shrunken, and looking like the ghost of Lear. He arrived from Venice and presumably he had not been in London since 1922! He refused to meet the press or indeed anyone, and did not once open his mouth. When I greeted him, he bowed very formally."[9] Giroux noted that Pound's silence, after all the years of over-talk, was "crushing." Though O'Connor never mentions in her essays or letters Pound's poetry and the influence it had on American poetry, she was aware of these visits, as she mentioned in a letter to Sally and Robert Fitzgerald in January 1956: "All my erstwhile *boy friends* visit Pound at St. Elizabeths and think he is mad and finished—he calls them all funny names and they think it's wonderful, touched by the holy hand, etc." (emphasis mine).

In fall 1948, before traveling with Lowell to New York to meet Giroux, O'Connor enjoyed the quasi-monastic privacy afforded by Yaddo, where she met, among other residents, Patricia Highsmith, then writing her first novel, *Strangers on a Train*; James Ross, the author of *They Don't Dance Much* (O'Connor called it a "very fine book"); and two African Americans, Chester Himes, then known primarily for his novel *If He Hollers Let Him Go*, and Arna Bontemps, a dominant figure in the Harlem

Renaissance.[10] Lowell described Yaddo to Elizabeth Bishop with an indirect reference to O'Connor: "Now there are an introverted and an extroverted colored man; a boy of 23 who experiments with dope; a student [O'Connor] of a former Kenyon class-mate of mine, who at age of six was in the Pathé News Reel for having a chicken that walked backwards; and Malcolm Cowley, nice but a little slow."[11] Lowell and Bishop, who suffered from various forms of alienation, whether mental or geographical, had an astonishingly private thirty-year friendship. Bishop, later a Pulitzer Prize recipient, struck up an extraordinary epistolary friendship with O'Connor, although they never met because Bishop relocated to Brazil.[12]

At Yaddo, O'Connor projected herself as being perceptive and rather reticent, as Lowell mentioned in a letter to Robie Macauley.[13] O'Connor survived her residency by keeping busy as much as she could and by not being apologetic about her Southern roots. In November, Lowell wrote to Caroline Gordon, then teaching a creative writing course at Columbia University, that she had an admirer then at Yaddo, a fellow Catholic by the name of Flannery O'Connor, who was looking for a teaching post. Would Columbia have a teaching position available?[14] This passing reference to O'Connor as someone familiar with Gordon's fiction provided enough assurance for Gordon eventually to take O'Connor under her pedagogical wing.

Giroux, too, had known and admired Gordon, particularly during the years she lived in Princeton, due partly to his sustained personal and professional friendship with Berryman, who taught at Princeton almost continuously for ten years beginning in the fall of 1943. Princeton had become, as it still is, an epicenter for internationally acclaimed creative writers, philosophers, scientists, and academicians of all sorts because of its intellectual history and preeminent academic resources, as well as its proximity to New York. Others identified with Princeton who would have a definite influence on O'Connor include Jacques Maritain (a professor from 1948 to 1952 who continued to live there until 1960); Maurice-Edgar Coindreau (professor from 1923 to 1961); Robert Fitzgerald (fellow, 1949 to 1951), Eliot (1948, fellow at the Institute for Advance Study), Tate (1939 to 1942, fellow in creative writing), and by extension Lowell and Stafford. Though never central to O'Connor's career, Berryman, a Pulitzer Prize–winning poet and one of Giroux's authors, sat in on Tate's lectures on poetry during his senior year at Columbia.

Giroux's caring nature in dealing with both Berryman's and Lowell's recurring physical and psychological problems reveals an incredible capacity for understanding authors whose talents needed to be fostered and advanced as far as humanly possible.[15] By midsummer of 1952, most likely through Giroux, O'Connor already knew Eileen Simpson, who earned a reputation as an NYU-trained psychotherapist. Simpson lamented that the strain caused by infidelity in the marriages of Lowell and Stafford, Tate and Gordon, and herself and Berryman eventually took its toll.[16] After fourteen years of marriage, dramatized in her 1975 novel *The Maze*, Simpson divorced Berryman in 1956, though she remained, as did her former husband, a lifelong friend of Giroux. When Giroux and I visited with her in her New York apartment, she often reminisced about her days in Princeton and the importance of those years to her.

It did not take long for O'Connor to find her place among the other writers and artists at Yaddo, though some had trouble understanding her heavy Southern accent. O'Connor, like everyone at Yaddo, knew who Robert Traill Spence Lowell IV was, for he had already achieved tremendous acclaim for his Pulitzer Prize–winning volume of poetry *Lord Weary's Castle*, judiciously critiqued in advance by his friend Randall Jarrell, edited by Giroux, and proofread by Berryman.[17] After Giroux had signed a contract for this book, Mrs. Lowell phoned from somewhere in the empyrean, as Giroux was wont to say.

"Is Bobby [she never called him Cal] any good?" When Giroux said her son was first-rate, she further asked, "Will his books make money?"

"It takes years to get established," he replied, "and ordinarily poems make little money at the start."

Her retort: "I thought so."

Alfred Kazin, a well-known literary critic, literary scout for Harcourt, Brace, and author of *On Native Grounds*, was one of a number of visitors at Yaddo while O'Connor was there. He described Lowell with great exuberance: "He was not just damned good, suddenly famous and deserving his fame; he was in a state of grandeur not negotiable with lesser beings. He was Lowell; he was handsome, magnetic, rich, wild with excitement about his powers, wild over the many tributes to him from Pound, [George] Santayana, his old friends, Tate, Jarrell and [Robert Penn]

Warren."[18] After O'Connor shared some manuscript pages of her novel, Kazin could barely retain his enthusiasm for her as well. "No fiction writer after the war seemed to be so *deep*, so severely perfect as Flannery," he wrote, though curiously he later voted against the novel's acceptance by Harcourt, Brace.[19] Ironically, Kazin went so far as to predict that out of the emerging crop of talented writers, O'Connor would become "our classic." He was quick to add that she "seemed to be attending Lowell with rapture."

Although O'Connor felt strongly attracted to certain men during her lifetime—John Sullivan in college, Robie Macauley in graduate school, and particularly Erik Langkjaer in the early 1950s—Lowell, whose pedigree was beyond impeccable, then and there captivated her, especially as he was both a brilliant poet and (at that moment) unmarried. Lowell was then writing his masterful *The Mills of the Kavanaughs*, which would be followed by *Life Studies*, *Phaedra* and *Figaro* (translation), *Imitations*, and *For the Union Dead*, all edited by Giroux. Lowell's father and grandfather had been navy commanders, and two distant cousins—Abbott Lawrence Lowell, who served as twenty-fourth president of Harvard University, and his sister Amy, a poet—likewise achieved national prominence. His mother, Charlotte Winslow Lowell, could trace her family back to Pilgrims on the *Mayflower*. O'Connor recognized in her new friend both a proven literary genius and someone seeking religious values in his life, a pursuit that grew in seriousness after his marriage in April 1940 to Stafford (Tate gave away the bride). Though Giroux edited the works of both Lowell and Stafford, he maintained a deeper and more abiding personal friendship with Stafford, particularly through some of the darker moments of her life.[20]

While a college student, Lowell had read such Catholic theologians and writers as Maritain, Étienne Gilson, Cardinal John Henry Newman, Gerard Manley Hopkins, S.J., and Blaise Pascal, some of whose works in various degrees exerted a great influence on his decision to convert to Catholicism in 1941. O'Connor—as did Gordon—refers to most of these same authors as significant figures who helped her better understand various facets and dimensions of Roman Catholicism. O'Connor would later think of Gilson as a more vigorous writer than Maritain.[21] As someone who rarely left the debates of the thirteenth century, Gilson maintained that Christian philosophy had important roots in a basic concept: Invisibilia Dei per ea quae facta sunt intellecta conspiciuntur (The mind perceives God's supernatural entities by means of created things).[22] As O'Connor developed as a writer, she placed a number of her protagonists in concrete situations that at first appear small, perhaps insignificant, until these characters experience their expansive nature and theological fullness. In this way, some of her protagonists gradually move closer and closer to an unspecified, but nevertheless mystical, beatific vision, though no one route is preferable to another in finding either one's heart or God—if that can, in the final analysis, be achieved. Still, Maritain and O'Connor both believed strongly in the spiritual unconscious that is part and parcel of the mysterious nature of the literary enterprise. By the time O'Connor arrived at Yaddo, she had read prolifically not only religious writers such as Georges Bernanos, Léon Bloy (Maritain's godfather), Graham Greene, François Mauriac (her personal library would eventually contain fifteen of Mauriac's books), and Evelyn Waugh, but also those who had made their mark on the world of literature from widely differing perspectives: William Faulkner, Katherine Ann Porter, Eudora Welty, Peter Taylor, Djuna Barnes, Dorothy Richardson, and Virginia Woolf ("Va. Woolfe," as she called her). Her interest in Russian and Polish fiction writers, including Dostoevsky, Tolstoy, Turgenev, Chekhov, Gogol, and Joseph Conrad (she read almost all his literary works), provides clear proof that her taste in fiction had a definite Catholic / catholic bias.[23] In much the same way, Lowell's interest in the works of explicitly Christian writers, in addition to more contemporary secular authors who had captivated him since his days as an undergraduate, could find striking echoes in O'Connor's own reading background. Each of them, in varying ways, could look through both ends of the telescope and thus make personal judgments about faith based in part—but only in part—on an awareness of important works of their Western literary heritage.

A faith commitment, no matter how often it is renewed, will bear fruit only if it emerges from the insights and experiences of the entire person, including the works of literature and the theology they internalize. Almost never in my experience as a Catholic priest are the works of one specific author the reason for someone's conversion to the faith. In the long run, personal prayer trumps intellectual acumen. I once asked Walker Percy why he had converted, and he replied that he had been led to the Catholic Church by reading Søren Kierkegaard. When I spontaneously remarked, "No one ever converted to Catholicism because of Kierkegaard," his face lit up and he thought for a minute before saying that he had actually been impressed by one of his North Carolina fraternity brothers who had the habit of rising early and going to daily Mass. During the twenty-three three-day retreats that Percy made during the course of his life at the Jesuit retreat house in Convent, Louisiana, he had many occasions to evaluate the various authors he had read and was reading. Conversion for him demanded ongoing acts of re-commitment.

O'Connor, a lifelong Catholic, stated explicitly in a letter to Helen Greene in May 1952 that her "philosophical notions don't derive from Kierkegard (I can't even spell it) but from St. Thomas Aquinas"— something that Percy would have appreciated, especially through his pro- longed studies of the medievally savvy semiotic philosopher Charles Sanders Peirce. It is worth noting that O'Connor explicitly states that her philosophical notions, *not* her theological ones—a crucial distinction— derive from Saint Thomas, though this distinction might not be all that clear-cut. Both Percy and O'Connor knew that religious commitment— and its transformation into works of literature—were a matter not just of accepting and repeating dogmas and decrees, but of interiorizing one's faith, sometimes in its ritualistic form, and allowing others to see that such faith not only can exist but also determine one's being, especially as a writer.

Lowell never forgot his first impression of O'Connor: "It seems such a short time ago that I met her at Yaddo, 23 or 24, always in a blue jean suit, working on the last chapters of *Wise Blood*, suffering from undiag- nosed pains, a face formless at times, then, very strong and young and right. She had already really mastered and found her themes and finely calibrated style, knew she wouldn't marry, would be Southern, shocking and disciplined. In a blunt, disdainful yet somehow very unpretentious and modest way, I think she knew how good she was."[24] Lowell undoubt- edly was taken by both O'Connor's disarming wit (deliciously sardonic at times) and determined commitment to her craft, even though later in her career she might work for months and throw everything away, not thinking that she had wasted her time at all.[25] While O'Connor might have been smitten by Lowell, no doubt prompted by his temporary re- commitment to Catholicism, their relationship, unlike the not-so-subtle amorous activities of some of the other Yaddo guests, never went beyond the bounds of propriety. It would have been clear to O'Connor that Lowell was reserving his expressions of affection for thirty-two-year-old Elizabeth Hardwick, also a Yaddo guest. Bishop had warned Lowell about not getting involved with Hardwick, someone he had known for a couple of years.[26] The marriage of Lowell and Hardwick on July 28, 1949, at his parents' house in Beverly Farms, Massachusetts, took place just after Lowell had been released from Baldpate, a small hospital in George-town, Massachusetts (where Giroux visited him), and before his stay at Payne Whitney Psychiatric Clinic on East Sixty-Eighth Street in New York, where Stafford had previously been hospitalized.

O'Connor and Hardwick seemingly had little in common and, in fact, never became close friends, though O'Connor considered her an excellent writer. Hardwick's background and lifestyle, had O'Connor even an inkling, would have astonished her. A native Kentuckian, the eighth of eleven children, Hardwick received a master's degree in English from the University of Kentucky in 1939 before heading off to Columbia to pursue graduate work for two more years. While living in New York in the early 1940s, she took up with Greer Johnson, a gay man she had known in Lexington. Her first novel, *The Ghostly Lover*, written while a student at Columbia, had been edited by John Woodburn, Giroux's good friend and colleague at Harcourt, Brace. In *Sleepless Nights*, published when she was sixty-two years old, the licentious protagonist, a Columbia student named Elizabeth, relates a decadent world that O'Connor could only have imagined in her wildest dreams:

> New York: there I lived at the Hotel Schuyler on West 45th Street, lived with a red-cheeked, homosexual man from Kentucky. We had known each other all our lives. Our friendship was a violent one and we were as obsessive, critical, jealous and cruel as any ordinary couple. The rages, the slamming doors, the silences, the dissembling. Each was for the other a treasured object of gossip and complaint. In spite of his inclinations, the drama was of man and woman, a genetic dissonance so like the marital howlings one could hear floating up from the courtyard or creeping up and down the rusty fire escapes.[27]

Lowell's famous poem "Man and Wife" recounts a moment, aided by a drug called Miltown, that reveals that his own out-of-control marriage with Hardwick had little chance of survival:

Man and Wife

Tamed by *Miltown*, we lie on Mother's bed;
the rising sun in war paint dyes us red;
in broad daylight her gilded bed-posts shine,

abandoned, almost Dionysian.
At last the trees are green on Marlborough Street,
blossoms on our magnolia ignite
the morning with their murderous five days' white.
All night I've held your hand,
as if you had
a fourth time faced the kingdom of the mad—
its hackneyed speech, its homicidal eye—
and dragged me home alive. . . . Oh my *Petite*,
clearest of all God's creatures, still all air and nerve:
you were in your twenties, and I,
once hand on glass
and heart in mouth,
outdrank the Rahvs in the heat
of Greenwich Village, fainting at your feet—
too boiled and shy
and poker-faced to make a pass,
while the shrill verve
of your invective scorched the traditional South.

Now twelve years later, you turn your back.
Sleepless, you hold
your pillow to your hollows like a child;
your old-fashioned tirade—
loving, rapid, merciless—
breaks like the Atlantic Ocean on my head.[28]

During their twenty-three years of marriage, Hardwick, always astonished at the depth of her husband's character, nursed him through his recurring manic-depressive episodes and hospitalizations. In many ways,
she became an articulate spokeswoman for those female writers who had
been seduced and then betrayed by the men they loved. One of her
greatest personal achievements was assisting Jason and Barbara Epstein
in founding the *New York Review of Books* in 1963, though most likely
O'Connor never knew about this publication.

As Lowell went through a process of metanoia, trying to retrieve a
faith that always seemed to escape his grasp, his behavior attracted attention. O'Connor's personal devotion to her faith undoubtedly awakened
something within Lowell. There was a bond between them that neither

defined with precision, preferring just to signal its presence. After he had separated from Hardwick in 1954, Lowell wrote to O'Connor, "Flannery, I love you very much," though he was quick to add that this was not a proposal.[29] Lowell repeated this word *love* in his tribute in *Flannery O'Connor: A Memorial*.[30] In a letter written in late 1957, he informs her that he considers her, Elizabeth Bishop, Peter Taylor, and Allen Tate as his "old friends."[31] Reciprocally, O'Connor continued in her own fashion to love Lowell, as she mentioned to Hester in a letter written in April 1956:

> I watched him that winter come back into the Church. I had nothing to do with it but of course it was a great joy to me. I was only 23 and didn't have much sense. He was terribly excited about it and got more and more excited and in about two weeks had a complete mental breakdown. That second conversion went with it, of course. He had shock treatments and all that, and when he came out, he was well for a time, married again a very nice girl named Elizabeth Hardwick, and since then has been off and on, in and out of institutions. . . . What I pray is that one day it will be easy for him to come back into the Church. He is one of the people *I love* and there is a part of me that won't be at peace until he is at peace in the Church [emphasis mine].

O'Connor's use of the word *love*, so honest and unnuanced, reveals a dimension of her life otherwise rarely seen, certainly not in her fiction, where she avoids depicting couples, young or otherwise, in love with each other, though she sometimes ended her letters to Maryat Lee with this word. What impressed Lowell was how O'Connor fused her habit of doing with her habit of being—particularly when focused on the process of conversion, as she wrote to Hester in April 1958: "It seems to me that all good stories are about conversion, about a character's changing. If it is the Church he's converted to, the Church remains stable and he has to change as you say—so why do you also say the character has to remain stable? The action of grace changes a character. Grace can't be experienced in itself."

Given her externally reserved personality, O'Connor had no intention of preaching to Lowell or serving as a catechetical mentor; she preferred just being present to him as a committed Catholic, continuing to express her faith as she had always done—in simple, unobtrusive ways that, of course, did not go unnoticed. In addition to going to Mass, as she had done almost every day at Saint Mary's Church during her three-year stay in Iowa City, she would soon start reading the breviary, a book used especially by priests and monks as they recited prescribed prayers and reflected on spiritual exhortations throughout the day. Since participation at religious services did not seem to be a priority for Yaddo guests, O'Connor accompanied Jim and Nellie Shannon, a caretaker and head cook at Yaddo, when they drove to Sunday Mass at Saint Clement's Church on Lake Avenue in Saratoga. O'Connor's devotion to the sacred liturgy was solidly based on its dogmatic, sacrificial dimensions. "Dogma," she informed Cecil Dawkins in December 1959, "is the guardian of mystery."

O'Connor had come to Yaddo not to find a husband, but to write and get published. Her first step in establishing herself as a professional writer was to write to Elizabeth McKee on June 19, 1948, indicating that she had been working on a novel "a year and a half and will probably be two more years finishing it"; at the suggestion of one of McKee's clients, Paul Moor, she asked McKee to become her agent. Though her relationship with McKee, a former editor at the *Atlantic Monthly*, provided her with a sustained conduit to the professional world of publishing, it did more than that: it helped to lessen her tendency to assume the responsibilities of a literary agent, mainly to guarantee control of the placement of certain stories.[32] McKee was a partner in McKee & Batchelder at 624 Madison Avenue in New York, as indicated on the inside address of O'Connor's first letters to her. She then joined Mavis McIntosh Riordan and Elizabeth Otis, a good friend of Giroux, at their firm of McIntosh & Otis at 30 East Sixtieth Street, which eventually became McIntosh, McKee & Dodds. When Giroux first met O'Connor, he had not yet met McKee; his contact had always been and would be for at least the next six years with McIntosh.[33] "Miss McIntosh," O'Connor wrote to Maryat Lee in early 1957, "is an old lady who sits at her desk with her hat on and Miss McKee is a youngish lady who speaks out of the side of her mouth like a refined dead-end kid"—perhaps, as Sally Fitzgerald once speculated, the result of facial paralysis.[34] Together, these two capable women would successfully represent such writers as William Styron, John Irving, Edna O'Brien, John Gardner, and Robert Coover.

O'Connor felt that the first chapters of her first novel were in no condition to be sent to anyone, certainly not a literary agent. She informed

McKee that the first chapter, "The Train," had been published (*Sewanee Review*, April–June 1948); the fourth chapter would appear in the new quarterly *American Letters* in the fall; another chapter had been sent to the *Partisan Review*, but she expected them to return it; and that a short story had been accepted by *Mademoiselle* for their fall issue. Wanting to become independent as soon as possible, O'Connor did not hide from McKee her concern about her personal finances: "I am writing you in my vague and slack season and mainly because I am being impressed just now with the money I am not making by having stories in such places as *American Letters*." McKee replied on June 23 that she would be glad to look at whatever O'Connor sent to her, indicating, too, that she was a good friend of John Selby at Rinehart & Company and could easily handle any contractual arrangements.

O'Connor probably knew little about Selby's background, especially his fiction, which most likely would not have appealed to her. By the time he came to know O'Connor, he had published four novels; the last, *Elegant Journey* (1944), concerned the Trace family history in his native Missouri from 1840 to 1880. After graduating from the University of Missouri in 1918, Selby worked as a journalist and music critic for the *Kansas City Star* until 1929. While living in France from 1929 to 1932, he furthered his interest in art and music, eventually working for the Associated Press. In 1944, he left the Associated Press to become associate editor and publicity director for Rinehart, assuming the role of editor in chief the following year.

McKee also contacted George Davis at *Mademoiselle* and asked him to send her the galleys of O'Connor's story. "Please don't let it worry you," McKee wrote to O'Connor, "that you are not a prolific writer, as that doesn't bother me at all. I know that you are sincerely interested and serious toward writing, and that is the determining factor in my attitude toward a writer."[35] In her letter dated July 4, 1948, O'Connor informed McKee that *Partisan Review* still had her story and that an unspecified story had been returned to her, but she thought it best not to send it to McKee. She mentioned to her agent that Selby had written her that he wanted to see the first draft of her novel before considering a contract, though she felt at that point that it would take six months to finish a first draft and then another year to finish the final version. She carefully kept McKee up to date about her progress. By mid-July, she noted she was working on the twelfth chapter of her novel and estimated that she would be kept busy with revisions for a while; in its final form, this chapter would run to 100,000 words. She enclosed a number of what she considered the best chapters, including "The Crop," which she asked McKee to try to place with a literary journal.[36] On July 21, before heading off to Milledgeville for six weeks, O'Connor thanked McKee for closely reading this story and returning it to her, but added that she did not want to fuss with it unless some publication expressed sincere interest. "I don't want an advance from Rinehart," she concluded, "until I finish the first draft and they see what they are getting—six or eight months hence."[37] Selby and McKee had lunch, as she mentioned in this letter, on Friday, July 30, just before McKee took off for a vacation in France. By early September, Selby had read O'Connor's story "The Turkey," which he returned to McKee, as well as some of the novel in progress, including chapter nine, "The Heart of the Park," which had been finally accepted by the *Partisan Review* (and was published in the issue of February 1949).[38] In her letter from Milledgeville, O'Connor informed McKee that she intended to be in New York later that month, staying at the Woodstock Hotel in Midtown Manhattan on her way back to Yaddo, and hoped for a meeting with Selby and Davis (about to resign as the fiction editor of *Mademoiselle*), who took her story "The Capture" for their November issue.[39]

Certainly Selby's hesitation about accepting the novel without reading it in its entirety had professional merit, but not the tone of the letter he sent to O'Connor. "What mystified John Selby," according to Virginia Wray,

is what was to become the essential nature of all of O'Connor's fiction beginning with *Wise Blood* and continuing up through her final and deathbed story, "Judgement Day." Invariably O'Connor uses her native deep-south Protestant homeland as setting for the development of religious themes. Every piece, no matter the cast of characters or the plot, explores the working of grace in a distinctly Southern territory occupied by the devil. Yet, ironically, both the Southern milieu and the religious themes are absent from the fiction prior to *Wise Blood*. A close reading of her early surviving works prior to *Wise Blood* suggests that only after O'Connor had left her native South was she fully imaginatively drawn to it—and embracing her southern home—to discover what she called her "true country."[40]

O'Connor's *Wise Blood* begins with the observation by Mrs. Wally Bee Hitchcock to Hazel Motes, "I guess you're going home," and ends with his landlady, Mrs. Flood, saying, after he had blinded himself like an American Tiresias, "I see you've come home!" Motes's final home is not, however, the house he returned to after the war; it would be an undefined spiritual place he had to discover. In effect, O'Connor's first novel, when completed, would explore her native literary and theological landscape. Her own personal, unexpected, definitive journey southward toward home lurked in the not-so-distant future. But now she was only beginning to locate her idiosyncratic dramatic voice and the locale in which this voice could best find expression. Since Selby had not seen the end of the novel, he could not have understood the importance of homeland in this text.

O'Connor commented more about *Wise Blood* in her letters than about any of her other fiction. In a March 1954 letter, for example, she wrote,

> Let me assure you that no one but a Catholic could have written *Wise Blood* even though it is a book about a kind of Protestant saint. It reduces Protestantism to the twin ultimate absurdities of The Church Without Christ or The Holy Church of Christ Without Christ, which no pious Protestant would do. And of course no unbeliever or agnostic could have written it because it is entirely Redemption-centered in thought. Not too many people are willing to see this, and perhaps it is hard to see because H. Motes is such an admirable nihilist. His nihilism leads him back to the fact of his Redemption, however, which is what he would have liked so much to get away from.

Though often solitary and reflectively intuitive like Hazel Motes, O'Connor had, it seems to me, more of the instincts of young Tarwater in *The Violent Bear It Away* as she moved steadily through her stories, her face set toward the dark city where the children of God lay sleeping. Her identification with Tarwater is clear from the way she signed some of her letters with variants of Tarwater's name—Tarblender, Tarsot, Tarbutter, Tarpot, Tarbug, Tarroot, Tarfunk, and, toward the end, Tarweary.

As O'Connor wrote day by day, following the lead of her characters and preferring not to outline this novel in advance, she continued to be upset by Selby's decision. The lack of funds continued to worry her, and she tried to do something about it. Davis agreed to write a letter of reference on her behalf for a Guggenheim application in 1948. She also asked for letters from Paul Engle, her mentor at the Writers' Workshop in Iowa; Robert Penn Warren, whom she had met briefly in April 1946 while at Iowa and who had publicly praised one of her stories; Theodore Amussen, who had been at Rinehart & Company before moving recently to Harcourt, Brace; and Philip Rahv, coeditor of the *Partisan Review*.[41] Of this group, Rahv is clearly the most atypical, mainly because of his family background and political convictions; he would publish two of O'Connor's stories, both chapters of *Wise Blood*, "The Heart of the Park" and "The Peeler" (December 1949).[42] The application was unsuccessful.

Feeling more relaxed and confident now that she had an agent, O'Connor wrote to McKee on September 18, 1948 "I am altogether pleased that you are my agent." With her newfound freedom, she started to rely on McKee's background and expertise. Not having time to retype "The Crop" as requested, she thought she could send McKee the first five chapters in about a month's time. Her progress to date pleased her. That September she met with Selby, who said that he needed to see six chapters before Rinehart would give her an advance.[43] On September 30 she sent McKee two copies of "The Geranium," the first story in her master's thesis, and one copy of "The Train," which she suggested be shown to Rahv—or anyone else. By early November, she changed her mind and said she intended to send McKee the first seven chapters, which comprised the first part of the novel. She finally sent "The Crop," reworked as "A Summer Story," to McKee.[44] On December 15 she wrote again to McKee: "Perhaps I shall get down [to New York] in January and perhaps before that send you the chapters I am working on. . . . I have decided, however, that no good comes of sending anything off in a hurry." McKee returned "A Summer Story" to the author with a polite note.[45] O'Connor sent McKee the first nine chapters of the novel, which she wanted her to pass on to Selby, on January 20, 1949. In the accompanying letter she raised a distinct possibility: if Rinehart rejected her novel, would Harcourt, Brace be interested in it, a suggestion made to her by Kazin. Little remained in her literary cupboard, but what she did have she wanted to have published; she herself would send chapter six to the *Kenyon Review*, and should they turn it down, then to the *Sewanee Review*. She informed McKee in a letter mailed eight days later that she could only stay at

Yaddo until April, but hoped to extend her stay through July and possibly return in the fall. As she worked away on her manuscript, her anxiety about the possible contract and advance from Rinehart did not diminish. Behind the scenes, McKee had apparently contacted Amussen at Harcourt, Brace and discussed an advance of $1,500. Understandably, O'Connor was anxious to discuss her tenuous situation with both her agent and Amussen. When she learned that McKee had talked to Selby, she was most concerned to learn about the outcome of their conversation.[46] Prompted by McKee, Selby wrote a letter to O'Connor in mid-February 1949:

> I think you are a pretty straight shooter, and I hope you won't mind if I work along the same line.
>
> You want to know about us, and we very much want to know what you need from us. I could assemble a large number of memos and give you almost paragraph by paragraph our own doubtless valuable ideas about the chapters we now have. I think this would be foolish, since what we need to tell you is basically simple.
>
> It is that you have an astonishing gift, that the chapters we have now don't seem to have the directness and direction that you probably feel yourself, and that here are probably some aspects of the book that have been obscured by your habit of rewriting over and over again.
>
> Do you want us to be specific and work with you the way we do with most of the writers on our list, or do you prefer to go it alone? To be honest, most of us have sensed a kind of aloneness in the book, as if you were writing out of the small world of your own experience, and as if you were consciously limiting this experience.
>
> I wish you would sit down and tell me what is what, so that you and ourselves will know on what basis to proceed.
>
> I also hope you won't mind this forthright letter.[47]

Incensed by Selby's critique of her writing habits and his overall evaluation of her work, O'Connor immediately wrote to McKee:

> I received Selby's letter today. Please tell me what is under this Sears Roebuck Straight Shooter approach. I presume Selby says either that Rinehart will not take the novel as it will be if left to my fiendish care

(it will be essentially as it is), or that Rinehart would like to rescue it at this point and train it into a conventional novel.

The criticism is vague and really tells me nothing except that they don't like it. I feel the objections they raise are connected with its virtues, and the thought of working with them specifically to correct these lacks they mention is repulsive to me. The letter is addressed to a slightly dim-witted Camp Fire Girl, and I cannot look with composure on getting a lifetime of others like them. I have not yet answered it and won't until I hear further from you, but if I were certain that Harcourt would take the novel, I would write Selby immediately that I prefer to be elsewhere.

Would it be possible for you to get the manuscript back now and show it to Harcourt, or does Rinehart hang onto it until we break relations. Please advise me what the next step is to be, or take it yourself. I'll probably come down week after next if you think it advisable. I am anxious to have this settled and off my mind so that I can get to work.

Thank you for sending the copies of my stories. They and the carbon of the novel have been sent to Mr. Moe [of the Guggenheim Foundation].[48]

Although O'Connor wanted the novel to be sent to Harcourt, Brace, she wondered if this could be done without a formal rejection from Rinehart. Clearly she was upset and wanted to settle the matter as quickly as possible and get back to writing, a normal procedure for her. She received McKee's reply on February 17, and promptly said that she would travel to New York soon. She wrote to Selby, stating her position about the novel, and made plans to be in New York City from February 24 to 26, staying at Hardwick's apartment, and hoping, if it could be arranged, to meet with Amussen or William Raney. "I have my doubt about the efficacy of a personal conversation with Selby," she mentioned to McKee, "as my experience with him is that he says as little as possible as vaguely as possible."[49] She believed that Selby's reply totally missed the point of the kind of novel she was writing. Lowell, too, had reacted negatively to Selby's letter, especially after he had read the first nine chapters and commented on them, but not without some reservations of his own.[50]

Resentful at being treated like a dimwitted child by Selby, O'Connor unconsciously—or perhaps consciously—was positioning herself, most likely with Kazin's and Lowell's concurrence, to approach Giroux at Harcourt, Brace. Her mid-February letter to Selby might have been meant to prompt him to abandon his interest in publishing her novel:

> I can only hope that in the finished novel the direction will be clearer, but I can tell you that I would not like at all to work with you as do other writers on your list. I feel that whatever virtues the novel may have are very much connected with the limitations you mention. I am not writing a conventional novel, and I think that the quality of the novel I write will derive precisely from the peculiarity or aloneness, if you will, of the experience I write from. I do not think there is any lack of objectivity in the writing, however, if this is what your criticism implies; and also I do not feel that rewriting has obscured the direction. I feel it has given whatever direction is now present.

While she might be amenable to criticism, it would have to deal with what she was actually trying to do. She concluded, "The finished book, though I hope less angular, will be just as odd if not odder than the nine chapters you now have." Willing nevertheless to keep the momentum going, O'Connor informed Selby that she would continue writing her novel, but only by following the interior pattern that the novel was in the process of establishing.

Clearly supportive of her new author, McKee set up an appointment for O'Connor with Selby on Tuesday, March 1, though O'Connor quickly replied that she would prefer a meeting on either Wednesday or Thursday.[51] "I am sorry you will have to break the Tuesday appointment with Selby," she wrote McKee. "I get in Tuesday night and will call you Wednesday morning. Any time after that will do for the appointment."[52] Once she arrived in New York, she learned that only Raney—who, along with Amussen when he was at Rinehart & Company, had assisted Norman Mailer with the publication of *The Naked and the Dead*—had apparently liked her novel (though even there, she mentioned, she only had secondhand evidence). She told Selby, as she mentions in a letter of April 1949 to Engle, that she would listen to criticism from Rinehart, but if it was not to her liking, she would disregard it. "That is the impasse." In the years to follow, O'Connor mellowed her tone, became more pliant, and even looked forward to receiving advice and comments about her work from those she trusted. But for now, she let her ego come forward and set the conditions for what she would or would not allow.[53]

The factor that precipitated the rather abrupt departure of Lowell, O'Connor, Hardwick, and Edward Maisel (a musicologist who took a fancy to O'Connor, though Lowell did not like him) from Yaddo that Tuesday morning had to do with Yaddo's creator and longtime director, Elizabeth Ames. The four had accused her of fostering an unfortunate friendship with Agnes Smedley, author of *China's Red Army Marches* and *Battle Hymn of China*. The events surrounding this situation become known nationally when Smedley was named as a Soviet spy by General Douglas MacArthur in the February 11, 1949, issue of the *New York Times*. (A few days later, the army admitted that it had no evidence for this accusation and the paper retracted its statement, though Smedley was later known to have spied on the Japanese for the Russians while in China.)[54] FBI agents visited Yaddo in mid-February, and when life there reached an intolerable point, the board convened a formal enquiry on Saturday, February 26, with Lowell assuming a leading role. During the session, O'Connor stated that she was leaving Yaddo the following Tuesday.[55] Robert Fitzgerald noted in his journal that the "day after the abortive meeting he [Lowell] went with Miss O'Connor, who is a Catholic, to [Sunday] Mass for the first time in over a year."[56]

After leaving Yaddo, O'Connor stayed with Hardwick at her apartment in the Devonshire House on East Tenth Street before moving to the Tatum House, an inexpensive YWCA residence on East Thirty-Eighth Street near Lexington Avenue. Lowell went to the Hotel Earle on Waverly Place, where, immediately upon his arrival on March 1, he sent an urgent evening telegram to Tate, then teaching at the University of Chicago, to come to his aid—no doubt signaling that he was in some type of acute emotional distress just as he was about to take O'Connor to see Giroux the next day.[57] When Lowell and O'Connor visited the Fitzgeralds in their apartment at 29 West 104th Street in New York on Ash Wednesday, Lowell announced that he had returned to the Church "after receiving an incredible outpouring of grace."[58] At this time, Lowell called Berryman in Princeton and asked him to join in some sort of "holy crusade," which Berryman summarily dismissed as a plea from someone who had drunk too much.[59] One can only imagine how Lowell had to control himself as he escorted O'Connor on Wednesday for their all-important meeting, during which he simply sat there, occasionally commenting on a number of people, but for the most part remaining silent.[60]

Thursday, March 3, as Ian Hamilton notes, was an incredibly disturbing day for Lowell; that morning he filled his bathtub and went into ecstatic convulsions praying to Saint Thérèse of Lisieux, whom Fitzgerald noted was O'Connor's patron. He then went to the Jesuit Church of Saint Francis Xavier on West Sixteenth Street and next to the Franciscan Church on West Thirty-First Street, still caught up in his excited state. He subsequently took a train to visit a Trappist monastery, Our Lady of the Valley Monastery, in Lonsdale, Rhode Island, in an attempt to achieve some spiritual equilibrium.[61] Fitzgerald immediately wrote a long letter to Tate and Gordon, giving his interpretation of Lowell's actions, fully aware of his friend's paranoiac tendencies.[62] Tate, who refused to travel east because Lowell had discussed publicly Tate's infidelities, subsequently saw Lowell in Chicago and wrote to Cleanth Brooks about Lowell's "delusional paranoia, far advanced religious mania (Christ, etc.) mixed up with sexual delusions."[63] In early April, Lowell, dirty and disheveled, took a train to stay with his old Kenyon College roommate and good friend Peter Taylor in Bloomington, Indiana; the two of them had dinner at a club. Afterward Lowell struck a policeman and spent time in jail. Eventually Lowell's mother, Lowell's friend John Thompson, and psychiatrist-poet Merrill Moore arrived and took him to Boston and subsequently to Baldpate.[64]

Lowell's odd behavior did not always remain secret. O'Connor later explained her thoughts about what had happened, considering it "revolting" that anyone would have shamelessly repeated the story, especially as Lowell was then close to a mental breakdown. She wrote to Hester in May 1960,

> He had the delusion that he had been called on some kind of mission of purification and he was canonizing everybody that had anything to do with his situation then. I was very close to him and so was Robert [Fitzgerald]. I was too inexperienced to know he was mad, I just thought that was the way poets acted. Even Robert didn't know it, or at least didn't know how near collapse he was. In a couple of weeks he was safely locked up. . . . Things went faster and faster and faster for him until I guess the shock table took care of it. It was a grief for me as if he had died. When he came out of it, he was no longer a Catholic."

In the spring of 1954, O'Connor informed the Fitzgeralds that she had previously written to Lowell, saying that his "not being in the Church was a grief to me and I knew no more to say about it. . . . I said the Sacraments gave grace—and let it go at that." Her subsequent sporadic letters to Lowell and his wife were fairly generic, and when she tried to be personal, she could be unexpectedly shocking, as when she revealed to them in March 1953 that she had lupus: "My father had it some twelve or fifteen years ago but at that time there was nothing for it but the undertaker." Though there existed a relationship in her mind between Lowell and death, as O'Connor mentioned in a June 1960 letter to John Hawkes, Lowell saw their relationship from a different angle, one that had its roots in a common bond that had to do with maddening, creative control: "I have been thinking that we perhaps have something of the same problem—how to hold one's true, though extreme vein without repetition; how to master conventional controls and content normal expectations without washing out all one has to say. This hurried way of saying it sounds cynical, but I think something like this happened to Shakespeare in moving from his clotted, odd, inspired *Troilus and Cressida* to the madder but more conventional *Lear*."[65] Because O'Connor did not want to become involved with Lowell's vacillating and irresolute personality—though she sometimes inquired of others about him—their friendship, which began so intensely and greatly impacted her future career, receded asymptotically, like one of Welty's undercurrents that over time seemed to disappear completely. Giroux continued seeing Lowell and communicating with him as he went through the process of editing his books.

The Lowell–Gordon–Tate relationship reveals a deep, swirling turbulence that existed before O'Connor went to Yaddo.[66] After two years at Harvard (1935–1937), and at the urging of Merrill Moore, Lowell went south to meet Ford Madox Ford, whom he had previously encountered in Boston.[67] Lowell felt that Harvard was not particularly interested in exposing its students to contemporary poetry. Thus he bivouacked for three months in a tent on Tate and Gordon's front lawn, a time described in his poem "An Afternoon in an Umbrella Tent at Benfolly." When he first arrived at Benfolly, a rather dilapidated Greek Revival mansion overlooking the Cumberland River near Clarksville, Tennessee, he realized that his world was about to change. He put aside thoughts of his native New England: "My head was full of Miltonic, vaguely piratical ambitions. My only anchor was a suitcase, heavy with bad poetry. I was brought to earth by my bumper mashing the Tates' frail agrarian mail box post.

Getting out to disguise the damage, I turned my back on their peeling, pillared house. I had crashed the civilization of the South."[68] Not totally pleased about his uninvited visitor, Tate wrote to Andrew Lytle that "the Lowell boy" turned up twice and seemed to be a potential nuisance.[69]

When Ford Madox Ford arrived to visit the Tates in May 1937, he again met Lowell, and not long afterward Tate, Gordon, and Lowell drove Ford cross-country for a literary conference in Michigan, as captured in Lowell's poem "A Month of Meals With Ford Madox Ford." Ford and Lowell then moved on to another writers' conference at the University of Denver, where Lowell first met his future wife Jean Stafford.[70] Feeling Tate's influence more and more, Lowell entered Kenyon College in Gambier, Ohio, to study with John Crowe Ransom, who had previously been Tate's mentor. This is the point about which Welty's image of the confluence unpredictably spirals. While at his new college, Lowell met Robie Macauley, later a close friend of O'Connor, and also began lifelong friendships with Randall Jarrell and Peter Taylor, both of whom would also have Giroux as an editor. (Taylor's short story "1939" concerns, in part, a Thanksgiving trip that he and Lowell took together in 1938. Lowell and Jarrell became roommates, a perfect match for two young men seriously aspiring to enter the world of poetry. It should be noted, too, that Ransom, who also taught Warren, Taylor, and Macauley, would later have an important role in the publication of O'Connor's short stories. While editing the *Kenyon Review* from 1939 to 1959, Ransom published four of O'Connor's stories: "The Life You Save May Be Your Own" [Spring 1953], "A Circle in the Fire" [Spring 1954], "The Artificial Nigger" [Spring 1955], and "Greenleaf" [Summer 1956]).[71] When Lowell undertook further studies at Louisiana State University in 1941, he came to know both Cleanth Brooks and Robert Penn Warren; the latter he considered the best teacher he ever had. Two important Brooks and Warren texts, *Understanding Poetry* and *Understanding Fiction*, shaped the methodological thinking of professional writers and students of literature, including O'Connor, for decades afterward.

Given this highly intricate social and literary network, which O'Connor might have discerned in her own way over the years, she would never have suspected how important Gordon—and, to a lesser degree, Tate—would be in evaluating the novel she was working on at Yaddo. More than any of Lowell's friends, except for Giroux, Gordon would have the most significant impact upon O'Connor's initial career as a writer, though a good part of their literary communication has been lost.[72] Above all, Gordon encouraged O'Connor to approach her fiction in a way that always seemed somewhat strange to the younger writer but, at the same time, not disassociated from what she had seen during her graduate school years. Gordon focused on what she considered the nature of literature, which integrated her Southern background with her religious convictions. Born in 1895 in southern Kentucky, near the Tennessee border, she brought to her reading of O'Connor's fiction strongly weighted values and experiences rooted in the postbellum South and the Western Frontier, later transformed by her knowledge of the philosophy and literary perspectives of the Southern Agrarians. She graduated from Bethany College in West Virginia in 1916 and then moved to Chattanooga, Tennessee, to work on a local newspaper. After moving home again, at age twenty-nine she met Tate, introduced to her by his former college roommate Robert Penn Warren. She and Tate married in a civil ceremony in 1925 in New York.

Though Gordon developed as an independent fiction writer, she is often discussed in terms of her collaborations with her husband, who in many ways overshadowed her. The youngest of three boys, Tate was born in 1899 in Winchester, Kentucky, and since his family moved frequently, he was forced to study a good deal on his own. With a quick mind and a discerning intellect he entered Vanderbilt in 1918; during his senior year he began attending gatherings led by Ransom and Donald Davidson, a member of the English faculty. Their journal, *The Fugitive*, for which Tate served as assistant editor in 1923, helped to introduce new and more critical approaches in post–World War I American literature. As these postwar writers became more numerous and vocal, their message served as a clarion call to Southerners (*and* Northerners) to reject industrialism in the South, arguing instead for agrarianism and the preservation and development of Southern literature, which reflected in its own way the wit and intelligence of the ancient classical age. In his well-known work "Ode to the Confederate Dead" (a "masterly poem," according to O'Connor, and subsequently translated into French by Maritain), Tate exhibits an inquiring intellectual posture steeped in Southern history, no doubt the result of research for his biographies of Stonewall Jackson and Jefferson Davis. In this poem, he depicts a former Confederate soldier ruminating on issues of honor, heroism, and mortality—in short, his place in the world—as he looks over a Confederate graveyard.[73] This powerful image implicitly embodies many of the questions Southerners were asking as they transformed their past, becoming less and less recognizable after the Civil War, into viable life structures that incorporated both old and new forms of identity.

With two such powerful minds not always working in synchronism with one another, it was inevitable—no doubt due, in part, to their wanderlust—that Gordon and Tate had significant marital troubles. Their two marriages had an imploding-exploding synergism that would have flattened lesser souls. In October 1928 they sailed to Europe on the SS *America*, and Tate visited Warren, then a Rhodes scholar at Oxford, and Eliot, a poet he had long admired, in London. When the couple arrived in Paris, they socialized with the transplanted American writers who often gathered in Gertrude Stein's famous salon on the Rue de Fleurus. They even rented a two-room apartment a few doors away from Stein's before moving into one owned by Ford. Urging Gordon to complete her first novel *Penhally*, Ford typed parts of her manuscript, requiring that she dictate five thousand words per day to him. In short, Tate and Gordon witnessed firsthand the avant-garde literary currents then in vogue in France. Gordon profited immensely from the advice and criticism of her literary mentor and was more than willing to assume the same role for Flannery O'Connor.

Tate gained considerable recognition at this point in his life with his important essay "Remarks on the Southern Religion," which appeared in *I'll Take My Stand: The South and the Agrarian Tradition*, a collection of significant essays by twelve Southern Agrarians.[74] This volume embodied their thinking about Southern culture, society, religion, industry, and the arts, not unlike what Matthew Arnold and Thomas Carlyle had done in a more sustained way about British culture for Victorian England. Most likely these essays did not influence O'Connor since she read them late in her life, but her acquaintance with a number of the principal actors in the Fugitive / Agrarian movement and their methodological concepts gave her the opportunity to view and evaluate her own fiction through this particular literary lens. The influence of the Agrarians on O'Connor, Katherine Hemple Prown notes, "stemmed from the central role they played in the dissemination and, eventually, in the institutionalization of the foundational theories and discourses underpinning the modern emergence of a self-conscious body of Southern writing and literary criticism and in the formulation of broader theories regarding the interpretation of literature generally."[75] It could be argued that the conversions of both Gordon and Tate to Catholicism reflected their disaffection with the Agrarian philosophy, especially after World War II and the burgeoning acceptance of industrial capitalism in the United States.[76] O'Connor never became an acolyte for the Agrarians, for she sought to give an explicitly transcendent foundation to her fiction. After the onset of lupus, she felt more attracted to some of the concepts of Saint Thomas Aquinas, which metaphysically grounded her in a way few of her literary contemporaries—Tate and Gordon perhaps being the exceptions in this case—felt they needed.

At this point, Welty's confluence continues to swirl and twist about. After a stint at the Women's College of the University of North Carolina from early 1938 to the summer of 1939, Gordon and Tate moved from Greensboro to Princeton and remained there until the summer of 1942. When Tate's contract as the first fellow in creative writing was not renewed, they moved to Monteagle, Tennessee, five miles north of the University of the South at Sewanee. One has only to read Tate's essay "Miss Emily and the Bibliographer," based on Faulkner's short story "A Rose for Emily" and delivered as a lecture in the spring of 1940 at Princeton, to sense the resentment Tate bore against certain Princeton faculty. Faulkner's Miss Emily refused to accept the death of her former lover and grotesquely kept his body in her bedroom. Tate writes, "It is better to pretend with Miss Emily that something dead [past works of literature taught at Princeton] is living than to pretend with the bibliographer [some colleagues at Princeton] that something living is dead."[77] The move south would prove fortuitous for O'Connor because Tate and Gordon reestablished ties with Lowell, who was beginning to come into his own as a writer.

Once in more congenial surroundings, the couple invited Lowell and also Stafford, then writing *The Outskirts*, later to become *Boston Adventure*, to live with them, and by March 1943 Lowell had written a good number of the poems that appeared in his first book, *Land of Unlikeness*, a collection of twenty-one intensely religious poems most likely influenced by the seventeenth-century metaphysical poets. Gordon worked indefatigably, publishing five novels and working on another, *The Women on the Porch*. This was not a pleasant time for Tate and Gordon, especially due to Tate's infidelities, and their marriage gradually fell apart. In August 1943 they moved to Washington, DC, where they invited Brainard

("Lon") and Frances ("Fannie") Neel Cheney, fellow Tennesseans they had known for a long time, to live in the downstairs section of their house. Lon had taken a position as advisor and executive secretary to U.S. Senator Tom Stewart of Tennessee, while Tate employed Fannie, a former student of Ransom at Vanderbilt University, as his assistant. She would later become president of the National Library Association. Tate enjoyed his role as poetry consultant at the Library of Congress (1943–1944) and was succeeded in this post by Warren, who later became the Library of Congress's first poet laureate. The Cheneys and O'Connor would become good friends, visiting one another's homes beginning in the summer of 1953 and subsequently entering into a warm and protracted correspondence. (Vanderbilt University's Heard Library contains 188 surviving letters and carbons, of which 117 are from O'Connor.)

When Tate took over the editorship of the *Sewanee Review* for two years beginning in October 1944, just as the war in the Pacific was building to a crisis, one of the first things he did was solicit and article from Maritain.[78] Though neither Tate nor Gordon was Catholic at this point, they were gradually heading in that direction, and while Maritain, who would greatly influence O'Connor's religious sensibilities, was an unusual choice as a possible author for this journal, Tate's initiative shows that he was willing to take risks just as he was beginning his new job.[79] When the Cheneys entered the Catholic Church in 1953, Tate and Gordon served as their godparents. In a minimal way, it might be said that Tate was searching for some moral and religious stability in his life—and reaching out to Maritain for an essay on Catholicism was simply a sign of this. After Tate and Gordon had another terrible fight in New York in 1945, Gordon rented a room in Princeton. Lowell and Stafford then offered her refuge in their home in Damariscotta Mills, Maine (a residence paid for by the financial success of *Boston Adventure*, edited by Giroux), and she accepted. Unfortunately, the three could not tolerate one another, so much so that Stafford once called the sheriff to intervene. These sometimes explosive conversations, about which we can only speculate, were part of the fabric of the lives of Gordon, Tate, Maritain, Lowell, Stafford, Giroux, and others who entered and exited this turbulence at various times.[80] Giroux often visited Gordon and Tate in Princeton, and they visited his home in Pittstown, New Jersey.[81] Thus he was fully aware of their marital difficulties. Little would O'Connor, as an up-and-coming writer, ever have imagined that a small core of people associated at various times with Princeton would have such a remarkable impact on her life and career. In effect, these writers and scholars were establishing a critical hegemony by mentoring, directly and indirectly, not only O'Connor but also other future literary stars. In retrospect, Lowell brought to Giroux's office not only O'Connor, but also Davidson, Maritain, Ransom, Stafford, Warren, and Berryman, as well as Tate and Gordon and, through them, their friends the Cheneys.

If Lowell gradually became a more and more distant part of O'Connor's life, the same was not true for Sally and Robert Fitzgerald, whom O'Connor first met when a mentally unstable Lowell brought her to their apartment on York Avenue in early March 1949. At this point, the confluence loops back and circles around. Robert had met Lowell in 1946 through Randall Jarrell during the first year that Robert taught at Sarah Lawrence College in Bronxville, New York.[82] "Fitzgerald is good on classics and good (very strident Catholic, though) on religion," Lowell wrote to Berryman in late August 1948. "Terribly patient and earnest and somehow surprisingly subtle at times—completely unselfish."[83] As with Jarrell, Giroux had a fine professional and personal relationship with the Fitzgeralds, both before and after their divorce. When he first started at Harcourt, Brace, Giroux came to know Robert Fitzgerald through Dudley Fitts. After finishing high school in 1928, Fitzgerald had spent a year at the Choate School in Wallingford, Connecticut, where Fitts was one of the masters. Fitzgerald went on to Trinity College, Cambridge University, from 1931 to 1932 and had a chance to meet T. S. Eliot, who encouraged him to write poetry. After graduating from Harvard in 1933, he worked at the New York *Herald Tribune* and *Time* magazine. Fitts tapped Fitzgerald as his cotranslator for a series of works of Greek drama, ending with Fitzgerald's fantastic solo rendering of *Oedipus at Colonus*.[84] Between translations, Fitzgerald served in World War II, assigned in late 1944 to the commander in chief of the Pacific fleet, first at Pearl Harbor and then in Guam. In fact, his naval career had certain similarities to Giroux's.

In late August 1949, at her own suggestion, O'Connor began living with the Fitzgeralds, then on Acre Road in Redding Ridge (adjacent to Ridgefield), Connecticut. There she would care for their two children and work on her novel.[85] Her room for approximately the next sixteen months, over an attached garage, had windows on three sides and looked out at the forest of oak, pine, and maple, so at odds with the locale of Taulkinham that she described in *Wise Blood*. The following May, O'Connor and Giroux acted as godparents for Maria Juliana Fitzgerald, becoming, in effect, a part of the larger Fitzgerald family. The O'Connor–Fitzgerald–Giroux relationship continued when the Fitzgeralds selected and edited *Mystery and Manners*. Robert wrote the introduction to *Everything That Rises Must Converge*, and Sally introduced *Three by Flannery O'Connor* and selected and edited O'Connor's posthumous collection of letters, *The Habit of Being*. In addition, son Michael Fitzgerald produced John Huston's 1979 film *Wise Blood*, with a script written by his brother, Benedict Fitzgerald. The 1988 Library of America edition of O'Connor's collected works was edited by Sally Fitzgerald.

As Robert Fitzgerald mentions in his introduction to *Everything That Rises Must Converge*, "Flannery was out to be a writer on her own and had no plans to go back to live in Georgia. Her reminiscences, however, were almost all about her home town and countryside, and they were told with gusto."[86] O'Connor rarely spoke about her three years in Iowa City while staying with the Fitzgeralds, but both husband and wife were aware of the work of Robie Macauley. In Redding, they all read and admired Andrew Lytle's classic essay on Gordon, whom the Fitzgeralds likewise knew. In addition, they read some of the works of Cardinal John Henry Newman and Lord Acton, as well as the Reverend Philip Hughes's *History of the Church*. After the children had been put to bed, O'Connor found time to read other important works, including the *Divine Comedy*, Maritain's *Art and Scholasticism*, *The Family Reunion* by T. S. Eliot (which had a successful Broadway run a few years before), and books by the French literary critic and traditionalist Émile Faguet. She eventually learned that Robert had been raised as a Catholic, but left the Church in his late teens. After his subsequent marriage outside the Church was annulled, he gradually reunited with Roman Catholicism. When O'Connor came to know Sally better, she also learned that she had been a convert. Like Lowell, Robert Fitzgerald had distinct memories of his first visit with O'Connor, "frowning and struggling softly in her drawl" as she chose her words with great care. "We saw a shy Georgia girl, her face heart-shaped and pale and glum, with fine eyes that could not stop frowning and open brilliantly upon everything. We had not then read her first stories, but we knew that Mr. Ransom [then editor of the *Kenyon Review*] had said of them that they were *written*."[87]

Based on the Fitzgeralds' and Lowell's support for O'Connor, Giroux intuited over the ensuing months that he could take a lot for granted, especially O'Connor's years of study and writing both in college and as a recipient of a graduate school scholarship in journalism at the State University of Iowa. Details about her educational and literary background would come later, once this initial encounter in his office was finished. O'Connor's great challenge now consisted in learning what type of professional posture she wanted to project, while remaining true to the not-as-yet-completely-articulated, deep-set values she had developed over the years. While in Iowa, she published an essay in the 1948 *Alumnae Journal* of the Georgia State College for Women concerning her experiences there, which contains a straightforward assessment: "No one can be taught to write, but a writing ability can be more quickly developed when it is concentrated up and encouraged by competent literary people than when it is left to wander. A graduate program for writers should give the writer time and credit for writing and for wide reading, and if his writing and reading are of high enough quality, it should offer him a degree."[88] O'Connor set out the basics but did not feel she had to be a publicity agent for the Iowa Writers' Workshop, considered by some to be the most successful of its type. Old-fashioned Southern charm worked well at white-gloved tea parties and polite gatherings in Milledgeville, where O'Connor had lived from age thirteen until the time she headed off to Iowa, but she was experienced enough to know that it would not sell on Madison Avenue in New York City. Since she had never had a *real* job up to this point, she had to learn how accommodating she should be before those, such as Selby or Giroux, who had the power to see that her works would or would not be published. Maps existed—one had only to read the biographical sketches of established writers—but she was not sure which road to take to get her where she wanted to go. "What first stuns the young writer emerging from college," she noted in the alumnae journal, "is that there is no clear-cut road for him to travel on. He must chop a path in the wilderness of his own soul; a disheartening process, lifelong and lonesome." Put succinctly, O'Connor felt the options were limited for someone with literary ambitions: either take writing courses or consider "the poor house" and "the mad house."

While not earthshaking, the initial meeting between O'Connor and Giroux proved to be a *callida iunctura*, although neither party was at all sure where it would lead. It would not take Giroux long to realize how focused O'Connor was on becoming a serious writer even at such an early stage in her literary development; she was absolutely convinced that she needed not only to work at her own speed but also publish as soon as reasonably possible—attributes that Giroux could only admire. During their meeting in his office, Giroux noted that though O'Connor was "very parsimonious with words," he "decided at that very moment that [he] was sorry [he] didn't have her under contract." He added, "You look at her when you're talking to her and she tells the truth, but she does it in her own way, which is very peculiar, of course. That was her gift."[89] Giroux found O'Connor direct, honest, and open, with wonderful, clear eyes that revealed much to him. Later he came to realize, as he mentioned in the O'Hare interview, that O'Connor's "intellect was superior to all the people she was dealing with and she knew it and it didn't bother her, that's rare, almost a unique thing in my experience."

At that point O'Connor had published more than Giroux suspected, though he had already been aware of her writing. After rejoining Harcourt, Brace in early 1946 subsequent to the completion of his tour of duty in the navy, he had traveled in March 1947 to the Women's College of the University of North Carolina at Greensboro, where he joined Warren, Taylor, Macauley, Ransom, Lowell, and Jarrell to select the winning story in a college fiction contest; it turned out to be one of O'Connor's stories.[90] Because of his involvement with the university and the Arts Forum, Taylor secured Warren as the main speaker. At the last minute, Giroux, who worked with Lambert Davis, Warren's editor at Harcourt, Brace, expressed interest in attending and was invited to join the select group. According to Giroux, the forum was a "rousing success," something like a family reunion for this particular group. Tate, to cite but one connection, had previously had the honor of giving away the bride, Eleanor Ross, when she married Taylor at Monteagle, Tennessee, in June 1943, with Lowell serving as best man.[91] Never one to miss a good business opportunity, Giroux talked with Taylor, whose books *The Long Fourth and Other Stories* and *A Woman of Means* he would later edit.

Though Giroux might have recalled O'Connor's winning story when they first met, neither was aware of the countless factors already at work on both sides, some quite subtle and never to be brought to the surface or made explicit, even if one or the other wanted to make it so. Over the years, they would come to know each other better, not just through personal conversations and visits and the comments made by mutual friends, but especially through Giroux's expert advice about O'Connor's fiction. By the time he retired, Giroux could easily be counted as among the very best editors produced in the United States, if one could make a judgment based solely on the number of his authors who received either the Nobel Prize or the Pulitzer Prize in literature.[92] Before leaving Giroux's office, O'Connor asked about Thomas Merton, the Trappist monk, and Giroux was most pleased to give her a copy of Merton's recently published *The Seven Storey Mountain,* which was enjoying tremendous success and which would become Giroux's best-selling book.[93] Later, Giroux linked Merton and O'Connor together, as did Sally Fitzgerald in her essay "Rooms With a View," since both monk and fiction writer had much in common, particularly, according to Giroux, a highly developed sense of wit, deep faith, and great intelligence: "The aura of aloneness surrounding each of them was not an accident. It was their métier, in which they refined and deepened their very different talents in a short span of time. They both died at the height of their powers."[94] Merton flourished in the seclusion of the monastery, due in large part to his searching imagination and his desire to communicate through the printed word. His vocation had many similarities with that of O'Connor. To those who believed that a Trappist monk should keep silent, both in and out of the cloister, Giroux would send a succinct six-word card he had printed: "Writing is a form of contemplation." O'Connor would have instinctively understood this observation.

CHAPTER TWO

Flannery O'Connor

1925–1948

Born when Robert Giroux was in sixth grade, Mary Flannery O'Connor (she dropped her first name about 1941) discouraged others, with no considerable success, from writing biographies of her, maintaining that "lives spent between the house and the chicken yard do not make exciting copy."[1] Given these limited parameters, who could argue with her? Yet, as intrepid letter writers tend to know, there is always the possibility that one's letters might become the basis of a biography. If that is true, O'Connor left a biographically ladened, albeit fragmented, paper trail: detailed, timely, witty, always personal, sometimes confrontational, occasionally repetitious as situations arose reminiscent of those in the past, yet always capturing the changes in her mind and spirit as she responded to the momentary stresses and strains of her correspondents. As far as I can determine, O'Connor, like Giroux, never indicated that she burned any of the letters she received, nor did she restrict future scholars' access to her manuscripts and typescripts, even for a limited period of time. She omitted, however, from the toss-away line about the house and the chicken yard an important consideration: she constantly sought to return to her writing table, where through her stories, novels, and essays, she allowed the fullness of her imagination to surface. As Robert McGill observes, "For O'Connor, fiction represented a safer mode of expression, even if it too could be autobiographically inflected."[2] Six of her thirty-one published stories focus on a mother-and-daughter relationship, clearly representing a specific area of her creative psyche, one so pronounced that she must have been aware of it herself.[3] And because O'Connor died in her late thirties, her relatives and classmates, not discounting her mother, who outlived her by thirty-four years, either stepped forward and wrote about her or shared their recollections through interviews.

Unlike Giroux, whose childhood Jersey City virtually transmogrified itself during the course of his life, O'Connor lived almost exclusively, except for the five years in Iowa, New York State, and Connecticut, in two cities in Georgia: Savannah and Milledgeville. Though Giroux never really left his hometown, Jersey City changed constantly before his eyes as new immigrants arrived and populations shifted. In contrast, Milledgeville, the state capital from 1804 to 1868, prided itself on having been spared General Sherman's wrath (although some residences, the Central Depot, and the town arsenal were destroyed), with the result that many of its stately mansions were not torn down and replaced with generically designed apartment buildings.

Though she rarely alludes to it in her letters, O'Connor lived in Savannah for the first twelve and a half years of her life. In "The Nature and Aim of Fiction," she commented, "The fact is that anybody who has survived his childhood has enough information about life to last him the rest of his days."[4] The city of her birth had a long and distinguished history, still apparent today in its topographical design and character. When General James Oglethorpe and 114 men, women, and children landed their galley ship *Anne* on a high bluff along the Savannah River in 1733, he named the thirteenth colony after King George II. Although Catholics ("Papists," as they were called) were originally banned from this British colony, a small group of Maryland Catholics settled in Locust Grove around 1790 in present-day Sharon, Taliaferro County, fifty miles west of Augusta. Eventually, the Irish began settling in small pockets in Locust Grove, as can be ascertained from several tombstones in the nearby small cemetery. How much O'Connor knew of her distinguished family history is not altogether clear, though given the Southern penchant for bringing up family genealogy one way or another in polite discussion, she would have been somewhat familiar with the history of Locust Grove.

In general, O'Connor seemed dismissive of her family's connections to Georgia's past. If anything, she seemed to enjoy mocking patriotic salutes to the past, particularly the springtime pilgrimages to the ante-bellum houses. Her delightful story "A Late Encounter with the Enemy" depicts in part an elderly gentleman who confuses in his mind Civil War stories with Hollywood movie premieres. No doubt because she was surrounded by layers of history, she took it for granted and later left it to others—one has only to think of Margaret Mitchell's *Gone with the Wind*—to explore imaginatively that territory. Had she so chosen, her own family history would have given her overwhelming creative material. Her distant cousin through marriage Alexander Ignatius Jenkins Semmes, for example, had an interesting history as a physician and priest. Born in Washington, DC, in 1828, he was one of thirteen children of Raphael and Mary Matilda Jenkins Semmes, both of Charles County, Maryland. His relatives included Admiral Raphael Semmes of the Confederate Navy, author of a number of significant works on naval history, and Confederate Brigadier General Paul Jones Semmes, who perished at Gettysburg.[5] Alexander Semmes studied medicine, became a resident surgeon at Charity Hospital in New Orleans, and at the outbreak of the Civil War joined the Louisiana Volunteers, serving as a surgeon with General Harry T. Hays's Louisiana Brigade. After the war, he taught physiology at the Savannah Medical College. When his wife, Sarah (née Berrien), died in 1872, he decided to study for the priesthood and was ordained at age fifty. He died in 1898 of a stroke in Charity Hospital, where he had worked as a young physician. From childhood, Flannery O'Connor was aware of the history of the Semmes family since Mary Catherine Flannery, whom she called "Cousin Katie," married Raphael Semmes, a nephew of Admiral Semmes, and after her husband's death in 1916 she inherited his wealth, in addition to over a million dollars her father had left her in 1910, some of which she donated to Saint Joseph's Hospital in Savannah for a building called the Flannery Memorial Wing.[6] In 1958, Cousin Katie willed to Flannery O'Connor the O'Connor house at 207 East Charlton Street, which was eventually fixed up and rented out to boarders.

The maternal side of O'Connor's mother's family also traces its roots back to Locust Grove and Patrick Harty from County Tipperary, who moved there in 1824.[7] His Irish-born daughter Johannah, who became Flannery O'Connor's great-grandmother, married Hugh Donnelly Treanor in 1848. Hugh Treanor moved in 1833 to Milledgeville, where he bought and operated a grist mill. "Mass was first said here [in

Milledgeville] in my great-grandfather's hotel room," O'Connor wrote in May 1963 to Janet McKane, "later in his home on the piano." After his death, his widow donated land in Milledgeville for the construction of Sacred Heart Church, completed in 1874, which eventually served as O'Connor's home parish.[8]

The history of O'Connor's father's family could have also been transformed into captivating fiction. After the Civil War, O'Connor's great-grandfather Patrick O'Connor, a native Irishman, came to Savannah, where he operated a livery service and manufactured wagons. His son Edward Francis, born in 1872 in Savannah, eventually established himself there as a prominent wholesale grocer and banker. But it was his son, Edward Francis Jr., the eldest of eight children, six of whom were boys, whose life touched Flannery O'Connor's most of all. Born in 1896 in Savannah and educated at a Benedictine school in Savannah and Mount Saint Mary's College in Emmitsburg, Maryland, the oldest Catholic independent college in the country, Edward seemed to enjoy life as a youth. As a member of the Junior Hussars, he made a dashing appearance whenever he put on his white linen suit and tilted his straw boater over his eye.[9] He served for just over a year in the Georgia National Guardsmen, beginning in the summer of 1916, mainly by patrolling the border of New Mexico against the rebel forces of Pancho Villa. But his life changed when he took to heart words spoken by President Woodrow Wilson in April 1917 to Congress: "The world must be made safe for democracy. Its peace must be planted upon the tested foundations of political liberty."

At the outbreak of World War I, Edward O'Connor, who was later to become Flannery O'Connor's father, joined the 325th Infantry Regiment of the 82nd Division of the American Expeditionary Forces, which had been organized at Camp Gordon, Georgia, before he relocated in late April to Camp Upton in Suffolk County, New York. What was about to take place in his life, though not unlike that which thousands of other soldiers experienced on both sides of the Maginot Line, proved to be ineffable—and later his daughter never even hinted about it in any of her writings. As each soldier from this regiment, including Private Dick Steenhoek of Company K, whose service record has been meticulously tracked, walked up the gangplank in Hoboken, New Jersey, Edward O'Connor responded to his name and was assigned to a compartment in one of the holds below.[10] The first and second battalions, consisting of 58 officers and 2,082 enlisted men, boarded the British ship HMS *Khyler*

Baltic, and the third battalion, with 45 officers and 1,406 enlisted men, boarded another British ship, HMS *Karmala*, which had been formerly used as an Indian freight vessel. The crews on both ships were mostly Portuguese and East Indians. From one of fourteen troop ships setting out to open sea, Edward O'Connor glimpsed the Statue of Liberty, reminding him of the mission that lay ahead of him.

When the convoy arrived in Liverpool, these soldiers bivouacked just outside the city before crossing the English Channel to LeHavre. From approximately June 25 to September 16, many of these troops fought near Toul and Marbache before advancing to Saint-Mihiel in northeastern France—the first time that military units composed totally of American soldiers fought in the war. The record of the First Battalion, 327th Infantry, is clear and precise. On October 11 they pressed on to the Meuse-Argonne region along the Aire River and "advanced as ordered, passing through elements of the other two battalions and the right of the 325th Infantry, and gained its objective about 7:00 p.m. Some of its troops withdrew from the summit of the ridge during the evening, but returned before midnight and organized the crest for defense." It is not too difficult to picture O'Connor trying to breathe as canisters of mustard gas were tossed at the American doughboys and the trenches filled up with rotting sandbags, stagnant mud, and discarded debris. During the last three weeks of October, the 325th, relieving elements of the 327th and 328th, fought against the Germans, as various companies took up strategic positions. "By the 18th of October," according to Steenhoek, "what was left of the 82nd Division was organized along a line from Châtel-Chéhéry, to Marcq and Champigneulle." After the Armistice was signed in November 1918, the 82nd Division was sent home on ships, departing from the ports of Brest and Bordeaux during the early summer of 1919. Lieutenant O'Connor returned home that May with a Victory Medal and a Victory button. However much he tried later in his life, how could he ever have explained sufficiently the months and months of sheer hell he had experienced? His division had spent 105 days in combat on the front lines, suffering 6,664 battle wounded and 1,413 battle deaths. It is not surprising that his subsequent work with the American Legion, particularly as the commander of Chatham Post No. 36, led him to a statewide position of prominence in 1936. The early stages of lupus, thought then to have been arthritis, soon after forced him to curtail his involvement with this organization.

Edward O'Connor adjusted to life after the war as best he could. He was fortunate to meet his future bride, Regina Cline, at the wedding ceremony of his sister Nan and Herbert Cline. After a short courtship, Edward and Regina married in Sacred Heart Church in Milledgeville on October 14, 1922. They first lived in the Graham Apartments, on Savannah's Oglethorpe Square, before settling into a three-bay townhouse at 207 East Charlton on Lafayette Square, which they rented from Cousin Katie. The square's brick-lined streets, azalea bushes, and cypress and elm trees created a genteel atmosphere, though the square itself, which served as an open-air market, had trolley tracks running through it.

Whenever Flannery O'Connor visited her playmate, Betty Jean McGuire, who lived nearby and whose picture can still be seen in the O'Connor house, now restored as a museum, she passed several architecturally significant buildings that exposed her not only to the history of the city but also to its remarkably symmetry. From her parents' bedroom, for example, she could see the Hamilton-Turner House, which was built for successful businessman Samuel Pugh Hamilton in 1873. Reflecting Second Empire baroque as well as Italianate architectural influences, it became, in 1883, the very first residence in Savannah with electricity. In 1929 Cousin Katie moved from Monterey Square to 211 East Charlton, next door to the O'Connors, bringing with her an unmarried cousin and two women friends. After Edward O'Connor bought his house, he conveyed it in a "debt deed" to Cousin Katie for $4,500; through default, the house eventually reverted to her. In effect, Cousin Katie owned this building, and, in doing so, became a principal benefactor to not only the O'Connor family but also many of her other relatives. The O'Connors hung over their fireplace an imposing, not-especially-flattering baby portrait of Cousin Katie that they had received as a gift—a daily reminder of her presence in their lives.

Whether rich and powerful or not, it was common for those living in and around Lafayette Square to have day help on occasion, allowing time for the families to visit, shop along downtown's Broughton Street, go to movies at the Odeon or the Bijoux, and take their children to school or to church—which for the O'Connors meant the French Gothic Cathedral of Saint John the Baptist, just beyond the square. The soaring twin spires of the original cathedral, whose cornerstone was laid in November 1873, dominated the surrounding area then as they continue to do today. Destroyed by fire in February 1898, the cathedral, which reopened in May

1912, featured five full-length stained glass windows executed by Austrian glassmakers on each side of the nave. It is worth stressing the importance of the spiritual imagery of these windows, especially when the sun makes them radiant. The window above the main altar portrays John baptizing his cousin, Jesus, who is standing in the Jordan River; on the lower left quadrant of the window a boy has his eyes fixated on Jesus—a scene that could well have lingered in O'Connor's imagination during her formative years, until it found its imaginative fruition in her story "The River." And yet, countless Catholic schoolchildren have given vivid testimony that being shepherded into a church by excessively vigilant nuns in long, black habits does not necessarily lead to deep spirituality. However, during Mass, especially on "holy days of obligation," the smoky arabesques emanating from the thurible and the Gregorian chant wafting to the ceiling created for each participant an atmosphere by which they could enter further into the mystery of the Eucharist being celebrated in the sanctuary.

Mary Flannery was baptized in this cathedral on April 12, 1925, received her First Communion there in May 1932, and was confirmed there two years later. Her mother's oldest sister, Mary Cline, noted for her long, aristocratic face and sweetness of voice, served as her godmother. O'Connor remained a faithful Catholic communicant for the rest of her life; private and liturgical prayer lifted up her inner spirits, creating a spiritual center from which she could live as authentically as possible. Many O'Connor critics correctly (though somewhat dismissively) note that she was a "devout Catholic," which too often, without any modifying explanation, sounds as though she were a mechanical and robot Christian, which was not the case. O'Connor simply could not have sustained an intense prayer life, especially when living with a deadly disease, without experiencing the efficacy of what she would have considered prayer-filled graces, coming at times, even as a young girl, when she least expected them.

Perhaps not surprisingly, O'Connor's Catholic school education seemed marginal in the formation of her spiritual life, but what she learned from the nuns who taught her had a profound significance in her life, no matter how cavalierly she tended to dismiss it. Her Catholic grade-school environment reinforced the piety she experienced at home, becoming the single most important factor that sustained her throughout her fairly brief adult life. The prayer journal O'Connor wrote while in graduate school would not have been possible without the prayer life that had been there from her earliest days. The Sisters of Mercy who had, since 1845, staffed Saint Vincent's Grammar School for Girls, the first of two schools O'Connor attended in Savannah, delivered what would have been considered an acceptable education in that period. Although the young women who entered this congregation had an extended period of spiritual formation, if not strictly theological training, they were expected to receive whatever college-level education they could during the summer months, which meant that they were in classrooms during almost the entire year. In addition, these religious women ran an orphanage, Saint Mary's Home, which closed in June 2010 after 135 years of existence. O'Connor remembered it as a desolate house on a dreary street.

Six-year-old Mary Flannery, hand in hand with her protective mother, started going to Saint Vincent's in 1931. The school was located a short distance from their house in a building near the cathedral on Lafayette Square. Sisters Mary Consuela and Mary Franzita, her first- and second-grade teachers, applauded her reading skills and knowledge of the *Baltimore Catechism* but were less happy with her mastery of arithmetic. Some of her former classmates, as well as third cousins Patricia and Winifred Persse, have shared memories of those early days. Their profile of Mary Flannery depicts a girl who was a good but not exceptional student, with a vivid, sometimes peculiar, imagination, and who liked to read and write (though she could not spell very well). Her third-grade teacher, Sister Mary Consolata, considered her an unremarkable student. Mary Flannery had a tendency to stay apart from the others, as if she did not feel all that comfortable in school. Given such comportment, it is understandable that she never took part in the school plays, though her cousin Katherine Doyle remembers that she wrote plays others acted out. Some of her friends, who were part of a small group called the "Merriweather girls," also recall that she wrote and read her stories aloud. The South, O'Connor wrote in her essay "The Catholic Novelist in the Protestant South," has a way of leaving a definite impression on the Southern writer from the time that one learns to distinguish one sound from another. Over the years, the Southern writer hears what is said and then finds those speech patterns and accents in his or her own voice, so much so that the senses automatically respond to the reality inherent in these sounds.[11] At a very early age, O'Connor was developing her own mimetic spoken and written voice.

Summer visits to Mrs. O'Connor's childhood home at 311 West Greene Street in Milledgeville gave young Mary Flannery a chance to know better her many relatives in the area. For reasons that remain obscure, she transferred in 1936, at the start of sixth grade, to the coeducational Sacred Heart School on Abercorn and Thirty-Eighth Street, run by the Sisters of Saint Joseph of Carondelet. Perhaps these sisters were better educated than their counterparts at Saint Vincent's; or perhaps, given the creeping effects of poverty in and around Lafayette Square, close as it was to downtown Savannah, Sacred Heart provided a slightly safer environment; or perhaps some of her friends, such as Lillian and Ann Dowling, suggested she transfer there; or perhaps students who attended Sacred Heart came from a higher social status and sought more visibility, something that might have appealed to Mrs. O'Connor and Cousin Katie. Sister Mary Maurice noted on Mary Flannery's seventh-grade report card that she received scores of 99 in Christian doctrine; 88 in reading; 78 in spelling; 82 in grammar; 98 in Bible history; 80 in arithmetic, and 108 in algebra, a grade that might indicate her interest in mathematical symbols and the rules for manipulating these symbols, providing a unifying thread of many aspects of mathematics.

The nuns during her grade-school years administered, as she wrote to Hester in January 1956, "True Faith with large doses of Pious Crap." In this slam-dunk evaluation of her early religious education, certainly shared by countless other Catholics of her day, O'Connor does not take into account the fact that these nuns supplied at least some theological basis that she could assess and deepen over the years. After later having met in Minnesota two groups of well-educated religious women (first at College of Saint Teresa in Winona, run by the Franciscan Sisters, and second at Saint Catherine's College in Saint Paul, run by the Sisters of Saint Joseph of Carondelet), she realized that these nuns were far different from the ones in her parochial schools. In addition, O'Connor became a strong advocate for poet Carol Johnson (formerly Sister Marya), both before and after she left the convent. Johnson would visit O'Connor with Ashley Brown, a professor of English at the University of South Carolina and a close friend.[12] By the end of her life, O'Connor's attitude toward nuns had softened further, as seen in her compassionate introduction for *A Memoir of Mary Ann*, about a girl with disfiguring cancer who benefitted from the care of Dominican nuns.

In addition to her early religious education, the Great Depression had a profound effect on O'Connor, as it did on all inhabitants of Georgia. O'Connor's stories are clearly rooted in this landscape and mindscape. Farmers, both black and white, suffered enormously as the price of cotton declined and the soil became depleted. Facing foreclosure and ruin, many farmers left the fields and took to the cities. It is estimated that on the eve of the Depression about two-thirds of the farmland in the state was operated by sharecroppers, who watched sadly as fields of soybean, peanuts, and corn withered before them. Since the mid-1920s, Franklin Delano Roosevelt had been a visitor to Warm Springs, seeking relief from his polio and seeing firsthand what was happening in Georgia. His New Deal, inaugurated in March 1933, attempted to provide economic relief and recovery for all Americans but saw only sporadic success in Georgia. And while his National Labor Relations Act of 1935 facilitated the unionization of the state's textile mills and factories and set minimum wages, working conditions, and working hours for industrial workers, Governor Eugene Talmadge set up significant countermeasures. Thus money remained scarce, and hope even scarcer. Bank failures were common, and opportunities for loans in small communities dried up. Small-business owners, such as Mary Flannery's father, were especially vulnerable. Working for his father for a while after the war, Edward O'Connor began a real estate business, called the Dixie Realty Company, in 1927, most likely with some start-up money from Cousin Katie. A few years later the company seemingly disappeared. Less money in circulation meant fewer paying customers, especially those buying, selling, or renting properties. As might be expected, however, Savannah fared a bit better than the countryside because it relied on trading ships coming and going to faraway places. Still and all, the city's businessmen cut back on the personnel they hired and the wages they paid. Mr. O'Connor suffered from ill health as well as great financial strain after another of his ventures, the C. F. Fulton Real Estate Company, folded in 1937. His choices were few, and he needed to follow any available leads to obtain employment.

After picking up several small jobs, including working again for his father, Edward O'Connor made a decision that would assure his family's continued well-being and accepted in March 1938 a position as a real estate appraiser for the Federal Housing Administration in Atlanta. Mary Flannery and her mother had only one option: they moved temporarily to the Cline family mansion in Milledgeville, where both could feel more at home. During the mid-1830s, this house had been rented to the State of Georgia for use as a temporary governor's mansion. Edward O'Connor joined his brothers-in-law Dr. Bernard and Louis Cline as a lodger at the Bell House, on Peachtree and Third Streets in Atlanta. On weekends, this trio could be seen making their way to Milledgeville.

At the beginning of the 1938 academic term, thirteen-year-old O'Connor entered her freshman year (or eighth grade) at Milledgeville's Peabody Laboratory School, an experimental high school run by the Education Department of Georgia State College for Women. From Monday to Friday she followed a set routine, as determined by her mother, her aunts Mary and Katie Cline, and her great-aunt Gertrude Treanor, who lived on the top floor of the mansion. Mary, a thin, pleasant, austerely dressed, businesslike woman known as "Sister," directed the household activities, as she had done in the past. She was given her nickname after being born into a family of five boys. Katie, a shorter, more vigorous individual called "the Duchess" by O'Connor, worked in the local post office. As O'Connor and her relations went to and from the house, they gave the distinct impression of moving among the aristocratic, genteel wealthy of the city. When her tall, good-looking, slightly mustached father arrived each weekend, O'Connor felt more relaxed; everyone who saw them together readily said they were a loving father and daughter. She was the absolute joy of his life. As an adolescent in need of two parents, she was now living not in her father's hometown but in her mother's, and was thus subject to visits by her mother's various and sundry relatives. Predictably, she worked at creating a comfortable niche for herself.

O'Connor's high school classmates and others who knew her during these years inevitably described the same portrait of her: quiet and unobtrusive; not prone to attracting attention to herself; unconcerned with wearing the latest fashions or getting involved in school gossip; solitary, and sometimes eccentric and rebellious in her own way; physically awkward at times; clever but not particularly interested in school subjects, except writing and art; exhibiting a dry wit when she felt like it; and disinclined to go out on dates. Her only diversion at home was raising different types of fowl, even to the point of giving names (Aloysius, Amelia Earhart, Herman, Hallie Selassie, Adolph, and Winston) to real and imaginary ones. O'Connor allowed her imagination to range freely, creating a world that few others wished to enter. The one group that O'Connor delighted in seeing were her four first cousins from Massachusetts, the Florencourt sisters (Margaret, Louise, Catherine, and Frances), daughters of her mother's sister Agnes. In hindsight, O'Connor reflected on the relationship between the community she lived in and her writing: "I don't feel that I am writing about the community at all. I feel that I am taking things in the community that I can show the whole western world, the whole edition [*sic*] of the present generation of people, of what I can use of the Southern situation."[13] In "The Temple of the Holy Ghost" (published in *Harper's Bazaar*, May 1954), O'Connor depicts in part the interaction of a naïve but perspicacious girl and her two chatty female cousins—a combination that strongly suggests an origin somewhere in O'Connor's own childhood.

O'Connor's father knew, however, that he and his wife and daughter should be together more as a family, and thus they moved to a rented house on Potomac Avenue NE, in Atlanta's Buckhead section. Once enrolled for the 1939–1940 academic year at North Fulton High School, a large, segregated public school, O'Connor began adjusting as best she could to this strange, new environment even as her father's health deteriorated even more. Atlanta proved not to be as welcoming as her father had hoped, judging just by one of O'Connor's stories, "The Artificial Nigger," in which young Nelson, forced to sink his head into one of Atlanta's sewers, thinks he is looking at the entrance to hell. Given the stress of this situation for mother, father, and daughter, the O'Connors returned to Milledgeville, where O'Connor enrolled as a tenth-grader at Peabody, certainly a more congenial setting. Since she spent the two remaining years of high school and three years of college in the same city and living in the same house, she knew every step of the way from her front porch to the nearby college campus, where Peabody was located. O'Connor very rarely used Milledgeville, an environment with little inherent drama, as a palimpsest for her fiction; one notable exception might be the murder sprees of Marion Stembridge in the late 1940s and early 1950s, which served as background to "The Partridge Festival."[14]

Peabody had an exceptional character about it. A predominantly female, experimental school, one of ten in the state whose pedagogy was heavily influenced by the philosophy of John Dewey, its teachers profited from the close mentoring and supervision of the college faculty. Placing great emphasis on pedagogical theory—sometimes to the detriment of the genuinely felt needs of the students—most teachers rotated from class to class every six weeks, making lasting teacher-student relationships almost impossible, particularly as the various subjects melded one into another. In chemistry, for example, a teacher might spend segments on photography and cosmetics rather than explaining the periodic table of the elements or proposing a useful framework to classify, systematize, and compare the many different forms of chemical activity. "I have found," O'Connor wrote in "The Teaching of Literature," "that if you are astute and energetic, you can integrate English literature with geography, biology, home economics, basketball or fire prevention—with anything at all that will put off a little longer the evil day when the novel or story must be examined simply as a story or a novel."[15] Given this atmosphere, Peabody students and faculty were not always in agreement about the type of education the school espoused. Some praised the innovative methods for encouraging students to think creatively; others had reservations or even outright criticism as students went through the academic cafeteria line, choosing those subjects that appealed to them at the moment. Mildred English, the principal, clearly could not please all the students and their families, however much she tried to meld traditional forms of education into more modern, innovative techniques.

O'Connor's high school transcript looks fairly ordinary. She took four credits in English and history, two in French, and one credit in Latin (certainly not enough to read later on a Thomistic theological treatise written in Latin), art, algebra, plane geometry, biology, home economics, and a half credit in arithmetic and commerce. One could well ask, Where were the four years of Latin that were being offered in other schools? O'Connor later lamented that she never received a classical education in high school (something that Giroux certainly had at Regis). In her lecture "Fiction Is a Subject with a History—It Should Be Taught That Way," prompted no doubt by the education she received at Peabody, she bemoaned the fact that the works of Homer and Virgil were no longer assigned in schools, with the result that young students do not have the wherewithal to deal with the past imaginatively.[16] She said, too, that novels should be assigned in eighth and ninth grade on a regular basis, rather than treating fiction haphazardly or burying it in a course on history. Fiction needed to be taught as a subject in itself, she maintained, with a close reading of the text and a subsequent, coherent analysis. Unless a student is familiar with the better works of writers such as James Fenimore Cooper, Nathaniel Hawthorne, Herman Melville, and Stephen Crane, and even some of the early works of Henry James, it is fairly useless to introduce them to John Hersey or John Steinbeck. Even before tackling any of these authors, they should have some familiarity with fiction of the better English writers of the eighteenth and nineteenth centuries. O'Connor shuddered to think that some students believed that President Lincoln was shot while watching a movie! Continuing in an Aristotelian vein, O'Connor wants readers to become engaged in the total experience of the fictional characters, their passions raised to new heights through order and clarification. Without some literary experience, a young reader might never be able to understand or resolve any of the passions that might emerge from reading a work of fiction. Furthermore, O'Connor praises the high school English teacher who focuses on literature as literature, and not as a sub-category of social studies from which students derive commonplace civic lessons or messages. Yet, what happens if students find that they do not enjoy reading excellent literature? While that would be most regrettable, O'Connor believed, students must understand that they are being formed and not necessarily consulted. Having expressed these sentiments, O'Connor admitted that she took little with her from Peabody: "About all I remember of those four years is the way the halls smelled," she said in an interview with Gerard E. Sherry, "and bringing my accordion sometimes to play for the 'devotionals.'"[17]

With little interest in academics, at least at Peabody, O'Connor focused on two extracurricular activities: writing and making linoleum blocks, thus launching interests highly significant for her later career. The *Peabody Palladium* newspaper in November 1940 lists her as its art editor and features two of her linoleum-block cuts and one of her poems. During her high school and college years, O'Connor produced more than 120 block cuts, evidence of the visual dimension of her creative imagination. Furthermore, one of her early unpublished stories in the O'Connor Collection at Georgia College is worthy of attention. It depicts a young girl named Caulda lamenting her dead rooster, Sillow, whom she thinks of as a brother. When her mother wants to take the dead rooster away, pointing out that Death is out to get her too, a conflict quickly erupts. How, one could rightly ask, could such a hostile tug-of-war ever be resolved, especially considering the weakening condition of O'Connor's own father, who would soon become an invalid and die?

Had you accompanied fifteen-year-old Flannery O'Connor to Sacred Heart Church in Milledgeville for her father's funeral on February 3, 1941, you would have entered a simple, Congregationalist-looking brick structure, topped by a steeple and surmounted with a cross.[18] This church would offer O'Connor great solace, especially at this traumatic moment of her life. Inside you would have been struck by the rather confined, unpretentious liturgical space, which allowed for close, almost intimate, contact between the congregation and the sanctuary. To the left, behind the altar rail, stood a baptismal font, and to the right a free-standing ambo, visual reminders to the congregation of the importance of both baptism and the proclamation of the Word of God. In the center stood the main altar at which the Reverend James E. King, wearing black vestments, celebrated the funeral liturgy in Latin with his back to the congregation. As a reminder of the sacrificial nature of the Mass, he could look up to a nearly life-size, loincloth-draped Christus plaintively staring down on him. O'Connor never shared in any detail her memories of her father; they remained bittersweet at best and terribly sad at worst:

> I suppose my father toted around some of my early productions. . . . My father wanted to write but had not the time or money or training or any of the opportunities I have had. I am never likely to romanticize him because I carry around most of his faults as well as his tastes. I even have about his same constitution: I have the same disease. . . . Anyway, whatever I do in the way of writing makes me extra happy in the thought that it is a fulfillment of what he wanted to do himself.[19]

Claire Kahane speculates that the loss of her father left O'Connor alone with her mother in a relationship of ambivalent interdependence at a crucial juncture in her life: "At a time when an adolescent girl is expected to disengage from the family romance which makes of a parent the most significant love object, while also consolidating her prior identifications with parental figures real or imagined, O'Connor had to deal with the emotional turmoil inevitably stirred up by the process of mourning, with the anger and pain of loss, feelings no doubt intensified by the sudden lack of a mediator to stand between her and Regina, who now ruled the roost."[20] In subsequent months and years, each time that O'Connor entered this church to attend Mass, what she saw and heard happening on the other side of the altar rail greatly enhanced her own spiritual life and helped her to grow. When she graduated from high school in May 1942, she felt little need to go away to college—war rationing was in effect, and her mother needed her at home—and besides, only one of her graduating cohort left to go to college elsewhere, someplace in Alabama. O'Connor hoped that her years in college, accelerated because the country needed young men and women to fight the Nazis in Europe, would be a genuine advancement over her previous educational experiences.

When O'Connor entered Georgia State College for Women that summer as a seventeen-year-old "Jessie" (the nickname derived from the first three letters in the college's initials, GSCW), she took the basic courses: social science, English, humanities, general mathematics, biology, health, and physical education. Tuition was reasonable: $67.50 a year. The faculty, most with master's degrees, reached out to their students as best they could. Katherine Scott, who reportedly taught a somewhat dull English 101, pushed O'Connor to write like Jane Austen; at the same time, she recognized in her someone who was a genius, if somewhat "warped." In English 102, Dr. William Wynn, likewise not among O'Connor's more scintillating professors, put pressure on her to write in a more traditional manner. As a result, she never declared English as a major; one class with Professor Wynn was enough. Hallie Smith's advanced composition classes, on the other hand, were more to O'Connor's liking. In some of her surviving writing assignments from this class, she received very high marks. Gradually, her efforts—initially several essays, including "Going to the Dogs" and "Why Worry the Horse?," plus a Poe-like short story, "Elegance is Its Own Reward," and a poem that mimics one of James Russell Lowell's poems—began appearing in the *Corinthian*, the college literary journal. O'Connor also became art editor in November for the *Colonnade*, the biweekly college newspaper, a post she held until she graduated. During the 1942–1943 academic year, she published more than twenty cartoons, sometimes with a slightly exaggerated self-portrait—an artistic trait that seemed important to her own creative development as a writer.

Beginning in the winter of 1943, the tone and tenor of the campus changed as Navy WAVES (Women Accepted for Volunteer Emergency Service) started arriving, some of them residing in the stately houses nearby. In a two-year period, more than fifteen thousand WAVES came to Milledgeville, altering campus life considerably. As O'Connor looked at these women in smart uniforms, her eye saw contrasts that she localized in one cartoon after another, sometimes focusing on the WAVES' appearance as perceived by the more socially minded coeds. In one she depicts a coed wanting to try on a WAVE cap, and in another she wonders whether one could make the dean's list if one were to rearrange the WAVES' caps on their numbered pegs. "Targets are where you find 'em!" reads a caption in one of O'Connor's cartoons in the March 27, 1943, *Colonnade*. This could well become her mantra for writing fiction. As Gerald Kelly notes, O'Connor's visual imagination anticipated her written one:

O'Connor's cartoons comment on the predictable range of student experiences: preoccupation with school holidays, dating, teachers, and exams. They target the anti-intellectualism and the various conceits of the students as well as the short-comings of the school that is the physical and historical setting. In her cartoons, however, O'Connor does not merely satirize the typical issues and events of student life, she documents the character of the students themselves, including settings from the college campus. These cartoons offer not only an accurate documentary of life at Georgia State College for Women but also a running commentary on the times. O'Connor's cartoons are a history in pictures, and her work largely functions as a social satire that clearly includes herself.[21]

Yet, if O'Connor were to get anything out of her college years, she needed to do well in her studies. She tackled with considerable energy the four courses in English, including a survey of English literature, the short story, and two further classes in English and American literature, plus two classes in French literature, which she took in her second year. Since she regularly made the dean's list, she did not feel guilty about submitting works to the *Corinthian*, including a story, "Home of the Brave," that deals with two gossipy hometown women discussing the fates of their war-bound sons, as well as two satirical essays: "Doctors of Delinquency," which laments the lack of moral education among young children, and "Biologic Endeavor," which focuses on modern dietary habits, particularly of those prone to overeating and then purging themselves with Tums or Ex-Lax. Her sardonic conclusion aims directly at schools such as Peabody. Given these college publications, O'Connor seemed to be hitting her stride and reaching out more than she had in the past. She wrote in July 1963 to her friend Janet McKane that she "enjoyed college," though the lack of specific details about these years might camouflage her real feelings.

During her last year in college, O'Connor wanted to complete requirements for a degree in social studies and thus engaged herself in a range of courses: current social and economic problems, American history and government, and finally comparative governments. She found her niche in editing the *Corinthian* with great competence and continuing to serve as the art editor for the *Colonnade*. (In this, O'Connor and Giroux showed parallel development, as writing for and editing a college literary magazine proved to be a hidden but significant bond that united them.[22]) However, O'Connor remained encircled only by her female peers. Since there were almost no men on campus, the only male student she "dated"—attending Sunday dinners at the Cline mansion or the occasional movie at the Co-ed or Campus—was John Sullivan, who would go off to war in the Pacific and later enter a Roman Catholic seminary.

O'Connor's final essay in the *Corinthian* (Spring 1945), entitled "Education's Only Hope," provides a not-too-favorable summary of the education she had received. Students, she believed, cannot face the future, especially in the waning days of World War II, if they are given only platitudes. Rather, faculty have a definite obligation to deal honestly with the realities in front of them by giving students a chance to explore and discern what has been and what remains important. In light of this, educational reform must be ongoing; otherwise students fall into apathetic trances. Her three final English courses, including contemporary literature and a course on Tennyson and Browning, made little lasting impression on her. All she could remember was the line "Come into the garden, Maud, for the black bat, Night, has flown," which she considered hilarious. Given these voids or more likely *longueurs* in her college education, she nevertheless was invited to join the prestigious Phoenix Society, members of which were chosen by faculty who were Phi Beta Kappa members. When she graduated with a degree in social science in June, she was fortunate to have had the support of George W. Beiswanger, a new faculty member with a Ph.D. from the State University of Iowa who had taught her "philosophical" Social Science 412, which used John Herman Randall Jr.'s *The Making of the Modern Mind* as its textbook. After applying both to Duke University and the State University of Iowa, she chose to go to Iowa because of a scholarship given to her in journalism—a path that Giroux had earlier considered.

In mid-September 1945, O'Connor agreed to have her mother accompany her to Atlanta, then by train to Chicago, and finally to Iowa City, the site of the university's sprawling 425-acre campus. It was not an easy time for Americans. After the *Enola Gay* dropped the first atomic bomb on Hiroshima in early August, Emperor Hirohito had his high military officers sign articles of surrender on the deck of the USS *Missouri* in Tokyo Bay. Although the UN Charter had recently been signed in San Francisco, the configuration and realignment of the postwar world could hardly be imagined. But one needed to look to the future. Thus both mother and daughter were eager to see the annex to Currier House on East Bloomington Street to which O'Connor had been assigned and where she would live for the next two years. This was the first time she had to share a room with a stranger, though she and Louise Trovato proved to be compatible. When Mrs. O'Connor left to return home, her daughter understood that she was to write to her every day; in return, she would receive comforting maternal letters and copies of the local newspaper.

Now a full-fledged Hawkeye in the Graduate School of Journalism, O'Connor chose her courses: magazine writing, principles of advertising, a course in political science, and advanced drawing. Her scholarship allowed for tuition remission and a stipend of $65 a term. She soon discovered that her heart was not in journalism; she simply could not see herself as a cub reporter working for some obscure newspaper, chasing ambulances or fire trucks or stopping by the local police precinct for the daily rap sheet. And how would she ever cope in the future with the subtleties of legal journalism or a daily routine of copyediting? Her college experience, especially reading English and American literature and writing for the college literary journal, had given her a taste of another type of writing—one that involved looking within herself and finding words that expressed her creative abilities. Thus, once she had a better grasp of the academic landscape at Iowa, she knocked on the office door of Paul Engle, director of the Writers' Workshop, who welcomed her but could not understand a word she was saying, so thick was her Georgia accent. "My name is Flannery O'Connor," she wrote for him on a piece of paper. "I am not a journalist. Can I come to the Writers' Workshop?"[23] After some discussion and a chance to look at writing samples, Engle admitted her. She thus added two more classes to her already heavy schedule, Understanding Fiction and Writers' Workshop. The first, using Brooks and Warren's *Understanding Fiction*, included William Faulkner's "A Rose for Emily," Caroline Gordon's "Old Red," and Nathaniel Hawthorne's "The Birthmark"—a story mentioned years later by O'Connor in *A Memoir for Mary Ann*. She later commented on one of Gordon's stories, "You read it and then you have to sit back and let your mind blend it together—like those pictures that you have to get so far away from before they come together. . . . You walk through her stories like you are walking in a complete real world. And watch how the meaning comes from the things themselves and not from her imposing anything. Right when you finish reading that story, you don't think you've read anything, but the more you think about it the more it grows."[24] Though O'Connor noted that the story is "impressionistic" with certain events "masterly" presented, it is quite disjointed, with little to no character development and no discernible plot. Gordon introduces the names of her characters and then seems to drop them from view, giving no insight into their personalities. What conflict there is seems inconsequential. It was expected that the students read such stories carefully and comment on them intelligently, without necessarily reading outside criticism or citing biographical information about the authors. O'Connor initially considered *Understanding Fiction* an uninviting textbook, but Paul Engle helped her appreciate its value. The earlier companion volume, *Understanding Poetry*, had the great advantage of taking a poem out of the hands of learned professors and putting it in the hands of students, who were encouraged to study the interaction of the various elements of the text, avoiding above all a too-facile paraphrase of one sort or another.

Engle provided the energy that drove the Workshop forward. Author of *Worn Earth*, a 1932 poetry book in the prestigious Yale Series of Younger Poets, and the 1934 collection *American Song: A Book of Poems*, and also a Rhodes scholar, he had assumed the directorship of the Workshop in 1942. Though the program was innovative, it was not complicated: rather than demonstrating a mastery of the history of literature or even of the works of certain authors, students were expected to write and submit creative work in order to receive a master's degree in fine arts. Engle wisely invited visiting lecturers and established writers to direct occasional seminars. When John Crowe Ransom, then editor of the *Kenyon Review*, came to campus that fall, he chose one of O'Connor's stories to read aloud—adding favorable comments at the end, which greatly enhanced O'Connor's standing among her fellow students. At one point, he suggested she replace *nigger* with *Negro*. Holding her own, she replied that such a substitution would spoil the story; after all, the people she was writing about would never use any other word.[25] But, according to Giroux, citing a letter he received from Paul Engle, she did change the word: "Flannery always had a flexible and objective view of her own writing, constantly revising, and in every case improving. The will to be a writer was adamant; nothing could resist it, not even her own sensibility about her own work. Cut, alter, try it again. . . ."[26] Herbert Nipson, an African American writer who joined the Workshop in 1946 and later went on to edit *Ebony*, remembered how O'Connor dealt with racial problems:

When Flannery read, there was little criticism of her writing. I think that everyone in the workshop recognized her talent. She had a way with words. Discussions usually centered on what she had to say. Other listeners read more into her stories than she would admit to. I remember her reading one of her stories set in a small Georgia town. After the reading one of the members complimented her on how she had treated one of the characters, a Black servant. The member felt that the servant had been treated in a dignified, human way and asked if she had done this to make a point. As I remember, Flannery's answer went something like this, "No. That was just the way he was."[27]

Though O'Connor was finding her voice and exploring her native locale, she would become much more flexible—at times malleable—when she realized that criticism, sometimes warranted and sometimes not, helped her to find what she really wanted to say in the first place.

Engle kept the classes small, and the students read their works aloud in class, seeing their own words reflected in the facial expressions and attitudes of their listeners. Through this process, repeated over and over, a student was forced to find some creative center, determine a personal written voice, and create stories that had genuine interest. The idea was so simple—and so pedagogically correct—that it was bound to succeed, and it became the preeminent creative writing program in the country, though rivals and imitators soon appeared. O'Connor came to know the other young women in the Workshop, but she had little interaction with a small contingent of slightly older men, many of whom had returned—with all sorts of harrowing stories to tell—from military service.

Unlike the WAVES in Milledgeville, these veterans planted an idea in her mind. What if one of them, for example, a local Tennessee boy named Hazel Motes, returned home from the World War II to Eastrod and, finding no one there to greet him, continued on to Taulkinham? After the train porter tells Haze, "Jesus been a long time gone," the story picks up on this theme and develops it with consummate intensity, mixed with unexpected moments of hilarity. Faulkner's first novel, *Soldiers' Pay*, concerns Lieutenant Donald Mahon's return to Charlestown, Georgia, after fighting in World War I, and *Wise Blood* begins with a similar premise. Curiously, while O'Connor could have drawn on whatever she might have gleaned of her father's wartime experiences in depicting Haze's, she seems not to have done so: that would have taken her down a road too painful to navigate, and, above all, the time gap between the two wars would have been too difficult to bridge. One discouraging note: when Engle made suggestions about the novel in progress, O'Connor did not feel that he completely understood what she was trying to do.

In order to see why certain works of literature were considered classics of their genre, students at the Workshop needed to have some background in literature. As O'Connor wrote her own stories, she was constantly reading, studying form and content, analyzing language and structure. At the same time, she had to avoid succumbing to the influence of other authors in order to find what made her style unique. In spite of having had a considerable number of literature courses in college, O'Connor felt, as she mentioned in an August 1955 letter to Hester, that her literary education really began in Iowa, no doubt aided by the intense literary interest and commitment of her peers:

> When I went to Iowa I had never heard of Faulkner, Kafka, Joyce, much less read them. Then I began to read everything at once, so much so that I didn't have time I suppose to be influenced by any one writer. I read all the Catholic novelists, Mauriac, Bernanos, Bloy, Greene, Waugh. I read all the nuts like Djuna Barnes and Dorothy Richardson and Va. Woolf (unfair to the dear lady of course): I read the best Southern writers like Faulkner and the Tates, K. A. Porter, Eudora Welty and Peter Taylor; read the Russians, not Tolstoy so much as Dostoevsky, Turgenev, Chekhov and Gogol. I became a great admirer of Conrad and have read almost all his fiction. I have totally skipped such people as Dreiser, Anderson (except for a few stories) and Thomas Wolfe. I have learned something from Hawthorne, Flaubert, Balzac, and something from Kafka, though I have never been able to finish one of his novels. I've read almost all of Henry James—from a sense of High Duty and because when I read James I feel something is happening to me, in slow motion but happening nevertheless. I admire Dr. Johnson's *Lives of the Poets*. But always the largest thing that looms up is *The Humorous Tales of Edgar Allan Poe*. I am sure he wrote them all while drunk too.

Long hours in the library and in her dorm room, especially while taking Engle's two-semester independent reading course, gave O'Connor the environment to figure out why certain authors succeeded and others failed. In effect, she was trying to discern how she could build on an incredibly powerful tradition of literary accomplishment.

When O'Connor returned from Christmas vacation in January 1946, she sent *Accent* two stories for possible publication: "The Geranium" (published in their summer issue) and "The Crop" (published posthumously in the April 1971 issue of *Mademoiselle*). The first story concerns an elderly gentleman forced by his daughter to move to New York, territory unknown to O'Connor at the time she was writing this story. A revision of this story, entitled "An Exile in the East" and published in the *South Carolina Review* (November 1978), and a final version, written just before O'Connor's death, entitled "Judgement Day," which was later included in *Everything That Rises Must Converge*, provide two related stories ("The Geranium" and "Judgement Day")—like bookends of O'Connor's entire career—showing her growing maturity in handling the themes of home, dislocation, alienation, black–white relations, and the Kingdom of God. Thomas Merton called "Judgement Day" "one of the best stories anybody ever wrote. . . . It is a great metaphysical poem of the South."[28] The story's first two sentences encapsulate these themes in a focused way, foreshadowing the story's dramatic ending: "Tanner was conserving all his strength for the trip home. He meant to walk as far as he could get and trust to the Almighty to get him the rest of the way."

In her book *Flannery O'Connor: The Obedient Imagination*, Sarah Gordon focuses extensively and appropriately on "The Crop" as a way of entering into O'Connor's creative imagination (see pp. 2–13, 17–22). In this story, Miss Willerton, a genteel Southern spinster and would-be writer, romanticizes sharecropper Lot Motun and his wife, and even their dog, endowing them with a dignity that she hopes will get her tale on the reading list of the Willowpool Female Seminary, from which she graduated. O'Connor, in relating the story of this female writer who imaginatively transforms herself into Lot's wife, might well be wrestling with her own double or having some type of interior debate with herself that has no resolution. "There were so many subjects to write stories about," as the story says, "that Miss Willerton could never think of one." The conclusion dispels any doubt that O'Connor accepts a rose-colored treatment of the South. When Miss Willerton "snaps out of her story," as if out of a trance, and later encounters a man and wife in a grocery store—her former literary creations now transformed into "real-life" sharecroppers—

she is only momentarily shocked. Before long, Miss Willerton decides to write a story about a completely different subject, one chosen again at random; she most likely will not finish it. This important female character never takes her art seriously and has no interest in the transcendent questions of human existence. According to Katherine Prown, in this story O'Connor adheres to some of the attributes of New Criticism by exploring trivial and trendy whims, characteristic of what some of her instructors at Iowa thought were appropriate to the genre.[29] Thus one of O'Connor's first significant stories revealed to her that she could successfully transfer the visual satire prevalent in her cartoons to her fiction.

After spending the summer in Milledgeville, O'Connor returned to Iowa in September, initially rooming in the Graduate House with Sarah Dawson, a former Women's Auxiliary Corps member from Des Moines, Iowa. Monkish O'Connor, no doubt fortified by her favorite concoction of coffee and Coca-Cola, worked hard in her room, sometimes pulling down the shades and writing under a single hanging light bulb, much to the astonishment of her friends. After spending Christmas with her mother, she had a new roommate, Martha Bell, a former WAVE and a graduate student in business education. During the entire 1946–1947 academic year, Engle spent a good deal of time away from Iowa, promoting the Workshop. Given this prolonged absence, it is not surprising that he and O'Connor drifted apart, unlike Robert Giroux and his mentor Mark Van Doren. Later—most likely in February 1950, as Lowell and Stafford were about to head off to Iowa City, where Cal would take over temporarily the directorship of the Workshop and then move on to teach summer school at Kenyon—O'Connor wrote to the Fitzgeralds, expressing a fear about Engle: "I hate to think that Cal may go out there and be Paul's *victim*" (emphasis mine).[30] When Paul Horgan replaced Engle in February 1946 as director, O'Connor took his Course 108 on imaginative writing but never felt that Horgan paid much attention to her, though she considered him a fine teacher. Horgan clearly remembered O'Connor: "The one student I had who later made an important name was Flannery O'Connor; but I hasten to add I don't think I taught her that much. She was already an artist—really an enigma, and a painfully shy person."[31] This was high praise indeed from such an accomplished writer.

Beginning in the spring 1947 semester, Andrew Lytle joined the Workshop as a guest faculty member; he would also serve as a faculty member in the spring 1948 semester, when Engle was again away. A professor at the University of the South, Lytle was lauded as editor of the *Sewanee Review* (1961–1973) and would later publish O'Connor's "The Lame Shall Enter First" (Summer 1962) and "Revelation" (Spring 1964). As O'Connor busily shaped her own fiction, Lytle increasingly played an important—though not necessarily consistent—part in her life. Their conversations were lively and informative. He thought O'Connor his best student (and James B. Hall, later a professor at the University of California, Santa Cruz, his second best), as he reflected on her published works: "The idiom of her characters rang with all the truth of the real thing, but the real thing heightened. It resembled in tone and choice of words all country speech I had ever heard, but I couldn't quite place it. And then I realized that what she had done was what any first rate artist always does—she made something more essential than life but resembling it."[32] Because Lytle served as O'Connor's mentor during this time, he was aware of the changes made in the final version of *Wise Blood*: "Included among these early chapters was the long section concerning Haze's sister Ruby," Katherine Prown notes, "which by 1949 had been omitted from the novel altogether."[33] Another of the visiting faculty in April 1947 was Allen Tate, who, after initially misreading a section of *Wise Blood*, offered to correct O'Connor's grammar and help her with what he perceived to be her dull style. In retrospect, he realized that his initial impression of her work was "irrelevant."[34] Tate and Warren, whose names are often associated with O'Connor, barely knew her personally. In addition to their encounter at Iowa, Tate saw O'Connor once more a few years later when both were guests of the Fitzgeralds. Warren, in addition to reading one of her stories at Iowa, also remembered meeting her in late April 1959, when he, along with Jesse Stuart and Murray Krieger, was part of a literary symposium at Vanderbilt University.[35]

Sometime before Christmas 1946, O'Connor felt honored that Paul Engle had submitted two of her stories to John Selby, the editor in chief of Rinehart & Company, for the Rinehart-Iowa Fiction competition. In June, at the end of her second year, she formally submitted six stories as her master's thesis, entitled "The Geranium: A Collection of Short Stories": "The Geranium," "The Barber," "Wildcat," "The Crop," "The Turkey," and "The Train." The lackluster dedication of her thesis to Engle indicates the growing distance between them: "To Paul Engle whose interest and criticism have made these stories better than they would otherwise have been." Later, Engle expressed displeasure over the choice of *Wise Blood* as a title and the fact that the Workshop had not been given appropriate credit on the novel's cover. Unlike those of some other authors, her stories were not published in the order they were written, thus preventing both general readers and scholars from seeing the artistic development of her work.[36] When she graduated that summer, she decided to use the Rinehart Fellowship she had received to stay on for another academic year. After a vacation in Milledgeville, O'Connor anticipated focusing on her novel in progress.

It is worth noting that O'Connor wrote a prayer journal in a Sterling notebook from January 19, 1947, to September 26, 1947, reflecting the time and energy she put into writing fiction as a graduate student—much of which resulted in undeniable bouts of frustration: "Dear God, I am so discouraged about my work."[37] The text of this journal centers on her life as both an unfulfilled fiction writer and a devout Roman Catholic who has no hesitation in addressing her Creator directly. Countless others have recorded their spiritual journeys in various ways, including four fellow Catholics whose lives were known to O'Connor: Thérèse de Lisieux (*l'Histoire d'une âme*), Gerard Manley Hopkins (in his "terrible sonnets"), Dorothy Day (in her autobiography *The Long Loneliness*), and Thomas Merton (in seven volumes of his published journals). O'Connor's journal, with Hopkins-like touches, is an unremitting and unpretentious cri de coeur, a sustained, passionate monologue beseeching God to help her reach her potential as a writer of Christian fiction. "Please let Christian principles permeate my writing and please let there be enough of my writing (published) for Christian principles to permeate" (5). Since these journal entries were meant for God alone, O'Connor addresses her listener forthrightly, often in the form of petitions that express her wholehearted belief in what the pre-Vatican II Catholic Church taught. Though she avoids debating with God or asking him to change his mind about what is expected of those who seek the kingdom, either proleptically on Earth or completely in heaven, O'Connor nevertheless questions and challenges aspects of her own personal faith. In all, however, one thing is clear: she had no intention of ever "becoming a nun" (6).

Written in her early twenties, O'Connor's text rushes from one personal observation to another with no calculated posturing. "My attention," she notes, "is always very fugitive" (4). She constantly vacillates, dashing off one sentence after another. The intensity of her writing is rooted to a great extent in the repetition of certain words or phrases: "Dear God" or "dear God" (37 times); "You" or "you" (40 times); "Lord" (18 times), and "Please" or "please" (19 times). Unlike in her published fiction, which she revised at times even on final galleys, O'Connor showed little desire to cross off sentences in her journal in order to craft thought-filled phrases, though a number of passages are excised.

O'Connor begins her journal with a sense of fear and trembling: "I am afraid of the insidious hands Oh Lord which grope into the darkness of my soul. Please be my guard against them" (7). Her mind, she says, is a little box down inside other little boxes. "There is very little air in my box" (17). Though she moves in this suffocating darkness, she nevertheless knows that light does exist: "To feel, we must know. And for this, when it is practically impossible for us to get it ourselves, not completely, of course, but what we can, we are dependent on God" (8). At the same time, she reaches out to feel God's loving mercy, approaching but not quite achieving the prayerful attitude expressed in Psalm 91: "Give me the courage to stand the pain to get the grace, Oh Lord," O'Connor writes. "Help me with this life that seems so treacherous, so disappointing" (10). Even when God assists her in writing a story, for which she is most grateful, she knows that she can too easily revert back to being "insecure" and "lax" (12).

Gradually O'Connor approaches a moment of honest resolution befitting any Christian writer who, though stymied on many fronts, desires to move forward: "If I ever do get to be a fine writer, it will not be because I am a fine writer but because God has given me credit for a few of the things He kindly wrote for me. Right at this present this does not seem to be His policy. I can't write a thing. But I'll continue to try—that is the point" (23). This act of the will, at once simple and direct, can only but energize her as a person and as a writer. "I must write down that I am to be an artist" (29). Experiencing greater friendship with—nay, love for— God would give her enormous bliss, not unlike that which mystics at times have experienced, as expressed on the next-to-last page of her journal: "If I could only hold God in my mind. If I could only always just think of Him" (39). Her final entry, however, completely undercuts these aspirations, returning us to the beginning of the journal: "My thoughts are so far away from God. He might as well not have made me" (40).

Although O'Connor provides very few autobiographical details, thus giving the impression that she did not want others to read this journal and perhaps judge her private life, one might suspect that she secretly desired that at some moment, certainly after her death, her journal would be discovered and published, thus revealing the theological and spiritual beliefs that would later be more carefully articulated in letters to several of her friends, particularly Betty Hester.

This prayer journal, written before O'Connor's major stories were published, is not a final synthesis of her spiritual life. In the mid-to-late 1940s, she could never have imagined the incredible setbacks and literary successes that would face her, nor the challenges and graces her "Dear God" and "Lord" would offer her, particularly during her secluded life with her mother at Andalusia, as lupus took a great toll on her day-to-day existence. She ends her journal in a whimsical way: "Today I have proved myself a glutton—for Scotch oatmeal cookies and erotic thought. There is nothing left to say of me" (40). Her prayer journal actually ends with six notes that, when played on a piano, progress upward, but in a dissonant way. Susan Srigley maintains that these notes form a clever palindrome: "The discordant tones of O'Connor's notation, the dislocation of the two staves by the misplaced bracket, the inversion of the bass clef and the double movement of the palindrome provide a metaphor for the dissonance and absence of feeling so plaintively noted by O'Connor throughout her prayers."[38] Had this journal been written at the end of her life, at age seventy as she imaginatively projects in the journal, it would have had a totally different shape and a more reflective character to it, as her fellow writer Walker Percy attempted to produce in his unpublished "Lenten Journal," written in part just before his death. O'Connor's most likely would have been filled with carefully articulated thoughts not about laziness, fear, and despair, but about genuine forgiveness and profound thanksgiving.

When she began her final academic year at Iowa as a postgraduate student, O'Connor became a teaching assistant with an office in the Old Dental Building. She moved to a boardinghouse on East Bloomington Street owned by Mrs. Guzeman and gradually met some of the new students, including Walter Sullivan, later a professor of American literature at Vanderbilt, and Paul Griffith and Robie Macauley, who were also instructors. Having studied under John Crowe Ransom at Kenyon College before joining the army, Macauley would eventually replace his former professor as editor of the *Kenyon Review* and accept O'Connor's "The Comforts of Home" (Fall 1960) for publication. Before long, the group coalesced and enjoyed Sunday evening gatherings in the home of Austin Warren, who was teaching a Henry James and James Joyce seminar. (Warren would later collaborate on *Theory of Literature* with René Wellek, who had taught at Iowa until 1946 before going to Yale.) As they read and discussed *A Portrait of the Artist as a Young Man*, which contains an explicitly Thomistic treatment of theology and literature, Warren called on O'Connor to answer questions about Catholicism in the text. Macauley grew close to O'Connor, going to movies with her and sharing an occasional meal in neighboring Amana, though he was engaged at that time to Anne Draper, then residing in New York. O'Connor knew of this engagement. He particularly enjoyed hearing O'Connor read her novel chapter by chapter, admiring her completely original style.[39]

With due admiration from her peers, O'Connor worked steadily on her novel. Writing chapters and then publishing them as stories formed a logistical puzzle for her. A slightly revised version of "The Train," for example, would be published in the *Sewanee Review* (April 1948) while serving also as the opening chapter of *Wise Blood*. "The Heart of the Park," which would become part of the fifth chapter, and "The Peeler," the third chapter of the novel, were accepted by Rahv for publication in the *Partisan Review*. Her story written in Iowa, "Woman on the Stairs," the fourth chapter of her novel, was published in *Tomorrow* (August 1949) and then revised to appear under the title of "A Stroke of Good Fortune" in *Shenandoah* (Spring 1953). By looking more conscientiously at her work, O'Connor realized that the stories were genuinely related to one another, forming part of a continuous whole. A pattern was developing before her eyes; her task was to allow the novel to develop on its own terms, giving freedom to her characters to grow as they should, without seeming to intrude on the novel's projected course.

It took O'Connor five years in all to write *Wise Blood*.[40] In addition to Haze, whose grit and determination dominate the novel, O'Connor presents a marvelous assortment of people: Mrs. Leora Watts, a warm, fun-loving, gap-toothed prostitute; Enoch Emery, an eighteen-year-old, manic, "sanctified crazy" zookeeper; Asa Hawks, a supposedly blind preacher; his nymphomaniac daughter Sabbath Lily; and smooth-talking Hoover Shoats, aka Onnie Jay Holy. Reacting against false religiosity all around him, Haze starts his own ministry, his Church Without Christ, suggesting that the former, two-thousand-year-old Church With Christ had not really done all that was expected of it. The story reaches a climax when Haze follows one of Onnie Jay Holy's consumptive pseudo-prophets, Solace Layfield, and afterward intentionally drives his Essex over him. If Hawks had failed to accomplish his mission of blinding himself, Haze succeeds. Like an early fourth-century Desert Father, an ascetic with no monastery, Haze desires to make up for all his past failings. His landlady, Mrs. Flood, wants to change him and schemes in her mind to marry him and gain access to his military pension. But this is not to be. After Haze flees her house and wanders about, he is finally found in a drainage ditch. As O'Connor was composing this novel, she might have been thinking of the rhythmically haunting sentences at the end of *The Great Gatsby*. When Mrs. Flood, thinking Haze is alive, gazes at his composed face, she looks into his deep, burned-out eye sockets. "She sat staring with her eyes shut, into his eyes, and felt as if she had finally got to the beginning of something she couldn't begin, and she saw him moving farther and farther away, farther and farther into the darkness until he was a pin point of light."[41]

When O'Connor left Iowa at the end of the academic year to go to Yaddo in Saratoga Springs, she remained in contact with a few of her Iowa friends but really never sought them out. Especially after she retreated to Andalusia, lupus determined how and to what degree she interacted with others. She wrote a fairly general essay, "The Writer and the Graduate School," in which she reflected simply and honestly on these three years of her life: "No one can be taught to write, but a writing ability can be more quickly developed when it is concentrated upon and encouraged by competent literary people than when it is left to wander."[42] She felt no need to be a publicist for Iowa, though she was one of the more successful students among her peer group. Indeed, she profited enormously from her education there, at times sharing her stories with well-known writers and men of letters. She also wrote, in "The Nature and Aim of Fiction," that there is no need to consider literature as an apologetic to prove one's faith or have it serve as a type of personal manifesto: "It is the nature of fiction not to be good for much unless it is good in itself."[43] Above all, she maintained in this essay that a successful literary work, always in touch with mystery, must be a very much self-contained dramatic unit: "This means that it must carry its meaning inside it. It means that any abstractly expressed compassion or piety or morality in a piece of fiction is only a statement added to it. It means that you can't make an inadequate dramatic action complete by putting a statement of meaning on the end of it or in the middle of it or at the beginning of it. It means that when you write fiction you are speaking *with* character and action, not *about* character and action. The writer's moral sense must coincide with his dramatic sense."[44] In this and other essays that discuss the value of literature in itself, she shows the influence on her work of the formal discourse of New Criticism, the important movement of which her Iowa connections Ransom, Warren, and Lytle were a part.

New Criticism moved away from Romantic subjectivity and Victorian moralism, allowing literary texts to stand or fall on their own and putting aside any *right* or *wrong* mode of interpretation. "The assumptions of the New Critics," writes Sarah Gordon, "that poetic or literary language differs from practical language and that the temperature of the text can be taken by analyzing its linguistic and metaphoric structures may have appealed to O'Connor's disdain for the subjective and sentimental and her established penchant for irony, satire, and caricature."[45] By separating works of literature from the category of psychological case studies, O'Connor knew instinctively that the imagination transforms in written words and structures something that nevertheless emerges from within the writer. Many, including her mother, wanted O'Connor to write about *nice* Southerners and not focus on poor whites or poor blacks who speak idiomatic English. At Iowa, O'Connor embraced the notion that the consciousness of the artist is so integral to the work of art that it cannot be excised and given an identity apart from the work of art. But as her formal education came to an end, she now wanted to join the ranks of the professionals, not an easy step to take for a reserved Southern woman. As she entered the public forum, she felt increasingly the need to return to her writing desk—probably the best sign of her determination to grow and become an accomplished, published author. Alas, it took until 1986 for the University of Iowa to recognize formally her talent and establish the Flannery O'Connor Chair.

CHAPTER THREE

Robert Giroux: CBS, U.S. Navy, and His Return to Harcourt, Brace

1936–1949

After receiving his college diploma from the venerable Nicholas Murray Butler in 1936, Giroux desperately wanted to become an editor and thus visited a number of publishing houses, without receiving a job offer. Through contacts made by Professor Mark Van Doren, he felt happy enough to start in August at $25 a week as an apprentice at CBS. He sometimes looked longingly from the CBS corporate headquarters on the corner of Madison Avenue and Fifty-Second Street to the Knopf offices across the street. He initially was assigned to short stints in eight different departments (Program, Special Events, Public Relations, Production, Traffic, Research, Television, and Executive) to allow him to gain a sense of the overall operation, something that would be immensely helpful in understanding the business world and evaluating a wide assortment of books for publication.[1] With a slightly exaggerated mannerism, Giroux wrote to his former classmate John Berryman shortly after starting his new job:

> My work at CBS is very steady and unexciting. But I am really grateful to have the job. There's a marvelous policy of laissez-faire here which leaves one's privacy unmolested, and if I get a few spare literary chores to do outside from time to time then I shall be happy

for the present. I am more fortunately situated than [Gilbert] Godfrey and [Robert Paul] Smith here, I think.[2] They do "creative" work in the script department—crap of purest ray serene, of course, and it is very harrowing (lists of adjectives and nouns for instance, from which they must choose in writing musical continuity: "exotic," "vignette," "lilting air," "measured cadence"—well, you've listened to the radio); while I work with statistics and other dispassionate paraphernalia and remain oh so detached.[3]

Day in and day out, he learned the value of meeting deadlines with the aim of producing a definite written product. With another new employee, Frank Stanton, who later served for over thirty years as president of CBS, Giroux worked for three years under the supervision of Victor Ratner, director of sales promotion, mainly assisting him in putting together a program guide every month. Two of these guides resulted in booklets entitled *Vienna, March, 1938: A Footnote for Historians from the Columbia Broadcasting System Crisis* and *Crisis, 1938: A Report from the Columbia Broadcasting System.* Though neither booklet listed him as the principal compiler, he was especially proud of the latter, which recounted Neville Chamberlain's "peace journey" and the ill-fated Munich Agreement.

During his time at CBS, Giroux was fortunate to meet Stanley Preston Young, a lively young playwright, then a senior editor at Harcourt, Brace, who introduced him to his colleague Frank Morley. Morley approved of him, and Giroux started working at Harcourt, Brace in early January 1940 as a junior editor in a newly arranged editorial bullpen with two desks placed on each side of a partition. He soon felt part of an important editorial team, though he knew that the U.S. book publishing industry might radically change due to the anxiety brought about by Hitler's invasion of Poland and the subsequent declarations of war on Germany by France and England. Still, Giroux wanted to know as much as possible about his responsibilities and the history of his new firm. It did not take long for him to become greatly impressed by Morley, a former Rhodes scholar at Oxford, who had worked as the London manager of G. P. Putnam's Sons and then at the new firm of Faber & Faber, thus becoming a good friend of T. S. Eliot some years before Giroux. Because of England's preparation for war, Donald Brace asked Morley to return to America in 1939 to become head of the trade department at Harcourt, Brace. Morley served as Giroux's personal mentor; he was, as Giroux said, "a wonderful teacher, not only because he knew so much and gathered so many interesting people around him . . . but because he was such an extraordinary human being."[4] Much to Giroux's astonishment, Morley had previously read Giroux's two CBS booklets and even wanted to publish them in England, but CBS would not allow it because they still were still receiving reports from William Shirer in Berlin and believed that the publication of these books would jeopardize Shirer's work.

Given the congenial surroundings at Harcourt, Brace, Giroux felt that he could easily approach the firm's owners. Both Alfred Harcourt and Brace were graduates of Columbia. A self-effacing individual who won the respect and affection of everyone who worked for him, Brace set a wonderful tone in the office, especially with his solid, avuncular advice. Giroux once repeated to me a piece of wisdom Brace had given him: "Bob, a book needs every support it can get and if you, the editor, like it, it starts out with one real friend. That's important. And that's a good reason never to take on a book if you don't like it."

When Harcourt resigned as president in 1942 because of poor health, Brace assumed his role. Giroux dealt with a dozen authors before his hiatus in the navy, including T. S. Eliot, Randall Jarrell, Bernard Malamud, William Saroyan, Jean Stafford, Eudora Welty, Edmund Wilson, and Virginia Woolf. Over the years, he developed his philosophy of editing based on his interactions with his authors. Bringing a sense of civility and probity to his work, he edited simultaneously any number of manuscripts without losing track of the mental and physical strengths of each of his authors and the contractual nature of each work. Aware that he was there to be of service to his authors, his firm, and the larger literary public, he needed to juggle all sorts of variables that, in the last analysis, had to make good human and literary sense. But he was most conscious of developing his own strengths. "Many elements go into the regular editor's making," he once noted, "starting with the accidents of background and schooling. But there are three qualities that cannot be taught, and without which a good editor cannot function—judgment, taste, and empathy. Judgment is the ability to evaluate a manuscript and its author. Taste is subjective and difficult to define, but we all recognize it when we encounter it. Empathy is the capacity not only to perceive what the author's aims are, but to help in achieving their realization to the fullest extent. The Pygmalion role, a desire to reshape the writer in the editor's image, is anathema."[5] To these three basic qualities, he added that "a little luck never hurts."

Given Giroux's developing awareness of his role as editor, the question could well be asked at this point: how did he know that O'Connor was a genius when they first met? "The answer is," he once said, "I really didn't know but had a hunch. Her demeanor, her reluctance to theorize about the book, her integrity impressed me."[6] And after he read nine chapters of her first novel, he was convinced of her potential. Over the years, he was not blindsided by O'Connor's often eccentric, outspoken characters, who seemed possible to some of her readers but seldom probable. Giroux often relied on his own spiritual insights and practices when reading O'Connor's manuscripts. Having moved beyond the foundational insights provided by the Catholic Catechism, Giroux searched for a spirituality that would sustain him day in and day out, one rooted in New Testament biblical texts, private prayer, and liturgical celebrations. O'Connor's fiction often gave Giroux moments in which to reflect on his own actions and beliefs. He lingered with her characters and their predicaments, however remote from his own, because he saw the underlining validity of what they faced. O'Connor's fiction did not teach him lessons as such, but rather allowed him to see the world as more complex—and relatively simple, at the same time—provided one could accept O'Connor's premises. Most importantly, he did not attempt to translate O'Connor's fiction into a hermeneutics of personal salvation.

As war ravaged Europe, Giroux felt he should put his life as an editor on hold and enlist to do what his country asked of him. Morley told him that he would have his old job at Harcourt, Brace when he returned from his stint in the navy. In fact, Morley, in his capacity as director of Harcourt, Brace, wrote a letter of support for Giroux, now editor in chief, to the Naval Reserve Office: "I can state without reservation that the intimate knowledge gained by working with him and seeing him outside of office hours has in every respect increased my opinion of him. He has to an unusual degree the qualities of intelligence, enterprise, character and discretion. His general deportment is excellent and he is at once quick-witted and thoroughly reliable."[7] Frank Stanton, then director of research at CBS, also wrote a glowing letter to the navy, as did Mark Van Doren, stating in part that Giroux's "character is sterling and attractive; his appearance is unexceptionable; he is famous among those who know him for his reliability and for the solidity of his deportment; he is tenacious in his intelligence; and his resourcefulness in several situations where I have seen him has been most admirable."[8] After Giroux applied for enlistment in late March 1942, he was interviewed by navy personnel and subsequently sworn in at the recruiting office in lower New York as an apprentice seaman. Not long afterward, he learned that Naval Intelligence was looking for college-educated men who needed to be at least twenty-seven years old. He felt qualified and, much to his surprise, no one in the intelligence office ever asked if he had applied for another military post. Thus, on April 18, he had his commission as a lieutenant (junior grade). After three months of training at the Quonset Point Naval Air Station in Rhode Island, Giroux was assigned during the summer of 1942 to the USS *Essex* at Norfolk, Virginia, which had been commissioned the previous December and was then being completed in a nearby shipyard. For almost two years, he served as an aide to Lieutenant Commander Charles D. Griffin, in charge of Air Group 9 aboard the *Essex*, which had a deck the length of three football fields, a crew of more than 3,400 men, and carried just over one hundred aircraft. On May 10, 1943, the *Essex* left for the Panama Canal and Hawaii. Though Giroux sometimes referred to his naval experience in the Pacific, he preferred not to put the spotlight on himself because he realized that he was but one of hundreds of thousands fighting for their country. He would always answer specific questions, but rarely went into detail about the maneuvers of the *Essex*, perhaps due to the secret nature of much of his work. In some analogous way, he shared Edward O'Connor's reserve about talking about his war experience. By the time the *Essex* pulled into San Francisco in early March 1944 for some R & R, it had participated in raids on strategic islands and atolls in the Pacific, including Marcus, Wake, Tarawa, the Gilberts, Kwajalein, and Truk—in short, in nearly every major carrier action in the Pacific from August 1943 until March 1944. The *Essex* returned to the Pacific theater in May.

Giroux, now tougher and more knowledgeable about the evils in the world, returned stateside after the Japanese signed the instruments of surrender aboard the USS *Missouri* in September 1945. He was decommissioned with the rank of lieutenant commander in the late fall of 1945. Resuming work at Harcourt, Brace in January 1946, he attacked his various projects effortlessly; his new boss, Eugene Reynal, confirmed him in his position as editor in chief. He picked up where he left off and began to line up new authors.

Giroux was surprised when Merton contacted him, this time with a book that would significantly change his life as an editor. Far away in the countryside of Kentucky, with the encouragement of Abbot Frederic Dunne, O.C.S.O., Merton had been writing his autobiography. In great peace and solitude, Merton had reviewed the events that led up to his arrival at Gethsemani Abbey and found a perspective that would later resonate with thousands of others, especially those who had been radically shaken by World War II. Both Merton and his agent, Naomi Burton, thought Giroux a good choice for the 694-page typescript (reduced from 800 pages by the Trappist censors), which was completed in December 1946. Giroux, as he mentioned to me, wondered whether he had gone out on a limb when he asked Brace to read the typescript:

"Do you think it will lose money?" the senior editor asked.

"Oh no," Giroux replied, "I'm sure it will find an audience. I don't think we'd lose any money, but whether we make any is problematic. Merton writes well, and I wish you'd take a look at it, Don."

"No, Bob," Brace said, "I'll read it in print. If you like it, let's do it."

The celebrated author Evelyn Waugh, who edited the British edition of Merton's *The Seven Storey Mountain* under the title *Elected Silence* and would later write a blurb for O'Connor's *Wise Blood*, wrote to Giroux on July 20, 1948, "I regard this as a book which may well prove to be of permanent interest in the history of religious experience. No one can afford to neglect this clear account of a complex religious process." Waugh's endorsement carried considerable weight, particularly within the Catholic community, which enjoyed his novels. In light of this and other superb comments, Harcourt, Brace increased the first printing from 5,000 copies to 12,500, knowing that they might still need more copies. In fact, its prepublication sale was 20,847 copies, with the original cloth edition eventually exceeding 600,000 copies!

Given his track record—he was particularly proud of editing Hannah Arendt's 1951 *The Origins of Totalitarianism*, brought to him by Kazin—Giroux was achieving all that he could imagine at Harcourt, Brace. But then William Jovanovich began to change things. Jovanovich, whom Giroux referred to as "Don Giovanovich," had joined the company in 1947 as a textbook salesman, becoming head of the school department and then president in 1955. Giroux feared that under Jovanovich's aegis the firm would become more and more a textbook publishing house and not continue as a literary one. (After thirty-four years at the helm, Jovanovich resigned in 1990 as chairman of Harcourt, Brace, due in large part to the company's burden of a $1.7 billion debt).[9]

One event in particular, involving J. D. Salinger, served as a prelude to Giroux's departure from Harcourt, Brace, as he recounted in part in an interview with George Plimpton. In December 1945, *Collier's* published a story written by Salinger entitled "I'm Crazy," about a teenager named Holden Caulfield. A year later the *New Yorker* published his "Slight Rebellion Off Madison," which Salinger had submitted to them a few years earlier. Salinger's *New Yorker* stories caught Giroux's eye, and in 1949 he wrote to him, care of the editor, William Shawn, about the possibility of publishing a collection of his stories. Receiving no response from Salinger, Giroux dropped the matter. Then one day, a shy, tall, Hamlet-like individual with pitch-black hair and very black eyes walked into Giroux's office.

"I can't publish a book of short stories," Salinger began, "because I've almost finished this novel, and the novel has to come first."

Giroux smiled and said, "You should be sitting here at my desk. You're a born publisher because it's true—short stories don't sell as well as novels."

"I'd like you to publish my novel."

"What novel?"

"Oh, it isn't finished. It's about a kid in New York during the Christmas holidays."

And on the basis of that and what Giroux had read in the *New Yorker*, author and editor shook hands in a gentlemen's agreement that Harcourt, Brace would publish this novel.

About a year later, as Giroux was eating in Grand Central's Oyster Bar, someone tapped him on the shoulder. He turned around and saw Jerry Salinger. "I didn't want to disturb you, Bob, but I have wonderful news. I just finished the draft of my novel. I've just come from Bill Shawn's office and the *New Yorker* is going to devote an entire issue to it." But in the ensuing months, the *New Yorker* reversed its decision, and a year later a messenger delivered the manuscript of *The Catcher in the Rye* to Giroux's office. He read it and was absolutely riveted. He thought how lucky he was that this incredible book had come into his hands. Immediately he wrote a rave report and turned it over to Eugene Reynal, who had become his boss after Morley returned to England. After not hearing back from Reynal about the matter for two weeks, he went to see him.

"Bob, I'm worried about that manuscript," Reynal began.
"What are you worried about?"
"I think the kid is disturbed."
"Well, that's all right. He is, but it's a great novel."
"I felt that I had to show it to the textbook department" Reynal said.
"What, the *textbook* department?"
"Yes, it's about a kid in prep school, isn't it? I'm waiting for their reply."
"It doesn't matter what their reply is, Gene. We have a contract for the book." He actually felt like saying, "This is the greatest insult to me that could ever be."

When the textbook department's report came back, it simply said, "This book is not for us, try Random House." So Giroux went to Donald Brace and recounted what had transpired, adding, "I feel that I have to resign from the firm." Brace had hired Reynal, one of the founders of Reynal & Hitchcock, in 1933, and would not overrule him. When Giroux later talked to Salinger on the phone, he shamefacedly admitted, "I don't have the power to sign the contract and my new boss won't do it, so I have to release it." As has been clear to generations of high school adolescents, literary history was made when Little, Brown & Company, published *The Catcher in the Rye*, edited by Giroux's good friend, John Woodburn.[10]

As the tremors at Harcourt, Brace grew more and more pronounced toward the end of 1954, Jovanovich tried to rectify the situation, first by easing Reynal out of the firm.[11] Unfortunately, Reynal thought Giroux was behind this maneuver, which was not the case. Feeling increasingly uncomfortable as month after month passed, Giroux bided his time. Another author caught unwittingly in the Reynal-Giroux crossfire, Bernard Malamud, caused Giroux added moments of anxiety. In the introduction to Malamud's *Complete Stories*, Giroux says he took Malamud's first novel *The Natural* as part of a two-book contract, though he did have some reservations about it.[12] He had first contacted Malamud in November

1950 at the suggestion of Catharine Carver and Kazin. Before the second novel, *The Assistant*, was ready, Giroux resigned from Harcourt, Brace. John McCallum, then vice president at Harcourt, Brace and someone who would be a significant figure in O'Connor's publishing history, turned down the novel, and Kazin suggested that Malamud migrate in the fall of 1956 to Farrar, Straus & Cudahy, where Giroux published it in 1957. A year later Giroux had his first National Book Award winner, Malamud's *The Magic Barrel*. The waffling back and forth, the lack of focus, and the arbitrary decision making now seemed the hallmarks of the firm under Jovanovich's direction. Giroux could no longer tolerate what was happening and wanted to resign in December 1954, but he waited patiently until the following April so he could obtain his pension rights.

CHAPTER FOUR

Flannery O'Connor, Robert Giroux

1949–1952

When Flannery O'Connor left Robert Giroux's office with Robert Lowell on March 2, 1949, she had no book contract in hand, nor even a written assurance of one, but she did know that Giroux had been favorably impressed by her and her accomplishments to date, and thus she felt more confident both about herself and her ability to negotiate the world of New York publishing. In the coming years she would learn that Giroux would do everything he could to promote her fiction, in spite of the twists and turns of office politics and the demands of his other authors. While in New York, she also met with Paul Engle and related to him her situation.[1] Not long after this meeting and a quick trip back home, she rented a room from April to September on the twelfth floor of the Manchester Apartments at West 108th Street on the corner of Broadway, just a block in from Riverside Park. On her own, she kept her routine simple and focused. She walked every morning to the Church of the Ascension on 107th Street, between Broadway and Amsterdam Avenue, said her prayers, and participated in the liturgy, enjoying her anonymity and having no desire to socialize with the other daily communicants. Motivated and disciplined, she spent a few hours writing each day. Though she had used New York as a locale in "The Geranium"—with its "swishing and jamming one minute and dirty and dead the next"—it became clear to her that this was not the city she would use as a backdrop for her later fiction.

About all she took away with her was that there was an *uptown* and a *downtown*—something apparent to even the most nonchalant tourist. If anything, living in this city gave her a keener sense of her home in Georgia.

Never caught up by the Bohemian spirit felt by many of the writers in Greenwich Village, O'Connor wanted merely to work in New York on her novel until her money ran out. Rinehart would not pay her until they had a good idea what the finished book would look like. One might ask why O'Connor did not test Rinehart to see if its previous decision might be reconsidered. The answer probably was not even clear to her, but according to some interior compass, she felt she needed to proceed further as a writer. Perhaps she subconsciously wished to emulate the accomplished fiction writers she met at Yaddo. She told herself repeatedly that she would not be hassled or directed by Rinehart; she had already been given $750 in prize money, after all, and an equal sum awaited her if Rinehart exercised their option. When she wrote to Engle on April 7 that other publishers "who have read the two printed chapters, are interested," she wisely gave no specifics. O'Connor was obstinate; she worked all the time and simply could not go any faster. "No one can convince me I shouldn't rewrite as much as I do." When news arrived that she had not received a Guggenheim Fellowship, she asked Engle to have her close friend Robie Macauley write to her; upset and uncertain where to turn, she clearly needed some advice from a trusted confidante who would not betray her.

Just as O'Connor was reaching this low point at the beginning of her career, Giroux was reaching a high point in his with the autobiography of Thomas Merton. When Abbot James Fox, O.C.S.O., invited Giroux and other of Merton's friends, including poet James Laughlin, educator Daniel Walsh, poet Robert Lax, and writer Edward Rice, to the monastery for Merton's ordination on May 26, 1949, Giroux brought along the 200,000th copy of Merton's book in a hand-tooled leather binding. In the introduction to the fiftieth-anniversary edition of *The Seven Storey Mountain*, Giroux reflected that "the combination of the right subject at the right time presented in the right way accounts for a good part of the book's success"—a formula that could well apply to O'Connor's novel. Giroux mused,

> Why did the success of *The Seven Storey Mountain* go so far beyond my expectations as an editor and publisher? Why, despite its being

banned from the [*New York Times* best-seller] list, did it outsell all other nonfiction books in the same months? Though few readers believe it, publishers cannot create best-sellers. There is always an element of mystery when it happens: why *this* book at *this* moment? The most essential element of success is right timing, which cannot usually be foreseen. *The Seven Storey Mountain* appeared at a time of disillusion, following the Second World War, when another war—the cold war—had started and the public was ready for a change from disillusion and cynicism. Second, the story Merton told was unusual: an articulate young man with an interesting background leaves the world and withdraws into a monastery. Third, it was a tale well told, with liveliness and eloquence. No doubt there were other reasons, but the combination of the right subject at the right time presented in the right way accounts for a good part of the book's success.[2]

Giroux often talked to me about the success of this book. He believed that Merton's journey through life was one of exploration, keeping his eye on God, on the eternal verities, and on the world God created—thus seeing all the relationships and the resulting congruities and incongruities. Giroux could easily have said the same about O'Connor's fiction. "Some people would say that Merton found a home in the monastery," Giroux once explained. "It may be true, but that doesn't take one iota away from his achievement. Many people have found homes in monasteries, but few have developed as remarkably as he did. The ambience never really explains the art itself."[3] In short, Merton was very much a man of his own times who had a deeply felt spirituality rooted in Cistercian forms of prayer and in the traditions and sacramental life of the Catholic Church. Except for some conflicting times toward the end of his life, when much to the dismay of his abbot, he became enamored with a nurse in a local hospital, he flourished in the seclusion of the monastery, due in large part to his searching imagination and his overwhelming desire to communicate through the printed word.

As Giroux balanced success and frustration at Harcourt, Brace, O'Connor's financial situation grew less than favorable. Given the uncertainty over the book contract, it made little sense for her to remain in New York, so she went to stay with the Fitzgeralds at their home in Redding, Connecticut. In mid-August she wrote to a friend, "Me & novel are going to move to the rural parts of Connecticut. . . . I am on a tight-rope somewhere between Rinehart and Harcourt, Brace. There should be some kind of insurance to take care of such cases." As it turned out, Rinehart never exercised its option to publish *Wise Blood.* When Mavis McIntosh wrote to Selby about this matter, he offered no immediate explanation. Giroux, as he explained it to me, thus became O'Connor's editor because Rinehart did not follow through on their option. She was delighted to receive Harcourt, Brace's provisional contract on October 6. She had established a relationship with a prominent publishing house and an editor who had just made history by publishing his best-selling book to date. Calculating that her novel would be less than 90,000 words, she wanted to have specifics at her fingertips for Giroux, not completely realizing that a *contractual option* from Harcourt, Brace was not a normal contract.

Indeed, it would have been naïve of Giroux to offer a contract on a first novel to an author who was, in many ways, just launching her career. O'Connor correctly surmised, in a letter to McIntosh in October 1949, that "since this contract is only to be looked at, I presume that is no consideration at present." The momentum nevertheless had shifted in O'Connor's favor, and she could write her novel at the Fitzgeralds' for about four hours each morning and look after their children as they needed her attention. Even better, Robert was then teaching medieval Scholasticism at Sarah Lawrence College, so she could dip into his library for his latest acquisitions of classical literary texts as well as the works of Aristotle and Saint Thomas Aquinas.

By mid-October, O'Connor still felt in a quandary, mainly because of a technicality: the lack of some formal letter releasing her from any ob-ligation to Rinehart. Giroux could not send a binding contract to her, via McIntosh, unless he was sure that he was legally and morally free to do so. The provisional contract was simply standard procedure. O'Connor expressed her frustration to her friend Betty Boyd, writing, "My pub-lishing snarl is still snarled. I have a provisional contract with Harcourt, Brace in my desk drawer but can't sign it because I am still unreleased by Rinehart; however all I really want to be about is getting this book fin-ished." Until she had something in writing from Rinehart or some other proof that they were dropping the option—and not just committing an oversight—she could not consider herself at liberty to place her novel elsewhere.

She finally received from Selby the sought-after statement of release, but it was not the clean break she desired: she wrote to her agent in late October, "I find it, like most of Selby's documents, in the highest degree unclear. They want it definitely understood that in the event of trouble with Harcourt they see the novel before any other publisher. This is no release. However, I suppose the best thing to do is sign the Harcourt agreement and hope there will be no further trouble; but I want it definitely understood that it is *not* definitely understood that in the event of trouble with Harcourt, Rinehart see the manuscript again." She remained anxious to know what had happened behind the scenes and what difficulties McIntosh might have had with Selby, who had described O'Connor in his statement of release as "stiff-necked, uncooperative and unethical."[4] The word *unethical* struck her the most because it was a moral judgment with implied legal overtones. Yet, enough was enough, and she anticipated no further contact with Selby; in her mind she had received what was probably the best Selby would or could say about this matter. Deeply offended by his handling of the matter, she had no intention of dealing with him in the future. She planned instead to visit New York again and talk with either McIntosh or McKee.

With one door definitely closed, O'Connor needed to put all her energies into her novel, which was going well, and thus open the door even wider at Harcourt, Brace. She was encouraged by the fact that she would soon be getting proofs for "The Heart of the Park" from *Partisan Review*, though she was curious as to the exact date of publication—and thus her payment. Still, she could not completely dismiss Selby and the feeling that she still was contracted, in some way or other, to Rinehart. Thus she wrote again to McIntosh at the end of October: "I think it is insulting and shows very clearly that I could not work with him. However, since they still feel that they have an option and that I am being dishonest, it seems to me that I should present them with more of the manuscript one more time." Incredibly, for all her strength of character, she could not completely sever her relationship with Rinehart. She asked herself as well whether she should sign the contract with Harcourt, Brace, knowing that she would not receive any money until the following fall—that is, providing they accepted the novel in the first place. The more she deliberated, the more incapable she felt of reaching a definite decision. She wondered, as she mentioned in the same letter to McIntosh, whether "it would be better all around to try to arrange something like this with

Rinehart: that next March, I show them what I have done up to that date. This will be considerably more than what they saw last year at the same time and the direction of the book will be more apparent." Should Rinehart turn her down again, she continued in her letter, they should release her in writing "without condition or any such malicious statement as accompanied the present release." Even so, she reiterated that she would never work with Rinehart if they insisted on an option of any kind. She felt certain that Rinehart would not want the book the following spring or at any date. O'Connor, to use a word that often occurred in Roman Catholic sacramental confessions in those days, was being *scrupulous.* Indeed, she was exhibiting a major characteristic of scrupulosity, asking the same question from various angles: "[I]f Harcourt doesn't take the book, we are back where we started from. If Rinehart will make this agreement with me, in writing, we might get the thing settled by summer and I would be free to work with an open mind, which I am certainly not now." Intending to see McIntosh in the very near future, she concluded her letter to McIntosh, "I wrote Elizabeth that I thought it would be best to go ahead and sign the contract with Harcourt, but this letter is the fruit of more thought."

When she returned to Redding in early November after two days in New York, she breathed a sigh of relief, as she wrote to Boyd, "There is one advantage in it because although you see several people you wish you didn't know, you see thousands you're glad you don't know." She received word in mid-December 1949 from Ted Amussen, who was about to leave Harcourt, Brace to become editor in chief at Henry Holt & Company, that he and Giroux were "very happy" about the contract with O'Connor.[5] Though O'Connor profited enormously from the discussions with her agent on this trip, her health began to falter not long afterward. After she complained about the heaviness in her arms, the Fitzgeralds quickly took her to see a doctor in nearby Wilton. Little did she suspect that her trip back to Milledgeville at Christmastime 1949, intended for an operation to correct a floating kidney, would inaugurate a lifestyle she most likely did not want or ever anticipate. Lowell and Hardwick met her at the train station in New York, but O'Connor felt depressed and had little to say, except for some small talk about Iowa as Lowell was about to travel to the Writers' Workshop to talk with Engle about teaching there.[6]

Once back in Georgia, she began adjusting to the restricting demands of her physical condition. Lyman Fulton, M.D., a New York acquaintance, termed her condition "Dietl's crisis," which is characterized by acute pain in the region of the kidneys accompanied by nausea and vomiting; it is usually associated with a floating kidney.[7] O'Connor went to the Baldwin Memorial Hospital in Milledgeville and returned home in an ambulance, as she wrote to the Fitzgeralds in late January 1950, and felt better afterward.[8] Walking up steps posed a problem for her, so she remained upstairs in the Cline mansion. Living at home did not seem right to her, and she expressed an interest in rejoining the Fitzgeralds in Connecticut.[9] Back in Redding in late April, she informed McKee that she had a letter from Giroux inquiring about the status of her novel. "This seems to be a question," she wrote with some irritation, "that extends itself over the years." She sent a chapter of the novel to McKee, with the request that it be sent to Frederick Morgan at the *Hudson Review*, but not to *Flair, Mademoiselle*, or the *Partisan Review*.[10] A month later she learned that the chapter had been turned down.[11]

Although she worked steadily in Redding, she could not keep up the same pace as before. "That October date for showing the manuscript to Harcourt will have to be put off four or five months," she informed McKee, "but I presume that will be no matter to anybody." Giroux met O'Connor that May at Maria Juliana Fitzgerald's christening, and at that point he spelled out more precisely what their professional relationship would be like and formally agreed to be her editor. She wrote to Macauley from Connecticut to inform him that she definitely had a new publisher, something that would have pleased him enormously: "The Brothers Rinehart and I have parted company to our mutual satisfaction," she wrote, "and I have a contract with Harcourt, Brace, but I am largely worried about wingless chickens."[12] In late September 1950, McKee received additional news from O'Connor: Harcourt, Brace was ready to formulate plans for the novel in early January 1951 and most likely start putting in place a timetable for its production. "The last time I saw Bob Giroux," O'Connor informed her agent, "he said he would push the date of the agreement up to the first of the year but that there was nothing magic in that date." At this point in her life, she realized that, given some health problems, she should return home to Milledgeville, but she was not sure if that would be her permanent residence.

Virginia Wray sets a positive tone about O'Connor's departure for Milledgeville: "No matter how radically the violent onset of lupus had affected the menial details and geography of O'Connor's life, it had essentially no effect on the nature and direction of her art. When she had boarded the train south in December of 1950, she had already completed a draft of her first novel, *Wise Blood*, a draft that she would revise only minimally for publication with help from her new editor, Robert Giroux of Harcourt, Brace, and from her new friend and mentor, Caroline Gordon."[13] O'Connor's health had in fact taken a decided turn for the worse, as she mentioned in a handwritten note to McKee. Because of what she thought was acute arthritis, she had gone to the Richard Bunion Clinic (associated with the Baldwin Memorial Hospital, or "horsepital" as she called it) and had started taking cortisone to reduce inflammation and the attendant pain. "Will be a couple of months before I can get back to Conn[ecticut] however," she admitted.[14] She had one welcome distraction: at Giroux's suggestion, she was reading Eliot's *Murder in the Cathedral* and enjoying it tremendously. In another handwritten note, this time from Emory Hospital in Atlanta, she told McKee that she felt much improved and was about to return to Milledgeville. "During the cortisone period, I managed to finish the first draft of the novel and send it to Mr. Fitzgerald in Conn. He is satisfied that it is good and so am I."[15] At about this time, Regina O'Connor called the Fitzgeralds and informed them, apparently without consulting her daughter, that Flannery was "dying of lupus."[16] The Fitzgeralds were stunned by the news and kept in contact with Regina, respecting for the time her wish to keep the news from her daughter.

For the next year and a half O'Connor stayed at Andalusia, unaware of the true nature of her illness. On January 25, 1951, Robert Fitzgerald sent O'Connor an honest three-page critique of her novel, which she valued very much.[17] By early March, Giroux learned from Robert that O'Connor had finished the draft of her novel; he asked if she would send it to him soon, since he would like to like to feature it in their fall catalogue.[18] She hired a typist in Atlanta to make copies for McKee and Harcourt, Brace, and on March 10 she sent Giroux his copy with a not-too-subtle suggestion: "I hope you'll like it and decide to publish it. I'm still open to suggestions about improving it and will welcome any you have; however, I'm anxious to be done with it and if it could be out in the fall that would suit me fine." Her tone had softened a bit over what she had previously written to Selby, but the underlying determination remained the same. Even though McKee thought some of the chapters might be salable separately, O'Connor had her doubts. In the meantime, she was pleased to receive Dr. Karl Stern's *A Pillar of Fire*, which Giroux had edited, a fortuitous choice given her need for sound spirituality from someone knowledgeable about medicine. Giroux regularly mailed O'Connor books he had edited, thus increasing her personal library and providing direction to her reading. He considered this aspect of an editor's job important, particularly as it gave the recipient a sense of the ongoing nature of his own work and of the texts he personally valued.

After sending the typescript to Giroux, O'Connor remained in a bit of a quandary, as she wrote McKee on March 10: "I wrote him [Giroux] that you or Miss McIntosh would see him. . . . If Harcourt doesn't want it, what about Scribner's?" She gave her agent some news about her medical condition, but shared little detail, except to say that she was full of ACTH (adrenocorticotropic hormone, a pain reliever derived from the pituitary glands of pigs) and feeling much better for it. She failed to mention that she had been in Emory Hospital for a month. Because she wanted to appear as normal as possible to her agent, she would have resisted articulating to McKee—and thus, perhaps, to herself—the extent of her physical, mental, and emotional state.

Her isolation began to produce anxious moments. Clearly miffed, she wrote to McKee on April 24, 1951, asking her to check on the typescript she had sent Giroux earlier in March, but for which she had strangely received no acknowledgment. "They ought to know by now if they don't want it or not, and I am anxious to get it off my mind. If they don't want it, please get the manuscript back and send it somewhere else." Her irritation mounted because she had so few people to talk to and, more importantly, so few people to listen to her, except her mother, who was just beginning to understand her daughter's career as a writer—and definitely not liking it at all.

Over the years, given her declining health and her mother's omnipresence, O'Connor had had little choice but to share her thoughts about her fiction in letters to friends (especially Catharine Carver, Cecil Dawkins, Robert Giroux, John Hawkes, Betty Hester, Maryat Lee, Janet McKane, Dr. T. R. Spivey [a professor of English at Georgia State University in Atlanta], Thomas Stritch [a professor of American studies at Notre Dame], and the Fitzgeralds, among others). Sally Fitzgerald provides a necessary observation in this regard: "Flannery O'Connor clearly had a gift for friendship, which she nurtured and developed with care and consideration, with full regard for the needs of others as they were gradually revealed, and with the candor that alone keeps open the lines of communication so that a friendship can remain fresh and viable."[19] Loneliness must have been a constant companion, especially as she had, except for her lecture trips, little outside stimulation (the O'Connors received their first television set in March 1961 as a gift from some of the Atlanta nuns she had befriended). Letters to her friends—never consciously meant for publication—should be considered a significant part of her published legacy, giving her an opportunity to touch the moment, however fallow or full it might be. Jeffrey Folks notes, "Perhaps the most distinctive quality of her letters, however, lies in something other than the cultural debate in which O'Connor participated or even the support for her art that she found from such correspondents like the novelist John Hawkes or her agent Elizabeth McKee. This quality entails something unique in the art of letter-writing: the pleasure of friendship; its discovery coming like a sudden and miraculous gift; its delight over months and years of exchanges; its inevitable end as correspondents drift apart, quarrel, lose interest, or inevitably die."[20] O'Connor's letters to her three editors and two agents complemented the work at hand, stressing its importance from various angles and allowing her to be a key player in the publication—and thus fruition—of what she considered essential to her life as a writer. Robert McGill's insightful essay on the posthumous publication of O'Connor's letters demonstrates that despite her desire "for her fiction to be discussed without reference to her life, she was often the first to conflate her life with her writing."[21] She had lived with one of her characters, Enoch, listened to him, and followed his every action, as she had noted, all the while trying to evaluate how mystery somehow enveloped his (and her own) existence.

O'Connor's main preoccupation had a threefold component: to safeguard what physical, psychic, and imaginative energies she had so that she could continue writing. She wrote Betty Boyd Love (now married) on April 24 that while in the hospital she gave "generous samples of [her] blood to this, that, and the other technician, all hours of the day and night, but now I am at home again and not receiving any more awful cards. . . . I have finished my opus nauseous and expect it to be out one of these days. The name will be *Wise Blood*." For O'Connor, the title of her first novel had a definite significance, as she wrote to John Hawkes in September 1959: "Haze is saved by virtue of having wise blood; it's too wise for him ultimately to deny Christ. Wise blood has to be these people's means of grace—they have no sacraments." But what would others think of this title, not knowing her stated intention? Should the emphasis be on *wise* or on *blood*, and what does the title mean when you put these two words together?

By early 1959, the French translator of the novel, Maurice-Edgar Coindreau, chose as its title *La Sagesse dans le sang*.[22] When O'Connor received a copy of the French edition in early January 1960, she wrote to Coindreau saying that she was going to read every word of it and that she was pleased that he had shown the book to Jacques Maritain.[23] Monsieur Coindreau told me in Paris that he had trouble selecting a phrase in French that provided a good translation for O'Connor's title. Why was *La Sagesse dans le sang* (The Wisdom in the Blood) better, I asked him, than some other translation, such as *La Sagesse du sang* (The Wisdom of the Blood) or, even a third possibility, *Sang sage* (Blood Wise, which could also be read as Wise Blood)? Coindreau had visited O'Connor a number of times and had a chance to talk to her about the novel, and I thought his choice of title might provide additional insight into its original meaning. He replied cryptically to me that the French title he chose suggested something innate about blood, while the first of my suggestions really does not readily call this to mind. He had not considered my second possibility.

No doubt part of O'Connor's growing anxiety about the acceptance of her novel, which as far as she and McIntosh knew, still had not been formally accepted as of early May 1951, stemmed from the fact that her confined residence the Cline mansion presented too many obstacles. Thus she and her mother decided to move permanently to Andalusia.[24] Out in the country, she could manage better living on the first floor alone; in addition, she would not have the solicitous intrusions of her elderly aunts Mary and Katie. Andalusia gave O'Connor a place, a locale, from which she could observe her own people with greater attention.

Giroux also tried to soothe her anxiety, writing on May 10, "I want your novel to have every consideration here, and that is taking time, so be please assured that it is getting our best attention. I think you have done wonders, myself, but it is not an easy book or one that elicits easy publishing judgments."[25] He wrote in early June to McIntosh that *Wise Blood* had been accepted and sent her the advance of $1,000.[26] Giroux subsequently forwarded to O'Connor the critique of the novel that Gordon had sent Robert Fitzgerald. "I have suggestions for revision, so do others here, and I'm sure you have definite revisions of your own in mind."[27] He recommended that she start with Gordon's comments. O'Connor had not taken sufficiently into account the Princeton-based Gordon–Tate–Giroux–Fitzgerald connection, to whatever degree she might have been aware of it. With O'Connor's permission, Fitzgerald sent the typescript of the novel to Gordon, "a friend for whose taste and artistry he had the highest regard" and who had read a few of O'Connor's stories "with great interest."[28] (It should be noted that at about the time Gordon was reading and reflecting on O'Connor's manuscript, Tate had been invited to become godfather to Peter Michael Fitzgerald, born on May 20, 1951, and thus could well have shared some of his ideas about this manuscript, a version of which he had previously read.) Gordon, then living in Princeton in a house on Nassau Street that she had purchased in fall of 1949, wrote to Robert Fitzgerald that O'Connor's procedure seemed sound: "She is, of course, writing the kind of stuff people like to read nowadays: about freaks. Her book, like those of most of the younger writers, is full of freaks, but she does something with them that [Frederick] Buechner and [Truman] Capote and those books seem to be incapable of doing. Truman's people seem to me to belong in some good clinic. Her characters started out real folk but turn into freaks as the result of original sin."[29] Giroux was undoubtedly aware, through either Fitzgerald or Gordon, of Gordon's interest in this manuscript and would have been among the first to have approved having an outside evaluator. Giroux knew that it would take some time for O'Connor to deal with the changes suggested by Gordon, and he let the process take its natural course. One way or another, O'Connor would learn that when others are involved in helping a novelist have a manuscript published, each person proceeds on his or her own schedule. It would soon be clear to her that both readers and editors work on many projects simultaneously. O'Connor simply had to content herself waiting for the mailman to deliver a letter from Giroux about specific plans for publishing her novel.

By early June 1951, the waiting was over; O'Connor had an official, signed book contract based on the typescript that Giroux had seen. But her irritation over Giroux's lack of communication had not totally disappeared, as she mentioned to McIntosh: "I am mighty pleased that Harcourt took the book and hope we'll get on with it now. I haven't heard from Bob Giroux but I suppose I will in whatever he considers the fullness of time." O'Connor's subsequent letter to Giroux, who was preparing to take a vacation, expresses her gratitude to Gordon, especially for her willingness to make more suggestions in the future. In a letter to Robert Fitzgerald, which begins "Dear Robert again," Gordon focuses on how the first scene ought to foreshadow the last: "We ought to see Hazel Motes before we hear him say anything or before we are taken into his thoughts. That business about the black hat looking as if it would bite you doesn't work because it comes too soon in the action; she begins playing tricks with us before she really got hold of us. The way Motes looks, particularly the way his eyes look, ought to be played up in the beginning."[30] By considering such criticism, however unsolicited, O'Connor would be in a better position to revise her work and make sure that her books would be understood by informed and intelligent readers. As she wrote to Giroux:

> I am much relieved that you are going to publish the book.
>
> I have been studying Mrs. Tate's notes. All her criticisms seem very much to the point to me and I would never have been able to see them myself without this help. I am indebted to her. Maybe she will look at the manuscript again after I have tried to do the things she has suggested.
>
> Probably the mummy needs to be disposed of. I hadn't thought about it but I will. As for Haze's past in the Army, I was afraid to fool with that: I don't know what goes on there. I think that opening up the first paragraphs as Mrs. Tate suggests (the business about the eyes) will help cut down the confusion about Haze. Anyway, I'll work on these things and hope you'll send me your own suggestions for revision when you get back.[31]

Robert Fitzgerald wrote to Giroux in late June from Redding, partly to chide him for being so slow in responding to O'Connor, but mostly to thank him for assisting her; he mentioned in passing that his friend Dan Walsh was assisting Merton with his next book.[32] Regina O'Connor, meanwhile, wrote in late July to the Fitzgeralds, giving them a fairly complete picture of her daughter's health. O'Connor was now under the care of Arthur J. Merrill, M.D., who would be her primary physician through her long ordeal with lupus. Regina felt confident that consultation with a new doctor would give them both reason to hope for the best. The trips from Milledgeville to Atlanta by ambulance had given clear evidence that O'Connor could not tolerate lengthy car rides. She explained,

I'm sending you by today's mail Flannery's corrected manuscript which she would like you both to read. She asked me to tell you both how grateful she is to you for all your help with the book and how much she appreciated Mrs. Tate's letter. I think Mrs. Tate's letter did a lot for her.

Monday I took her to the hospital here, in the ambulance, and it waited, while we had chest x-rays, blood work and an electrocardiogram made. This was so we could send a report to Dr. Merrill. There was no trouble with the chest or heart and the blood was about the same. However she still has fever but it is not so high as it has been. She is taking rather large doses of ACTH which makes her nervous and keeps her awake.

Dr. Merrill has been in touch by phone with a doctor in Wis[consin] who has had very good results with a new drug (taken by mouth). I don't know the name of it but anyway he phoned Dr. [C. B.] Fulghum [a local physician] that he would have a good room for me at Emory by Friday and be ready to give the new medicine at that time. This seems very encouraging. We will have to go in the ambulance as Flannery has been in bed about six or seven weeks. This new drug is given with the ACTH but you are able to give very much smaller doses of the ACTH, which will make Flannery much more comfortable.

I will try to keep you posted as to how she is doing. I have no idea how long it will take to adjust the doses. I guess the length of time we stay at Emory will depend on this.

Thanks again and keep praying. Hope the children are well. Send a snapshot of them sometime.

[P.S.] I may not get the manuscript off today as I want to make a copy of the corrections. This is the only corrected copy and she won't be able to do it so I will try to.[33]

Behind the scenes, Gordon delighted in finding a new author whose works she could mold according to her own literary tastes. When Giroux returned the typescript to O'Connor, he noted that he had no other points to make that had not been mentioned in their correspondence and in the Gordon letters.[34] When Gordon learned a few months later that the novel approached completion, she wrote O'Connor directly from Minneapolis, where she had moved after Tate accepted a position at the

University of Minnesota, offering, "I shall be glad to read it whenever Robert [Fitzgerald] sends it. I am going to write to Robert Giroux, too, and tell him that I want to review it when it comes out and that I would like to do anything I can to help—though, of course, there is little that one can do, or needs to do to help a good novel."[35]

If beauty, sentimentality, and truth were Romantic and Victorian ideals that influenced nineteenth-century Southern writers who looked to English models, Gordon wanted to share with O'Connor some new norms for looking at culture and literature, especially those influenced by the more structured and objective classical authors. A listing of some of her own published novels up to that point undoubtedly allowed her to speak authoritatively: *Aleck Maury, Sportsman* deals with a retired classics professor, most likely based on her father, who devotes himself to outdoor sports and activities; *None Shall Look Back*, a Civil War novel, focuses on General Nathan Bedford Forest; *Green Centuries* is set in the Kentucky frontier during the American Revolution; and *The Women on the Porch* concerns a woman who returns home to Tennessee after her marriage has failed. But more was at stake, especially Gordon's missionary zeal; she had converted to Catholicism in November 1947—as did Tate in December 1950 (Sally Fitzgerald was present, and Raïssa and Jacques Maritain served as godparents)—giving her life a new spiritual focus, but one that was never easy for her to sustain.[36] Gordon's literary theories tended to fuse Aristotelian concepts of plot, classic Greek and Christian mythology, Jungian thought, and the four levels of biblical interpretation—literal, moral, anagogic, and allegorical—favored by many nineteenth-century Scripture scholars. Eventually O'Connor would be attracted by this fourfold approach to Scripture, as clearly articulated by Gordon's close friend Father William Lynch, whose book *Christ and Apollo* O'Connor read.

In spite of receiving a Guggenheim Fellowship in 1932 and an O. Henry Award in 1934, Gordon never achieved the popular success that might have been hers, and perhaps due in part to the feeling of inadequacy that prompted her to reach out to O'Connor. Gordon manifested a desire to ghostwrite parts of O'Connor's fiction, giving it a character that O'Connor wanted to avoid. Katherine Prown notes, "If O'Connor is to achieve her ambition, Gordon made it clear, then she must learn to curb her tendency to reveal, through her inappropriate use of narrative voice, her own identity not as a scrupulously objective man who speaks Johnsonian English, but as a carelessly subjective woman who speaks with a southern accent."[37] Gordon also had a penchant for focusing on technique and grammar, whereas O'Connor, as she articulated in several important essays in *Mystery and Manners*, felt that the notion of mystery emerging organically from a story always took precedence. O'Connor was in the process of discovery, and she well knew that her lack of a classical education did not sit well with Gordon. As she was finishing *Wise Blood*, O'Connor incorporated into it a theological view of the world that would become more pronounced during the ensuing years. Her fictive journey through life was motivated by a desperate desire to affirm a basis for human existence that transcends the waywardness and willfulness of the individual human self—something Gordon was not educated from birth to believe and would struggle to understand.

O'Connor would have understood the views of her Iowa faculty and interiorized them from discussions with her peers, but now she needed to test the validity of their views in a very practical way. While open to new ideas, she had enough of a metaphysical and spiritual center at this point in her career not to bend to a proposition that did not convince her. She had known the value of comedy and caricature from her days in college and been praised for her early published efforts. Moreover, she had developed a strong visual imagination that gradually shifted to the oral—especially in repeating the local idiom she heard, giving it its proper context and sequence. Her letters are peppered with neologisms and slant spellings, strong indicators of what she was hearing and the way she heard it. But Gordon had something entirely different to offer O'Connor: a model of a married, Catholic-convert female writer immensely concerned with assisting younger writers. Yet Gordon, it would seem, overstepped the bounds appropriate for a mentor. O'Connor gradually developed ambivalent feelings about Gordon, whom she liked and saw periodically, even as she lay dying in a hospital bed. She found Gordon's critical theories, as she wrote to Hester in March 1956, a bit apodictic and rigid: "She takes great pains and is very generous with her criticism. Is highly energetic and violently enthusiastic. When I am around her, I feel like her illiterate grandmother." As a disciple of Henry James, Gordon felt it important that novels have a "central intelligence"—that is, an omniscient narrator. In a letter to Maritain, Gordon noted that O'Connor had "more in common with Henry James than almost any other American writer."[38] Yet O'Connor felt too restricted by this because discussions about point of view, especially of a character's perceptions, limited the spontaneous development of a story or novel. She just wanted to sit down and write her fiction. It is not difficult to surmise that Gordon's letters (many of which, alas, were given by Gordon to a graduate student and never returned) were peppered with insights based on the fiction from James, Conrad, Forster, and Flaubert.[39] O'Connor absorbed it all, seeing some value in what Gordon wrote, but in the end, it was not the guidance she needed. Nevertheless, because O'Connor had few genuine literary confidantes who had actually published fiction, Gordon's voice often dominated for lack of anything better. O'Connor seemed always to be trying to withdraw unobtrusively from Gordon's classroom, for she wanted to avoid a confrontation with someone who had been kind to her, knowing as she did that Gordon had absorbed the traumatic periods of her marriage and remarriage to Tate.

Before Giroux flew to England in fall of 1951 to see friends and publishers, especially Thomas Burns of Hollis & Carter, he reread O'Connor's typescript. O'Connor informed McIntosh in early September 1951 that both Giroux and Gordon had made some suggestions about the book, though, according to Prown, no copy of Gordon's first set of suggestions survives.[40] Sally Fitzgerald has noted that Gordon's initial response is available through a letter she wrote to Robert: "I'm quite excited about it. This girl is a real novelist. (I only wish that I had as firm a grasp on my subject matter when I was her age!) At any rate she is already a rare phenomenon: a Catholic novelist with a real dramatic sense, one who relies more on her technique than her piety."[41]

Prompted by such criticism, O'Connor set about the task of rewriting parts of her novel, as she mentioned to McIntosh, anticipating having yet another draft in a few weeks. She was not familiar with the necessities or the niceties of sending a final draft to the publisher, and thus she queried if it was acceptable to send the copy she had with inked-in corrections on it. Moreover, she wondered if the deadline for the spring printing had already passed. Since she had been in and out of the hospital during the summer, she felt too depleted to type even a hundred and fifty pages a month. Making multiple copies with carbon paper not only was time-consuming, but also demanded energy, attention, and organization. One can almost hear her groan as she discussed the whereabouts of various drafts. Though she wrote, "I hate to think of that other draft batting around at British publishing houses when this improved version exists," she doubted that a British firm would buy it. "Giroux sent me the other ms. back," she continued in her letter to McIntosh, "and I have been inserting the additions and corrections, etc., into it and that is the copy I'll have in a few weeks. He said they would like to have it as soon as possible, but that is nothing definite." Given the amount of time she spent just on the mechanics of typing and retyping this novel—her word *nauseous* is most appropriate in this case—she clearly needed a sympathetically objective view and thus took the initiative in mid-September, as she had previously indicated, to take Gordon up on her earlier offer. She sent it to the Fitzgeralds, writing, "Enclosed is Opus Nauseous No. 1. I had to read it over after it came from the typist's and that was like spending the day eating a horse blanket. . . . I sent it on to Giroux and said if he thought it was alright to go on with it but I doubt if the poor man puts himself to reading it again. Do you think Mrs. Tate would? All the changes are efforts after what she suggested in that letter and I am much obliged to her." Another letter to the Fitzgeralds in late September makes it clear that her health would not permit her to keep typing draft after draft. Enduring two moderate shots of ACTH a day, down from four large ones, she had almost completed the end of novel.

In late September 1951, O'Connor wrote again to the Fitzgeralds: "I am working on the end of the book, while a lady around her [*sic*] types the first part of it. I think it is a lot better but I may be mistaken and will have to be told."[42] To distract herself, she told the Fitzgeralds, she was reading Samuel Johnson's *Life of Dryden*. She sent Giroux, still in England, her revised manuscript in mid-October 1951, explaining, "I've tried to clear up the foggier places and to make the changes suggested by Mrs. Tate. It looks better to me but I have no one here to read it who could tell me. If it seems all right to you, or to her, please go on with it; if not, I'd like to work on it again." She noted that she was awaiting the suggestions from the Fitzgeralds. O'Connor, at this point, had considerably softened her attitude toward accepting criticism, even though it took an additional toll on her health. About the same time, she wrote to Boyd Love that she had finished the last draft of *Wise Blood* and hoped to "start another novel," no doubt an early reference to *The Violent Bear It Away*.

Had O'Connor asked Andrew Lytle if she could learn something from Gordon's fiction, he would undoubtedly have replied, "I know of no writer of fiction that other writers can study with greater profit."[43] Gordon subsequently sent back, on November 12, 1951, which she noted was Saint Didacus's feast day, nine pages of densely packed comments, which O'Connor read with utmost care and gratitude. (Sally Fitzgerald later recorded them in their entirety in the essay "A Master Class.") "Your manuscript has come," Gordon began. "I spent yesterday reading it. I think it is terrific! I know a good many young writers who think they are like Kafka. You are the only one I know who succeeds in doing a certain thing that he does. . . . I do not mean that it is in any way derivative of Kafka. In fact this book seems to me the most original book I have read in a long time. But you are like Kafka in providing a firm Naturalistic ground-work for your symbolism." Her rather rambling letter incorporates comments on homosexuality, childishness, freakishness, and fatherlessness, as well as reflections on the works of Truman Capote, Anton Chekhov, Hart Crane, Stephen Crane, E. M. Forster, Henry James, Marcel Proust, William Butler Yeats, and Stendhal.

In all, Gordon admired the unflagging, dramatic action in the novel, but she asked O'Connor to consider two important principles in novel writing. First, O'Connor's novel might gain something by not being so bare, but rather having the core of the action surrounded by some contrasting material. She gave the image of a spotlight that a burglar uses, which focuses almost exclusively on the safe in front of him. "It would be better, I think, if you occasionally used a spotlight large enough to illuminate the corners of the room, for those corners have gone on existing all through the most dramatic moments." Second, her novel should avoid making excessive demands on the reader. Like the old-timey preacher, Gordon advised, O'Connor should be clear in her preaching style: "First I tells 'em I'm going to tell 'em, then I tells 'em, then I tell 'em I done told them." There is no need to hurry through crucial moments, as, for example, when the patrolman pushes Haze's car over the embankment, because it is important to give the reader ample time to absorb what is happening. Supplying sensuous details might add to the impact of certain scenes. In addition, she noted that O'Connor tells the reader what Enoch did every day before she showed him in the act of doing it. Gordon had read the manuscript carefully and then discovered what she wanted to tell O'Connor as she wrote the letter. It goes from one thing to "and another thing" to "and another thing" with jerky rapidity as she cites specific passages that O'Connor might reconsider in revising the text yet again. Gordon was well aware that her comments might not be easy for O'Connor to absorb. "Once you learn how to do one thing you have to start learning how to do something else and the devil of it is that you always have to be doing three or four things at a time." Finally, she congratulated O'Connor on writing a "wonderful book" and she would write to Giroux expressing her admiration for it.

"Thank you for sending the ms. to Caroline," O'Connor wrote to the Fitzgeralds in mid-November. "She sent it back to me with nine pages of comments and she certainly increased my education thereby. So I am doing more things to it and then I mean to send it off for the LAST time." O'Connor also noted in a letter to Giroux in late November 1951 that Gordon had written another long letter, expressing still more reservations about the novel. Incredibly, O'Connor was willing to stick to her word and rework the text once again: "I suppose it is not set up and if not, I would like to do some more to the three or four places she has mentioned. Would you let me know? I apologize for all this shilly-shallying. And keep on doing it." Giroux replied, expressing a hope that she could make the changes that Gordon had suggested on the galley proofs, for he had already sent off the typescript to the printers. He noted that he had made a few emendations of his own, which she could restore on the proofs if she wished. "One further possibility," he added. "Send me carbons of the sheets in which there are changes, and I'll try to get them substituted in the manuscript at the printer's, who may not have reached those parts."[44] Unless there were major changes, O'Connor would not be charged for "author's alterations."

In her essay "Rebels and Revolutionaries," Gordon reflected on certain aspects of O'Connor's fiction ten years after the author's death. As might be expected, she initially focuses on the literary qualities found in the works of O'Connor and Henry James, though she seems more taken with James in linking these two authors. Because her critique is not clearly organized, she never probes specific aspects of either writer in detail. She maintains that "both James and O'Connor are masters of illusionism—that is to say of those techniques which it is necessary to master if the reader is to be lured into that world of imagination which exists only in the author's imagination. In the fiction of both James and O'Connor, one finds a faithful reflection of the world they live in."[45] In particular, Gordon praises O'Connor's use of dialect and the rhythms of everyday speech. Furthermore, she notes that these two authors share a similar trait: a desire to upset conventional, expected order through violence. James's fiction explores the unconscious, subterranean chambers of the human spirit, so magnificently found in the Greek tragedians, whereas O'Connor depicts the rural South fictionally through the eyes of Roman Catholic theology, often putting her characters in conflict with their surroundings. While not especially original in her approach, Gordon's comparisons merit attention. O'Connor herself had no desire to read James, as she mentions shamefacedly in a letter to Betty Hester: "Which brings me to the embarrassing subject of what I have not read and have been influenced by. I hope nobody ever asks me in public. If so I intend to look very dark and mutter, 'Henry James Henry James'—which will be the veriest lie, but no matter."[46] To Gordon she explained, "My method is more liable to be affected by my mother's dairyman's wife than by Mr. Henry James. She hangs around all the time and all her sentences begin: 'I know one time my husband seen. . . .' It works like you say. He sees everything and she sees twice as much as he sees but she has never looked at anything but him. They both read my book and said: 'It just shown you how some people would do.'"[47]

O'Connor was not the only one at this time to receive Gordon's critical attention. Most likely in early December 1951, Gordon sent Walker Percy a telegram in which she praised his novel *The Charterhouse*.[48] She later wrote to him that she had never before been as impressed by a first novel as she had been by his: "Perhaps it is having read so many that has sharpened my pleasure in your book."[49] Percy, she believed, had found his own voice. As was her wont, Gordon then added twenty-one single-spaced pages of very detailed criticism and suggestions. These, more than any other critique that Percy received, prompted him, as he told me, *never* to see the novel through final publication. His thank-you letter included a check for $200. Gordon wrote to Brainard Cheney and shared with him some of her views about the first novels of both O'Connor and Percy:

> I have put my money on a good many horses, in my time, as you know. Scatter-brained though I be, I occasionally get a glimpse of the wheels going around. I saw them revolving in this study several months before Christmas. When I was working on Flannery O'Connor's novel and when Walker Percy sent me his novel. He's got a lot to learn that boy, almost everything, but reading that novel was like suddenly getting down on your knees on a long dusty walk to drink from a fresh, cold spring. His novel and Flannery's suddenly convinced me of something that I had been feeling vaguely for a long time. The Protestant mystique (which is what everybody who isn't a

Catholic, even Communists, are writing of, whether they know it or not) is outworn, sucked-dry, beginning to rot, to stink. That accounts for the curious dryness which almost everybody remarks in homosexual novels. There's no juice left in that orange. Everybody has suspected it for some time but the fact is now being brought out into the open. Flannery's novel—as grim a picture of the Protestant world as you can find—and Walker's novel, which is the story of a man's desperate effort to stay alive spiritually will be sensations when they come out. They will show so clearly that the tide has turned.[50]

Though immensely appreciative, Percy decided not to follow Gordon's literary advice. However, one can glean from Gordon's advice to Percy what she might have said to O'Connor in her first letter, since both critiques were written about the same time.

In order to give a larger context to her critique, Gordon referred Percy to her essay "How Not to Write Short Stories" in the anthology *The House of Fiction*, which she and Tate published. Her intention was to help Percy form good habits of writing. First and foremost, she stressed the need for direct representation, and in attempting to put it into language that Percy would understand, she compared writing to a human body. Gordon also cautioned Percy to slow down and not to jam ideas together; he needed to control the relationship between thought and action. Gordon lamented that Catholic fiction had not been good up to the present, since most Catholic writers were poor technicians. She concluded her long letter by citing a number of texts helpful to fiction writers, including Percy Lubbock's *The Craft of Fiction*, Flaubert's *Madame Bovary*, Jacques Maritain's *Art and Scholasticism*, and her own *The Strange Children*—and by offering more encouragement, something that O'Connor, who dealt with Protestant "mystics," might not have appreciated:

And as I said at the beginning of this letter, the only way one can really understand a fundamental principle of the craft is by an illustration from one's own work. It seems to me that you need to learn a few things—a few tricks of the trade, as it were. Once you have learned them, once you have got out of a few bad habits and set up in their place some good habits I do not see what there is to stop you. You have an enormous—an incalculable—advantage over most people writing today: you know what it is all about. The saints, the mystics are the proper companions of the fiction writer, for, as Jacques Maritain points out in *Art and Scholasticism*, "they alone know what is the human heart." And the mystics are, particularly, the artists of artists. But the Protestant is cut off from most of the saints. When one is writing out of the Protestant mystique, which is what everybody who isn't a Catholic is doing—even the Communists, I think—one has the responsibility of setting up a new heaven and a new earth as one goes. But a Catholic knows that God has already created the universe and that his job is to find his proper place in it.

For all this criticism, the novels of Percy and O'Connor were the finest first novels ever to come Gordon's way.

When O'Connor contacted Giroux in early December 1951, she enclosed what she hoped were the final changes and suggested he could get them substituted at the printers. She thought the additions made a good deal of difference. She still envisioned some for the first chapter but presumed it was too late to add them. Gordon, she mentioned, thought that in some places the story moved too fast and that the reader needed more preparation to understand the significance of the title. Knowing that fifteen percent of the cost of composition would be charged against her royalties (an expense O'Connor wished to avoid), she asked for the actual number of paragraphs she could insert. Not wanting to call attention to herself, or to the debacle with Selby at Rinehart, her biographical statement for the book's jacket was bare bones, with a few words about raising ducks and game birds, and a brief mention that her stories had been published in *Accent, Sewanee Review, Partisan Review, Mademoiselle*, and *Tomorrow*. Giroux liked the changes and agreed to make them, thinking especially that the ones suggested by Gordon were "magnificent."[51] When he sent O'Connor the complete galleys, he mentioned his assistant: "Catherine Carver, who did the copyediting, has answered some of the printer's queries and I don't believe you will encounter many problems. . . ."[52] He asked that the typescript be returned to the printer, along with the marked galleys, in order to proceed with the pagination. She would have a publicity picture taken and sent off soon. O'Connor sent the corrected galleys and typescript of her novel to Giroux in late January 1952, indicating that all the corrections and insertions she had included had been suggested by Gordon, though she added a few clarifications of her own: The shrub Enoch sits under in galleys 20 and 21 is *abelia*, not *lobelia*. Also the buzzard on galley 53 would have to stand on a roof if a television aerial in 1946 could not support him. She liked the sample page and wondered when the book would actually be published.

As might be expected from Giroux's perspective, the more advance attention the novel could receive, the better. In January 1952, Arabel Porter of the New American Library sent Giroux a formal letter of agreement for "Enoch and the Gorilla," which she wanted for the first issue of *New World Writing* to be published in April.[53] Giroux, perhaps unwisely, had not informed O'Connor about the possible publication of this section of the novel, though he was in fact in charge of serial rights. Her letter of enquiry to her editor read, "The enclosed, sent on February 5, 1952 [GIROUX ASSURES US NEW AMERICAN LIBRARY AGREEMENT ON WAY STOP KINDLY RUSH IF NOT. (VICTOR) WEYBRIGHT—(ARABEL) PORTER] came for me yesterday but I don't know what it's about. Could you enlighten me?"[54] Giroux did enlighten her and also informed her that he had just completed an agreement with the same firm for a paperback reprint edition of *Wise Blood*.[55] Porter further explained the situation to Giroux, including a seemingly low payment for the story:

I took the liberty of wiring Miss O'Connor direct because I didn't want to bother you any more than I already had, and because hers was the only agreement still unsigned, and *New World Writing* had already been sent off to the printer. (The thought of tearing her story out of 100,000 copies of *New World Writing* was too awful to bear, if anything should go amiss!)

Just in case Miss O'Connor has misplaced the agreement, I'm sending another set. To save further time and trouble, will you simply sign both copies for Miss O'Connor? I believe this is common enough practice. In any case, since you have scheduled the book for June, we are now buying first, not second serial rights, and will pay at 2½ cents a word, not at 2 cents a word. This means that our payment would be in the amount of $83.08, not $66.46, as before. If you'd be good enough to ask Miss O'Connor to return the original check, we shall send along the new one in the proper amount, or if she has already cashed the check, we shall be glad to send a separate check for $16.62.[56]

Giroux immediately wrote back with a copy of an agreement covering their use of this story and formally requesting for the reassignment of copyright in the name of the author after publication in *New World Writing*. When he brought O'Connor up to date on the arrangement with this literary publication, he also told her of his own efforts to promote her work:

> I'm sorry you were bothered by the mysterious telegram. We have sold reprint rights of the "Enoch and the Gorilla" chapter to *New World Writing*. This is a paper-covered anthology which will sell for twenty-five cents and will be published by the New American Library (the U.S. branch of Penguin). Victor Weybright, their editor, told me he wanted to include the best young writers in the U.S. I told him in that case he couldn't publish without something of yours. He and Arabel Porter, who wired you, liked the Enoch episode enormously. They pay two and a half cents a word based on an edition of 100,000 copies; they pay more if they print another edition. I've signed the agreement and I've written Mavis about it.
>
> Page proofs are due in two weeks. I'll send them to the Savannah address if there's time to get them to you by February 22nd; otherwise to Milledgeville.[57]

Giroux's subsequent letter to McIntosh also included news about a possible agreement with the Book-of-the-Month Club.[58] He also requested that O'Connor return both the galley proofs and the marked page proofs together, adding, "The unmarked page proofs you may keep. And, of course, the sooner you can return the proofs, the nearer we shall be able to keep to schedule. I would be most grateful if you can give them your attention right away."[59] These pro forma letters back and forth reassured O'Connor that Giroux was handling the production of the novel in a timely fashion. Further, he was not upset at her incessant reworking of the text, something understandable, but not desirable, in the case of a first novel. O'Connor returned the two sets of proofs within days, noting that she made insignificant changes that could be dispensed with if they would cost the printer any unhappiness or herself any money. She was glad to hear about the New American Library paperback reprint.

Up to this point, O'Connor had received little financial recompense for all the effort she had put into her writing, a good deal of it due to the length of time she expended in writing her stories and her novel. McIntosh wrote to Giroux on March 7 about O'Connor's financial situation: "I haven't had any luck trying to reach you by telephone, but I do want to put a request to you. Knowing that *Wise Blood* has been sold to New American Library for reprint, and that the advance is $4,000, I wonder if Harcourt, Brace would give Flannery her half of the first payment, just as soon as possible? Flannery needs money so badly—as you may know—that I am sure you will do what you can to arrange to make this a special case."[60] Giroux replied three days later with a check for $500 as a further advance against O'Connor's book, as discussed between McIntosh and Reynal. He would also send O'Connor another check from New American Library once it was received.[61] Meanwhile, O'Connor sent McKee an episode from something longer she was working on and mentioned that she was feeling well and might even go to Connecticut in May or June.[62] She was most pleased that her two agents had been successful in obtaining some money for her, but she really did not want to accept it if she would have to repay anyone any of it.

For his part Giroux pursued having the novel distributed by various book clubs, first by writing to Dan Herr, president of the Thomas More Association in Chicago. The reply on March 10 was not too encouraging: "We would be glad to take a look at the galleys of *Wise Blood* although I must confess that I'm a little doubtful about our using it."[63] The proofs were sent to Herr three days later, but his evaluation of the novel was negative. Giroux wanted a quick reply because he was about to head off to Cuba for two weeks. "I can't share your enthusiasm for *Wise Blood* by Flannery O'Connor," Herr wrote. "Three of our staff have read it and we all agree that it's not for us as a book club selection. There must be something in it that we missed but I don't know what it is."[64] Giroux sent a quick note on March 12 to Douglas Jerrold, care of the Hotel Plaza in New York, hoping to discuss *Wise Blood* with him in person.[65] Jerrold, a prominent British Catholic author and publisher, would become noted for his book *The Lie about the West*, which critiqued Arnold Toynbee for not sufficiently taking into account the heritage of Christianity in Western civilization. In addition, Giroux wrote to Harrison Smith, formerly of Smith and Haas and one of the men responsible for launching Faulkner's career. In writing to Smith at the *Saturday Review of Literature*, he was reaching out to a decidedly non-Catholic audience: "Knowing your keen interest in new novelists, I am sending you the first novel of a brilliant young writer, Flannery O'Connor. It is called *Wise Blood* and it is a satire on Southern evangelism. Parts of it appeared in *Partisan Review*. We publish the book on May 19th."[66] The most important letter Giroux wrote to promote *Wise Blood* was to someone he felt could profoundly influence Catholic readers of fiction on both sides of the Atlantic, Evelyn Waugh, residing at Piers Court, Stinchcombe, Gloucestershire, England (he also sent a similar letter to Graham Greene, at 5 St. James Street, London):

Dear Mr. Waugh:
The enclosed novel, *Wise Blood*, is the first work of Miss Flannery O'Connor, a young Catholic writer. I send it in the hope that it may interest you sufficiently to warrant your sending us your comment. The setting is the South, the word Catholic never occurs, the characters are obsessed with religion but only in the form of blasphemy; in short the book is a commentary on American protestantism, in the evangelical forms peculiar to the South. I think it is a book which will make many readers squirm. I think that the writing has kick, humor, and compassion. I should be most interested to know what you think, and I would be very grateful for any trouble you may take on behalf of the book or its author.

PS. Caroline Gordon has written, "I was more impressed by *Wise Blood* than any novel I have read in a long time. Her picture of the modern world is literally terrifying. Kafka is almost the only one of our contemporaries who has achieved such effects. I have a tremendous admiration for the work of this young writer. An important novel."[67]

Giroux's bold approach worked. Waugh not only replied with a blurb that was used on the book's jacket, but could also be given credit for the book's production in England. Giroux liked powerful endorsements that could catch the eye of a potential reader. When the novel was later reissued by Farrar, Straus & Cudahy in 1962, Giroux personally chose a publicity quote by William Goyen, taken from the *New York Times Book Review*, to be featured on the inside flap: "There is in Flannery O'Connor a fierceness of literary gesture, an angriness of observation, a facility for catching as an animal eye in a wilderness, cunningly and at one sharp glance, the shape and detail and intention of enemy and foe."

After a local bookstore owner showed the Harcourt, Brace copy to O'Connor before she actually received her own copies, she commented in a letter to the Fitzgeralds, "The book itself is very pretty but the jacket is lousy with me blown up on the back of it, looking like a refugee from deep thought. It has Caroline's *Imprimatur* on it so that ought to help." Her mother asked, "Who is this Evalin Wow?" Giroux informed McIntosh in mid-April about the event they all had been waiting for: "It's a pleasure to send you advance copies of *Wise Blood* by Flannery O'Connor, which have just come from the printer. We have slated publication for May 15th. I have already sent to Flannery her ten author's copies. If you have any suggestions for writers and critics to whom advance copies might profitably be sent, I'll be glad to have them. I wonder if you could have lunch with me on Wednesday, April 23rd? It's been much too long since we've met."[68] O'Connor liked the general appearance of the book, except for the thunderclap moment when she saw her unsmiling photo on the back cover. She found that very grim, indeed. The cover, with a light-cream-colored background, featured the word *Wise* on a red oval and the word *Blood* on a black oval; oddly, both words seem to be sinking into a whirlpool created by wavy circular lines.

In an internal Harcourt, Brace memo, dated April 4, 1952, a query was made as to who should receive copies of the novel, as Giroux hoped to elicit comments and encourage scholars to write articles that might focus on this novel. Suggested recipients included John Aldridge, James F. Powers, William Styron, Jean Stafford, Katherine Anne Porter, Eudora Welty, and Professor Francis X. Connolly at Fordham University.[69] O'Connor soon added more names: Gordon and Tate, the Fitzgeralds, Robert Lowell and Elizabeth Hardwick (who had married in 1949, after his marriage to Stafford ended in 1948), Mr. and Mrs. John Thompson (Thompson, author of a book on English prosody, roomed with Peter Taylor at Kenyon College and was a friend of Lowell and Macauley), Mr. and Mrs. J. D. Way, and Engle, who did not like the title. In late October, O'Connor wrote to Macauley, noting that Engle thought the end was clear, "but otherwise he thought it was fine etc. etc. and he would permit himself 'only one note of harshness,' to wit: from the jacket nobody would have known I had ever been at Iowa WHEREAS my book had really been 'shaped' there and this was a 'simple honorable fact that I should have thought of myself.'" The novel would soon be in the hands of influential critics, and O'Connor could do little more with it. It now had a life of its own, and she had to simply and graciously accept that fact.

The publication announcement prompted a friend of O'Connor's, a librarian, to write to Giroux, though she asked that her name not be revealed. Since this letter was not solicited, it has a personal, honest tone about it, filling in some of the gaps missing from the first O'Connor–Giroux meeting in March 1949:

I'm taking it upon myself to write to you, *sub rosa*, about (Mary) Flannery O'Connor whose book *Wise Blood* is to be issued by your house May 15th next. . . . She won a fellowship, upon graduation here, to Iowa State University, where she studied under Paul Engle and took her Master's degree. She afterwards won scholarships at Yaddo—I think she was there about two years, off and on—and she also won a scholarship offered by the Cummington press. I remember she came up here to the library for me to look up something about Cummington for she couldn't go there "unless it was a large enough village to have a Catholic church" for she could not miss going to Mass. I've forgotten whether she went there or not.

She was working on her book with and living with some friends in Connecticut when she was suddenly stricken with something like acute arthritis. She came home and was just desperately ill in Emory University Hospital for months: the only thing that saved her life was cortisone and ACTH which she expects to have to take for the rest of her life. How she ever finished *Wise Blood* and got the proofs read, no one knows, except that she has always known exactly what she wanted to do since she decided to be a writer at the age of six and nothing has prevented her from driving herself to that end.

She was tearfully nervous and frail after she had recovered enough to leave the hospital, even the telephone ringing disturbed her, so she and her mother (who is the "Regina" of the dedication in *Wise Blood*) went to live on a dairy farm that Regina owns, three miles from town on a hill. It is an old plantation called "Andalusia" and is an ideal spot for a writer to live. The whole house is geared to Mary Flannery's regime, and her rigid diet and hours of rest are taken care of as they were in the hospital. She has practically entirely recovered and has a whole flock of ducks, geese, pheasants, chickens and even a frizzled chicken (one with feathers grown backward—the negroes considered them a good-luck fetish) which she takes to. You may remember a story called "The Capture" which was published in

Mademoiselle in the November 1948 issue which describes a turkey hunt in the greatest detail. Her absorption in fowls has always been very interesting to me. Besides the dairy farm and cattle, Regina raises Shetland ponies, and their existence is idyllic with no phone and no interruptions during the morning hours when Mary Flannery does her writing. . . . How the child can write as she does after living the extremely sheltered-ivory-tower existence that she has, I don't know except that she has the spark of genius.[70]

Giroux's courteous reply unfortunately failed to inquire about the nature of the fellowship of the Cummington Press, which most likely was a type of apprenticeship or a guarantee that one of O'Connor's stories would be published by them.[71]

Concerned, as first-time novelists tend to be, that her book was not being featured in ads, O'Connor wrote to Giroux on April 30 approving of Macauley to write a review. She mentioned, too, that Gordon had informed her that she could not review the book since someone had told her she couldn't because of her blurb on the jacket."[72] Later Gordon did review the novel in *Critique*. Highly praising O'Connor as one of the most original writers of her day, she did not focus on the novel as such, but took a number of detours in comparing the text with Capote's *Other Voices, Other Rooms* and with Faulkner's *A Fable*. Fixedly, O'Connor tracked reviews in the *Herald Tribune* and the *New York Times*; though the May 19 issue of *Newsweek* gave her a "good review," she told Boyd Love in late May 1952, "I ain't seen any cash yet." She was upset that Isaac Rosenfeld of the *New Republic* found her novel completely bogus. After Lon Cheney's positive review of the novel in *Shenandoah* (Autumn 1952), O'Connor wrote him on February 8, 1953, as William Sessions describes:

> "I only want to tell you that I like the review." She added sardonically: "There have not been many good ones." Flannery had been "surprised again and again to learn what a tough character I must be to have produced a work so lacking in what one lady called 'love.'" Apparently "the love of God doesn't count or else I didn't make it recognizable." In fact, many reviewers thought her novel "just another dirty book and enjoyed it for that reason." But Cheney had read her book and written about it "so carefully and with so much understanding" that she made copies of his review "to show to some of

my connections who think it would be nicer if I wrote about nice people."[73]

Giroux had done all he could to make sure that O'Connor's novel would be a success; he sent out press releases and wrote to important people who might promote the book, but he could not nor would not manipulate the reaction of critics. He appropriately cleared out his files on this book, informing McIntosh that he would return to her an early draft of the novel, which might, had O'Connor thought about it, become a source of revenue for her at some later point.[74] O'Connor well knew that her $1,000 advance for *Wise Blood* would not go a long way. It was determined that the initial run would be 3,000 copies, each at a price of $3.00. In addition, she would receive 10 percent of the list price up to 5,000 copies; 12 1/2 percent to 10,000; and 15 percent thereafter.

After having typed approximately two thousand pages of various drafts of this novel, now archived in the O'Connor Collection at Georgia College, O'Connor just seemed tired with it all. Even though she had published her first novel, the experience had exhausted her and she was still dependent on her mother's income for support. Giroux stood in awe of what she had achieved and was sure that she would continue to accomplish even more in spite of her physical limitations. "In the three years following the publication of *Wise Blood*," he recalled, "Flannery's development as a writer of stories was amazing. Despite her illness, lupus, her writing became better and better."[75]

CHAPTER FIVE

Flannery O'Connor, Robert Giroux

1952–1955

Needing a respite and a change of scenery, O'Connor visited the Fitzgeralds in June 1952, most likely to avoid confronting polite but intrusive
comments about her novel from family and friends in Milledgeville.
When she arrived in Redding, Robert, now the father of four children,
noted that she came "looking ravaged but pretty, with short soft new
curls."[1] Her stay in Connecticut was not without some strain; Sally was
experiencing serious prenatal problems, and Robert was away for part of
the time in Indiana. On her return trip south by way of New York,
O'Connor had a chance to visit with Gordon, whose novel *The Strange
Children* she had recently read. Gordon brought up the possibility that
her friend, British poet and art critic Herbert Read, might help in finding
a publisher for O'Connor's novel in England, something that apparently
had been in the works for a while.[2] Encouraged by Giroux, she set about
finishing "A Late Encounter with the Enemy," which was soon accepted
by Alice Morris for the September 1953 issue of *Harper's Bazaar.* Morris
offered her own suggestions for improving the story, thus widening the
circle of those commenting on O'Connor's fiction. Now that O'Connor
had reached her goal, the publication of her first novel, she could quietly
bask in her achievement, knowing at the same time that her life would
continue to change.

Giroux's life, too, was advancing in a new and somewhat unexpected direction. In 1952 he married Doña Carmen Natica de Arango y del Valle, known more informally as Carmen de Arango, in Greenwich, Connecticut. The daughter of a Cuban aristocrat, Don Francisco de Arango, the third Marquis de la Gratitud, and his wife, the former Doña Petronila del Valle, Doña Carmen became the fifth Marquise de la Gratitud after the death of her sister Mercedes. An alumna of Manhattanville College of the Sacred Heart with an M.A. in English from Columbia, she worked for the Vatican delegation at the United Nations. She most likely met Giroux through some connection at Columbia. Her father had been a statesman and political economist in Spain and Cuba, and given this background it was not surprising that she had memberships in the Greenwich Country Club in Connecticut and the Havana Yacht Club.

The wedding party included Giroux's nieces Kathleen Healy and Roberta Rodriquez as bridesmaids; Charles Reilly as best man; and Lester Giroux and Dan Walsh as ushers. "Half of Cuba arrived yesterday for the wedding," Giroux wrote to Merton. "There are enough Consuelos and Juanitas and José Marias and Conchitas to people a Spanish novel. I can hardly wait for Friday afternoon to greet Father Abbot at the Westchester airport. . . . I can't tell you how grateful Carmen and I are for your wedding present of your Mass this Saturday."[3] Dom James Fox, Merton's abbot, presided at the liturgy on August 30, 1952, in Saint Mary's Church in Greenwich. Giroux had mentioned Cuba in passing to Merton but never shared any personal feelings about it, thus raising the possibility of having doubts about his forthcoming marriage: "The trip to Cuba was part of my vacation and I had a most wonderful time. It is, as you found it to be long ago, a wonderfully religious country in the very best sense. I hope it did me some good."[4] Following a reception at Hickory Hill, the bride's family's residence, the married couple spent their honeymoon in Murray Bay, Québec, an area known to Giroux's ancestors, before moving into Giroux's apartment on East Sixty-Ninth Street.

On several occasions, Giroux referred obliquely to me about his marriage, its canonical dissolution on October 25, 1968, and his divorce a year later. He personally invited O'Connor to the wedding ceremony, which she could not do for health reasons, though Jean Stafford, the Fitzgeralds, and the Berrymans did attend.[5] Eventually it became known to a number of Giroux's friends that Doña Carmen had been an epileptic for years. Giroux, worn down by his efforts to get her professional medical attention, was absolutely distraught when his wife simply left him and returned home to her parents. Marriages can break down for a number of reasons, and in this case those reasons were never discussed publicly in interviews or in print; those directly involved kept what happened to themselves. This marriage most likely was destined not to succeed from the beginning, though Giroux was grateful for the love and support of his lifelong friend and companion Reilly, who subsequently lived with him while working as the director of personnel for the State of New Jersey and then as the editor of *Films in Review*. Giroux's relationship with Reilly, I believe, played a significant part in his desire to seek this divorce. It should be noted, however, that Giroux went through a process of serious discernment, certainly from a spiritual point of view, during this critical stage of his life.

By September, O'Connor felt reenergized and ready to resume a writing schedule. "I am up again now," she wrote Gordon in September 1952, "and looking forward to a recessive period of my come-and-go ailment. It's very good working again. I am just writing a story to see if I can get away from the freaks for a while." By mid-October she sent a corrected version of "The World is Almost Rotten" (later "The Life You Save May Be Your Own") to her agent with some concerns. If *Discovery* did not accept it, then she wanted it sent to the *Sewanee Review*. As expected, royalty payments from Harcourt, Brace were also on her mind. Would she have to pay any money back if the novel was not selling well? When would she receive the rest of the money from the reprint sale? How long was it going to take to receive a royalty statement? Her concerns translated into another search for a fellowship, prompted, no doubt, by learning that Engle had recently received a Ford fellowship. When John Crowe Ransom, who had read and been impressed by *Wise Blood*, wrote O'Connor to recommend that she seek the Kenyon Review Fellowship in Fiction, subsidized by Rockefeller money, and noted that in doing so she would have the backing of Robert Fitzgerald and Peter Taylor, she immediately saw a good financial option.[6] Having finished "The Life You Save May Be Your Own," she sent a copy of it to Sally Fitzgerald in November, writing, "I have been working on it two months & it's cold as a fish." After Sally replied, O'Connor reworked the story in light of her comments; it became part of her fellowship application along with "the first chapter of what proposes itself to be a novel—the one with the hero named Tarwater [*The Violent Bear It Away*]." Clearly O'Connor was hitting her stride, moving forward with her fiction, and trying desperately to become as financially independent as possible.

By late November 1952, however, O'Connor's mood had changed. Since she had started her second novel, she experienced moments of frustration that expressed themselves in unforeseen ways. Above all, she felt powerless in being unable to manage the placement of her stories as she wanted, harboring the feeling that neither Harcourt, Brace nor her agent was working hard enough on her behalf. When she sent McKee her story "The River," which she suggested be forwarded to the *Hudson Review*, she asked to know when *Harper's Bazaar* would bring out "A Late Encounter with the Enemy" (published in September 1953). She seemed incapable of containing her irritation: "What has happened to Mr. Shiflet [of "The Life You Save May Be Your Own"] and where is my royalty statement that they were supposed to send in October?"[7] Since Ransom had informed her that he would take either "The Life You Save May Be Your Own" or "The River" for publication, O'Connor told McKee in late December that she wanted the first one definitely sent to him at the *Kenyon Review* (if it had not already been done so). As a result, the second, sent out initially to *New World Writing*, was published in the *Sewanee Review* (Summer 1953). O'Connor was reluctant to mention money to Ransom and wanted to avoid asking him to send a check to McKee; but if money were sent to Milledgeville, she would certainly send McKee her ten percent. Not long after, she breathed a sigh of relief when she received both the *Kenyon Review* fellowship and the long-awaited royalty check.

Her increasing agitation was quite understandable. During O'Connor's six-week visit to the Fitzgeralds in June and July of 1952, Sally had relayed to her the fact of her lupus diagnosis.[8] In addition to suffering from the effects of shingles at Christmastime, she now became more conscious of the relentless effects of a death-in-life disease, which caused her hair to drop out and her face to swell. She thought intermittently about the manner in which her father died and how she might not be able to fulfill her writing and publishing dreams. Others were moving forward— Lowell was about to take Engle's place again in February 1953 at the Writers' Workshop, and the Fitzgeralds were making plans to go to the University of Notre Dame, where Robert would do some teaching and writing—and O'Connor wanted similar advancements in her own life. She wrote to the Fitzgeralds in early February, informing them that her new novel seemed to be going well, though she was reluctant to reveal the plot: "I have a nice gangster of 14 in it named Rufus Florida Johnson." Rufus Johnson also appears in "The Lame Shall Enter First," implying a connection between her novel and this story. In her letter to Lowell and Hardwick in Iowa City in mid-March, she thanked them for their kind comments about one of the stories she had sent them, and she mentioned directly that she had lupus, writing, "it comes and goes, when it comes I retire and when it goes, I venture forth."

Fortified by her religious beliefs, O'Connor never seems to have gone through a period of denial about her illness but instead accepted her condition, thinking that ACTH might bring about some type of cure. Though sustained by private prayer, she thought that reading Gabriel Marcel might give her more of a philosophical-theological grounding in understanding the nature of her illness as it might shape her future life, as she mentioned in a letter to the Fitzgeralds in early June. But it was to no avail: "I certainly like it but oncet [sic] the book is shut I have no idea what it's all about."

O'Connor worked slowly on her novel during the hot Georgia spring and early summer, and by mid-June 1953 she had something to report to her editor about her progress:

I was surprised that the pocket edition should be out so soon and that the cover was no worse than it was. I had expected Mrs. Watts to be on it and was hoping the new Georgia Literature Commission would take it off the drugstore racks. We have a fine new literature commission in this state, composed of a preacher, a picture-show manager, and some other worthy who I keep thinking must or should be the warden at the state penitentiary.

The review you enclosed was of considerable interest to me and I appreciate your sending it. I have 50 or 60 pages of the [new] novel but I still expect to be a long time at it. It's a theme that requires prayer and fasting to make it get anywhere. I manage to pray but am a very sloppy faster.

At this point her health seemed to be stable, if not improving, allowing her to venture forth from Milledgeville. She mentioned to the Fitzgeralds in a series of letters that summer that she had flown to Nashville to see the Cheneys and that she would accept the standing invitation of the

Fitzgeralds to visit them. Her flight to Newark Airport on August 11 was the beginning of a much-needed three-week vacation. Warm conversation flowed easily as her hosts talked about their stay at Notre Dame and how the children were faring. O'Connor had missed having a family of her own and delighted in the spontaneous give-and-take with dear friends. The Fitzgeralds were then planning to depart for Fiesole, Italy, a country they loved and in which their children felt comfortable, in mid-October. As O'Connor mentioned in a thank-you letter to them, she had lunch in early September 1953 with Giroux, who suggested that she might consider the publication of a book of her short stories for the fall of 1954. He was, she observed, agreeable and vague, and in all "a perfect publisher."[9] She obtained from him a sense of how she stood with the firm. When she learned that two hundred and eight copies of *Wise Blood* had been returned before the first statement but only two hundred before the second, she noted flippantly in a letter to Macauley in mid-October that it was only a difference of *eight*. Giroux did not tell her that Merton's *The Sign of Jonas* had already sold more than eighty thousand copies.[10] She had lunch again with Giroux in Atlanta in late December or early January, and they talked about her novel and her health problems. Giroux noticed a change in her physical state; though she did not use a cane, she was insecure on her feet. (As she wrote to Elizabeth Fenwick in mid-February 1954, she had the appearance of being a little drunk all the time.) These brief meetings were incredibly important for Giroux, who afterward could better determine how O'Connor would proceed with her work and what tone his letters to her should take. He renewed his efforts to make sure that O'Connor's works would reach a larger audience. He worried when Neville Armstrong, director of Neville Spearman, Ltd., of London, enquired about the British rights to *Wise Blood*, along with O'Connor's next title.[11] In mentioning to McIntosh that he had never heard of this firm, Giroux hoped to signal to her that dealing with an unknown publishing firm usually presented hidden problems.

Despite her poor physical condition, O'Connor seemed to be hitting her stride and wanted to share the news with the Fitzgeralds. "I have been sending poor Caroline stories by the dozen it seems to me," O'Connor wrote to her friends in mid-November 1953. "I have written three in a row, all in the interest of excusing myself from writing on the novel. But now I have seven good stories and two lousy ones for my collection." She was definitely contemplating putting together a volume of her short stories before publishing her next novel. This collection took on more and more importance; as she wrote to Lowell and Hardwick at the beginning of 1954, "I'm writing a novel but it's so bad at present that I'm writing a lot of stories so as not to have to look at it. . . . I'm getting up a collection of stories that I'm going to call *A Good Man Is Hard to Find.* I send them all to Caroline and she writes me wherein they do not meet the mark." Yet focusing on a novel might have been easier than writing and organizing a collection of stories. In late March she informed Giroux that, for one reason or another, she had "forgotten about the manuscript for the collection of short stories, but the last story ["The Displaced Person"] has just been sold to the *Sewanee Review* [for their October 1954 issue] and I don't think they will be able to print it before next spring; so I don't see any need to startle myself into activity about making up the manuscript. I have eleven stories anyway." As was his wont, Giroux sent with his reply copies of two books O'Connor might like: Taylor's *The Widows of Thornton* and Eliot's *The Confidential Clerk.*[12] She worked hard at Andalusia, sharing little with other friends of what she was doing, as often happens with writers who do not want to put a jinx on the project at hand. In the months that followed she began assembling her manuscript, and by early September she wondered if the collection could be published in the spring, assuming she could get her stories to Giroux by October. "Of course I'll be anxious to get it out of the house," she wrote, "and I have the manuscript practically ready. I enclose a list of stories. One or two of them might be left out, according to what you think." On another front, McKee had signed a contract with Neville Spearman, "which I know may be the British equivalent of Gory Stories. . . . I am anxious to hear from you about this collection." O'Connor's intuition about its similarity to the pulp magazine *Gory Stories* proved more accurate than she suspected.

When O'Connor again met with Giroux in Atlanta on October 26, 1954, she wanted him to know that she was rewriting "The Artificial Nigger," with the intention of incorporating suggestions made by Gordon in a four-page, single-spaced letter.[13] She also reworked "The Displaced Person," especially one of the key scenes between Father Flynn and Mrs. McIntyre, and as might be expected she sent it to Gordon mid-November. "I am doing very well these days except for a limp which I am informed is rheumatism," she wrote Gordon. "Colored people call it 'the misery.' Anyway I walk like I have one foot in the gutter but it's not an inconvenience and I get out of doing a great many things I don't want to do."

Approximately a year from the time she first thought about this collection, she informed Giroux that she had sent off the manuscript to McIntosh, with a request that she forward it to him within two weeks. She included the long version of "The Displaced Person," hoping it would be placed last, but if Giroux did not like it she would send him the short version. She also included the story published in *Mademoiselle* under the title "The Capture," though after rewriting it, she had given it a new title, "An Afternoon in the Woods." Finally she enclosed the latest version of "The Artificial Nigger," not the one she had sent to Ransom. O'Connor wondered, too, when she should send the new version, since the corrections she was working on could not really be made on the proofs. "I am sorry about this shilly-shallying," she wrote Giroux in late November, "but the story will be much better in consequence of it." Gordon had asked O'Connor to send her the proofs of the collection so she could review it at the request of the *New York Times*. Giroux replied in early December that he would accommodate her wishes and thus he sent O'Connor a new publication schedule. She promised that she would absolutely have it to him just before Christmas, including new material for "The Displaced Person." The final typescript exceeded the prescribed length, unfortunately, so Giroux suggested that one of the stories be dropped, and O'Connor agreed; nine stories, she said, ought to be enough, especially as "The Displaced Person" was long. "However, if it must be one or the other, I think I would prefer leaving in 'A Stroke of Good Fortune,'" she wrote on December 11, "because it seems more tied in with the others thematically. I may be wrong; I'm not wildly fond of either and I leave it up to you. I would really like both left out." She mailed him the revised version of "The Artificial Nigger" and included the new first two pages of "The Displaced Person," both of which arrived in his office by mid-December. Among her Christmas gifts were a check for $200 for winning second place in the O. Henry prizes (Engle, as judge, had given the first place award to Jean Stafford) and a contract for *A Good Man Is Hard to Find*, for which she would receive an advance.[14]

Though O'Connor expressed concern about the placement of her stories and the payment due her, she had not paid too much attention to the problem of copyright. That was about to change. She communicated an initial concern about this in a letter to McIntosh in early January 1955, writing, "I enclose the signed contract with many thanks to you. I don't know who has the copyrights on these stories—me or the magazines they were printed in. Nobody has asked where they first appeared; however, I presume Harcourt, Brace takes care of that. Please let me know when the New American Library makes up its mind if it will take the collection or not. The novel takes on some steam now and I am well."[15] McIntosh promptly contacted Giroux, raising an important contractual matter that Giroux would later deal with when considering the reissue of *Wise Blood*:

> Here is your copy of the contract with Flannery O'Connor for *A Good Man Is Hard to Find*, signed by the author. She tells me that the novel was beginning "to get some steam into it," which is good news.
>
> One point about the contract struck me after I had sent it off for signature, and I wonder if you will consider a change at this point; it isn't critical but it might be a nuisance we have found in other cases. This concerns your clause 12, about letting the book go out of print and the reversion of rights to the author. Can we assume that even if the author does not buy plates and stock, all rights revert to her if the publisher destroys plates and so on? If not, we would like to use the clause we have worked out and had accepted by many publishers, a copy of which I enclose. It is fairer, we feel, and avoids complications when certain rights may become valuable years after the book has been abandoned in the trade edition. Let me know if we could get this into Flannery's agreement somehow.[16]

When Giroux replied to McIntosh, he enclosed a reformulation of the clause:

> In the event that the Work shall at any time be out of print, the Author or his representative may give notice thereof to the Publisher, and in such event the Publisher shall declare within thirty (30) days in writing whether or not he intends to bring out a new edition of the work; if he shall declare his intention to bring out such a new edition, then such edition shall be published not later than six (6) months from the giving of such notice. If the Publisher shall not within thirty (30) days declare in writing that he does so intend, and shall not within six (6) months bring out a new printing of the Work, then all rights granted hereunder shall terminate and revert to the Author at the end of such thirty (30) days, or six (6) month period, as the case may be.[17]

O'Connor had no difficulty in accepting the reformulation and in the process started learning about some of the technical aspects of publishing, which she would master as best she could. She soon faced an analogous situation: In mid-January, T. H. Carter wanted to reserve the right to publish "A Stroke of Good Fortune" in *Shenandoah*.[18] Carter's intentions were not all that clear, however, and Giroux dealt with the problem in a subsequent letter. Then, when sending McKee a copy of "An Exile in the East," a version of which had been published as "The Geranium" in *Accent*, O'Connor wanted to make sure her agent knew that the story had been revised considerably; she did not want to be accused of having the same story published twice.

The collection seemed ready for publication, but such was not the case. O'Connor wrote to Giroux in late February 1955, hoping that her book had not gotten too far into production, because she had just written a twenty-seven-page story called "Good Country People" (published in *Harper's Bazaar*, June 1955) that Tate and Gordon both considered the best story she had ever written.[19] They encouraged her to include it in her collection. Gordon's three-page, single-spaced letter to O'Connor begins by calling it a "master piece," though she did not hesitate to mention a few reservations about the story.[20] In addition, Tate's letter to O'Connor says the story is "without exception the most terrible and powerful story of Maimed Souls I have ever read. . . . You are a wonderful writer, and you started out with the first instinct of a good writer: you write only about the life you know."[21] Giroux wisely wanted at least one story that had not been printed before, and this fit the bill. O'Connor wrote a joint letter in early March to Tate and Gordon, thanking them for their opinions of the story.[22] She admits that "by the grace of God" she escapes being Hulga.

Soon thereafter, Giroux wrote to propose the order in which the stories should appear: "A Good Man Is Hard to Find," "The River," "The Life You Save May Be Your Own," "A Stroke of Good Fortune," "A Temple of the Holy Ghost," "The Artificial Nigger," "A Circle in the Fire," "A Late Encounter With the Enemy," "Good Country People," and "The Displaced Person." He also described the connections he had determined between the stories:

> "Good Country People" is a marvelous story and I'm glad there was just time to include it in the book. We are dropping "An Afternoon in the Woods" and "An Exile in the East." It appears that we'll be able to keep "A Stroke of Good Fortune" and still keep within 256

pages. Galley proofs are expected in today and will be sent right off to you. The publication schedule is now extremely tight, of course, and I wonder if I may ask you to return the marked set (with the manuscript) by March 14th?

"Good Country People" will reach you a little later in separate proof. Incidentally, while I agree with the Tates that this is one of your best stories, I wonder if it wouldn't be made better by having the mother and / or Mrs. Freeman appear again at the very end. Their points of view are so predominant in those marvelous opening pages and indeed up to the final scene between Hulga and the Bible salesman, that it might be worth considering a few final sentences which get them back in—the mother observing the man's departure as she observed Hulga and him together, or some such thing. You may not want to change it at all, of course, but if you do you can make alterations on the proof. . . . [Giroux then gives a list of the stories] The book should certainly end with "The Displaced Person" and, that being so, the best place for "Good Country People" is next to last, don't you agree?

I also assume that there won't be time for "Good Country People" to appear in a magazine, and we'll have a first in the book, which is all to the good. In that connection, *Shenandoah* magazine has not responded to our request for a copyright assignment of "A Stroke of Good Fortune." This is all legal redtape, but we must have it if the copyright of the book is to be valid. We've sent the necessary papers to the magazine. Will you ask them to return them to us, and explain how urgent it is that they do so? With regard to the *Shenandoah* anthology, about which you wrote some time ago, I was not sure from your query whether Mr. Carter wants *exclusive* right to use "A Stroke of Good Fortune." If so, I don't see why he should have it, do you? If he means he wants the *first* use of it after it appears in your book, that is another matter and we can accommodate him if he doesn't hold up his publication more than a year. Don't you agree that this last provision is reasonable? Anyway, when you write him please ask for clarification of these points.

Many thanks for that unexpected self-portrait. We might release it if one of the review media (it will probably be *Time*) asks for something "different." However, I don't think we need a picture of the author on the jacket. We want to run quotes about *Wise Blood* on the back panel.[23]

In her reply on March 7, O'Connor was most eager to follow Giroux's lead. By now she had seen that intelligent criticism could only help her:

> I like the suggestion about the ending of "Good Country People" and enclose a dozen or so lines that can be added on to the present end. I enclose them in case you can get them put on before I get the proofs. I am mighty wary of making changes on proofs.
>
> I wrote the editor of *Shenandoah*. I don't know what ails them. They didn't even have to pay for that story and they should be polite enough to fill out the papers at once. However, I don't think the collection needs that story and I wouldn't care if you dropped it along with the other two.
>
> As for Mr. Carter, I don't know what he wants and he probably doesn't either; but I think he ought to take it up with Harcourt, Brace, not with me. Anyway I don't think he will ever get around to such a collection.
>
> The proofs have not come but I will try to get them off by the 14th.[24]

Giroux told me that of all the suggestions he made to O'Connor, the one about the conclusion of "Good Country People" was the most significant; he thought that the story ended abruptly and needed, to use film terminology, a certain "fading away" motion to allow the events that had taken place between Hulga Hopewell and Manley Pointer to be absorbed and rendered less disconcerting. In the revised conclusion, the additions of the "green speckled lake" and the action of Manley heading "across the meadow toward the highway" permit the reader to have a calmer feeling about the recent events in the barn, while the world of Mrs. Hopewell and Mrs. Freeman remains as it has been all along. The repetition of the word "simple" returns the reader back to the larger context of the story, one filled with marvelously insightful bromides and formulaic trite expressions. This new ending suggests that nothing of real importance had taken place during the course of the story—but the reader knows far different.

During the third week of March 1955, O'Connor learned that there was still time to add this ending to the manuscript. She would next see this story in proof form, even though the proofs of the rest of the book had been sent to her a few days earlier. In timely fashion, the book's composition, as Giroux wrote to O'Connor, was taking final shape:

The corrected proof and the manuscript of "Good Country People" arrived this morning. Many thanks for getting them back so promptly. I think the new ending is perfect.

Since we have already started on the page proofs, it is too late to delete "A Stroke of Good Fortune." However, I think that it should be a part of this collection, and I can't believe that the *Shenandoah* people won't assign the copyright to you in time for book publication. I hope you'll write them again and explain that it's pretty much of a technicality; they won't lose their rights in any way. We'll continue to pester them from this end.

Page proofs will begin to come through around March 29th. We'll send you a duplicate set, which it will not be necessary to return. Our proof-readers here are going over them again and I'm sure they won't miss anything, but in the unlikely event that you should find some out of order send us a collect telegram.[25]

E. Gerald Hopkins, business manager at Harcourt, Brace, informed O'Connor that the matter of the copyright for "A Stroke of Fortune" had been taken care of in early March and that she was not to worry.[26] With this technicality solved, Catharine Carver—*not* Giroux, it should be noted—wrote to McKee on March 30, "I am sending you over herewith a set of page proofs of Flannery O'Connor's book, because I do want you to have a chance to read the stories you haven't seen." A copy of the first edition (numbering 2,500 in all) cost $3.50; between 1955 and 1972, Harcourt, Brace produced 13,000 copies of the book. Carver's appearance in the production process of this book signaled that something unusual was happening at Harcourt, Brace.

On March 31, 1955, Giroux officially resigned from Harcourt, Brace. Denver Lindley became the new editor in chief, and O'Connor was assigned to Carver by John McCallum.[27] Once Giroux had finished the task of getting *A Good Man Is Hard to Find and Other Stories* into page proofs, and had put his other projects to rest, he packed up all the books in his office, said his goodbyes, and quietly left Harcourt, Brace forever. Adhering to his own sense of propriety and tact, he said little about it, preferring not to do or say anything that might hurt others or endanger his career. But in his own time and in his own way, he reached out to a few select friends and authors to explain why he had left Harcourt, Brace.

What had happened was far more dire—and religiously intolerant—than missing out on publishing Salinger's *Catcher in the Rye*. Blunt and outspoken, William Jovanovich had told Giroux that Harcourt, Brace had no intention whatsoever of making him a director. Giroux mentioned to Frank Morley that Jovanovich and McCallum, then vice president at Harcourt, Brace, had given him one day to pack up and leave. After some reflection, Giroux's final assessment was to see his departure in a positive light: "What blessed, blessed relief after weeks of anxiety. . . . They're so blindly confident of their own superiority and ability to take over unfinished business, that an hour's conference seemed sufficient transition."[28]

After lunching with T. S. Eliot, Morley, who had previously resigned from Harcourt, Brace, wrote to Giroux from England, "If the overconfident J & M [Jovanovich and McCallum] think they are going to hold such as Tom [Eliot], they'll have some new thinks [sic] coming. What the hell did the text-book boys ever do to help Tom when he needed help, except get in his hair, and mine too, incidentally?"[29] It had been a wrenching experience for Giroux, but he felt that his departure was inevitable. Giroux also wrote to Paul Horgan, one of his authors and O'Connor's former instructor at the Writers' Workshop, explaining in part that because he was a Catholic he was not considered "eligible material for the board of directors. . . . The firm was quite content to publish Catholic authors, yes; Catholic money was acceptable, yes, but a Catholic director? No."[30] Morley, as Giroux mentions in this letter to Horgan, had initially suggested to Giroux that this might happen, but it took a fair while for Giroux to realize the truth of the matter. Horgan subsequently suggested to McCallum that he contact his agent, Virginia Rice, because he would like to go with Giroux to his new firm; he did so soon afterward.[31] (In September, Giroux met up with Horgan in London and made plans to see Eliot.)[32]

In his three-page letter explaining the change to Jessamyn West, well known for her collection of stories *The Friendly Persuasion*, published by Harcourt, Brace in 1945, Giroux explained that he felt the need to resign because of "bigotry and religious prejudice. . . . I was shocked at being given 24 hours and pointed out to McCallum that there were a good many items of unfinished business and he said, 'We'll have an hour's meeting today and go over the list'—one hour for fifteen years' work." He also mentioned that Lindley had said that he, too, wanted to resign, but had no other job offer in hand.[33]

On Maundy Thursday, in early April 1955, Giroux wrote on Farrar, Straus & Cudahy stationery to Thomas Merton at Gethsemani, deeply regretting the misunderstanding during his last weeks at Harcourt, Brace that had resulted in the final corrections not being made in the first printing of *No Man Is an Island.* "I am grateful to Harcourt, Brace for having released you from their contract, and I know that their doing so is due mainly to Naomi's skill and tact in an extremely difficult situation."[34] In a postscript, he added that T. S. Eliot had confirmed that he would be joining Giroux's new firm. Revealing a new energy and ready to start afresh, Giroux wrote a "private and personal" letter to John Berryman, then in Minneapolis, Minnesota:

As you may have heard, I have left Harcourt, Brace after fifteen years to join this firm. I had thought my troubles were over when [Eugene] Reynal resigned last December, but this was a miscalculation; his leaving only confirmed the ascendency of the textbook people. William Jovanovich (or Don Giovanovich as I like to think of him) and John McCallum are The New Men. Denver Lindley, an old one whom I have always liked, will last as long as they can use him.

In any event, here I am loaded with honors (vice-president, member of the board of directors, stockholder) and as excited as Alfred Harcourt and Donald Brace must have been when they left [Henry] Holt in 1919. I've known Roger Straus since we were in the Navy together; John Farrar and Sheila Cudahy are old friends. We're a young firm, and at the same time the oldest survivor (perhaps the only, now that [William] Sloane [Associates] has fragmentized) of the postwar publishers. We publish [François] Mauriac, Edmund Wilson, [Alberto] Moravia, Colette, [Marguerite] Yourcenar, Alec Waugh, and [Giovanni] Guareschi among others.

I want to build up the American list in general (I think our European list has great distinction), and the poetry list in particular. I would like to start with *Homage to Mistress Bradstreet.* I can now sign contracts myself, and there will be none of the Harcourt, Brace ambivalence—editor proposing and management disposing. May I publish your poem? . . . We are going to do Eliot's new play (he staggered me by cabling "I will come along with you"), and Cal Lowell has agreed to publish the prose book he is working on (a memoir) with us; his poetry, alas, is tied up (I tied it up, of course).

So come on, and join your friends. Will you wire me collect and tell me we can submit a contract for the Anne Bradstreet; I'll offer you good terms.

I plan to come out your way in early May for a brief visit; I have to get back by May 11th when Uncle Tom [Eliot] arrives from London to stay at my apartment. It will be good to see you, and to talk over lots of things, but meanwhile let me know about the poem, by telegram preferably.[35]

When Merton's agent, Naomi Burton, learned of Giroux's situation, she introduced him to Sheila Cudahy, who set up a dinner meeting. In February 1955, Giroux was formally invited by Roger W. Straus Jr., John Farrar, and Cudahy to join Farrar, Straus & Company, soon to become Farrar, Straus & Cudahy, on a five-year contract. According to the new arrangement, under Straus as president and owner, Giroux would hold the positions of vice president and editor in chief, and also be a shareholder and member of the board of directors. Cudahy, who had previously owned a publishing firm in Italy with her husband, Giorgio Pellegrini, retained her post as vice president. She continued to focus on children's books, as well as books that might appeal to Catholics, until her resignation in November 1962.

When Giroux arrived at his new first-floor office at 101 Fifth Avenue at Seventeenth Street, he found the firm poorly managed and thus spent considerable time establishing a decent house library and archives so that copyrights could be properly filed. Approximately seventeen authors followed him to his new firm, including John Berryman, T. S. Eliot, Jean Stafford, Paul Horgan, John La Farge, S.J., Robert Lowell, Thomas Merton, Jack Kerouac, Peter Taylor, Randall Jarrell, and eventually Flannery O'Connor and Bernard Malamud. Just before he left Harcourt, Brace, he was proud to have edited, most likely with Carver's assistance, *The Recognitions*, by William Gaddis, an author he admired and whose works eventually received two National Book Awards, but who decided not to follow him. When Eliot cabled his desire to remain with Giroux as his American editor, Giroux saw it, he once told me, as a rare act of generosity and friendship. Donald Brace simply handed Giroux the telegram that Eliot had sent and left Giroux's office without saying a word. Roger Straus later said that Giroux's arrival in 1955 was "the single most important thing to happen to this company."[36]

Giroux was anxious to become acquainted with his new colleagues. He already knew that Straus could count on family financial resources: his mother was a Guggenheim; his father's family owned Macy's department store; his paternal grandfather Oscar Straus was secretary of commerce during the presidency of Theodore Roosevelt. While serving in the U.S. Navy, Straus had started planning his own publishing firm and enlisted James Van Alen to help get it started in 1945, but because of pressure from his family Van Alen never became fully involved, preferring to put his energies into promoting professional tennis. Straus and Giroux had met in New York during World War II, during the latter's time on the *Essex*. On leave in New York, Giroux approached Straus, then an ensign and a censor for the navy, with an account of the experience of Lieutenant George M. Blair, a pilot from the *Essex* who had been shot down at Truk on February 18, 1944. Straus approved the article, and "Rescue at Truk" appeared in *Collier's* (May 13, 1944). Thus the Giroux-Straus friendship was formed, though Straus's often coarse language and personal insults would cause tension for Giroux later on. But in the beginning both were eager to advance the firm, which they did with great éclat. The other member of the firm, John Farrar, a friend of Straus's, was a Yale graduate who had worked for the *New York World* and subsequently established himself in publishing circles as editor of *The Bookman*. In addition, he had started the Breadloaf Writers' Conference at Middlebury College in Vermont in 1926. As a former editor in chief of the George H. Doran Company and a founding member of Farrar & Rinehart, he too had the background Straus needed.[37]

After Giroux landed safely in a new position, should he have spoken out against the discrimination he faced at Harcourt, Brace? Given that he was going through a traumatic period of transition, one that could have had unforeseen negative consequences, should he have reacted other than he did? What would have happened to him—and his future career—if he had put the public spotlight on his predicament and allowed rumors to circulate? How much time and effort would he have expended to dampen these rumors, if ever that could be done? Certainly, the past could not be rewritten, but he wanted to have as much say in damage control as possible. And thus, for better or worse, he chose a path that would not demand hours and hours of explaining and reexplaining what, in the long run, would only be counterproductive. For now, with Merton, Berryman, and others aboard, Giroux wasted no time getting back to editing. That spring brought him some notable works: *The Vagabond*, by Colette; *The Selected Letters of Anton Chekhov*, edited by Lillian Hellman; *Flesh and*

Blood, by François Mauriac; *A Ghost at Noon,* by Alberto Moravia; *Keats,* by John Middleton Murry; and *Island in the Sun,* by Alec Waugh.

Giroux decided to contact O'Connor not directly, but rather through their mutual friend Robert Fitzgerald: "I have felt tongue-tied about writing Flannery for a number of reasons," he wrote to Fitzgerald. "First, her new book, which is marvelous, is about to come out (fortunately I was able to see it through the press) and I don't want to do anything to lessen H[arcourt,] B[race]'s enthusiasm. . . . I don't want Flannery to do any-thing in mid-publication so to speak (and perhaps she may not want to [change publishing firms]), but I want her to know the facts and if, as her good friend, you think you can give Flannery the background without unduly disturbing her at this point, I hope you will do so."[38] Fitzgerald, writing from Genoa, Italy, agreed to contact O'Connor about the matter.[39] When O'Connor returned in early April from a trip to the Woman's Col-lege of the University of North Carolina in Greensboro, where she had caught up with Robie Macauley and met Randall Jarrell and Peter Taylor, she had no intimations at all of the changes taking place in New York. Fitzgerald broke the news to her in a letter in which he repeated what Giroux had told others, though adding, "HB wouldn't have had sense enough to publish *Wise Blood* if it hadn't been for Giroux."[40]

CHAPTER SIX

Flannery O'Connor, Catharine Carver, Denver Lindley

1955–1958

Because O'Connor had learned to accept so much so quickly during her adult life, particularly the reverses imposed by her illness, she would have been upset, but not devastated, by not receiving directly the news of Giroux's sudden resignation from Harcourt, Brace. O'Connor simply continued with her life as usual, anticipating that at some point she would be given a rational explanation. For his part, Giroux, as he told me, knew that he could contact his authors by telegram or phone, or, as happened in most cases, leave it to word of mouth. Given her Southern background, sense of discretion, and sincere gratitude toward those who had helped her, it is no surprise that O'Connor never directly contacted Giroux. She knew it was crucial to establish a positive relationship with Catharine Carver, whom she had never met. She expressed a vague hope that she would see her new editor in a year or two, which could seem like an eternity to a writer, especially one who constantly dealt with medical problems that diminished her physical energies. In the meantime, she anticipated a visit from Lindley, who would provide an interim liaison with her publishers.

For many of her contemporaries, Carver was always a bit of an enigma, due in large part to her incredible work schedule and reluctance to enter into the social arena of the publishing world.[1] Born in 1921 in

Cambridge, Ohio, she received her B.A. degree in 1943 from Muskingum College in New Concord and two years later obtained a job at the publishing firm of Reynal & Hitchcock in New York. During the spring and summer of 1945, Carver served as business manager of the *Partisan Review*, and then over the years as its managing editor, editorial assistant, and then as assistant editor and associate editor from the spring of 1956 to the fall of 1957. She was also an occasional book reviewer, which proved important for O'Connor's career because Carver was already familiar with her work and could look at fiction with a critical eye.[2] In the late 1960s she went to London and worked for Chatto & Windus, Victor Gollancz, and Oxford University Press.[3] Aware of Carver's background at the *Partisan Review*, Giroux hired her, most likely as an editorial assistant, sometime around 1950, fully aware of the workload involved. She was often the first to read O'Connor's stories before passing them on to Giroux.[4]

Over the years, O'Connor grew in her admiration of Carver. In late March 1959, for example, she sent Carver, then an editor at Viking, a copy of the typescript of her second novel, *The Violent Bear It Away*, and took to heart her subsequent critique.[5] Carver visited O'Connor and was her guest at a conference of the Georgia Council of Teachers of English in Atlanta at which O'Connor was a featured speaker. O'Connor commented about Carver in a March 1960 letter to her friend and fellow fiction writer Cecil Dawkins, author of *The Quiet Enemy*, "I wouldn't want a woman editor unless she was someone I knew and liked already. Catharine Carver is a great friend of mine and I would have her for my editor in a minute, but some strange woman—no." In June 1961, she mentioned Carver in a letter to another close friend, Maryat Lee, recommending, "She's brighter than the lot of them put together. Listen to anything she has to say." But O'Connor's final written observation about Carver, made before Christmas 1963, less than a year before she died, and perhaps one that she regretted writing, reveals a harsher and more dispirited evaluation: "She's a Yankee and a stoic, a woman whose only happiness seems to be in work and endurance, and that is not real happiness but just non-misery."[6] Yet if one substituted *Southerner* for *Yankee*, it might be possible to imagine that given her declining health, O'Connor was holding up a mirror to herself.

Giroux, who worked closely with Carver, considered her "a great editor."[7] After the death of T. S. Eliot, he wrote to Valerie Eliot and suggested that she might meet Carver, then in England, as a source of editorial assistance in gathering and organizing her late husband's papers. "She is a very sensitive person and extremely well informed on American writers and publishers," he promised.[8]

O'Connor continued to consult with Carver about her stories, even when she was terminally ill, knowing that she would always receive honest and intelligent evaluations. The more O'Connor came to know Carver and her editorial skills, the more she relied on her assistance and advice. Their relationship developed this strength because Carver, who lacked job security over the years and must have felt vulnerable at times, never felt the need to dominate O'Connor as Gordon had, but instead remained discreet and helpful whenever called upon.

After Giroux's departure, Carver wasted no time in writing O'Connor a detailed letter in late March 1955 in which she expressed the hope she could successfully take his place: "I've worked closely with Bob on both your books, had a hand in the suggestions he made you about the final choices and arrangement of the stories for the new book, and edited the copy on both books myself. . . . I believe in your work very strongly; I think what you're doing, particularly in these latest stories, is very powerful, often profound, and absolutely *sui generis*—it seems to me about the most interesting work coming from any young writer in the country right now."[9] Carver sent to Gordon, McKee, and O'Connor page proofs of *A Good Man Is Hard to Find*, anticipating that O'Connor would not return them unless she wanted to make corrections. O'Connor's first letter to Carver, written from Milledgeville in early April and addressed in proper form, clearly indicates that O'Connor had expectations about how her new editor should deal with advance copies of her story collection. In paying Carver a compliment for having worked hard in helping Giroux edit her collection of stories, she was acknowledging in her own way that it was (and is) fairly common for junior editors to copyedit a manuscript after the senior editor had gone through the entire text.

Even though Giroux had left Harcourt, Brace, he had dealt with O'Connor's collection of stories up to the point of its physical publication; in effect, he always considered himself, as he mentioned in his letter of reference for her Guggenheim Fellowship, as the one "to have seen her book of stories *A Good Man Is Hard to Find* through the press"—in sum, its editor.[10] O'Connor, in any case, did not want any mix-up with this new book, especially when it concerned her professional friends and acquaintances. The list of possible recipients of the finished book indicates how carefully she had kept track of individuals who could help promote her work.[11] Lowell, for example, highly praised O'Connor's collection: "*Wise Blood*, I think, is impossible to improve on; but your stories are almost exhibition pieces of how a story should be written."[12] O'Connor wanted to make sure that Carver knew she appreciated her contribution to her collection, and perhaps overstated the case in order to establish a good rapport with her new editor:

> Dear Miss Carver,
> I had not heard that Bob Giroux had left Harcourt but since he has gone, I am very glad that you will be my editor. He told me once that you did all the work anyhow, which was what I might have suspected. I appreciate your interest in my writing and I will rely on you to tell when what I do needs more doing. The last time I was at the Harcourt office, I stayed around longer than I was expected, hoping you would come in, but I had to leave before you returned from lunch. I don't expect to get to New York this year or next. If you make any of these trips that editors seem to make, I hope you will include Milledgeville. Meanwhile, perhaps I'll see Mr. Lindley. . . .
> I wish you would let me know which of these you do not send books to as I will want to send them then myself. Do you still send books first and charge them to the author and enclose the card? If so, I will send a list of people I would like books sent to and charged to me. . . .
> And I'll be particularly glad to see any [reviews] that come in on the British edition as I can't fancy what the British will make of *Wise Blood*. You probably noticed in the Neville Spearman catalogue that they said I was finishing my second novel—and they would publish it in the fall. I am not finishing it or anywhere near finishing it and it is fortunate they don't say which fall.
> Many thanks for all your kindnesses to me.[13]

Still unsure about her new editor, O'Connor's reverted to old, nervous habits to make sure her stories were placed in appropriate journals. In early April 1955, she followed up with a second letter instructing her agent to send a chapter of her new novel, "Whom the Plague Beckons" (eventually called "You Can't Be Any Poorer Than Dead") to *New World*

Writing, which seemed to favor novels in progress, but if *Harper's Bazaar* would pay more for it, she wanted it placed there, since she was "all for the money." Above all, she wanted it understood this submission should be considered a *chapter*, not a story, though even Sally Fitzgerald was not able to discern its plot.[14]

Just about to turn thirty, O'Connor had done remarkably well, having finished one novel and a collection of short stories, and was now working on a second novel. Undeterred, she would move forward making as few waves as possible: "I am sorry Giroux is elsewhere but I will like Miss Carver fine," she informed McKee that April. Wanting to do exactly as O'Connor wished, Carver replied with a formal note and enclosed, as was normally done, the front matter of the book, so that O'Connor would have the time to react to it in advance:

Dear Miss O'Connor,
Thanks for your very straight and agreeable letter.
We'll have bound copies of the book on or about April 27th, and I'll see that one goes out to each of the people on your list, as well as to many others I can think of. I'll also see that all the Georgia newspaper people have review copies well in advance. Yes, we will send copies, to be charged to you, to anyone you like. Remember that you have ten free copies coming to you, and any over that number will be charged to you at a discount. If you'd like to send me special cards to be enclosed in these personal copies, I'll try to see that the right card gets into the right book. . . .
I can't think of anything else at the moment, but I will be in touch with you again soon.[15]

Meanwhile, in addition to coping with Giroux's departure and anticipating Lindley's visit (provided he could deal with transportation to Andalusia), O'Connor attended a breakfast for women writers in Atlanta and had to sit next to her *almost* editor, John Selby, for two excruciating hours!

Lindley's visit would fall through, but he knew the importance of making contact. With Giroux casting his net wider and wider to bring new writers into his firm, Harcourt, Brace wanted to make sure that O'Connor would *not* follow her former editor. She needed to be reassured personally that she was appreciated and admired where she was. In his letter to O'Connor, Lindley expressed regret at not managing to see her at Andalusia, though he hoped she would come north and confer there with her publisher. And, once they knew one another on a personal basis, he could look forward to another trip to the Deep South. "My recent experience was so brief as to be tantalizing, though I did manage a whole and very pleasant day in Jackson."[16] He might have been to Jackson in part to see Eudora Welty and persuade her, too, not to follow Giroux, who had recently edited one of her books at Harcourt, Brace.[17] In his letter to Welty, Lindley was most circumspect: "Unless Bob has already sent you his news, it will come as a surprise to get this letter from me instead of him."[18] He explained that quite suddenly at the end of the previous week Giroux had resigned from Harcourt, Brace to become a vice president at Farrar, Straus & Cudahy. "We who have worked closely with Bob feel his going as a personal loss. The new prospects for him, however, are bright and we can only hope that the move will an auspicious one for him."

By the time Lindley had returned to New York, copies of O'Connor's book had arrived at his office. Just as McKee was reading a chapter of O'Connor's new novel, Carver sent copies of *A Good Man Is Hard to Find* to O'Connor on April 28, 1955.[19] Lindley's letter, dated the same day, had an indifferent tone that would not ingratiate him to O'Connor: he wanted her to know that if he could be of any service to her, or if she had any questions about the company she would like to ask, he hoped she would not hesitate in contacting him.[20]

O'Connor, however, was more interested in making sure that her story "Good Country People," marvelously stitched together with Mrs. Hopewell's platitudes, would be ready for the June 6 issue of *Harper's Bazaar* than she was in making new friends. In a second, unpublished letter to editor Alice Morris on April 28, O'Connor innocently mentions a Danish acquaintance: "The picture I sent you was taken by a Danish friend of mine and he didn't leave the negative with me. He is now in Copenhagen—so I guess that takes care of that one. After I received your letter this afternoon, I bought some film and got a friend to take no less than eight pictures of me."[21] Erik Langkjaer, the Dane in question, had worked as a salesman for Giroux, visiting bookstores and meeting authors throughout the South. O'Connor's former college professor Helen Greene, whose English history textbook was published by Harcourt, Brace, had taken Langkjaer to meet O'Connor in May 1953. As O'Connor had earlier enjoyed the attention of John Sullivan, Robie Macauley, and Robert Lowell, she became enamored with Langkjaer and looked forward to those times when they could drive out into the Baldwin County countryside and spend time together. As Langkjaer admits, O'Connor was "mildly in love" with him.[22] Mark Bosco, S.J., notes in his essay "Consenting to Love" that Langkjaer was Danish on his father's side and Russian on his mother's. He had graduated from Princeton and finished two years of graduate studies in philosophy at Fordham University before deciding to begin a career in publishing.[23] Since "Good Country People," in spite of O'Connor's comments to Gordon and Tate in her letter of March 1, 1955, is often considered her most autobiographical story, critics tend to see Manley Pointer, the gigolo Bible salesman in this story, as based on Langkjaer.[24] (O'Connor once wrote Langkjaer about this: "I am highly taken with the thought of your seeing yourself as the Bible salesman. Dear boy, remove this delusion from your head at once. And if you think the story is also my spiritual autobiography, remove that one too.")[25] Pointer, whose name has not-so-subtle phallic overtones, pretends to take a fancy to Hulga Hopewell, a one-legged Southerner with a Ph.D. in philosophy (O'Connor had recently been using aluminum crutches), but mistreats her and then suddenly departs. Clearly taken by Pointer's apparent charm, she shares a kiss with him before they climb into the hayloft of a nearby barn. As Pointer continues his amorous encounter, Hulga begins to resist his advances, especially his request that she remove her artificial leg to prove that she loves him. She soon realizes the ruse being played upon her. As Pointer puts her leg into his suitcase, he leaves Hulga stranded, alone with what the reader can only imagine to be thoughts of deep abandonment and rejection.

O'Connor had had been quite taken with Langkjaer and gradually had to work her way out of her feelings of being rebuffed by him. Would Hulga, as devastated as O'Connor was after Langkjaer departed, ever find it within herself to attempt to come close to another man? The reader cannot but see Hulga's luminous moment of insight, but could she, now a castoff, ever find a love that might sustain her? O'Connor, as author, had brilliantly raised the question, but even more brilliantly had not attempted to answer it. In pursuing this topic, Bosco notes that Sally Fitzgerald focused, appropriately, on the significance of this friendship as the last and "most seriously painful, instance in which the old pattern of unrequited love was to reappear," continuing,

Having located Langkjaer in Denmark, Fitzgerald interviewed him for her biography of O'Connor; Langkjaer, in turn, shared with her the twelve letters that O'Connor had sent him after he departed from the South. Fitzgerald noted a qualitative difference in these letters, which reveal a depth of feeling seen nowhere else in O'Connor's correspondence. She quotes a handwritten postscript in one such letter to Langkjaer as indicative of O'Connor's feelings for the young Dane: "I think that if you were here, we could talk for about a million years." The poignancy of this revelation lies in its timing, for her letter to Langkjaer was sent shortly before the arrival of his own letter to her announcing his engagement to marry. O'Connor, Fitzgerald notes, instantly withdrew into her customary reserve, and the letters sent to Langkjaer thenceforward were warm but very correct in their southern manners.[26]

One of the letters quoted by Bosco from O'Connor to Langkjaer, dated October 17, 1954, shows a vulnerable side of O'Connor that she had never before revealed: "You are wonderful and wildly original and I would probably think you even more so if I didn't still hope you will come back from that awful place. . . . Did I tell you I call my baby peachicken Brother in public and Erik in private?" It seems that O'Connor and Langkjaer had decided not to break off their relationship after a lengthy discussion; rather, on their last night together, they kissed a few times as he told her of his summer plans.[27] Her father, her editor, and now her *boyfriend* (to apply a word she probably would not have used), *had left her*. She concluded another letter to Langkjaer, "I haven't seen any dirt roads since you left & I miss you."[28] Although O'Connor had invested so much of herself in writing this story, she was able to distance herself from the immediacy of the experience, focusing more on the story's literary qualities. One could well ask if her relationship with Langkjaer might be one of multiple reasons why O'Connor does not depict mature single men or happily married couples in her fiction, though Paul Engle remembered one story she wrote earlier "involving a scene between a young man and a young woman about to make love."[29] Once they had a chance to discuss the story in private, Engle concluded, "It was obvious that she was improvising from innocence."

After Langkjaer's departure, any consolation, however small, would help. When the finished books arrived in early May 1955, O'Connor wrote to Carver saying that she liked them. She noted that the first chapter of her projected novel, "Whom the Plague Beckons," had been sold to *New World Writing* (the title was later changed to "You Can't Be Any Poorer Than Dead"). Carver, for her part, felt it important to meet personally with O'Connor and see how they could work together. After talking with her by phone, she started making arrangements for O'Connor to meet other people in the New York publishing world, even planning for her to make a foray into public television. Carver wrote, in mid-May,

> It was good to talk to you on Friday and to hear that you are willing to come up for the program on the 31. I hope it won't be too disagreeable.
>
> I made a reservation for you at the Woodstock [Hotel], and I'm enclosing our check for what the airlines people tell us the round-trip fare from Atlanta will come to. I will meet you at whatever airport you say and whatever time Monday, May 30.
>
> I've spoken to Harvey Breit [assistant editor of the book section of the *New York Times*], and he would like you [*sic*] to have an early lunch with you at noon on the 31, in order to get your signals straight for the program, which begins at 1:30. The only other plan I've tentatively made for you is for dinner on Monday evening with the Lindleys. Denver hopes thus to make up, as early in your visit as possible, for not having met you in Georgia. John McCallum—as I had forgotten when I talked to you—is leaving the 28 for London, so you won't meet him, and I know he is sorry about this. I've left a message with Elizabeth McKee that you are coming, and I'm sure she'll count on seeing you sometime. Arabel Porter, a good friend of mine, wants very much to meet you, and I'll try to arrange this too.
>
> It will be good if you can stay over at least until Wednesday, June 1, as I see there are already more engagements threatening than you can possibly manage in the course of Monday and Tuesday.
>
> I'm afraid I always get a little excited over talking long distance, and tend to forget important things. So I forgot, in the course of our conversation Friday, to tell you that I had read "You Can't Be Any Poorer Than Dead," and that Denver has also, and that we both think it is an amazing piece of work. It looks to me as tho [*sic*] the novel is really going to be *something*! I'm anxious to read more, when you're ready to have me do so. Meanwhile, if you agree, we would like to go ahead and make a contract for this next book. I'll talk to Elizabeth McKee about this, and to you when you get here.

Thanks again, so much, for your willingness to make the trip. Please let me know if there are any other things I can do in advance to make it more pleasant. I do look forward to seeing you on the 30.[30]

O'Connor was thus prepared to visit the set of Harvey Breit's *Galley-Proof* TV show on WFCA, an NBC affiliate, which would dramatize the opening scene of "The Life You Save May Be Your Own" (published in the *Kenyon Review*, Spring 1953). This broadcast would be important for determining whether O'Connor's fiction could be translated into other media. This would, of course, be successfully done for the film version of "The Displaced Person" as part of the American Short Story Series in 1977; by John Huston for the 1979 film *Wise Blood*; and by Cecil Dawkins in her compilation of several O'Connor stories presented as a theatrical piece at the American Place Theatre in 1965 under the title *The Displaced Person*. O'Connor's upbeat reply to Carver was both informative and witty, revealing that she now felt more at ease with her new editor:

I have a reservation on Flight 514, Eastern Air Lines, which will arrive at the Newark airport at 4:20 P.M. EDT, May 30. I think as long as I am up there I will stay through Friday, however, I naturally don't expect Harcourt, Brace to pay the hotel bill for these extra days, but any engagement you want to make for me will be all right. I have long wanted to meet Miss Porter and meant to the last time I was in New York but got sick and had to go home.

If you could tell me what time this program is going to be and on what channel I would be obliged, as my mother insists upon no- tifying her connections and I have no information to pacify her with. People here feel that since I am going to be on a television program I must be a better writer than they thought. Competing now with the Lone Ranger.

Your letter and telegram arrived simultaneously so I had no time to be worried.

I'm glad you like the chapter. The new title is fine and is just the way I feel every time I get to work on it.[31]

Carver replied, giving basic information about the television show but not going overboard in supplying details. Not having met O'Connor, she did not want to give her a chance to reverse herself and stay at home. As an act of kindness, Carver took it upon herself to greet O'Connor at the airport.[32] In her efforts to be informative and congenial, Carver, however, had not been entirely forthright with O'Connor, perhaps revealing that dimension of her personality "whose only happiness seems to be in work and endurance," as O'Connor phrased it.

Behind the scenes, Harcourt, Brace was trying to figure out the type of contractual arrangement they should have with O'Connor, so they could talk to her in a businesslike fashion at some point during her visit, as revealed in a previously unpublished, two-part, internal Harcourt, Brace memorandum from Carver to McCallum. O'Connor might have been surprised by Carver's business acumen and her desire to embrace O'Connor's work in progress wholeheartedly:

> We are proposing to make a contract now for Flannery O'Connor's new novel, of which we have seen one chapter, but which—the author estimates—will not be finished for some two years. She works slowly and carefully; if this first chapter (of which I enclose a copy, in case you'd like to read a little way into it) is any indication at all, the novel when ready will be an extraordinary piece of work. These opening pages of it have more power, I think, than any writing of hers I've yet seen; they represent a considerable advance over any of the stories in *A Good Man Is Hard to Find* and I think those stories are superior to anything in her first novel *Wise Blood*. She's improving steadily in control and in what I suppose might be called the imaginative projection of her themes; the theme of this new novel, as prefigured here, is a very strong one.
>
> We've learned this week the kind of attention reviewers will pay to a book of stories by Flannery O'Connor; I think any novel she publishes from here on out is assured of a lot of attention if not all praise; I think we might even sell the next book. We're offering the same terms for this novel, as we did for *Wise Blood*, except that the advance asked by the agent is $1,250, and it was $1,000 for *Wise Blood*. There was some talk of putting $750 of this advance against general royalties, but this the agent has refused. Flannery O'Connor is in town this week (I hope you may be here to meet her on Friday around noon) and it would be good if the contract could go through for her signature while she's here.

Do you think we *could* split the O'Connor advance, putting the $500 to be paid on signing against this book [her new novel], and the other $750 into general royalty. I've thought about this, and talked to Denver, and it does seem very hard to put it *all* into general royalty. There is a chance of the stories earning her a little, since the advance was so small, but signing this contract now with the whole new advance put into general royalty, means that she wouldn't get any of whatever small proceeds there are on *A Good Man. An argument, in fact, for not signing up the novel* [emphasis mine]. I think we ought to believe in her to the extent of the $500. She's not likely to draw the balance for some years. (The reviews of *A Good Man* look promising; incidentally, I attach some exhibits.)

What a parental relation an advance (yours and mine)! I feel like I've just asked you for an advance on my allowance.

[Counter-signed by JMC:] *OK Katy. Whatever, we need to keep her. John*[33]

Carver then outlined in detail what she thought Harcourt, Brace should offer O'Connor, based on past contractual arrangements:

A Good Man Is Hard to Find, 10 percent of the list price to 10,000; 15 percent thereafter. Advance: $250 on signing, accrued royalties on publication, ⅔ of movie, television, etc., royalties to author. Now, shall I offer the same terms for the new novel as on *Wise Blood*, making the first $500 of the advance payable on demand (since she may be years still on this new novel), and including an option for her next full-length work? I expect Mavis McIntosh might ask for 15 percent after 7,500 instead of after 10,000, but I would think we ought to start from the *Wise Blood* terms.

It should be noted that at this point McCallum and also Jovanovich, who added a postscript to the memorandum, were actively involved in Harcourt, Brace's dealings with O'Connor; their future communication with her would be based on a knowledge of her contractual situation with their firm.

Given that Harcourt, Brace had determined in advance its contractual offer, all that remained was a serious discussion with O'Connor, though it is not too clear from the following letter how much information was transmitted to her by this time. In late May 1955, O'Connor

wrote to Carver, glossing over to her detriment any contractual information that might have been sent to her. Rather, she focused on the difficulties she would have were she required to walk a good deal while in New
York. Carver, as she notes in a letter, continued to be most attentive to
O'Connor's needs:

I haven't written to you sooner because I've been closeted in the
semi-annual sales conference. But I did take care of the hotel reservation change. I've made a reservation for you at the New Weston
Hotel which is just next door to the office, at 49th and Madison. It's
a nicer and quieter place than any of the hotels near Grand Central,
and naturally I think it will be more convenient for you for many reasons. It has a couple of pleasant lobbies, where you can talk to the
people who want to see you without having to go out of the building.

I'll save all the other things I have to tell you till I see you at
Newark on Monday. I do hope it's going to be a good trip for you. . . .
The Lowells are here and Elizabeth will be staying on through part
of next week, so you'll see her. Cal [Lowell] was so sorry to miss you,
he has to be in Iowa for some reason next week.

Don't worry about the television thing (if you *are* a worrier) because I'm sure it will go quite smoothly. . . .

Oh yes, the Celestine Sibley column [in the Atlanta *Journal &
Constitution*] is *very* nice. It looks to me like you are appreciated
more than you think at home.[34]

While in New York, O'Connor went one evening with Carver to the
Morosco Theatre to see *Cat on a Hot Tin Roof,* which featured Barbara
Bel Geddes as Maggie; Ben Gazzara as Brick; Burl Ives as Big Daddy,
and Mildred Dunnock as Big Mama. It received considerable acclaim,
winning the Pulitzer Prize for Drama in 1955. "I didn't like Tennessee
Williams's play," O'Connor wrote McKee at the end of June. "I thought
I could do that good myself. However, on reflection I guess it is wise to
doubt that." In fact, as she later made clear, Williams made her "plumb
sick."[35] O'Connor's reluctance to talk positively about this production
might stem from the fact that there is little evidence that O'Connor attended the theater with any frequency, something that seems strange
given the highly dramatic nature of her fiction, especially the perfectly
pitched dialogue.

O'Connor survived the television show and the ambient notoriety, but she still did not feel totally comfortable with Harcourt, Brace. She and Giroux had arranged a quiet meeting at the New Weston Hotel, which Giroux talked to me about and which O'Connor discussed in a letter to the Fitzgeralds.[36] Giroux told O'Connor that she would always be welcome at his new firm, where he would continue to be her editor, and that he would be glad to give her any assistance as she parsed her Harcourt, Brace contract. Not wanting to promote himself, he probably did not tell her about his current workload of twenty-four books, three of which he was particularly proud (*Five Novels* by Alberto Moravia; *God in Search of Man* by Rabbi Abraham Joshua Heschel, and *Seven* by Colette). After this meeting, he wrote to O'Connor a "personal and private" letter on June 6 from his new apartment at 219 East Sixty-Sixth Street—a clear sign that this letter came from him as an individual and not as an editor at Farrar, Straus & Cudahy. It would have been improper for him to woo O'Connor away from Harcourt, Brace without somehow informing them of his intentions. He could plant a seed in her mind, as he indicates in a letter to O'Connor, and yet would always give her complete freedom to consider any options:

> Mavis [McIntosh] told me on the telephone today that after hesitating HB has finally capitulated and would guarantee Catharine Carver as editor of your novel. I am delighted to hear this, for her sake as well as yours, but I have one further friendly suggestion. Before you sign the contract, will you send me at this address the exact wording of this clause?
>
> It's possible to be offered something which sounds like a guarantee but which really isn't. It ought to state that the contract is "void unless. . . ." Since there is no rush on your part to conclude the contract, now is the time to assure yourself of every aspect of the matter, and I'm uniquely qualified to be of help.
>
> It was good seeing you at the New Weston. I'm delighted to see the book is getting good review space and attention.[37]

Reacting immediately to Giroux's advice, and thus acknowledging his ongoing presence in her literary career, O'Connor wrote to him from Milledgeville, flummoxed by her Harcourt, Brace contract:

I have just gotten your letter about the 'void unless . . .' business. They have not sent me my copy of the contract yet but I don't believe there was any void unless on it. I had her [Carver] call Elizabeth McKee and read the clause to her and Elizabeth said it would be all right to sign it, so I did. I certainly hope I have not got myself tied up. As I remember it, it said that "It is understood that Catharine Carver will be my editor and that if she leaves, the option can be broken upon repayment of the advance." I have only signed one copy of the contract and I am supposed to sign another. Could you find out about this from Elizabeth McKee or—Mavis? This is very stupid of me but of course I know nothing about legal wording, and was relying on the agent.

They agreed to the clause with a great cry of pain. Said they had never done such a thing before and if they had to do it with every author, they would soon be out of business, etc.

I am satisfied there as long as Catharine Carver is my editor. I liked Denver Lindley very much but one against the tide would not be enough.

I'll certainly appreciate your continued help on this. They want to put a time limit on this contract but have not done that yet. Could that be an avenue of escape for me if the clause proves not to be?

I had a letter from Robert Fitzgerald saying that if he had a book of poems out, you would be the one to do it.[38]

Upset by the unresolved implications in her contract and her own inattention, O'Connor immediately sat down and wrote a letter on June 9 to McKee, indicating that she had gone ahead and signed the contract, though only one copy of it. She also sent Carver a thank-you gift of peacock feathers for dealing with the clause in question; in her accompanying letter she indicates that she still had not completely mastered the details of her contract: "Please tell me this: I get bills from Harcourt, Brace for books that the agent has ordered. Am I supposed to pay these as they come or will they be taken off my statement? I have been saving them, presuming they would be taken off the statement, I mean deducted from the royalty check or whatever it is."[39] O'Connor also shared with the Fitzgeralds in mid-June some news, all of it positive and upbeat, of her visit to New York, mentioning that she had seen Giroux, who looked in good health and adding, "I liked Denver Lindley fine and am satisfied at Harcourt, Brace as long as he and Miss Carver are there." She had also spent a weekend in Connecticut with Caroline Gordon, whose review of *A Good Man Is Hard to Find* would appear in the *New York Times Book Review* (June 12, 1955), and met Malcolm Cowley and "dear old Van Wyke [*sic*] Brooks" who later remarked that it was a shame that someone with so much talent should look on life as a horror story. Cowley simply wanted to know if O'Connor, like Hulga Hopewell, had a wooden leg.

Not completely aware of what had taken place at Harcourt, Brace about revising the contract because he had been out of town, Giroux instinctively sensed that he was the appropriate person to serve as O'Connor's guide as she dealt with one signed contract and another in the process of having a new clause added. Writing again from his apartment, he followed through on his previous letter, wanting to make sure that all would be in order to forestall any unforeseen consequences with the publication of her new novel:

Many thanks for your letter of June 8th which arrived this morning. I am a little concerned about your recollection of the clause, because if it states what you say, namely that "the option can be broken upon repayment of the advance," then it really doesn't cover the novel. In other words, I assume they have given you a new contract for the novel with an option for the book after that. If the editor clause refers to the *option*, I wonder where that leaves you with the novel? I am reluctant to discuss this matter with Elizabeth McKee or Mavis. After all, they presumably know their business, and strictly speaking it is none of my business, and they would be justified in telling me so. However, as a personal matter between you and me, I don't see why it isn't possible to get complete clarification. When the other copy of the contract arrives please copy out the clause in question and I'll be able to study the exact wording.

I am further puzzled by your saying they want to put a time limit on this contract, "but they have not done that yet." How is this possible, if you've already signed it? And a time limit on what—delivery of the manuscript? I cannot understand the terrific rush with which they have handled the matter or why, for example, they sent you only one copy of the contract.

Once they swallowed hard, and agreed to the edited clause in principle, they did not have to worry about me anymore (if they were worrying and they obviously were), I should think the final agreement could have been drawn up in a leisurely manner. Anyway, don't worry your agent about it, but, when the final document comes, for legal, personal, historical, pastoral, and tragical reasons, I'll be eager to see it.

The good old New York *Times* came through this morning with a fine review [of *A Good Man Is Hard to Find*]. Good for them. It was unsigned, but it sounds like Orville Prescott—and if it is that's really a revolution!

I visited the Lowells on Tuesday [June 7] and stayed overnight at their new house in Duxbury [Massachusetts]. We had dinner with Eliot in Boston and it was a very pleasant occasion indeed. Yes, we're going to do Robert's [Fitzgerald] poetry.[40]

Giroux returned to New York elated because the contract he had just signed with Lowell had historic significance: it was the first one he signed at his new firm. In New York, Giroux planned on reserving time to be with Eliot and assist him as needed. He especially wanted to make sure that his poet-friend would find time to join him and Martin D'Arcy, S.J., a noted British writer and academic, for dinner at Sheila Cudahy's apartment.[41] O'Connor would eventually own five books by Father D'Arcy, including *The Mind and Heart of Love* (1947), passages of which she underlined.[42]

Knowing that Giroux would continue to mentor her through her new contractual arrangement with Harcourt, Brace, O'Connor wrote to him again, aware that she could not let the moment pass without mastering this important document:

I wrote Elizabeth McKee last week and without mentioning your name told her I had heard the contract should say "void unless . . ." and asked her to check on it. I am sure it didn't but as soon as I hear from her or get my copy from Harcourt I'll send you the exact wording.

As for the time limit, Catharine said, I believe, that they had forgotten to put that in and that it was only a formality. It was a time limit for the manuscript to be delivered. She wanted to put three years and I think I said they could put what they pleased, that the manuscript wouldn't be delivered until I had finished with it, which might be three years, five, or ten. This discussion took place after I had already signed the thing.

I'll keep you informed in any case.[43]

Giroux again wrote O'Connor from his apartment, this time adding some good news: She had a new fan—T. S. Eliot:

Thanks for your letter of June 13. I am glad to know that the time limit has to do only with the formality of the delivery date, which is never taken literally. I'll be mighty curious to see the wording of the "void unless" clause when you get your copy of the contract.

Eliot picked up my copy of your book yesterday in my apartment and told me how much he admired the opening story. I told him that your work deserved a first-rate English publisher, and I won't be surprised if Mavis receives an inquiry from Faber & Faber. He may read the other stories this morning before he sails on the *Queen Elizabeth*.[44]

In a letter to Merton in late June, Giroux wrote that Eliot had just returned after a month's visit. His presence and his advice had, as usual, done Giroux a world of good.[45] O'Connor tracked Eliot's work carefully; her library would contain twelve of his books. Sally Fitzgerald believed that Eliot was perhaps the greatest literary mentor in O'Connor's life, particularly in the way "The Waste Land" influenced the writing of *Wise Blood*.[46]

O'Connor would have a chance to see the contract in its final, revised form, which Carver sent to McKee. Carver also informed O'Connor on June 14 that her book had sold almost five hundred copies the previous week:

Don't count on being a best-seller; but feel as encouraged as you [do] by this spurt, which has excited us all. We are repeating the ad in the *Times* today (enclosed), substituting a quote from [Orville] Prescott's review—which, as Denver told you, is for him truly ecstatic (and may very well explain the 300 copies sold on last Friday alone).

I wish Caroline [Gordon] had said a little more about the book and less about the symbols, but still, her review is very nice. Oh yes, he is Brainard Cheney, the same name as the Lon Cheney to whom you suggested we send a copy? (I'm sure we addressed him as Lon, or was this a monstrous error on our part? I have heard of Brainard Cheney.) Said Cheney sent a very good letter, from which I quote: "I consider the title story the most dramatic comment on nuclear fission that I've encountered. 'The River' and 'Good Country People' can keep company with the best that have been done in this century. But they all are very exceptional—all, are only to be expected from the hand of Flannery O'Connor, whom I nominate the Oracle of the Cold War." How does it feel to be called an oracle?

I am enclosing a copy of the contract, for you to sign and keep. The advance will be going off to Elizabeth in a day or so.

About the book bills. Ignore them, they are not meant to be paid. They'll take them off your royalty statement every six months. I don't know why they send out these monthly memoranda, something to do with keeping orderly books. But they are only tokens, not real bills.

Things seem to be quieting down a little up here, since we're not publishing any more books for a few weeks. But the excitement about yours was all very nice, and I hope it continues.[47]

Contract in hand—and with a chance to look at it more carefully— O'Connor decided not to respond to its legal ramifications, but simply thanked Carver for sending it. But the issue lingered on. She soon wrote Giroux, giving him the exact information he needed to extend his expert opinion: "My copy of the contract came today and I see the clause reads as follows: 'It is understood Catharine Carver will act as editor for this book. If, for any reason, she is unable to do so, the author shall have the option, upon repayment of the advance, of cancelling this contract.' There is no 'void unless' . . . but it is not as bad as I had remembered it. The time limit she put on it is five years, during which time Mr. Ivonovitch [Jovanovich] may decide to sell textbooks exclusively or Miss Carver may take the veil or I may join Uncle Roy and his Red Creek Wranglers."[48]

McKee, prescient in retrospect, raised an interesting speculation in a letter to O'Connor about what would happen if Carver ever left Harcourt, Brace:

I talked to Katy about the cancellation clause in the contract. She doesn't think much can be done about it now and actually I believe the way it is now written not only adequately but completely protects you. If Katy leaves the firm and you decide that you do not want to remain there, all you need do is tell us that you wish to have the contract canceled. Its automatic cancelation might be a great nuisance for, God knows, by that time anything might have happened and you might wish to remain.[49]

Carver remained unaware that Giroux's behind-the-scenes efforts had put the contractual matter to rest. Once Giroux had a chance to review the contact, he wrote to O'Connor, again from his apartment, not without some barbs of his own:

It's a pretty good clause, and more or less fulfills your intention. It puts the burden on you of taking action ("the author shall have the option") whereas the "void unless" clause would have been automatic. But it serves.

I am delighted to hear about the second printing. The book is getting a wonderful press—much more so, it seems to me, than *Wise Blood*, which reverses the usual pattern of the reviewers favoring novels and not favoring books of stories.

Poor Father [Omer] Englebert [author of The *Last of the Conquistadores: Junipero Serra*, 1956], who is trying to get a release from Harcourt, Brace on the grounds that [Eugene] Reynal guaranteed I would be his editor, has just been told in lofty words by Jovanovich: "We have no knowledge of such a guarantee and no record of it. In any event, it is not the kind of special guarantee which we ever make to an author." This is under the date of June 10th, when your contract presumably had been signed. This is the man who, according to *Publishers Weekly*, "once served briefly as an Anglican altar boy." It must have been at Halloween.[50]

Now savvier about contracts, O'Connor thanked McKee for the final version, feeling more comfortable with the stipulations that had been added. She also received a copy of Victor Gollancz's letter from London, as well as a note from Neville Armstrong of Neville Spearman saying *Wise Blood* would be published in England in the very near future. She wondered if she were obligated to Armstrong for her next book of stories, since she felt that only he had an option on the novel. O'Connor asked McKee to return "An Exile in the East," which was not included in the new collection, as she would like to rework it. "I gather it is too much still like it was in *Accent* to be published anywhere else." Her instinct, even at this point, was to account, one way or another, for stories that might go into a *second* collection of stories.

Unfortunately, O'Connor had not asked bottom-line questions about her British publisher, and now she felt the effects of her inattention. In early July, Carver had less than encouraging news: "No, Neville Spearman hasn't gone bankrupt, to the accumulated sorrow of all of us. Elizabeth is trying, as she probably told you, to get another English publisher [Gollancz] to bid enough for the stories to dislodge the option on them from Spearman, and so far a number of other, *good publishers* are interested, so it may yet turn out. McCallum reported that Spearman's London office was practically a rat hole (which doesn't necessarily mean he is poverty stricken, I gather, but certainly he is 'marginal'). Well, we shall see."[51] When Giroux went to London in mid-September, he met with Gollancz and no doubt brought up O'Connor's name.[52] McKee avoided taking responsibility for the Spearman fiasco and suggested in a letter that O'Connor had not paid sufficient attention to the details in the contract, writing,

> Spearman tied you up in an extremely involved manner in the option clauses of his contract with you. He has the right to have first offer of your next novel and also first offer of publishing a volume of your short stories but . . . shall not be bound to give their decision to publish such a volume until they shall have had the opportunity of considering the above mentioned option novel. You will remember that you agreed to sign this contract only after all the leading English publishers had (short sightedly) refused the novel. Gollancz was one of them. The great hope now is that in some manner or other our corresponding agents, A. M. Heath, who handle the British end of our affairs, will be able to persuade Neville Spearman to release you. It's too bad that Gollancz did not "come to" until after you had had your big American press.[53]

Letters at this time from author to agent to editor went back and forth, often filled with niceties, but never showed O'Connor's sharper, more creative side, as if she were holding back for some reason. Likewise

Carver's dutiful replies revealed at this point only moderate interest in O'Connor. "Yes," Carver wrote, "it has been beastly hot, though I hate to admit it because usually I take such pride in being oblivious to the weather. But if your letters from me sound more and more like your institutional fan mail, you will know the reason why. I hope the thirteen peachickens all live to grow tails as splendid as their forefathers, now gracing my mantelpiece. Somehow I think peacocks must manage never to notice the weather."[54] O'Connor, for her part, simply refused to communicate with her editor about what was going on in her creative imagination. As the following exchange demonstrates, both wanted to avoid putting into writing what was really happening in their lives:

Thank you from my mother for the pictures. For myself I think they're horrible but she is overjoyed. I am glad you are not going to use either of those. They are not suitable for anyone but a parent. Thanks for sending one to Neville Spearman. I am wondering if he is ever really going to publish *Wise Blood*. . . .

I have been asked to talk on The Significance of the Short Story (UGH) at a wholesale gathering of the AAUW in Lansing, Michigan next April. It will take me from now until next April to find out what the significance of the short story is. Have you any ideas? I think I will just tell them that this is no concern of the short story writer.

Did you all publish Karl Stern's book, *The Third Revolution*? If you did, the next time Harcourt, Brace elects to send me a book, I wish they would send me that.

The total of peachickens is 16 today.[55]

I am sending you under separate cover a copy of your own book which a man in Chicago terribly wants you to sign. It seemed to me as the simplest thing to do was to send it to you in what we call a "jiffy bag" already stamped and addressed to this man. So all you have to do is sign the book inside, seal up the bag and mail it. . . .

I sent you a copy of Karl Stern's book, along with something else which I thought you would enjoy.

If I ever had any idea as to what the significance of the short story is, the August weather has driven it out of my head. But I'm sure you will do well in Michigan in April.

Can't think of another thing, significant or otherwise [emphasis mine].[56]

———

Here at last are the small glossies. And I am so sorry it has taken such a long time.

Robert Penn Warren wrote today to say how much he liked your book, and to ask us to tell you so. That makes it a clean sweep, I should say.[57]

———

Today I got a letter from a man who said he had spent his childhood among characters such as I had portrayed. Poor man. He said since he had seen them in print they burdened his conscience less.

I would be much obliged if you would send me and charge to me five copies of *A Good Man*. My mother again. She wants to send them to sick friends.[58]

Despite their routine correspondence, Carver forgot to inform O'Connor about subsequent printings of her collection of stories. By late August, O'Connor wondered whether Carver had seen the British edition of *Wise Blood*: "A horrible printing job but a very funny jacket, which I think would stop anybody in a fog."[59] O'Connor learned that a total of 5,500 copies of the American edition were in print, of which about 3,900 had been sold to date.[60] Prompted by the sight the British edition, O'Connor immediately asked Carver about commissioning a French translation, noting, "Apparently the French are interested in Southern literature."[61] Carver's reply offered not the slightest bit of encouragement to O'Connor, a sign that her work as an editor had lost its appeal, most likely due to the same angst that Giroux experienced. In an undated note to McCallum about O'Connor, Carver hinted that she might be formulating plans to leave Harcourt, Brace:

Nothing doing at the moment, and her novel may take 3 more years to finish. Meanwhile, her health worsens. DL [Denver Lindley] should handle, of course, since she met him and liked him, and said jokingly that if I left she would settle for him. The silly clause ought to be changed at once to name him (Mavis McIntosh can handle since Elizabeth McKee will be abroad till January), and I can't imagine Flannery would raise any objection to doing so. If she does I'll try to persuade her personally. Elizabeth McKee was perfectly reasonable about this when I talked to her. Ch.1 of Flannery's novel is in the safe.[62]

One could easily imagine at this time that O'Connor's lack of interest in writing personal, probing letters to her editor might be due to some writer's block or psychological funk, but her letters to Betty Hester beginning about this time are among the most captivating and poignant she ever wrote.

Bolstered by enough good reviews for *A Good Man Is Hard to Find* and the fact that it had been selling well, O'Connor decided to apply again for a Guggenheim Fellowship. Were she to receive this grant, she would have more funds to assist with her medical expenses, as well as the stature she desperately wanted as a writer making significant contributions to American literature. She wrote to Denver Lindley—*not* Catharine Carver—asking for a letter of reference.[63] Lindley replied positively to O'Connor's request in early September and mentioned that the sales figures for *A Good Man Is Hard to Find* had broken 4,000 and were proceeding steadily.[64] In asking Giroux to write a letter of reference—he gave her a high recommendation—she brought him up to date about the British edition of her first novel: "*Wise Blood* finally came out in England and has gotten good reviews. It is printed in off-set and looks as if it will come apart in the hand but has such a jacket as would stop the blindest Englishman in the thickest fog. I think Neville Spearman will do the stories next and not wait on the novel as I have given him to understand it will be a long wait."[65] With a Guggenheim in hand, she would have more incentive to work steadily on her new novel, but unfortunately she was not among the recipients, which included future Nobel Prize laureate Saul Bellow and Civil War historian and novelist Shelby Foote (Walker Percy's best friend).

In early September, as O'Connor was working on chapter two of the novel and feeling as though she were on a treadmill, she informed Macauley that her agent was trying to find a French publisher for her collection of stories. Before long Gallimard had signed a contract to this effect.[66] At the end of the month, she wrote to Carver and also to McKee to explain how her physical condition was affecting the progress of her new novel: "I have been put on crutches on account of this hip of mine and told I will have to use them for a year, possibly two. It's a great nuisance and I am very awkward. . . . It requires a major decision for me to make up my mind to cross the room. However, this may speed up the novel as, once I am seated at the typewriter, I am loath to leave it."[67] Carver responded most sympathetically, though she had no idea of the true extent of O'Connor's illness:

> I am so sorry to hear that you are on crutches—that seems very bad luck. But of course I hope that the doctors may be wrong about how long you will have to stay on them. . . . And of course I hope the novel will go ahead well—for one quite selfish reason: I'm so anxious to read it—but I hate to have literature being served by your discomfort.
>
> I enclose a review from the *Catholic World*, which I think will interest you. It seems a little truncated, but I don't understand the deprecatory tone of the first paragraph. But still, I think it will please you. . . .
>
> Maybe if you just sit very quietly for a while the hip will get better, then you won't need the crutches. I hope so.[68]

Thanks in part to Carver's diligence, O'Connor was kept abreast of reviews of her book, which always interested her. In late October, Carver wrote, "I am enclosing the reviews, which I expect you may have seen from the *Kenyon*, and from the *Sewanee* reviews. I am awfully pleased that the stories are getting this kind of serious attention, however belated. . . . I'm so glad you are getting around more easily. I hope the crutches won't last too long."[69] Carver had served as O'Connor's editor for seven months, and though she had seemingly earned the author's trust, there is almost no evidence from her letters that she understood either the nature of O'Connor's lupus or, at least initially, the direction that O'Connor hoped to take with her fiction. If Harcourt, Brace, as a firm, felt that O'Connor was among the better writers in their stable, then a more concerted effort should have been made to ensure that she knew, in some deeply felt way, that she had its total support. But something was wrong in New York, and it was bound to manifest itself one way or another. When Carver returned the typescript of *A Good Man Is Hard to Find* in mid-November with a polite but laconic note, O'Connor might have sensed that her editor was cleaning out her files.[70]

Giroux had taken a late fall trip to Europe, and while in Rome he had a pleasant meeting with Gordon, as he informed O'Connor in early December: "We strolled through the beautiful gardens of the American Academy, high above the city. She was hoping you would make a trip abroad before her return in February."[71] Giroux sent O'Connor two of the thirty books he edited recently: *The Grand Mademoiselle*, by Francis Steegmuller, and *The Selected Letters of Henry James*, edited by Leon Edel.[72] This contact reassured O'Connor that her former editor continued to think about her. She needed such support when she read Carver's unforgettable letter in early December, one that she most likely sensed was coming:

> No point in a preamble: the fact is that I resigned from Harcourt, Brace as of December 15. It was not a sudden decision, and it was essentially a personal one: I haven't much liked myself in my role here for some time. Having decided, it seemed simpler just to get out, and then think what to do next. I have no plans at the moment: I'll have to get a job, of course, since I have to eat, but I have no idea whether or not it will be in publishing. I'll let you know what happens to me. Of course I'd like very much to keep in touch with you. . . .
>
> I know this will be disturbing news for you, and I'm glad I was able to tell you before Elizabeth takes off for England. But please understand that this is merely my personal gesture, and no great upheaval in Harcourt, Brace. Everything here remains as it is. Since you know Denver Lindley, I am sure you know that your interests here are perfectly safe with him. He'll be writing you soon. And I'll write you myself when this paroxysm somewhat subsides. I'm so glad you came up last summer and that I did get to know you; I'm just very sorry I couldn't continue to work with you here. I do answer letters, in private life, so please write. And all the best to you.[73]

Understandably, O'Connor had little recourse but to contact her agent, not wanting to deal at this point with anyone at Harcourt, Brace. Three days after this letter was written, she informed McKee about Carver's departure and indicated that she would stay with the firm on one condition, that Lindley become her editor, though clearly her feelings were quite ambivalent at this point. "Will you please talk to Giroux about it," she suggested, "because I wouldn't leave Harcourt, Brace unless he was willing to take me on." Naturally she contacted Giroux directly, expressing her exasperation, not knowing exactly what to do but indicating that she would wait until McKee returned from England in mid-January 1956 before making a decision. "I like Denver Lindley," she wrote, "but he is the only one there now that I know anything about; I mean anything about good. In any case that is the situation and I thought you would like to know about it."[74] O'Connor's relationship with Lindley up to this point had seemed more social than anything else. Perhaps because Lindley, who clearly felt comfortable with European authors, inherited O'Connor on the rebound, he and O'Connor had a most tenuous relationship.

Noted eventually for his translations into English of works by Thomas Mann, André Maurois, and Erich Maria Remarque, Lindley, a graduate of Princeton, joined *Collier's* magazine in 1927, where he served as fiction editor. He then was hired by Appleton-Century in 1944 as editor in chief of the trade books division, and two years later he moved to Henry Holt & Company and eventually to Harcourt, Brace. In his letter to O'Connor, Lindley said they were "a good deal startled by the suddenness of her [Carver's] decision to go" and he hoped that O'Connor would be willing to accept him as her new editor.[75] About all that one can say is that Lindley's letters to O'Connor were always dutifully professional, fairly generic, and normally ended with a polite greeting to O'Connor's mother, whom he twice met. It was only a matter of time before he, too, would be further caught up in the Harcourt, Brace maelstrom.

O'Connor had to make one of the most important decisions of her career as the year ended. She had met once Lindley in New York but never had a genuine heart-to-heart discussion with him and had no idea if he would really prove to be the editor she needed. Wasting no time, Giroux wrote O'Connor an honest, thoughtful letter, including a contract offer, which pleased her very much. He sketched out the important variables that were part of the equation that O'Connor would have to solve. Also important, Giroux, as mentioned in a letter to O'Connor, had taken the time to visit with Carver, precisely to understand the nature of her situation and thus how best to help O'Connor:

I heard the news about Katy [Carver] on Friday, and the next day had a long talk with her at her apartment. I understand perfectly her reasons for deciding to leave; they were to some extent my own reasons for leaving. But Katy needs a job and it was principally to talk about that that I called on her. The best prospect seems to be with Anchor books at Doubleday. She also has a chance at one of the big magazines, but I hope she stays with book publishing. I have always admired Katy, and I admire her more than ever for a decision which took courage.

I think, as she does, that Denver Lindley is a fine person. However, you ought to know that Denver has never liked your books. He and Alfred Kazin both voted against *Wise Blood*; this was before Katy joined the staff. In the end, he raised no objections in view of praise from Caroline Gordon, whom he admires very much. Naturally he will now want to publish your books, and certainly he is never going to admit that he had anything but the highest regard for your work from the beginning. But you want to know the whole truth. At the same time I admit that Denver is a man of good will, and he will do his utmost to protect your interests at Harcourt, Brace, but the real character of the firm is becoming only too evident. They simply should not have allowed Katy to go. Elizabeth McKee is right in saying you're not obliged to leave Harcourt, Brace. Yet the very thing you protected yourself against in your contract has now happened.

If Katy goes to another publishing house, you will doubtless want to go with her. I hope, for your own sake, you will not stay with Harcourt, Brace. I will be ready to draw up a contract on the same terms as your present one, including a guarantee that I will be your editor, whenever you say so. I have never met Elizabeth McKee; I arranged all your contracts with Mavis McIntosh. I am therefore at a disadvantage. But the decision is up to you and I urge you to exercise the action which you (rather than she) insisted on having in the contract. The news of Katy's resignation must be very upsetting, and I don't want to upset you further. Yet in honesty I must give you the whole background and, if you don't go with Katy, I hope you will come with us. It was good of you to write me, and I thank you. I cordially hope the Guggenheim comes through without delay.[76]

Had O'Connor known, she might have been consoled by the fact that Lindley had turned down Walker Percy's first novel *The Charterhouse* in 1953, which Allen Tate, at the urging of his wife, Caroline Gordon, had submitted to Harcourt, Brace. Nevertheless, with this offer of a contract from Giroux, plus having him as an editor who admired her work and was most willing to stay the course with her at his successful firm, O'Connor wrote to Lindley on December 16. She must have reflected long and hard about this letter, which manifests loyalty to the firm that had published her two books, though she addresses Lindley reservedly: "I was much distressed to hear from Catharine that she has left and I think the loss is Harcourt, Brace's. I'll be very glad indeed to accept you for my editor; the only question in my mind, after having two such respected ones depart from under with the year, is how long you will be my editor. My sense of the stability of editorial positions at Harcourt, Brace is not being increased with time."[77] She went on to say that she had written to McKee and asked her what she thought she should do. In reply, McKee informed her that the terms of the contract did not call for any action on O'Connor's part, something that gave her some relief, especially as McKee would be in England during any contractual changes that Harcourt, Brace might wish to negotiate. O'Connor wanted Lindley's name substituted in the clause she had put into the revised contract, since it was only his presence there that inclined her to stay. Thus O'Connor's response, less than enthusiastic, prefigures her future conduct should the nature of her contractual relationship with Harcourt, Brace change in the slightest.

Unwilling to play both sides at once, O'Connor wrote to Giroux in early January 1956 as she went through a serious process of discernment, admitting,

I have not heard what Catharine is going to do but for myself I have decided that any change right now would be upsetting; and since both you and she say that Denver will look after my interests, I have decided to do the same thing you advised me to do last summer, that is, make them put a clause in the contract saying he will be my editor or I can leave. This will still keep me one step removed from McCallum, etc.

As to Denver's not liking my books, that doesn't bother me. I guess they are disliked by some of the best people; anyway, I won't embarrass him by consulting him on their merits.

When he leaves there, you will doubtless be hearing from me again, and in the meantime I'll always be very grateful for your help and advice.

Robert F. [Fitzgerald] sent me the first seven books of the *Odyssey* and they seem very fine.

The best new year to you.[78]

Lindley was quick to respond to her acceptance, making overtures to visit her in Georgia—though both remembered that he had once before failed to show up at Andalusia. He made a request about Gordon's novel: as Harcourt, Brace would be publishing Gordon's *The Malefactors* in early March, he wondered in a roundabout way if O'Connor might like to give a blurb after reading the advance page proofs. He added, "My projected trip is already taking shape and I hope it may be possible for you to spare me an hour or two sometime fairly early next month—with proper warning of course."[79] O'Connor replied with reserve and caution. After Sue Jenkins, a literary agent and Gordon's friend, informed O'Connor about the publication of this book, she said she would be willing to send Lindley some names of people who might like to receive a copy.[80] How seriously would O'Connor approach Gordon's novel? She had written Betty Hester in August 1955 that Gordon is "as good as anybody [writing fiction], though I have not read much of it myself." This astounding admission by O'Connor shows how little she looked to Gordon as a model fiction writer even after all the time and effort Gordon had spent reading and analyzing her fiction. She subsequently backed away from giving the blurb because she did not think the novel entirely successful. She did, however, write a review for the Savannah-Atlanta diocesan *Bulletin* (March 31, 1956), stating, "Making grace believable to the contemporary reader is the almost insurmountable problem of the novelist who writes from the standpoint of Christian orthodoxy. *The Malefactors* is undoubtedly the most serious and successful fiction statement of a conversion in this country to date." Her comment to the *Bulletin*'s editor reveals more of what she actually thought: "Most of your readers wouldn't like *The Malefactors* if it were favorably reviewed by Pius XII."[81] O'Connor had the luxury of accepting or rejecting such invitations and of regularly deciding which books she wanted to review for the *Bulletin*. In quantifying these reviews, Carter Martin noted that O'Connor chose a broad range of works, reviewing 143 titles in 120 separate reviews between 1956 and 1964. The works are distributed as follows: fifty religious and homiletic, twenty-one biographies and saints' lives, nineteen books of sermons and theology, seventeen fiction, eight literary criticism, six psychology and science, four history, four literary letters, three intellectual history and criticism, and one art criticism.[82] These reviews constitute hidden testimony to O'Connor's deep desire to grow intellectually—and most notably in the formation of her faith.

At least for the moment, O'Connor had made up her mind to stay with Harcourt, Brace, though her heart seemed to be holding back on her decision. As he noted, Giroux understood her dilemma:

> Thanks for letting me know your decision so promptly. I understand and sympathize with your desire not to move from a list which already has two of your books on it. Changes are upsetting, and I only hope that Messrs. J. [Jovanovich] and M. [McCallum] know it. I am glad you've decided to put in that clause (but don't be surprised if they balk at it again); you really do need it. When we talked about Catharine that day at the New Weston, it was inconceivable that she'd leave, but she did. Incidentally she's had offers from Little, Brown, the *Atlantic*, and Doubleday but said no. I hope she'll find what she wants. As for Denver not liking your books (I only know about *Wise Blood*, actually), I am sure his ignorance is not invincible.
>
> Cal [Lowell] is here for the meeting of the poetry judges of the National Book Award. In the fiction department, Cal and I both hope the award goes to *A Good Man Is Hard to Find*.[83]

In January 1956, Lindley dictated a letter to O'Connor, maintaining the necessary contact with her. He had talked to McKee on the phone and agreed to have the substitution of names carried out in her contract, and he assured O'Connor that, as far as he was concerned, there would be no more changes made. "Barring what the underwriters rather shockingly call an act of God, I intend to stay right here, a place I like very much."[84] He appreciated her willingness to help with Gordon's book and looked forward to reading her comments. "My trip, by the way, has been postponed again and now," he continued, "it seems likely I will turn up in Atlanta about the twenty-third of February. I hope these changes do not suggest a weather vane: the present one was made necessary by the fact that Eudora is coming here for the opening of *The Ponder Heart* play." To balance that bad news, he reported that in a phone call with Gordon in Princeton he had learned that Maurice-Edgar Coindreau had just made a great discovery, "A most brilliant young American writer whom he intended to translate into French—Flannery O'Connor. I have known Coindreau quite well for years and I would like to say for what it's worth that I think there is no better translator—however slow he may be in making his discoveries."

O'Connor wrote to Lindley again on January 15, 1956, reconfirming her commitment to him and Harcourt, Brace:

> I have read Caroline's novel with all my usual admiration for everything she writes. I look at it from the underside, thinking how difficult all this was to do because I know nothing harder than making good people believable. It would be impertinent for me to comment on the book, simply because I have too much to learn from it.
>
> I am enclosing a list of people that I think ought to know about it. I know you have a list of all the obvious people so I've included on my list only the ones I think you may not have. They are not important people in any literary sense but are people I feel for one reason or another will talk or write about the book and its implications. Robert Fitzgerald would know of a few more if you asked him. His current address is: La Mandrella, Sestri Levante (Genoa), Italy.
>
> Am I supposed to return the page proofs? Also does Caroline know I have seen them? I would like to write her that I like the book but not unless she knows that I have read the page proofs. If it would be better to wait until the advance copies have gone out, I'll wait.
>
> It would be good to be translated by a Maurice Coindreau but I suppose that is up to Gallimard. I have just read an unpleasant book called *The American Novel in France*, which says that the translations are usually terrible and that the French think Erskine Caldwell is a great writer [Giroux edited seven of Caldwell's books]. Apparently they (the publishers) get any translator who cares to call himself one.
>
> I sent my copy of the contract to Elizabeth yesterday.[85]

Lindley, not surprised that O'Connor had liked Gordon's novel, related that Gordon indeed knew that O'Connor had seen the page proofs.[86] As Gordon left Princeton to teach in Kansas, she was glad to learn from Lindley of O'Connor's friendly support. Curiously, both women shared the same editor at this point in time, though not for long. In the case of Gordon, it had to do with Dorothy Day, a saintly Catholic peace activist who absolutely did not want *The Malefactors* dedicated to her. Having received page proofs from Lindley, Day had been incensed by what she perceived as Gordon's references to so-called Black Masses.[87] O'Connor wrote to her new editor about Day's reaction, "I wish Caroline had dedicated the book to 'My Dog, Spot,' or anybody."[88] Day's name was removed before the book was finally published. As Paul Elie notes, "*The Malefactors* was an example of the kind of Catholic novel O'Connor would never write, one in which good and thoughtful people discuss the quandaries of religious faith in an earnest and intelligent way."[89] After the publication of *The Malefactors* and a party in her honor in Kansas, Gordon left Harcourt, Brace and returned to Viking.

Jovanovich, in his role as president of Harcourt, Brace, wrote to O'Connor making clear his interpretation of the clause in question: Lindley would act as editor of her next book, and if, for any reason, he was unable to do so, O'Connor would have the option, upon repayment of the advance, of canceling the contract.[90] O'Connor's courteous reply closed the matter, at least temporarily: "I am pleased too that this revision could be settled upon as my association with Harcourt, Brace has always been very pleasant."[91] Jovanovich was pleased to learn that O'Connor hoped to have another collection of stories ready, the first of which would be entitled "You Can't Be Any Poorer Than Dead," before she finished her novel, though she was still contemplating using that story as the novel's first chapter.

It was clear to O'Connor, who was willing to act as the gracious hostess at Andalusia, that the letters from Lindley did not address even her basic imaginative concerns. In his reply he thanked her for her support of Gordon's novel and told her that the dedication had been removed at the joint request of Caroline and the dedicatee. Day was relieved by this and even more by the removal of the objectionable reference. He continued, "*At the risk of boring you to death with my plans*, let me say that they now look pretty definite. I'll turn up on your doorstep around noon on Friday, February 24th. My plan is to drive from Macon and take you to lunch, if I may. Should this for any reason be inconvenient for you, please don't hesitate to let me know. I am leaving here on the afternoon of the 23rd" (emphasis mine).[92] O'Connor let Lindley know that she was expecting him and gave him tongue-in-cheek directions: "Just to insure your arrival at my doorstep on the 24th, I think I'd better tell you where it is: four miles outside of Milledgeville on the road to Eatonton—a two story white farm house without television aerial. It's not hard to find if you know where you're going."[93] Lindley's visits to Georgia and Kansas seem to have been quite successful, though Gordon must have been going through some trying moments of her own, as O'Connor mentions in a letter to Lindley dated March 18:

> We hope by now you have safely returned yourself to New York and also that you'll come to see us again. My mother enjoyed your visit very much and so did I. I hope you didn't have to look at too many local monuments. . . .
>
> I was sickened by the *Time* review of *The Malefactors* but someone wrote me there was a good review in *Books on Trial*. I am reviewing it for the Georgia diocesan paper, *The Bulletin*. This is read only by the clergy and elderly laity of the diocese of Savannah-Atlanta and I am allowed only one double-spaced typewritten page and my effort will mostly be in vain, but I'll send you a copy. Thanks very much for the issue of *Critique*. I managed to quote from it in my review.[94]

Some of those who received copies of the novel at O'Connor's suggestion were offended by the book, though most seemed to rally behind it, writing favorable reviews.[95] Undeterred by Gordon's problems, O'Connor continued to work steadily, and by mid-March she had finished writing "Greenleaf" and sent it to John Crowe Ransom; it would be published in the *Kenyon Review* (Summer 1956) and win a first-place, three-hundred-dollar O. Henry award. She stayed fixed on her work and refrained from involvement in any outside distractions, such as the politics of the Cold War. In no way did she want to offend her country or embarrass herself, and thus she turned down emphatically any publication of her work in communist Poland or Czechoslovakia.[96]

Giroux—busy editing twenty-seven books for the fall catalogue, including one that pleased him immensely, Berryman's *Homage to Mistress Bradstreet*—was then planning to assist T. S. Eliot, who was arriving in New York in late April on the *Queen Mary*.[97] As usual, Eliot had made appointments in advance, particularly to go to the University of Minnesota, at the invitation of Tate, before heading to Washington, DC, Boston, and finally, in early May, back to New York, where he would return to England in early June.[98] Giroux thoroughly enjoyed these visits from his English friend, though they required an investment of considerable time and energy behind the scenes.

O'Connor's luck with her British publisher continued to trouble her, and even McCallum could not resolve the situation. Neville Spearman was not really good enough for O'Connor, he believed, yet they had an option on *A Good Man Is Hard to Find*. In early June McCallum assured O'Connor that he had done and would continue to do everything possible to get her work into the hands of a topnotch British publisher. "I doubt even now that there is a single one in London who hasn't heard about *A Good Man Is Hard to Find*," he wrote.[99] O'Connor's response was to the point: "I had supposed that Mr. Neville Armstrong would be bankrupt before he got around to publishing my stories but it seems he manages to hang on. I grudgingly admire his tenacity even while I would like a better English publisher. In any case, he has no option on the next book. My mother and I enjoyed Denver Lindley's visit to us in February and we hope that if you find yourself in this direction you will stop by too."[100] When O'Connor wrote to Lindley in early July, she mentioned that she had just returned to Houghton Mifflin a contract for reprinting "The Artificial Nigger" in a Martha Foley collection. When he next wrote O'Connor, his first two sentences undoubtedly brought a smile to her lips: "Sins of omission are my stock in trade. You, on the other hand, are probably just as glad not to be bothered by letters—*especially when they have nothing to say*" (emphasis mine).[101] Though these conversations had diminished to a trickle, O'Connor was nevertheless pleased to receive from McCallum the three books she had requested: Moore's *The Life of Man with God*, Eliot's *Essays on Elizabethan Drama*, and Forster's *Aspects of the Novel*.[102]

O'Connor was at a low point in her life, and her relationship with Harcourt, Brace was disastrous, barely rising above the trivial. Her lack of verve at this time is quite understandable; her illness had reached such a stage that she was prompted to consider the end of her life on this earth, as she wrote Hester in late June 1956: "I have never been anywhere but sick. . . . Sickness before death is a very appropriate thing and I don't think those who don't have it miss one of God's mercies." She had reached a stage even in her spiritual life where she rarely articulated her thoughts about lupus, except to her friend Elizabeth Fenwick Way, who had a milder form of the disease. O'Connor's search for spiritual equilibrium as she entered a very dark night were undoubtedly occasioned by a greater understanding of the demands of her illness—and how it had affected her father toward the end of his life. More than ever before, she had to keep her focus clear and sharp and not be dragged down by New York's lack of response to her work.

Nevertheless, it was difficult for O'Connor to keep an even keel, especially when her work took on a visibility she could not have foreseen. After a Hollywood TV writer wanted to acquire the rights for a production of "The Life You Save May Be Your Own" but the initial offer fell through, the Music Corporation of America's Revue Productions increased their offer from $850 to $1,000. O'Connor agreed, thinking that either *General Electric Theater*, hosted by Ronald Reagan, or *Schlitz Playhouse of Stars* would be a good showcase for her work. The new contract for *A Good Man Is Hard to Find* unfortunately gave Harcourt, Brace control of the TV rights and also one-third of the sale price. Once McKee had the approval of Lindley and McCallum, as well as O'Connor, the play went into rehearsal.[103] But when O'Connor saw the *Schlitz Playhouse of Stars* production, which had been delayed until March 1, she was definitely not pleased, calling the performance, in a letter to George Haslam written immediately afterward, "slop of the third water." She had initially treated the proposal with indifference, as if it would just happen and she would not feel any repercussions, except to gain financially from the production, but she miscalculated how her story would be adapted and produced. "Elizabeth McKee," O'Connor told Lindley in a letter of early September 1956, "wrote me that Harcourt, Brace had waived the one-third [share of rights sale] and substituted the 10 percent agreement on television rights to my stories. This was very nice and I appreciate it. We don't have a television so I'll be spared the viewing of the story."[104] As she finished her story, "A View of the Woods" (published in *Partisan Review*, Fall 1957), she informed Lindley that he would be welcome again at Andalusia; the total peachicken population had reached twenty-seven, but they had not started ganging up on visitors yet.[105] Lindley continued to vacillate, informing O'Connor that he might cancel the visit.[106] One could well wonder which of O'Connor's categories—Very Irksome, Medium Irksome, Rare Irksome, Non-Irksome—she might have applied to Lindley at this point in their relationship.

Not uncharacteristically, Lindley's fuel gauge, like Carver's at the end of her employment at Harcourt, Brace, seems to have been running close to empty. Like Giroux and Carver, he never communicated to O'Connor the problems at Harcourt, Brace. In late October, he visited Toccoa in northeast Georgia but found no time in his schedule to make his way to Milledgeville.[107] Connor's Christmas greeting to him stayed light and courteous.[108] Lindley's tardy Christmas note, however, reveals that he had seen O'Connor's fellow Georgian writer Lillian Smith, then working on her manuscript of *One Hour*, at her home on Old Screamer Mountain. The two writers had met in December 1955 but had little in common.[109] Though snubbed by Lindley's apparent indifference to her, she was still aware that she had Giroux's friendship and support. And Giroux was doing well: having finished editing twenty-three books for the spring 1957 catalogue, he was busy preparing the fall list.[110] One of the books that pleased him most was *The Diary of "Helena Morley,"* by Elizabeth Bishop, a copy of which Bishop would send to O'Connor.

Lindley visited O'Connor a second time on May 21, 1957, though according to her next letter to him, nothing of great importance was discussed about her work in progress or what she hoped to accomplish in the coming years. "We enjoyed your visit and look forward to the next one," she wrote. "You came a day too soon as far as the excitement was concerned as on Wednesday, Mr. Parker discovered a rattlesnake near the chicken yard; but all he did was throw a crate on top of it and run, so it is still at large and maybe we can produce it the next time you come."[111] Subsequent communications between them focused on inconsequential farm talk, revealing nothing about O'Connor's literary activity. Nevertheless, O'Connor continued to compose page after page, knowing that her writing depended on her quiet inner strength. She mentioned in a letter to Maryat Lee in June 1957 that she was "glad to be a hermit novelist." By late September the novel showed signs of progress but was not anywhere near finished. She wrote to Betty Hester in late October, "I have put up the novel for a short spell and am writing a story and it's like a vacation in the mountains." Judging solely by the Lindley-O'Connor correspondence from this time period, one could infer that O'Connor had retreated into a very private part of herself, but such was not the case. She maintained regular contact with friends. Her correspondence for the year 1957, especially to and from Maryat Lee, a rather eccentric, definitely flamboyant, and often outrageous playwright living in New York, whose brother was the president of Georgia State College for Women, reveals the expansive side of O'Connor's personality as they discussed matters of race and religion. In addition, her letters to Betty Hester,

Louise Abbot, Cecil Dawkins, and Elizabeth Fenwick Way show the wide range of her thoughts and problems. Still, she believed that she needed to work as steadily as she possibly could. When and if another office shuffle occurred at Harcourt, Brace, she would be ready. This was not a time to slack off, inventing excuses for non-productivity because of the lackadaisical attitude of others.

By late November, she was reworking "The Enduring Chill," a draft of which she had finished a few weeks before, and was undecided whether she liked it or not. After Gordon and Tate read a copy of this story, O'Connor wanted to send Gordon another draft, though before Christmas she tore it up and was redrafting it again.[112] The story, which eventually appeared in the July 1958 issue of *Harper's*, might be a reflection of her own psychological state: it deals with a young man, Asbury Fox, returning from school in New York, who has premonitions of his own death. "He saw that for the rest of his days, frail, racked, but enduring, he would live in the face of a purifying terror. A feeble cry, a last impossible protest escaped him. But the Holy Ghost, emblazoned in ice instead of fire, continued, implacable to descend."[113] Thoughts of death, particularly a sense of her own mortality, weighed heavily on O'Connor's psyche. Reluctantly, she agreed to join her mother and a group of Catholics making a seventeen-day pilgrimage to Rome and Lourdes, a trip that just might have restorative effects. As she planned for the trip to New York and then Europe, she made an appointment to see her editor on April 22, 1958; she wanted to show her mother the new Harcourt, Brace offices at 750 Third Avenue.[114]

Lindley, however, had vacated his old office permanently and taken a position at Viking.[115] It could not have come at a more awkward time for O'Connor, yet her note in early April to the Fitzgeralds shows that she was taking things in stride: "Denver Lindley has just left Harcourt, Brace so I am in search of a publisher. Two or three are in search of me and tomorrow the new forces at Harcourt are coming down here for 'tea.' I called my agent up to ask her what she thought and she said, 'Put some poison in it.'" Lindley's treatment of O'Connor, while superficially cordial, had not boded well for their continued relationship. Unlike Giroux and Carver, he must have felt incredible pressure at work simply to leave and not to reach out to her with some explanation. Calmly, O'Connor accepted McKee's counsel and made up her mind to back away gracefully from everyone at Harcourt, Brace and accept Giroux's long-standing offer. She informed McKee,

On second and better thought I am going to take your advice about not seeing Dan Wickenden [an editor at Harcourt, Brace]. Don't make the appointment with him. Since I have already made up my mind to leave them, there is no need to go through that; also would be unfair to him as they would think I was going to leave because I didn't like him.

I'll write Mr. McCallum a note and say I prefer to be with Giroux, as on the two previous books, and that you will see him about the whatever.

I don't want this hanging over me in Europe.

Ask for what you want from FS&C but don't get me owing them anything or paying income tax etc. That money is nothing to me.[116]

Upset by O'Connor's decision, McCallum, accompanied by colleague George L. White, flew to Atlanta and then drove to Milledgeville to have a heart-to-heart talk with O'Connor. She agreed to see them, but without necessarily acquiescing to their invitation to remain with the firm. Much wiser than before, she held her ground, though she briefly equivocated about seeing Wickenden.[117] In his letter to O'Connor, White gives the impression that none of the three parties seriously addressed Lindley's resignation or O'Connor's decision not to remain with Harcourt, Brace. He and McCallum had enjoyed the wonderful Georgia weather, he noted, especially the tour of Andalusia, and hoped the delightful springtime might serve as a prelude to O'Connor's trip to Europe. His plan seemed relatively guileless: after O'Connor had talked to Wickenden in New York about the possibility of staying at Harcourt, Brace, she and her mother might have lunch with him. White wrote to O'Connor that he did not want to inconvenience her in any way, either physically or emotionally. She should feel totally free to leave Harcourt, Brace as her publisher, and if she did so he wished her a happy trip.[118]

Before beginning her journey, O'Connor wrote to her good friend Ashley Brown on April 14, "It appears that my connection with Harcourt, Brace is about to be severed. Denver Lindley has left them, and I have an escape clause in my contract that says I can leave if he is not my editor. I think I will take up where I left off when they began changing editors so fast—with Bob Giroux at Farrar, Straus." (Her decision to leave seems likely to have been a good one. Years later, Eudora Welty, greatly upset with the way that Wickenden wanted to edit her novel *Losing Battles*, left Harcourt, Brace, as she explained to him when they met in New York.[119]

Before his departure from Harcourt, Brace, Giroux had edited three of Welty's books. O'Connor would have been astounded to realize the similarities of their publishing histories at crucial times in their lives.) Once this weighty decision had been made in apparent great peace, O'Connor could turn her attention to preparing for her spiritual journey and making new friends in New York as she became acquainted with the editorial staff at Farrar, Straus & Cudahy.

CHAPTER SEVEN

Flannery O'Connor, Robert Giroux

1958–1964

Greatly pleased at becoming once again O'Connor's editor, as he mentioned to me on several occasions, Giroux immediately drew up a contract for *The Violent Bear It Away*. For her part, O'Connor took great comfort in being welcomed to a distinguished publishing house by an attentive editor who, season after season, had published the works of celebrated authors. Communication among the principal parties now moved at a rapid pace, in an exchange beginning in mid-April 1958:

> Dear Flannery,
> I can't tell you how happy I am that we shall be publishing your novel.
>   I have sent the contracts off to Elizabeth McKee this afternoon. I assure you that we shall do the very best publishing job of which we are capable.
>   As you know, I am escorting the Eliots to Texas on Monday, and I shall be able to see you in New York before your departure for Europe. Roger Straus and Sheila Cudahy share my enthusiasm for your work, and they are anxious to meet you, but they thoughtfully suggest that it might be an imposition and an inconvenience during your short stay in New York. If it is agreeable to you, they would prefer to make it on your return, when I too look forward to seeing you.

Incidentally, I don't want you to get the idea that publishers without Madison Avenue addresses are slouches. We should be very happy to provide a limousine to meet you at the airport on Tuesday, if you would like it. Just pick up the nearest telephone and send me a collect telegram stating your flight number and arrival time and a limousine will be there.[1]

Dear Mr. McCallum and Mr. White:
It was very nice to see you both last Friday in spite of what was for me the very distressing news you brought.

I had thought that I would wait until our trip to Italy is over before I made up my mind what I wanted to do about the situation that has presented itself. However, since this is a considerable worry, I do not want it hanging over me for the next three weeks.

My association with Harcourt, Brace has been so pleasant that it is indeed painful to break it off now. However, I feel that a second novel is a crucial time for any writer and that it will be to my own best interest to be with an editor I have had before. Mr. Giroux is an old friend and has worked on both my books and so I am going to ask his firm to take me on.

I have talked to Miss McKee about this over the telephone and she too believes that this is the thing for me to do. She will see you about the return of the advance and such details as may come up.

Thank you for your kindness and interest and know that I am very pleased to have at least two books on your list. I also hope you will come to see us again the next time you are in Georgia.[2]

Dear Bob,
I'm delighted with these arrangements, and feel as if I am properly back where I started from.

I am going to stop in New York on my way back, only just long enough to get through the customs and get a plane to Atlanta, so if Miss Cudahy and Mr. Straus are not busy Tuesday I'd like to try to meet them then.

Editors seem to move about so perhaps you will be down this way sometime and I can talk to you about the novel itself.

The limousine to meet us at the airport would be a great help as I am on crutches and haven't attempted the city before in this fashion. We come in Monday on Delta flight 120 at 4:34 in the afternoon at Idlewild.

I hope you and the Eliots enjoy Texas. A man I know in Austin sends me a paper called the *Lone Star Catholic* and I have a mental picture of what a lone star Catholic should look like.[3]

Though Giroux informed O'Connor that his flight for Texas would be departing just as hers was arriving from Europe, his assistant Anne Brooks Murray met her and her mother before their outbound journey and took them to the Vanderbilt Hotel. She met with Sheila Cudahy and Roger Straus on Tuesday, as arranged by McKee.[4] In spite of a trying schedule, Giroux made every effort for O'Connor to be properly welcomed by her new publishers.

Not accepting defeat easily, McCallum wanted to keep his hat in the ring, even trying to curry her favor by ranking O'Connor among her peer group (she was, he wrote, one of their three or four best writers and certainly in the top five or six writers in the country). In their discussion at Andalusia, he had told her of his belief that a writer of her attainments should not have to be concerned with such secondary problems as what editor and what publisher handles her work. He was deeply upset that she had been troubled during the past weeks by these very problems. The letter she had written him disturbed him in a way that he felt he could not let the situation drop: "I am forced to say—as I think—that you are unfairly punishing Harcourt, Brace. Mr. Lindley's resignation was literally a resignation; he was not dismissed. Accordingly, I feel that we should not be chastised because of his resignation."[5] He asked O'Connor to defer her final decision until after she returned from her trip abroad and perhaps had a chance to talk to him again. Her scheduled talk with Wickenden, he believed, would give her a fuller sense of their high regard for her. But O'Connor would not be persuaded otherwise, even thinking it best not to see Wickenden.

Dear Mr. McCallum:
I am sorry that you consider my leaving Harcourt, Brace unfair, but I believe it was clearly understood when I signed the contract for the novel in 1955 that Mr. Lindley's leaving the company for whatever reason would void the contract.

Since 1955 I have had three editors at Harcourt, Brace. Mr. Wickenden would make the fourth. This is just too many.

I decided not to see Mr. Wickenden because it might then appear that I was not staying with Harcourt, Brace because I did not think he would make me a good editor. I am sure he would but I want to be somewhere where the editorial position is longer lived. All these changes are very upsetting and I have regretted each one.

Please be assured that I regret this one also but that I cannot reconsider my decision to leave.[6]

In her letter to Hester about leaving Harcourt, Brace, O'Connor cited for herself the very reason why Giroux had originally left Harcourt, Brace: "I have a new publisher. My editor at Harcourt, Brace resigned suddenly. Three editors I have had resigned from there in 3 years. It seems the place is being taken over by the textbook end of the firm and these men don't know anything about literature. . . . Tuesday in New York I'll sign a contract with Farrar, Straus & Cudahy. I'll be back with the editor I had at Harcourt for both *Wise Blood* and *A Good Man*. He was the first one [of my editors] and the best and a very nice person, so I am cheered by all this. They have given me a much better contract and when I get home, I'll bear down on getting this novel finished." While in New York, O'Connor also met with Gordon and had a chance to explain her return to Giroux.

Given Eliot's preeminent stature among poets and playwrights, it is not surprising that Giroux decided to keep his commitment to the Eliots over this meeting with O'Connor, especially as O'Connor's decision to change publishers had occurred unannounced. Once the Eliots arrived in New York, they stayed at the River Club, located at Fifty-Second Street and the East River. Eliot wanted to limit his engagements, just seeing old friends such as Marianne Moore, Reinhold Niebuhr, and Djuna Barnes. He and his wife, Valerie, had a private dinner with Giroux and Charles Reilly, and another with the Strauses, who invited Edmund and Elena Wilson and Jacques Barzun. Giroux accompanied the Eliots to Southern Methodist University in Dallas, where Eliot never faltered as he read his poetry with great attention while a violent rainstorm raged outside.[7] Eliot also traveled to Cambridge, Massachusetts, where his sister lived, spending three weeks there before returning to New York. He sailed to Southampton on the *Queen Elizabeth* at the end of May.[8] To ensure that each segment of Eliot's trip was prepared in advance, in addition to orchestrating the demanding tasks of his own office, Giroux had to use all the organizational skills he possessed.

Having taken care of the business at hand with great aplomb, O'Connor and her mother joined Monsignor T. James McNamara of Savannah and ten others on a scheduled pilgrimage to Europe. The O'Connors altered the itinerary to suit their own desires, particularly as they wanted to meet the Fitzgeralds in Milan on April 24, 1958, and then drive south to their home in Levanto, where they spent a delightful four days.[9] Sally subsequently accompanied the two women to Rome (a round-faced O'Connor appears in several official photos standing just behind Pope Pius XII), then by plane to Lourdes in southern France (where William Sessions, a convert to Catholicism, joined them), and finally to Paris. Staying at the Hôtel de la Grotte, seeing infirmed pilgrims on the grounds at Lourdes, walking in an evening procession around the basilica with Sessions for about an hour saying the Rosary, and taking a quick dip in the cold waters had a positive effect on O'Connor as she witnessed firsthand the faith of many who had come from distant places seeking a cure. The town of Lourdes, however, did not merit her unfettered praise; she found the village pockmarked with shops selling religious kitsch—right up to the entrance of the grotto. "Here the heavy hand of the prelate smacks down on free enterprise and it's a pity the whole town can't be controlled the way the grotto is," she wrote to Elizabeth Bishop.[10]

A few days later Maurice-Edgar Coindreau, who had been working on the French translation of *Wise Blood*, accompanied Regina O'Connor and Sally Fitzgerald on a whirlwind tour of the Champs-Élysées, an area of Paris he told me he had not seen since the days of World War II. O'Connor informed Coindreau later that year that she hoped Gordon would not become involved with this French edition: "The French are too intelligent to need telling what a book is about and I am sure an introduction would only irritate them and put any discussion of the book on a factional plane. I have written Caroline and explained that I think a living author should allow his book to stand on its own and that I prefer not to use an introduction. I think she will understand."[11] O'Connor would later return to this issue.

Upon her return to Milledgeville, exhausted by all the traveling, she took time to rest. In a polite note written in mid-May, she informed McCallum that her capacity for staying at home had now been increased to one hundred percent.[12] When up and about, she read two novels by Kingsley Amis and with renewed vigor focused on her novel. As she returned to her writing routine, Giroux wanted her to know that he looked forward to publishing *both* her second collection of stories and her second novel, thus giving her added encouragement and motivation:

> I've just read "The Enduring Chill" in *Harper's Bazaar* [July 1958] and I think it one of the best stories you have ever written. Father Finn (like all the characters) is perfect. I hope you intend to include this story in your next collection. . . .
>
> I haven't yet succeeded in meeting Elizabeth McKee. We made a lunch date, and I got the grippe. Then she went abroad. Now I'm about to take a vacation, as she returns. I spent all summer in town ("New York *is* a summer festival"), and I can't wait to get to Maine in September. I expect to see Cal Lowell at Castine; he's been teaching all summer at Boston U. and winds up tomorrow.
>
> I'm glad to hear that the novel is coming along well, and that a first draft may be ready this year. It will be wonderful to be publishing you again.
>
> Sheila Cudahy is now at Salzburg, after Italy and the Grecian Isles (my idea of a perfect vacation). I'm glad you liked Bernard Malamud's stories. I'm sending you some more FS&C reading matter: the new La Farge book, Carlo Levi, Erika Mann, and Jean Hougron [*A Question of Character*], which I hope you enjoy.[13]

Steadily O'Connor worked on her novel, and by late October she felt she had begun to understand its final direction. She informed the Fitzgeralds at the beginning of January 1959 that she would only have to bear with the prophet Tarwater for about a dozen more pages: "At least I will be through with a first draft then and will have to start bearing with him again from the beginning; but it is a very good feeling to see the end in sight even if I don't know whether it's any good or not." She completed the novel in mid-January, typing the final pages on a new portable typewriter; she attributed her ability to do this to whatever graces she had received at Lourdes the previous summer.

O'Connor wanted Hester, Gordon, and the Fitzgeralds to have copies of the typescript, knowing that she would profit from any criticisms they made. She was relatively satisfied with the title, *The Violent*

Bear It Away, but not completely so with the text. After working on it for seven years, she had no intention of finishing it quickly. The title was taken from the Douay-Rheims translation of the New Testament, "From the days of John the Baptist until now, the kingdom of heaven suffereth violence, and the violent bear it away" (Mt. 11:12), though after its publication she heard it referred to as *The Valiant Bear It Always* or *The Violets Bloom Away.* Scripture scholars have noted that a variant of this saying also occurs in Luke's Gospel (16:16), though it is not clear which version is the basic one. Nor are scholars unanimous about its meaning. It might suggest that the kingdom does violence as it makes its entrance into the world; those who wish to enter the kingdom will exhibit appropriate violence to force their way in, perhaps through renunciation or mortification. It could be, too, that the kingdom has always experienced violence at the hands of its enemies and is now still under attack. Or perhaps it refers to the vehemence manifested by the Zealots, who wished to establish the kingdom by violence. O'Connor highlighted a passage in her own copy of Emmanuel Mounier's *Personalism,* in a chapter called "Confrontation," that could shed light on her own interpretation. It reads, "The person attains self-consciousness, not through some ecstasy but by force of mortal combat; and force is one of its principal attributes. Not the brute force of mere power and aggression in which man forsakes his own action and imitates the behavior of matter; but human force, which is at once internal and efficacious, spiritual and manifest. Christian moralists used to give this dimension to their conception of fortitude, and the great aim of this fortitude was to overcome the fear of bodily evil—and beyond that, of death, the supreme physical disaster."[14] In O'Connor's spiritual economy, according to Connie Ann Kirk, an individual realizes his or her true potential through confrontation and the use of moral courage.[15] O'Connor might have believed that the violence in this novel forced her characters to accept the reality in their lives, but more than that, it prepared them to accept moments of grace. In a territory ruled by the Devil, the use of violent force might be the only way to seek and find the Kingdom of God.

It was just as well that O'Connor held off sending a copy of her typescript to New York as Giroux was again preoccupied with Eliot—this time his January 1959 visit in connection with his play *The Elder Statesman,* which had completed a most successful week's run in Newcastle before opening in Edinburgh.[16] The Eliots continued on by ship from New

York to Nassau, where Giroux and Reilly joined them for the first two weeks of February. Neither Giroux nor Reilly had ever been to Nassau, and both felt honored to vacation there with the Eliots, especially as they knew that New York winters would take their toll on Eliot's health. The Eliots planned to return on the *Queen Mary*, departing New York in mid-March. Since the corrected galleys for Eliot's play had arrived at year's end, Giroux would see its American publication through the press as expeditiously as possible, with a publication date set for April or May.

By mid-February, O'Connor had received a two-year grant of $8,000 from the Ford Foundation, and was pleased that Robert Fitzgerald and Caroline Gordon had similar grants (from a total of $150,000 divided among eleven people). Gordon read O'Connor's typescript with enthusiasm, and since O'Connor wanted a more tempered view, she sent it to the Fitzgeralds. In rewriting the 45,000-word novel, O'Connor was not sure if it worked or if it was the worst novel ever written. Because the text had not fully gelled, she did not want to send it to Giroux, as she informed Carver, now at Viking. Given her declining health, O'Connor knew that it was not wise to send her editor a manuscript that had not been read and commented upon by others whose opinions she trusted. She would not have wanted to rush a less-than-perfect manuscript into print. Her literary reputation, she intuited, needed to be sustained, not diminished by lessening her imaginative powers. Yet, the more O'Connor looked at her work in progress, the more she saw its weaknesses. When Carver also read the last pages of the revision toward the end of March, she was a bit surprised by O'Connor's ominous reference to death in the accompanying letter: "When the grim reaper comes to get me, he'll have to give me a few extra hours to revise my last words. No end to this." In spite of her uncertainty about the novel's merits, O'Connor found enough energy to finish typing a second draft, though she wondered whether an electric typewriter might be more beneficial in the future. She was now ready to welcome Coindreau to Andalusia, where there was little to show him except some local monuments, the reformatory, and, as she called it, the insane asylum. As would Giroux, Coindreau amused himself by filming her peafowl with a movie camera he brought with him.[17] On April 7, she signed a copy of *Wise Blood* to him, partly in French; Coindreau prized this book and later took it back with him to Paris, where he gave it to his dear friend, likewise a translator of Southern fiction, and my colleague at the Université de Paris VII, Michel Gresset.

O'Connor soon received word that Giroux, who wanted to find out about the progress of the novel, had started making plans to visit Andalusia, the first and only time he would do so. He wrote to her,

I have made arrangements to visit [Thomas Merton at] Gethsemani on the weekend of May 2–3, and I wonder if it would be possible to pay you a visit either on Friday, May 1, or on Tuesday, May 5. I assume, if it's the latter, that I can get a plane from Louisville to Atlanta, but I'm not sure how to get from Atlanta to Milledgeville, and I would appreciate your advice.

I was delighted at the news of your Ford Foundation grant; congratulations. It was a very distinguished list altogether, except for the mysterious Tillie Olsen [*sic*]. Has anyone discovered who she is? . . . We are publishing *The Elder Statesman* by T. S. Eliot and *Life Studies* by Robert Lowell during April, and I am sending you advance copies under separate cover.[18]

Carver's astute comments, seconded by Robert Fitzgerald's critique sent from Italy, prompted O'Connor to return to her typewriter: "Everything you say," she wrote Carver on April 18, "makes wonderful sense to me; in fact, your first note made sense and I started at once rewriting Part II, doing about what you suggested in your second letter." In all, O'Connor seemed satisfied with the end of the novel but would go about reconceiving its middle before sending it again to Carver (and also, curiously, to Denver Lindley). "It occurred to me that people at FS&C might take it amiss that I have sent it to someone at Viking," she continued in her letter to Carver, "even though it was to a friend and nobody's bidnis [*sic*] but mine. You have done me an immense favor that nobody else could have or would have done. Caroline read it but her strictures always run to matters of style. She swallows a good many camels while she is swatting the flies—though what she has taught me has been invaluable and I can never thank her enough." Given her previous unproductive relationship with Lindley, who never seemed to display more than a halfhearted interest in her work, it seems most odd that she would seek him out at this point in her life. But as an editor of the works of well-known writers, he had a professional track record that O'Connor could count on, even if they had never been more than casual friends. It is a tribute to O'Connor that she had grown to such a point that she was willing to reach out to Lindley and profit from his editorial skills, something she had never experienced before. She explained to the Fitzgeralds in late April the main problem with the text had been the character of Rayber. She needed both to portray his reactions more dramatically and revise the middle section. Dejected by what she was reading herself, she asked the Fitzgeralds to tear up the typescript, promising, "I am going to renovate the whole thing." It should be noted that O'Connor did not say that she would destroy her copy of the original typescript, but rather that she would rework it. To distract herself, she started reading as many of the works of Lord Acton as she could find, plus a two-volume work on Saint Catherine of Genoa written by Baron Friedrich von Hügel, which Fannie Cheney had sent her and which she reviewed in the Savannah-Atlanta diocesan *Bulletin* (August 31, 1957).

Unaware of O'Connor's conflicted, deep-seated feelings about her novel, Giroux flew from New York to San Francisco first to visit Jessamyn West in Napa and then to Louisville to see Merton on the first Saturday of May. While there, Giroux learned that Merton thought very highly of O'Connor's fiction. From the monastery, Giroux called O'Connor and relayed to her Merton's best wishes. When Giroux repeated his desire to visit her, O'Connor extended an invitation to stay with her and her mother at Milledgeville. Thus, Flannery and Regina drove to the Atlanta airport to meet him, and on the return trip the three of them stopped at the Trappist monastery in Conyers, then under construction. For the rest of his life, Giroux remembered distinctly seeing O'Connor climbing with great agility over piles of construction material.[19] The new monastery, financed in large part by the royalties of *The Seven Storey Mountain*, had more impressive buildings, Giroux thought, than those at Gethsemani. Merton had suggested that Giroux might like to meet some of the monks there, especially Paul Bourne, O.C.S.O., who sometimes censored Merton's books for the order. Giroux and his companions also encountered William Sessions, who engaged them in an animated conversation.

When Giroux arrived at Andalusia for his three-day visit, he noticed that the peacocks were slow in crossing the road, and the rear part of their long trains got caught under the O'Connor car; these elegant birds had to wait patiently until released. "When I was taken to my guest room," he wrote, "I found plenty of bookshelves and good books, though none of Flannery's. The next day we were invited as lunch guests, in Milledgeville, by Regina's older sister. The Cline's [*sic*] white-pillared antebellum mansion stood in the center of town and I was told that Milledgeville had served as the temporary capital of Georgia during the Civil War."[20] During the luncheon, which was served by a young African American man with white cotton gloves, O'Connor acted the quiet, dutiful daughter, sitting "stiff as a pole" and "absolutely poker faced," though Giroux realized that she was upset by the display of Southern manners.[21]

Prompted by the gift from Giroux of a copy of the beautifully designed edition of Merton's *Prometheus: A Meditation*, O'Connor asked a number of questions about Gethsemani.

"Was Merton allowed to talk to Giroux?" she wondered.

"Yes, without restriction."

"What was the daily routine like in the monastery?"

"The monks first gather for community prayer, beginning with Matins at two a.m., then they pray together at certain times during the day, and finally at sunset they say Compline before retiring to bed."

O'Connor listened intently to Giroux's replies, trying to enter into the rhythm of Merton's life and subconsciously comparing it with her own. Giroux also brought with him a recording of Edith Sitwell's quirky *Façade*, which Merton had played over and over, laughing so hard that tears ran down his cheeks. Giroux recited, at O'Connor's insistence, some of Sitwell's poems, rendering his own version of "Daisy and Lily / Lazy and silly" in her poem "Valse," "Long Steel Grass" (pronounced, as he said, as *Grawss*), and "Black Mrs Behemoth."[22] O'Connor's face lit up with a big smile at his silly performance.

Countless times Giroux related to me an incident that took place during this visit. When he went downstairs for morning coffee on Tuesday, wearing his plaid shirt and moccasins, he found Regina O'Connor already in the kitchen on the back side of the house. As she served him breakfast, she asked, "Mr. Giroux, why don't you get Flannery to write about *nice* people?" He tried to explain that Flannery herself was a nice person and thus she wrote in an appropriate way about others she knew, etc., etc. Mrs. O'Connor would have none of this literary psychobabble and abruptly left to go outside for her morning chores. When O'Connor entered the kitchen a few minutes later, she asked, "Bob, what did *The Mother* say this time?"[23]

The question should be asked: if Giroux felt that O'Connor was one of his most important authors, why did he not visit her more often? And why did he not invite Charles Reilly to accompany him to Milledgeville, as he was inclined to do when visiting the Eliots? On a practical level, travel to Andalusia was complicated by the fact that Giroux did not drive, nor did O'Connor once her lupus became pronounced, so he would have had been required to take buses or hire cars. While O'Connor traveled extensively while giving talks and escorted the occasional visitor to local sites of interest, she never seemed to afford herself the time, unlike Giroux, to take extended vacations with friends. But beyond these challenges, one can only speculate about this, given Giroux's reluctance to talk about his private life, but it has to do, in my opinion, both with his distant relationship to the male members of his family and the developments in his life after his divorce. Only in his most guarded moments did Giroux, in my presence, speak about his two sisters and two brothers, particularly Arnold, who was thirteen years older than him and whom he barely knew. After graduating from high school, Arnold, winsome and handsome according to one member of the family, worked as a welder on the Jersey docks, where he had to contend with rape at the hands of some coworkers. As a result, he had severe psychological problems and was placed in a psychiatric facility, the Hudson County Insane Asylum in Secaucus. He never recovered from the depression brought on by this trauma; his death at age fifty-seven in August 1958 from cancer was hastened by the ingestion of asbestos that he wrapped around pipes, most likely as a work task in various buildings on the grounds.[24] Giroux gradually drifted away from his other brother, Lester, as well, though all were proud of his avocation as a photographer and of his work at a Jersey City radio station and its sister station, Channel 13. Lester spent his senior years living in Morris Plains, New Jersey, before entering a group home. Sadly, Giroux did not know about Lester's death until four years after the event, as he mentioned in a note to his sister Josephine.[25] What saddened Giroux most was that his brother had not listed any next of kin. Thus Giroux never became close to the three men in his family, including his father. He simply put them out of his mind during his adult life, for none of them ever talked to him on a one-to-one basis about the deficits in their lives or the challenges they faced.

After his divorce, Giroux rarely traveled without Reilly as his constant companion, and he probably sensed that Andalusia could not have easily accommodated two men staying overnight for a few days. He would have anticipated Regina O'Connor's feelings about having Reilly stay at Andalusia—or even in a motel in Milledgeville—and concluded that it was better to avoid any potential embarrassment Reilly's presence might cause.

The friendship of these two men was based on mutual love and reverence. During the twenty-plus years that I knew Giroux and Reilly, I rarely saw them apart. Cultivated, deeply knowledgeable about opera, well read, and informed about current events, Reilly had an abiding commitment, as did Giroux, to the Catholic Church and its precepts. Giroux's Catholicism had a certain tenor to it; he told me that as he faced certain obstacles in his life—not having regular contact with his brothers and sisters and the family rituals that sustain such relationships; neither hiding nor feeling the need to explain his relationship with Reilly; not having a circle of Catholic friends in Jersey City, other than Reilly—he had to develop a private prayer life and spirituality that made ongoing sense to him. Prayerful in his own way, he understood over the years his growing readiness to accompany Reilly to church on Sunday. He profited enormously from the writings of five friends whose works he edited: Madeleine L'Engle, Bernard Häring, C.Ss.R., Rabbi Abraham Joshua Heschel, John La Farge, S.J., and Xavier Rynne (pseudonym for Francis X. Murphy, C.Ss.R.). Had O'Connor experienced the maturing vision of the Church as a result of the decrees of Vatican II, she and Giroux would have had, I believe, many fruitful, open-ended discussions about how the Church, in the words of the Protestant theologian Karl Barth, who was officially invited to attend the sessions of Vatican II, might always seek to reform itself (*ecclesia semper reformanda est*).

During Giroux's visit in Milledgeville there was some discussion concerning O'Connor's revision of her novel based on the critiques of her friends. Both author and editor were fully aware that the novel would progress at its own speed. In no way would Giroux have pushed O'Connor to work faster; he saw her physical condition and had only the highest respect for her ability to negotiate the rising currents that pulled her down. His thank-you note mentioned that he sent her Turgenev's *The Torrents of Spring*, Erich Heller's *The Disinherited Mind*, and Muriel Spark's *Memento Mori* published by Macmillan.[26]

After Giroux left—not knowing, of course, that it would be the last time he would see her—O'Connor went back to her novel and also started reading *The Image Industry*, by Father William Lynch, whose theological works would have a significant impact on the way she dealt with theology and literature. O'Connor also followed through on Giroux's suggestion about visiting Conyers, writing in May,

> As the chief fruit of your visit we have at last got to visit the monastery. Tom Gossett went there shortly after you left (with a religion class from Wesleyan where he teaches) and asked for Fr. Paul. The brother told him that Fr. Paul couldn't see anybody that day; he was much disappointed but while they were being taken around, he happened to see a priest digging in the flowers and he asked the one taking them around if he could talk to that one. That one turned out to be Fr. Paul. Tom was much taken with him and decided that he must take me and Regina up there. We went Friday. Fr. Paul had a letter from you that he had just got. We were much impressed with it all and with Fr. Paul. I am going to give them some peacocks for the place if the Abbot decides they can have them. They could contribute volume to the choir—from a distance.
>
> We really enjoyed your visit and hope you will come again when you don't have to hurry.
>
> Thanks for the books. I am particularly enjoying *The Disinherited Mind*.[27]

O'Connor could now see the completion of her writing project, writing to Maryat Lee in early July, "I am about convinced now that my novel is finished. It has reached the stage where it is a pleasure for me to type it so I presume it is done."[28] She wrote to Giroux on July 17, "I have mailed the manuscript of my novel to Elizabeth McKee and she will send it on to you. She may be on her vacation or something so if it doesn't show up in a reasonable time, I'd be obliged if you would inquire about it. Catharine says it's all right, but anything that you find rough, I'll be glad to think about further."[29] Giroux had been in Santa Fe, visiting Paul Horgan, O'Connor's former instructor at the Iowa Writers' Workshop, and planning for the publication of his *A Distant Trumpet* before Horgan took up a post at Wesleyan University in Connecticut. Once he was back in the office and had a chance to look at the mail that had piled up in his absence, he congratulated O'Connor in late July on the good news about her completed typescript: "I called Elizabeth, who has received it, and she promised to send it to me by Tuesday or Wednesday next week. Catharine has told me how much she likes it, and I can't wait to read it. I managed to get to the Grand Canyon from New Mexico; staggering. I refrained from going down on mule back and staying 'on the floor,' as they say, overnight."[30] O'Connor almost gloated over her accomplishment, especially pleased that Robert Fitzgerald had thought the second version he had seen was immensely better than the previous one, though it had taken a tremendous toll on her physically and psychologically. Hester's comments arrived too late to be used in restructuring the novel, but O'Connor was nevertheless grateful. Writing this novel had taken a great toll on her. And then there was the inevitable letdown of having leisure time, which left her feeling as if she had been fired from her job; she discovered that not writing was more difficult than writing.

McKee sent the typescript to Giroux with a covering letter, stating, "Here is Flannery O'Connor's novel, *The Violent Bear It Away*. The title is a magnificent one for the book. Flannery's talent has become even more powerful. When you have read it, of course, I am anxious to hear what you have to say about it. I think you will note one slight repetition. There is no use going into that for I am sure you will catch it."[31] When O'Connor wrote to Bishop in early August, she mentioned that Carver had thought the novel too short in the middle. Thus O'Connor added three more chapters.[32] Giroux's August 6 reaction to the novel, delivered by telegram, was quick and positive: CONGRATULATIONS ON NEW NOVEL. I THINK IT IS YOUR BEST BOOK. HOPE WE CAN PUBLISH IN FEBRUARY. LETTER FOLLOWS. BOB GIROUX.[33] As might be expected from a seasoned editor, Giroux had some suggestions to make in a letter he wrote the same day:

> I'd just sent off a wire telling you that I thank you for it is your best book. It's really an amazing work, an accomplishment of which you should be proud. One of the best things, in my opinion, is the characterization of Rayber. This I take to be the middle section which you spoke about on my visit. I think it makes a great difference; it's hard to imagine the book without it. Also includes one of the books "big" moments—the girl evangelist's tabernacle talk, with Rayber watching. I find the ending quite moving—Tarwater's vision of the multitude sitting down to be fed, his receiving a command, and his progress towards the city. The book is full of all kinds of surprises, in

dialogue and action. If I began to list the scenes that remain vivid in my mind, I'd be making a summary of the book.

I made notes about a lot of minor points as I went along, which I enclose on the attached sheet. Elizabeth raised one point about the repetition of the fountain scene on pages 131–32 and 146–47. I understand this to be deliberate, presented from Rayber's point of view first and then in retrospect from Tarwater's. However, I enclose copies of the sheets in question, for re-examination. Perhaps the pluperfect tense could be used for second time to underline the fact that it is intentional.

Now that I've read the book, the title is quite wonderful. The complete text of Matthew as epigraph on the title page will help, too. We would like to publish in February, and go into galley proofs just as soon as I have your replies to the editorial queries. *The Violent Bear It Away* is certainly not light summer reading! The winter of 1960 seems right, and I hope you agree.[34]

Three days later O'Connor sent Giroux a new page 104, commented positively on his suggested corrections, and added some minor changes of her own. She sent further, minor last-minute adjustments to Giroux by mid-August.

With the novel totally completed, O'Connor could now return to writing shorter fiction, including "The Partridge Festival," which seemed to come easy to her. By the end of September 1959 she had two sets of galley proofs of the book, followed by specimen type pages in Caledonia font, which she accepted as "fine."[35] In the letter, she wondered whether chapters of the book should be sent to the *Partisan Review* or *Mademoiselle*, though she was not sure that anybody would be encouraged to read the whole book by reading only a part of it. She thanked Giroux for a copy of Mauriac's *Questions of Precedence*, which, in her mind, ought to have been a play rather than a novel. Giroux replied with instructions to return just one marked set of proofs, noting that he did not return the typescript because he thought she would not need it, but would do so if she wanted it back. He was of a divided mind about publishing chapters in magazines and felt *Partisan Review* might help, but doubted if any of the others would. "The book is so integrated that I think it would be better to avoid magazine publication. Incidentally, can you tell me where the first chapter appeared? I seem to have missed it, and we shall have to get an assignment of copyright in your name for the book."[36] ("You Can't Be Any Poorer Than Dead" had been published in *New World Writing*, October 1955.) In her reply, O'Connor brought up a new topic: three years earlier she had corresponded with Robert Jiras, who had visited her in August 1956 and wanted to use some of her fiction as the basis of a film.[37] Jiras had recently contacted Giroux as well, as Giroux mentioned in a letter to O'Connor, requesting a copy of the proofs of her recent novel. She replied,

> I guess it is all right to let Mr. Jiras have the proofs but I wish you would ask him either to keep them to himself or return them to you when he has finished reading them, as I don't relish the thought of his passing them around among his friends and disciples. Mr. Jiras is a young man who has written a movie out of three of my stories [including "The River," published in the *Sewanee Review*, Summer 1953] and his consuming ambition is to produce it himself. . . .
>
> If the proofs are not awkward to handle I would be much obliged if you would send a set to Caroline, but if they are the long kind that flap, don't do it because it would be an imposition I am afraid.
>
> I'll get the marked set back to you shortly and I won't need the manuscript.[38]

Much later she mentioned that she had signed a contract with Jiras to make a movie of "The River," though she had no idea what would become of it. The film was finally produced and directed by Barbara Noble for Phoenix Films in 1976.

As O'Connor corrected the galley proofs in early October, she again found it depressing to see her work in print. It was dull and half-done and she could not blame anyone for not liking it. Giroux had helped a jittery O'Connor before and knew that an update on the book's progress would serve as a soothing antidote. "We have an extra set of book-club-type proofs, the kind that are bound, and I'll send it off to Caroline Tate," he promised. "It will be quite easy for her to handle, almost a book. As for Mr. Jiras, I think it might be better to wait until we are closer to finished books. Perhaps a set of sheets would be best, just before the book is sent to the binder."[39] A more relaxed O'Connor promptly returned the proofs, noting,

I am returning the proofs today. I have not made many changes but the ones I have made are important and I hope I will get page proofs to check them again. I have taken out a few sentences and added two. I have also changed the Biblical names to fit the King James version. The Tarwaters read the King James and the omniscient narrator reads the Douay. I should have thought of that before but it is good I thought of it at all.

I would be very much interested in reading James Purdy's novel [*Malcolm*]. I didn't know you published him. I read the stories and thought this was a most interesting talent and wondered what he would do with it.[40]

As with her first novel, O'Connor reworked her second even after the proofs had been completed. When her friend and fellow fiction writer John Hawkes gave her a detailed evaluation of the novel, she wrote to her editor immediately:

After I sent the corrected proofs back to you, I had a letter from a friend to whom I had sent the manuscript. He was alarmed at the number of "as ifs" and "seems" and other flaws in the prose of the middle section. So I am wondering if you could keep the proofs back from the printer until I can send you some more corrections on the set I have here. They could be transferred to the set I have already sent before you give it to the printer. They are not many but they are important. I sent the other proofs fourth class but I will send the second ones first and you should get them by Monday. I'll only send a few galleys. I figure it will be easier to make the changes now than on page proofs. I hope not too many people will have to see this thing until it gets in page proofs. Thanks for putting up with this inconvenience I am causing you.[41]

In his response Giroux proved to be most accommodating; he would await her corrections, glad that they were caught in time to be added to the galleys.[42] Such unruffled matter-of-factness on Giroux's part, the result of dealing in a most understanding way with hundreds of authors, calmed O'Connor's prepublication anxiety and strengthened the bond between them.

O'Connor busied herself with making changes and corrections and sent them off to New York, where Giroux collated them into the final page proofs in mid-October 1959.[43] She appreciated that Gordon, too, was sent a copy of the galleys. Not long after, Gordon drove to Milledgeville with Professor Ashley Brown from Columbia, South Carolina, to spend the weekend with O'Connor and her mother. True to form, Gordon took her friend aside and gave a long lecture on her writing fiction. When O'Connor wrote to Coindreau about the visit, she merely said that Gordon was in good spirits, considering her recent divorce: "After having done battle these many years, I shouldn't think she'd be tempted to marry again, unless she lost the use of reason."[44] Gordon suggested that the finished book be sent to Elizabeth Bishop, Granville Hicks, Alfred Kazin, Andrew Lytle, Robert Penn Warren, and Robert Lowell and Elizabeth Hardwick. O'Connor decided that a copy should also be sent to Paul Engle. In late October, Giroux felt that he had received the final version of the novel and acted accordingly: "I enclose herewith the page-proofs, containing all the revisions. The marked set must be returned as soon as you can conveniently go through it. The duplicate set may be retained."[45] Yet, as had become part of her mode of composition, O'Connor made further textual modifications, as she explained in a letter to Giroux:

I am returning the proofs today with, I am afraid, a good many more corrections, mostly deletions, on them. I am sorry to have to make these on the page proofs but the prose seemed even lamer to me on this reading. I hope they will not cause too much bother.

I am not sure that some of my directions on the proofs are clear so I enclose a sheet with some of the doubtful ones typed out. In case any of these do not seem to you to be improvements, you can let it stand as it is. At this point I don't know whether I am a good judge. The book entirely fails to move me, except to disgust.

Also I have discovered another error, this also my fault: the Biblical quotation is not "From the time of John the Baptist etc.," but "And from the days of John the Baptist etc." This means that the designer will have to get three more spaces in the top line. I enclose it. I think it's very nice.

Next Saturday Billy Sessions is going to bring Fr. Paul and a friend of Fr. Paul's who is visiting him from the West Coast down for lunch. This is presuming he can get permission to come, but Billy seems to think he can as the excuse is to look at some of my mother's plants. We wish you were about to join this gathering.[46]

O'Connor altered 346 lines in the galleys and 460 lines in the page proofs, costing her a total of $308.67.[47] Giroux did not comment on the changes because he was preoccupied from mid-October to mid-November by yet another visit from T. S. Eliot—this one going from New York to Washington, DC, Boston, Chicago, and St. Louis, and then back to New York. Social events included a quiet dinner party hosted by the Strauses for the Eliots and Giroux.[48] Since Giroux remained in New York for the most part during Eliot's visit, however, he was able to inform O'Connor in early November that the production schedule of her book was on time and few difficulties were anticipated:

The page proofs and your letter have arrived, and after checking over the sheet which you enclosed, I have turned them over to the printer. There may be one or two places where copy will be short, but I'm not certain of this. Only if the printer runs into difficulties (and I don't expect this to happen) will I bother you again. I'm sure the title-page epigraph can be corrected without difficulty also.

Your prose style seems as good as ever to me. Prepublication letdown is a familiar symptom. I see it often and I don't know any good writer who doesn't have it.

I wish I could join you and your guests next Saturday. I hope Father Paul gets permission for the visit. It's a great event for them to break the routine occasionally, and I'm always abashed by Father Louis's [Thomas Merton's] delight over visitors; not having any family to take advantage of the one-visit-a-year privilege, he counts on his friends for this.

I'm sending you Father [Martin] D'Arcy's *The Meaning and Matter of History* and Elizabeth Jenkins's *Jane Austen* by separate cover.[49]

O'Connor replied,

Thanks so much for the two books which I shall enjoy immensely. I would like to be able to say I enjoyed the Purdy book. I certainly expected to because there was much of interest in his stories. But that novel left me behind.

Fr. Paul got permission to come, came, and I think enjoyed himself thoroughly. He said the Abbot said to pave the way for him, so the next time, we hope to get both of them down. The excuse for the Abbot to come will be to look at Sister's [O'Connor's aunt's] peephole fence in town—they want to build such a fence at the monastery, or at least Fr. Paul thinks they ought to.

I find that Fr. Paul too is a great admirer of Baron von Hügel. He thinks that some American publisher ought to bring out a volume of von Hügel's essays—selected to be a kind of antidote to some of the less worthy aspects of American Catholicism. I wish I could interest you people in the notion.[50]

O'Connor still had anxious moments about her novel, fearing, of all things, that it would not be controversial enough. She anticipated negative reviews before the book dropped gently out of sight. Tarwater in the final analysis was neither a caricature nor a monster in her mind, and she would have done everything he did had she had been in his place. She bided her time and waited.

Giroux had pleasant news to send O'Connor in late November, about a paperback edition and the book's appearance, which prominently featured the book's title in white letters encapsulated in red and set against a gold background. (Giroux believed, as he told me, that a book's jacket accounted for more sales than any publicity given to a book.) They arranged the details in a swift exchange:

I am delighted to report that Arabel Porter of New American Library has offered us a reprint contract for *The Violent Bear It Away*, at an advance of the $3,500 payable half on signing and half on publication. I am writing to Elizabeth McKee today to give her the particulars. The paperback edition cannot appear earlier than one year from ours.

I enclose the proof of the jacket copy, which I hope you like. I found it extremely difficult to summarize the story without giving everything away. The others here, John Farrar, Sheila Cudahy and Roger Straus, like this. I've decided to use the back panel for the Caroline Gordon quote by itself. We have plenty of other good reviews to quote on *A Good Man Is Hard to Find*, but I think we should limit it to [Granville] Hicks and [Orville] Prescott on the front flap and delete the *Time* quote on the back flap.

Our publicity department wants to use the photograph showing the self-portrait. They ask if they can have one additional photo and are interested in the one in *Harper's Bazaar* in which you are wearing glasses. Can you supply a copy of this?[51]

I'm glad to hear that the Mentor people have bought the novel. I have forgotten the figure but I don't believe they paid so much for the last two. Their Gory Jacket Division should have a field day with this one.

I like the jacket copy fine. There are one or two small changes that I would suggest. On the front flap, would you consider changing it as follows, beginning with the fifth sentence:

"Another crucial prophecy he makes is to Rayber, his nephew, a schoolteacher, about Rayber's son, Bishop: either he himself or Tarwater will baptize the child—'if not me in my day, him in his.' At the old man's death, little Bishop, thanks to Rayber's alert opposition, remains unbaptized, and on Tarwater falls the burden of baptizing him. A struggle over Bishop begins between Tarwater and Rayber."

I'd prefer not to have "dimwit" or "atheist" used or Tarwater and Rayber too much characterized.

Then I'd be obliged if you'd take out "shocking and violent climax" and say only, "The story moves inexorably to its climax and an outcome which neither Rayber nor Tarwater could foresee."

I don't have the book with Caroline's quotation before me but I think she said "one of the more important writers of our age" instead of "most."

The picture with the glasses was a passport picture and I don't like it. I'll try to have another made. I take it you already have a copy of the other.[52]

I have made all the changes in the jacket copy you suggest, save one, and I think they improve it. It is much better without "dimwit" or "atheist" and without characterizing the climax. However, I did not change the old man's quote in prophecy (even though it varies slightly from the text) after testing it on some of the people here. It seems to confuse them. I'm not really happy about this sentence, but I don't see any better way of stating the relationships.

Caroline's article was on hand here, and she does say "one of the most important writers." I rechecked the whole quote to make sure. And of course she's right in saying "most."

I don't think you should go to the trouble of another photograph now. You gave me the copy of the other, which is unusual and is bound to be reproduced widely. There isn't any photographer credit, however, and if you'd like us to run it we'll be glad to.

I will send you a color proof of the front of the jacket soon. It seems to me that the artist has done an excellent job. If the Mentor people have the good sense to use it in the reprint edition too, you have nothing to fear.

P.S. Did you know that Katy Carver has found a spot with Lippincott? I'm happy she is back in book publishing.[53]

———

Thanks for getting rid of the "dimwit" and the "atheist." I don't think it makes too much difference about the quotation since, if they get that far, they will see that it is different in the book.

I have written the girl who took the picture you have to find out how exactly she spells her name and I'll let you know what the credit should be as soon as I hear from her. I'll also send you that list of names of people I think should be sent the book.

I was much cheered when Catharine wrote me she was at Lippincott and she was certainly much cheered herself. We invited her down for Thanksgiving but she did not have enough time. She says she will come and I would like very much to have her.[54]

———

Many thanks for the photographer's name. We have decided, as you know, to use the Caroline Gordon quote on the back of the jacket; the photograph will be sent out with review copies and Miss [Blythe] McKay's name will be properly credited on each copy. Thanks also for the list of people to whom advance copies should go. If you think of any additions, let me have them.

I enclose herewith a preliminary color proof of the jacket sketch. I hope you like it. I'm also enclosing a facsimile of the revised jacket copy. I'll send the finished jackets, in which the corn color will be nearer to the artist's original, in about three weeks.[55]

Thanks so much for the NRF [*Nouvelle Revue Française*] bulletin. The Gallimard book [*La Sagesse dans le sang*] itself just arrived today from M. Coindreau. He has an introduction in it about the traveling preacher in American life. I hope you will see it and give me your opinion as my French only hits the high spots.[56]

I enclose a photograph that your publicity department can use.

The *Partisan Review* sent me some galleys of Chapter 2 in which they had excerpted a part that they wanted permission to print if they had room in their winter issue. It was a very random excerpt, made I felt to fit their possible space, and so I did not agree to their printing it. I also hope to see the book soon.[57]

As the nation anticipated the announcement by John F. Kennedy of his candidacy for the presidency, O'Connor, too, could look forward to the challenges that awaited her. First of all, she finished "The Partridge Festival," eventually published in *The Critic* (February–March 1961), which she had converted into a peanut festival, but that would not work. By early December she sent both Gordon and Carver copies of "The Comforts of Home" (published in the *Kenyon Review*, Autumn 1960); the former liked it but the latter had serious reservations, prompting O'Connor to rework it because she felt it was not dramatic enough and contained too much superfluous material.

The year 1960 began with the rather routine news that the book, priced at 3.75, had been published. Giroux wrote,

I have just sent off to you by air the first copy of *The Violent Bear It Away*, which reached my desk this afternoon. Your other author copies follow.

In case you haven't seen the enclosed note in the Paulist magazine, *Information*, I am sending it to you.

Publication has been set for February 24th and I will keep in touch with you about all the goings on. Review copies will be going out shortly, and I will send you advance copies of reviews as they come in.[58]

O'Connor replied,

> Thanks for the book, which came this morning. I'm glad it's out but I don't think I'll read it. . . . Also please send a copy to Rev. Robert F. Quinn, C.S.P., Paulist Information Center, Five Park Street, Boston 8.
> The Paulist clipping was interesting. It will be up to them now to decide whether Tarwater belongs in a Catholic novel.[59]

Although O'Connor had seen the page proofs, she held back her real feelings from Giroux about certain aspects of the book's production, which she expressed to Dawkins: "The title page is a real mess. They try to be fancy and just create confusion. I haven't read it for misprints because I don't have the courage, but you will soon see. If you mark any misprints, let me know." O'Connor was quick to point out a typo to Giroux, "a bad typographical error on page 242, line 19 of my book. Instead of 'he heard the command,' the book has it 'he heard to command,' which destroys the sense at a crucial point. I know nothing can be done about this now but I wish you would be sure that when proofs go to the New American Library and Longman's, Green this is corrected. I am sure there won't be another printing of this book, but should there be, I hope this can be corrected."[60] Nothing seemed to please O'Connor about the appearance of this book; as she wrote Hester in September 1960, the proposed cover of the British edition of *Wise Blood* was even worse: "Sabbath is thereon turned into Marilyn Monroe in underclothes." There was, unfortunately, no one to blame but herself for the first cover, for she had seen the rough version in advance. Conversely, she was pleased by the proposed British jacket of *The Violent Bear It Away*: "Apparently they have taken to heart my reply about the meaning of Tarwater's encounter with the man in the motor car. They wanted to be sure the jacket was not a wrong interpretation of the book."[61] As O'Connor grew more experienced, she often projected her doubts and fears about the quality of her writing onto the appearance of the book in its published form, as if the publishers lacked interest in her work—which was certainly not the case with Giroux, who had carefully guided her through each step of a book's production.

The first review O'Connor saw appeared in *Library Journal* (January 1960), often consulted by professional librarians and booksellers as to which books they should order. Though it was completely unfavorable, she was not dismayed and asked that additional copies of the book be sent to Allen Tate in Minnesota, Francis Fergusson at Princeton, and fiction writer Thomas Mabry in Guthrie, Kentucky.[62] Her letter to Lowell in early February 1960 contains some of her more tempered reactions to seeing her novel published. Perhaps the novel would even have a sequel, she mused: "I am not through with prophets, though. I think the next one will be about how the children of God finish off Tarwater in the city; and that one may finish me off."[63] A letter from Andrew Lytle at this time lifted her spirits because he was one of the few people whose judgment she trusted. A February 5 telegram from Giroux also helped: RAVE REVIEW FEBRUARY CATHOLIC WORLD BY ALBERT DUHAMEL CALLING IT QUOTE GREAT NEW NOVEL UNQUOTE AND STATING IT QUOTE CHALLENGES COMPARISON WITH THE GREATEST UNQUOTE. CONGRATULATIONS. LETTER WILL FOLLOW. REGARDS. BOB GIROUX.[64] True to his word, Giroux followed through with a letter, giving her the full critique by Duhamel and apologizing for the typo, which would be corrected in future British and American editions.[65] O'Connor read the reviews in the Sunday *New York Times*, the *Herald Tribune*, *Catholic World*, and *Saturday Review*, as well as Prescott's in the weekday *New York Times*. With the exception of the *Saturday Review*, the reviews seemed so predictable; as she wrote Dawkins, "It is to them all a trip in a glass-bottomed boat."

At age thirty-four, O'Connor had accomplished a good deal, but maybe at that moment this was not apparent to her. She was, in fact, about to enter the final phase of her life on Earth. Though Giroux had spent time with her and had seen her use crutches, he did not entirely grasp the seriousness of her illness, being under the impression that medication would lessen its effects or at least provide unchanging mobility. As was his wont, he continued sending her reviews, most of which she had seen, though he tried to situate them in context as candidly as possible, more than O'Connor would have done for herself. Of a batch in February, he noted, "From a publishing point of view, they are all in the favorable if not rave class. From any other point of view, they don't seem to have much of a grasp of the book's intention."[66] In all, O'Connor dismissed most as idiot reviews. In an unpublished internal Farrar, Straus & Cudahy memo to Straus, dated June 20 [1960], Giroux notes, "It's been a tough book to sell, and we've had no extra (book club) help. But I still think it has a chance at the National Book Award, if a certain literary kind of judge presides at the novel selection." O'Connor's fixation on negative reviews seems appropriate because, in a deeply personal way, they could serve as a gauge of whether she should continue to write in the same vein or consider a new direction. One bright note: in mid-March 1960, Carver visited her and together they spent some time with Maryat Lee's brother.[67]

O'Connor on occasion commented to others about her own work, perhaps as a way to explain to herself what she considered important. In a two-page, single-spaced letter, she shared her insights about *The Violent Bear It Away* with John J. Quinn, S.J., who taught English at the University of Scranton in Pennsylvania. O'Connor noted that she preferred that the novel be referred to as a "mystery" story rather than a "salvation" story for two reasons:

1) [Francis Marion] Tarwater's salvation still hangs in the balance even though at the end he has accepted his mission, and because 2) the word "salvation" kills off readers like Flit does flies. I may one of these days write another story about how the children of God finish off Tarwater in the city. Then it would be more in keeping to talk about his salvation (as he would attain it by a kind of martyrdom.) . . .

I think the reason Tarwater and [his uncle] Rayber deny the force in them is not because it is bitter, or anyway I think why it is bitter requires some explanation. Of ordinary bitterness they could both take a good deal. What Tarw. can't take is the fact that Christ is more than pure spirit. Tarw. wants to hear the voice of the Lord "out of a clear and empty sky." He wants it untouched "by any human hand or breath." Any human involvement is a lowering of himself. He has a sense of the Incarnation which terrifies him. When he feels the presence of Christ through things, he quickly turns away. As for Rayber, for him to accept the force in him would mean accepting Bishop. He believes the love he has for Bishop is senseless and takes away from his human dignity. Bishop has no spiritual or intellectual potential of his own. Christianity is repulsive to Rayber because it means loving and sanctifying what is intellectually valueless. Rayber is woefully wrong—but to what extent can you call him a sinner? This is the main question about modern man and I can't presume to offer any answer. Take [Albert] Camus. I think of him as a good man. Tarwater now really knows that he is running away from his vocation. He has a bad conscience. He perceives Christ even in the silence.

I think it is too pat to say Bishop [Rayber's son] is the sins of the father visited on the child. It's more complicated than that. . . . Tarwater's friend and mentor is the Devil. And it is an actualization of the Devil who gives him a lift at the end of the book and shows him what it means to deny the bread of life. [For] some this episode is going to be considered arbitrary, but the end would not have been possible without it.[68]

She continued by saying that she did not think that the dominant emotion was tragic; Rayber is more of a fanatic than old Mason Tarwater, though more tragic than Mason's great-nephew Francis Marion Tarwater, she believed. If Tarwater's prototype might be Jonah, with some Jacob added, as O'Connor noted, he would really like to be Moses speaking to the Lord in the burning bush. "Even if this burning bush is only the woods which he has set on fire himself," she concludes, "it is only after he has acknowledged Christ that he can see God in the woods burning." At the end of the novel, Tarwater realizes that he has fulfilled old Mason Tarwater's request to be given a proper burial and that his young cousin Bishop be baptized. Empowered by this, he accepts his prophetic calling: "Go warn the children of God of the terrible speed of mercy."

Given her rapidly declining health, O'Connor had to face a weighty decision: what should she now do with her time and waning energy? Since her bout with lupus had become a topic of interest to others, she needed to consider whether she should really start writing a third novel, as she had intimated doing, and thus possibly face more negativity? Given O'Connor's reluctance to discuss her personal feelings, it would have been difficult for Giroux to discern in her letter to him exactly what she intended to do. She wrote,

Apparently *Time* received some letters contradicting some of the statements they make about me in their review. They had the man in their Atlanta office call and ask a lot of questions, such as did Caroline Gordon and Maurice Coindreau really visit me and had I really been to lecture at various colleges and had they really described my illness in the wrong way. (The kind of lupus I have is not the skin disease as they said.) I put them straight on these questions but I don't see why they should be concerned about it now.

I hope you have a nice vacation and maybe get to Florence and see the Fitzgeralds.[69]

Prompted by another visit from Coindreau, she read as carefully as she could the reviews of *Wise Blood* in French. "One full-page one from *l'Observateur* illustrated in the middle with a picture of Billy Graham," she wrote to Dawkins, "one review of my book and [Nelson] Algren's (*A Walk on the Wild Side*, in French *La Rue chaude*) with the favor going to mine. The reviews indicate it is a good translation and I was very pleased, so was M. Coindreau. He is now going to translate the last novel." She did not know at this point that future Nobel Prize laureate J. M. G. Le Clézio would write the preface. Coindreau had told her that he had given a copy of the French translation of *Wise Blood* to Maritain, who was so taken by it that he wanted to have a discussion about it.[70]

It was a heady time for the country as John F. Kennedy, O'Connor's choice for president, took the country by storm, traipsing as he did from state to state on his campaign trips. The O'Connors listened to his speeches on a radio because they did not yet possess a television. O'Connor, however, had to keep any interest she had in politics in perspective, focusing instead on what physical, imaginative, and spiritual forces she could muster.

Before Giroux headed off to Europe for an extended vacation, O'Connor became deeply involved in a project that would develop into the last book she saw to completion. In early May 1960, after spending time in Emory Hospital, Father Bourne and Abbot Augustine More of Conyers had lunch with her at Andalusia, and for the first time the subject of Mary Ann Long came up. Later, in July, six nuns from Atlanta, all Servants of Relief for Incurable Cancer, a religious congregation founded by Rose Hawthorne (daughter of Nathaniel Hawthorne), plus the intrepid community superior Sister Evangelist, visited O'Connor to resume the discussion about this young girl with face cancer whom the nuns had nursed for nine years, from age three until she died at age twelve. The group descended on O'Connor to ask her support for the book Sister Evangelist was writing. As O'Connor informed Hester, "She don't write like Shakespeare but she does well enough for this. What will come of the book, I wouldn't know but I am convinced that the child had an outsize cross and bore it with what most of us don't have and couldn't muster."

As O'Connor began to understand the implications of what the nuns were demanding, she saw the wisdom of helping them. She discussed the Mary Ann book with Gordon in late July before Gordon continued on her way to see her aunt in Chattanooga.[71] At the end of September, O'Connor wrote Giroux a long letter explaining in detail the Mary Ann project and above all stating that she would like his professional advice about it. Many people in Atlanta knew about Mary Ann and were most impressed with the way she had coped with her illness. Once the nuns heard about O'Connor through the monks at Conyers, Sister Evangelist contacted her. It is not difficult to see O'Connor throwing up her hands as she explained the situation to her editor: "Just my kind of thing." She really wanted the nuns to write the book themselves—just a factual account of the girl and her death at the home. Once finished, she would be glad to review it and supply an introduction if that would help. "I thought that would be the last I'd hear of her. Never underestimate them. They forthwith sat down and wrote it and they are hellbent to see it through." Toward the end of October 1960, after participating in a panel discussion on recent Southern fiction at Wesleyan College in Macon, O'Connor entertained, among others, Caroline Gordon, Ashley Brown, Katherine Anne Porter, Madison Jones, and Louis Rubin. When the Mary Ann book came up in conversation, Gordon felt it should be published by a secular press. Once Giroux had been consulted, he agreed to read the final version.

Caught in a lull after the publication of her second novel, O'Connor continued with the Mary Ann project, and by the end of November she sent Hester a copy of the introduction, including the comments that Gordon had made. From O'Connor's perspective, the introduction was mostly finished, though she wanted to remove some of the references to herself because she believed the focus should be kept on Mary Ann. In early December she submitted the book to Giroux, writing in the cover letter,

The enclosed jolly treat is the Sister's manuscript. If you think there is any possibility at all of its getting published anywhere, I might be able to get them to improve it. After I had got the thing all typed for them, they decided there were "a few other little things" they had forgot to mention. So I told them to write them down and I would insert them. Today they sent me the insertions, three of them. Two I have inserted and the other I am sparing you. It had to do with Mary Ann eating some apple sauce.

Caroline proclaimed that this should be called *Death of a Child*. I presented this to the Sisters but they did not take to it at all. They then got together to think of titles and came up with some that would curl your hair: *The Bridegroom Cometh, Song Without End, The Crooked Smile*. The Abbot, who is in on this too, came up with the worst: *Scarred Angel*. I informed them that none of these would do, and suggested the title I have put on it [*A Memoir of Mary Ann*]. They accept this reluctantly but think it is very "flat."

Now that they have produced a book, Sister Evangelist thinks a movie should be made about Mary Ann for their postulants. They are serious. I have declined to take part in the production of the movie.

I am entering the hospital in Atlanta Tuesday to have my bones inspected as they are not doing well, but I am sure I'll be spared at least until I find a publisher for the Sisters as they are all praying for it.

I hope you will have a Merry Christmas and thank you very much for reading this. I think there is a great deal in this child and wish her book were written better but I don't know anybody who would write it.[72]

After the holidays, Giroux replied,

We have decided to go ahead with the Mary Ann book. I read your preface at once; it's marvelous. Then I read the story, with a few misgivings which somehow are not important. Then Sheila Cudahy read it and Claire Costello; yesterday we decided we'd want to publish it—provided the sisters gave us a free editorial hand, in the purely routine sense of the phrase. The question now is, with whom do we draw up a contract?

If you think I should write the sisters directly, I will do so offering royalty terms on a rising scale of 10 percent to 7,500 copies; 12
percent to 10,000; and 15 percent thereafter. If you will let me know
which Sister I should write to (preferably the one who will sign the
contract or get it signed), and where, I'll do so at once. For the work
that you have done and for the writing of the preface, you should
share in the royalty, it seems to me, and I will propose this with your
permission.

We like your suggested title, *A Memoir of Mary Ann*, and we
would want to publish the book in early fall. Ed Rice tells me that
Jubilee is running your introduction in their April issue. They can an-
nounce the book at that time.

I enclose an excellent review of *The Violent Bear It Away* in the
new issue of *Kenyon Review*. It seems to me we should get out some
kind of brochure with the best quotes; your novel is my candidate for
the National Book Award and even if the judges don't agree with me,
I want them to see the excellent press *The Violent Bear It Away* has
had. . . .

I am sending you *Memoires Interieurs* by François Mauriac under
separate cover. It's one of my favorites on our spring list, and may
well be one of the great books of any season.[73]

O'Connor felt glad that she had done her part in promoting the publication of this book. Giroux remarked that O'Connor's "introduction made
me realize that the book could, not only could be published, but ought to
be published. I didn't think it was going to be a best seller or anything like
that; it was simply deserving of publication. It was such an extraordinary
story."[74]

Just before Christmas 1960, after O'Connor returned home from another stay in the hospital, where she had been reading Proust, she worked
on "Parker's Back" (published in *Esquire*, April 1965), which would pre-
occupy her until her final days. It concerned a man who had a large tattoo
image of Christ Pantocrator on his back, something he carried with him
each day but could never see. She described the source of this story in a
letter to Bishop: "A few years ago, I cut out of the paper a picture of a
man who was having a head of Christ tattooed on his back, I have been
mulling this over ever since, thinking I'll someday write a story about
him, but I haven't thought up the right thing yet."[75] When Christians see

this portrayal of Christ in Eastern Orthodox iconography as the *Panto-crator*, the "Almighty" or "All Powerful" (see Saint Paul's letter, 2 Co-rinthians 6:18), they sense that he both blesses and judges them by all that is written in the New Testament. O'Connor found in this majestic image a synthesis of much of the theology that served as the basis for her fiction.

At the start of January 1961, O'Connor had not returned to full ca-pacity, and she felt that her latest story was not coming along well because too much humor dominated its serious theme. Still and all, the accep-tance of the Mary Ann book picked up her spirits, revealing an ebullience rarely seen in her letters. She had found a new mission, not to try to in-struct or convert someone, as she had done with great intensity with Hester (who would commit suicide in 1998), but to help the cause of a girl she had never met and whose life story needed to be told. Because of her own infirmity, almost no one ever asked O'Connor for assistance; when it happened in the case of Mary Ann she responded with great dispatch, serving at times in the role of editor, writer, advisor, and intermediary as she addressed various aspects of this book, including the contract and royalty payments.

Since O'Connor had come a long way in understanding the pitfalls in the publication of a book, she counseled the sisters to have the Longs sign a statement indicating they did not object to anything in the book. Knowing that the sisters could be a bit naïve in dealing with contracts, she made sure that she would do everything possible to facilitate mat-ters before retreating from the scene. "It seems to be all right with the powers at Hawthorne [the location of the congregation's motherhouse]," O'Connor wrote Giroux in February, "if Sr. Evangelist is the one to sign the contract."[76] Giroux, as he explained in a letter to O'Connor, worked as expeditiously as she did:

I expect to get the contract to Sister Evangelist this week. I have to leave New York on February 22nd and I'm hopeful it will be signed and sealed before then.

I have gone over all the corrections and have made them all except one which is not clear and which I am writing Sister about. The Bishop's sermon is adequately quoted in the last page; one word more would kill it. *Brief Candle* is out as a title for lots of reasons but I wonder if they know it was once used by Aldous Huxley? The

Shakespeare quotation [*The Merchant of Venice*, V, i] doesn't seem right—too coy in its reference to "a naughty world." The poem by Mary Ann's sister is pathetic; it would serve no good purpose in the book that I can see. . . . Incidentally, I am proposing that the royalties be divided two-thirds to the Sisters and one-third to you.[77]

———

The Mother Superior in Hawthorne told Sister Evangelist she would have to send the contract to a lawyer before she signed it, which Sister Evangelist did. The lawyer, lawyer-like, has made a number of observations about it, most of which I think are obstructionist and can be ignored. Sister Evangelist has sent me his letter and the signed contract but doesn't want me to send the contract on to you until I am sure that the points he makes are negligible. Will you look his letter over and if anything in it makes sense, would you alter the contract accordingly? The only thing I see that might be done is to give the Sisters the right to approve other types of publications—since Orders are always concerned with their public image etc., they might not want any and every kind of publication.

If it were left up to me, I would send the contract signed to you at once, and I will if you will assure me that there is nothing in it which at a future date could cause the Sisters any trouble. . . . I am not cut out to be an agent.[78]

———

Lawyers will be lawyers. The contract I sent is, of course, our printed contract, the same as you have signed and all our authors and their agents have signed. It is approved by the Society of Authors' Representatives, who had a whole battery of lawyers go over it when it was agreed to some ten or more years ago.

I checked with Elizabeth before sending it. She is aware of and agrees to the division I suggested. She also agreed that neither you nor she had a legal reason for being a party to the contract, though I'd be delighted to have you sign it too, as Mr. [Alex] Smith suggests. That's the most important part of his letter and he and the Sisters can be assured that your agent is wholly apprised of, and in agreement with, the contract.

[Responding to the lawyer's observations:] None of his other points is important. Author's alterations allowance beyond 10 percent of the "cost of publication" is, of course, based on the "cost of composition." He misread this clause. We do not plan to go bankrupt, but if we did there would be no difficulty about assigning copyright, as Clause 15 provides. We cannot clear punctuation in advance; they can change the proofs, if they disagree, which they won't. We do not allow T. S. Eliot (or Bishop [Fulton] Sheen) to examine our records and books; we assume mutual trust. We take out Canadian copyright as a matter of routine; in Canada the book will be published by Ambassador Books, our partners there. We would naturally not want to make any arrangements for subsidiary rights, including movies or paperbacks, unless they are first-rate and in good taste. We must maintain control of these rights, however. Please assure the Sisters of our good faith in this, as in all the other matters.[79]

O'Connor wasted no time in returning the contract, which she did not sign herself because she was not the author of the text. Giroux responded quickly, thanking her for the contract and letting her know that the anticipated National Book Award had been given to Harper Lee's *To Kill a Mockingbird*, a novel O'Connor summarily dismissed as a child's book.[80] In spite of this, Giroux, Straus, and their editorial team had made such enormous strides in the world of literary publishing that they moved to new offices, located on several floors at 19 Union Square West. Giroux's compact, fourth-floor office looking out over Union Square gave him even more of a sense of the vitality of the city.

O'Connor now had to deal with an expected problem: the canonical aspects of publishing a work written by a Catholic nun whose bishop insisted on both a nihil obstat and an imprimatur (in case Mary Ann should eventually be canonized). Though O'Connor hated to see the clerical finger in the pie, she felt it inevitable.[81] Given Giroux's considerable experience in obtaining ecclesiastical permissions for Merton's books, he knew exactly what to do.[82]

Occasionally O'Connor mentioned to Giroux that she was still in touch with Carver, who had been looking for employment in England: "I hope that if Catharine doesn't get something in London she can get something with the Library of Congress. I think myself that would be better. She has just bought a story from me for *New World Writing* [published in October 1961] called 'Everything That Rises Must Converge.'

This is what I want to call my next collection of stories. I have six now."[83] Buoyed by this accomplishment and her participation in the Mary Ann book, particularly having resolved the question of ecclesiastical approval, and knowing that her previous work had competed with the very best for the National Book Award, O'Connor planned her next volume of stories.[84]

Giroux accompanied the Eliots to Ocho Rios, Jamaica, which he noted in a letter to Thomas Merton "was a very British corner of the island complete with carefully manicured lawns practically down to the ocean side. . . . It's a technicolor island, and the average daily temperature was 80 wonderful degrees. It was good to get away from the longest and dreariest winter I've ever known in New York. Eliot said the climate there was too perfect for work."[85] After an Easter visit from Robert Fitzgerald and reading the galley proofs of the Mary Ann book, O'Connor was pleased to learn that Giroux, now back in his office, had worked out an agreement with McKee for his firm to take over the reprint rights of *Wise Blood*, once the present stock had sold out. "We will draw up a new contract with Elizabeth, paying an advance of $500 and 10 percent royalties to 2,500; 12 ½ percent to 5,000, 15 percent thereafter."[86] He questioned whether a preface by Gordon might be appropriate, though he had no strong convictions one way or another, and stated, "I haven't told you that I think the title of your new collection is excellent. *Everything That Rises Must Converge* is not easy to forget." O'Connor felt pleased by the possible reissue of *Wise Blood*, which would give her added visibility as well as more financial independence. "I am rather wary of introductions," she informed Giroux in mid-April 1961. "I didn't like the introduction Caroline wrote for the French translation of *Wise Blood* and had the embarrassment of finding a way not to have to use it. I don't know anybody else who likes the book well enough to write an introduction. However, if I think of anything, I'll let you know."[87] At this point, O'Connor heard a welcome voice from the past: Giroux had enjoyed a dinner with Cal Lowell as he recuperated from a hospital stay. "He seemed relaxed and better, and he was delighted to hear that we are reissuing *Wise Blood*. He called it one of his all-time favorites."[88] When Harcourt, Brace finally agreed to transfer the rights to O'Connor's first novel, she and Giroux hoped they might do the same for her second book.[89]

In writing to John Hawkes at the end of June, O'Connor said that she really had nothing to say in a note to be included in the reprint of *Wise Blood*. Her words reveal, above all, a distancing from this novel. Were she to write something for it, she would have to look back in time and locate within herself her literary posture when writing that novel. She asked Giroux to consider various options: "I'd like to talk to you also about *Wise Blood*. It seems to me that some kind of note to the second edition would be in order, if only to point out that this *is* a second edition and that the book has survived for ten years anyway. But I haven't succeeded in writing anything about the book. I think an introduction by Caroline would do more harm than good and I don't know anybody else who would be willing to write one. If I did find someone to write an introduction, how do you work that financially?"[90] She preferred to look forward, especially as she was in the middle of advancing a book that would have great personal significance for her. She kept abreast of the developments of *A Memoir of Mary Ann*, especially when *Good Housekeeping* magazine featured it in a Christmas issue, for which she received $1, 275.[91] Via his ongoing relationship with Tom Burns in England, Giroux sought out one of the best English publishing companies to publish this book there. When they accepted the book, they asked that the title be changed to *The Death of a Child*.[92] On July 7, 1961, O'Connor replied that the sisters were most pleased with the London publisher and had agreed to let them change the title.

Another visit from Gordon and Brown proved quite strenuous for O'Connor. Gordon had read "The Lame Shall Enter First" and felt it was, among its many faults, completely without a sense of drama, something that O'Connor lamented would take three months to change. She and her mother planned on going to Boston for a Ford Foundation conference and then New York in late August, where Giroux had invited her to share a cocktail and further discuss the reprinting of *Wise Blood*, but the trip was canceled. Knowing that she had to conserve her energy, O'Connor was not disposed to travel further than really needed. In mid-November, she, her mother, and two friends made the short trip to the monastery at Conyers for dinner, and in passing met Charles English, O.C.S.O., a survivor of the London Blitz, who appreciated O'Connor's fiction. This monk, as some of his fellow monks once told me, never adjusted well to life in the cloister; they felt he was more attracted to the Bohemian lifestyle in New York, where he had a number of friends. He would sometimes call Walker Percy in the middle of the night, which prompted Percy, as he told me, to use him in part as the basis for the character of Father Simon Smith in *The Thanatos Syndrome*.

In mid-January 1962, Brown sent O'Connor a copy of *The Movie-goer*, as eventually did Thomas Merton; it was the only novel of Percy's that O'Connor read. Though she once mentioned that she and Percy had corresponded over the years, these letters have not surfaced.[93] When Percy won a coveted prize for this novel, O'Connor penned him a short note of congratulations in late March, writing, "I'm glad we lost the War and you won the National Book Award. I didn't think the judges would have that much sense but they surprised [*sic*] me." Though they once had a brief conversation when O'Connor spoke at Loyola University in New Orleans, these two literary figures never really knew each other all that well, in spite of the fact that they are often linked, appropriately, in scholarly literary articles and books.[94] Percy considered O'Connor, as he once wrote to Shelby Foote, "a truly remarkable lady, laconic, funny, tough, smart, hard-headed, no-nonsense, the very best of us, South and Catholic."[95]

O'Connor's health was not improving, and she was questioning whether she should try to have a piece of her bone from one of her legs grafted onto one of her hips. During this time, her letters in general are informative but lack any genuine spark. A bout with the flu in February had not helped matters, though she knew that keeping to a predetermined schedule would get her through the tougher moments. Giroux anticipated that the reprinting of *Wise Blood*, by an offset process using the original Harcourt, Brace plates, would be ready for the 1962 summer–fall season. He asked in mid-October if she wanted to make any changes or corrections in the text.[96] "There are no changes I want to make in *Wise Blood*," she replied. "I haven't read it in ten years and I'm not going to read it as I might want to rewrite the whole thing. Let it go as is and any way you want to reproduce it will be agreeable to me."[97] Giroux opted to let the matter sit a while.

O'Connor sent Giroux a copy of the letter that Sister Evangelist had written to him about the publication of the Mary Ann book. The nuns had been kept busy reading more than two dozen wildly enthusiastic letters, as well as adding up the needed donations.[98] Giroux, who had recently talked to Jacques Maritain at the Campion Award dinner in New York, had more good news for O'Connor in early December 1961: the book would be published in paperback by Dell, no later, according to the contract, than December 1964.[99] At the suggestion of a cleric from Georgia, he wondered whether O'Connor might write a book for young readers, perhaps based on her interest in peafowl.[100] Though O'Connor liked the idea in general, she needed to focus on a story she was writing for Lytle, as well as a couple of talks she would give in the spring. As Giroux followed through on every aspect of the Mary Ann book, in addition to editing twenty-two other books for the spring 1962 catalogue, he wanted to give O'Connor as much leeway as possible. He was juggling many commitments, including managing the finances for T. S. Eliot's next trip to New York. The Eliots had decided not to vacation in the West Indies in October, but instead to visit the United States toward the end of November, staying as in the past at the River Club. Though Eliot had a full schedule, he spent Christmas 1961 with his sister in Cambridge and also held readings at Boston College, Harvard, Yale, the New York Poetry Center, and Columbia.[101] The Eliots then went briefly to San Juan, St. Thomas, and Barbados, where Giroux and Reilly joined them in late February, before the Eliots returned to England in March.

Not long after her thirty-seventh birthday, O'Connor received a letter on April 19, 1962, from Giroux, again mentioning a possible foreword to the reissue of *Wise Blood*. Carefully, he noted,

We are going ahead with publication of *Wise Blood* for the fall. Although we've discussed this point before, I'd like you to reconsider from another point of view doing a new prefatory note for this edition. What I had in mind, aside from the help this will give us with reviewers who might simply ignore the book as just a "re-issue," is that it will allow you to renew the copyright as of 1962.

This may not be a big point, but I felt at least that I should bring it up. Even a paragraph or two would take care of the copyright thing.

I'm expecting a jacket sketch of our edition next week, and I think that we should make good use of quotes on the flaps. Please let me know if there are particular reviews which I should not overlook. I am afraid I will not get much help from Harcourt, Brace on this, since they have all the files.[102]

O'Connor agreed, though not happily:

I'll write some kind of preface for the new edition if you think it will help. When will you have to have it? I have a sort of full schedule ahead of me. I'm going to Rosary College and Notre Dame next week, the next week I have taken on a lecture to the Methodist students at Emory and after that I have to go back to Notre Dame to get a degree they are going to give me at St. Mary's College; so with all this I doubt I will get down to it before the 1st of June unless something special occurs to me.[103]

Despite her time concerns, O'Connor soon wrote an introduction and sent it to Dawkins, indicating that it was about as much as she could write. She sent the tentative author note to Giroux in early May and said she would redo it if he so wished. Giroux wrote back suggesting two minor changes, which she was grateful to receive: "Thanks for the jacket, which I like. The change in the author's Note is all right with me. Since the book is going to cost so much, I hope you will print it in a paperback edition. A lot of schools would like to use it but, of course, students can't pay $4.50"[104] Giroux thought that their Noonday version, when printed, would cost $1.95 or less.[105]

When O'Connor received a copy of the reissued *Wise Blood*, she liked the simple red dust jacket that pictured a man wearing dark glasses with the title printed over the lenses. She was glad Giroux, as she told him toward the end of June, had insisted on the author note.[106] In his reply, Giroux mentioned he had sent copies to Gordon, Carver (who resigned from Lippincott in late August 1962), Granville Hicks, Anne Fremantle, Paul Kneeland (the *Boston Globe*), Frank Daniel (the *Atlanta Journal*), Ralph McGill (the *Atlanta Constitution*), Joel Wells (*The Critic*), and Maurice-Edgar Coindreau in Sweet Briar, Virginia.[107] Above all, this exchange of letters shows that O'Connor again took an active role in the promotion of her books, as she had in the past, perceiving that copies of the reissued novel in the hands of influential critics and authors would go a long way in building up her reading public.

O'Connor now saw two possible routes before her: finish her third novel or compile a second collection of her stories. By mid-July, she had chosen to work on a short novel. The clock was ticking away, and O'Connor did not hesitate to reveal to Hester in late October some thoughts about her future demise. "I want to simplify my life," she wrote. "If the doctor were to say you have five years to live, it would take me all five to get my room in such shape that I would leave it." At this point, however, her direction changed: Giroux proposed that she work on her collection of short stories, for which she had already chosen a title, explaining,

We are now preparing our spring list, and I can't help wondering if it would be possible to add a new Flannery O'Connor book. Your long story, "The Lame Shall Enter First," is surely one of the best things you have ever done, and could be a central story of another collection. Have you thought of it as part of the book you once called by another story title, "Everything That Rises Must Converge"? (Incidentally, I've heard that there's an English anthology about Teilhard de Chardin, one section of which is entitled *Tout ce qui monte converge* [*Everything That Rises Converges*]).[108]

O'Connor resisted the suggestion, replying,

I have seven stories but I don't think there is enough variety in them to make a good collection. I might as well wait and see what I come up with in the next year or two. I'm not in any hurry. I still want to call the book *Everything That Rises Must Converge*. Right now I am writing on something that may prove to be longer than I'd like. It's tentatively called "Why Do the Heathen Rage?" It's been inevitable I get around to that title sooner or later. . . .

Mr. Coindreau [who had visited O'Connor in late October] tells me that he thinks [noted French writer] Julian [*sic*] Green would be interested in seeing the Mary Ann book. He also thinks the Spanish would print it and is going to mention it to a Spanish publisher he knows. The Sisters had a letter from someone in Brazil who wants to put it into Portuguese.[109]

While at Andalusia, Giroux had mentioned that he had been personally impressed by Pierre Teilhard de Chardin, S.J., whose works in French (*Le Phénomène humain* [1955]; *l'Apparition de l'homme* [1956], and *Le Milieu divin* [1957]), some of which dealt with his controversial views on human fallibility, had created a theological storm within the deep recesses of the Vatican. O'Connor, who owned three books written by Teilhard, plus four others about him, positively reviewed *The Divine Milieu* (Savannah-Atlanta diocesan *Bulletin*, February 4, 1961), *The Phenomenon of Man* (*Bulletin*, February 20, 1960; also *American Scholar*, Fall 1961), and *Letters from a Traveler* (Diocese of Savannah's *Southern Cross*, April 27, 1963). She noted that in *The Phenomenon of Man* Teilhard's scientific expression reflects what the poet is attempting: to penetrate matter until spirit is revealed in it, something she would not have written had she thought his theology was, as one literary critic of Southern literature phrased it, "vapid New Age babble."[110] This remarkable man, cited approvingly by Pope Francis in his encyclical *Laudato Si': On Care for Our Common Home* (May 24, 2015), postulated that the universe is constantly developing toward new levels of complexity and consciousness, drawn by what he terms a personal, transcendent Omega Point, which can be interpreted as the Christian *Logos* or Christ.[111] O'Connor wrote in her review of *The Divine Milieu* that "it is doubtful if any Christian of this century can be fully aware of his religion until he has reseen it in the cosmic light which Teilhard's vision has cast upon it."[112] O'Connor would undoubtedly have been impressed that Giroux had not only briefly met this Jesuit, who stayed with the Strauses on and off for over six years, but also attended his funeral in April 1955 at Saint Ignatius Church in New York, the very church he had regularly prayed in as a high school student at Regis.[113]

In early January 1963, O'Connor wrote to McKee that she had enough stories for a collection, but she wanted to have more from which to select. She was in no hurry, especially as she thought too many people were publishing too much. Given this go-slow approach, she let the "Thing," as she then called her new novel, fall somewhat into abeyance. In starting a friendship with Janet McKane, a New York primary school teacher, she returned to considerations of Teilhard de Chardin at the end of February 1963; she now considered him a "very great man" and was quite taken by his comments on "passive diminishments"—"those afflictions you can't get rid of and have to bear." (It is interesting to note that she was writing, however obliquely, to someone she had never met, and yet was willing to share some of her deepest physical and spiritual concerns about final acceptance and resignation.) At this time, in addition to reading *Atheism in Our Time* by Ignace Lepp, she was trying hard to absorb the ideas in *The Theology of Death* by Karl Rahner, S.J., a German theologian whose densely reasoned articles and books had a great impact on the Second Vatican Council.[114] She said she could read him once a year and still not know exactly what he said—and by no means was she alone in this. She no doubt followed the news of the death of Pope Jean XXIII and the events leading up to the election of Cardinal Giovanni Montini as Pope Paul VI in late June 1963, but such changes in Rome would have had little impact on her day-to-day spirituality.

In November, O'Connor finished reconceiving "The Enduring Chill," having worked on it all summer, but she had doubts about it where it would fit in to her proposed collection and thus set about writing "Revelation." "I'd really like to turn 'Why Do the Heathen Rage?' into a long story, without the 'Enduring Chill' section," she wrote Dawkins in early November, "and use it in the collection, but this all takes time." Just as she was coping with the contents of a new book, she heard a voice from the past: Sister Evangelist wrote to her about a new book project concerning meditation and Scripture that she thought, with O'Connor's help, Giroux might find interesting. In a fairly detailed exchange of letters with her editor, O'Connor agreed that this project was not viable and should be considered by a publishing house that dealt mostly with Catholic texts, such as Paulist Press.

As the entire country, and indeed the world, learned of the assassination of President Kennedy, millions saw one television playback after another of Jack Ruby shooting Lee Harvey Oswald and then felt overwhelmed with grief in viewing the president's funeral. An era had seemingly come to an end. Though a certain degree of adjustment eventually pervaded the United States, the Montgomery bus boycott in Alabama and the Greensboro sit-in in North Carolina still remained in the consciousness of many Americans. By no means had political or racial harmony been achieved in the United States. O'Connor returned to her story "Revelation," which had emerged from such instability and turbulence. The story pleased her very much. Carver judged it to be one of her most powerful stories and probably her "*blackest*."[115] Most notable about this story is that the protagonist, Mrs. Turpin, has an incredible hierophany of a "vast horde of souls . . . rumbling toward heaven. There were whole companies of white-trash, clean for the first time in their lives, and bands of black niggers in white robes, and battalions of freaks and lunatics shouting and clapping and leaping like frogs." This joyous conclusion, a depiction of the apocalyptic end time, affirms O'Connor's view that all people on this earth, including many she had portrayed in her stories, are rising in glory, climbing Jacob's Ladder, as it were, ready to meet the Lord who welcomes them.

After an exhausting 1963 Christmas trip from West Lafayette, the home of Purdue University, to Chattanooga and then Princeton, and finally back to Indiana, Gordon wrote a six-page, single-spaced letter to O'Connor recounting the trip and the broken-down railroads and misconnected buses and obsolete airplanes she had experienced.[116] "She may be old," O'Connor wrote to her friend Thomas Stritch in January 1964, "but that woman has Vitality; or maybe it's just recklessness. I sent her a copy of a story I wrote before Christmas, a real good one too, better than I have pulled off in a long time, and she wrote me another six-page letter about that, or rather all about grammar which I ain't got the principles of besides not being able to spell anything. She was crazy about the story. . . . I improved the story from her letter, good as it already was. I don't always carry on so over my own stories but in this last one I got confidence, as you can see." After reworking this story, she sent Gordon a second version and then wrote to Giroux,

> I am about ready to turn my attention to a collection of stories. I have just completed another story, which I think may possibly round it out. This makes eight finished and I am working on another which may or may not turn out. They are on the whole longer stories than in the last collection and I am wondering if there is any limit on the number of pages; whether it might be better to select six of these stories, or just what. I want to do some more rewriting on a few of them and I don't know when I can have it ready. Is there any particular time you would prefer to bring it out?[117]

Pleased, Giroux promptly replied,

> That's very exciting news about the stories. We would like to publish the book this year, in September or October if possible. That would mean manuscript delivery by late May. Does that seem feasible to you? There would be no particular limit on the number of pages. Eight or nine stories sound about right, even if they are all long. I think the basis ought to be that you are satisfied with them all. Is there a working title for the whole collection yet—one of the stories presumably? Let me know if you think May is a possible delivery date. We'd be very pleased to have a book of yours on our fall list.[118]

Just as O'Connor had reason to rejoice about a new book in 1964, she entered the darkest period of her life, exacerbated by an anemic condition caused by a benign but debilitating fibroid tumor. She informed Giroux that she was not sure whether she could have the book ready by late May or not. "I had thought I'd call the collection *Everything That Rises Must Converge* and use that for the last story."[119] In February, she entered Baldwin County Hospital for an operation, rather than traveling to Atlanta, as her mother was also caring for her ailing aunt Mary Cline. O'Connor's operation on February 25, for which they administered cortisone, activated her lupus, which had remained dormant since 1951.

In spite of these incredible setbacks, O'Connor corrected while in the hospital the galleys of "Revelation," which would soon appear in the *Sewanee Review* (Spring 1964), and had every intention of preparing her collection of stories for publication. Her words to Hester, written years before on June 28, 1956, had a special ring to them now: "I have never been anywhere but sick. . . . Sickness before death is a very appropriate thing and I think those who don't have it miss one of God's mercies." Having lived so long with lupus, she was reconciled to the graces that would occur before her death.

At this point, the last thing that O'Connor needed was the possibility of being involved in a lawsuit. George and Dollie Long, Mary Ann's parents, had hired D. H. Robinson of Louisville, Kentucky, to act as their attorney. Both O'Connor and Giroux, as expected, were upset to learn that the Longs had retained a lawyer in order to claim damages for the seeming unhappiness they had been caused to suffer by the publication of the book. O'Connor conveyed her thoughts to Giroux about this situation in a handwritten letter on March 7, 1964:

> I have just got out of the hospital after having had serious surgery and I am not yet up to the typewriter. I am shocked and disgusted by this turn of events. Of course the Longs knew the book was being written and they offered no objections. As soon as your letter came, Regina called Sr. Josephine. She was looking through their files then for the letter written by the Longs saying they had no objection to the publication of the book. She said the letter *had* been written and she knew they had it. She said she was going to send everything they could find on to Mother Elizabeth who would have it photostated at Hawthorne. We suggested she have it all photostated before she sent it as well, as it might get lost in the mail. I don't know whether she intends to follow that advice or not, since Mother Elizabeth told her to do it the other way and they do what they are told.

We asked her if the Longs had been cool to them lately. She said, by no means, they had just recently sent the Longs $200. I think the Longs have just fallen into the hands of some shyster lawyer. They may not even be fully aware of what he is doing. Last summer the Sisters brought down Mr. and Mrs. Long and two of the girls and one of the girl's [*sic*] husbands. They were feeling no harassment then that we heard of. They spent the afternoon with us and were very pleasant. Plain poor people and simple enough to get taken in. Sr. Josephine said Mr. Long had been trying to get Social Security but hasn't been able to.

Don't count on my book for the fall now. I'm not up to it. Cancelled lectures.

Please keep me posted on this Long mess because it certainly worries me.[120]

Though Giroux was busy with yet another of Eliot's visits, he did not put aside addressing the details of this legal issue, which was eventually dropped.[121] In order to calm O'Connor's spirits, Giroux followed up on an earlier telephone call from Straus:

The Longs' lawyer has not replied to our lawyer, and it may be that he now realizes what an untenable position he is in. I enclose our lawyer's letter of March 10 and also my letter to Sr. Evangelist. It's really shocking to see how simple people can be preyed on and used to others' advantage. It probably comes down to his telling them, "Let me see if I can get you some money. It won't cost you a cent, and we'll split the proceeds," or something like that. Please don't give this anymore worry. I'll let you know the outcome, of course, but we are now inclined to think the matter will go no further.

Roger is right in saying that the main thing is for you to get well and conserve your strength. We shall publish the book when it is ready. The important thing now is to rest.[122]

But O'Connor's health simply would not allow her to focus on the forthcoming collection since she had to stay in bed most of the time. Giroux did not want to cause her further anxiety by telling her that his mother had died in mid-April. When O'Connor wrote to Coindreau in mid-May, she told him that her February operation had been a success, but that it had activated her lupus, noting, "This is one of these diseases where you are allergic to your own protein or some such foolishness."[123] Given her gradual decline, she really could not foresee the possibility of reworking any of the stories for a collected volume; that would demand too much effort, though she might be able to make some changes on the proofs. She made a list of stories she wanted included: "Greenleaf," "A View of the Woods," "The Enduring Chill," "The Comforts of Home," "The Partridge Festival," "The Lame Shall Enter First," "Everything That Rises Must Converge," and "Revelation"—though not in this particular order.[124] Seemingly having forgotten her previous decision about the title of the collection, she implied that she intended to choose one in the near future. Giroux wrote back, reminding her in mid-May 1964 of the title she had chosen as early as April 1961:

> Elizabeth sent me a copy of your recent letter, and I want to tell you at once that of course we want to go ahead right away with the stories. I am collecting copies of those I do not have, and we will go right into galley proofs and send them to you. We can still make it for late fall publication, I am sure; certainly January at the latest.
>
> I shall get the contract to Elizabeth at once. As far as title goes, I have always thought of the book as *Everything That Rises Must Converge*, as I think you have. Unless you now feel otherwise, I think we should proceed under that title. I don't think it could have a better one.[125]

As Giroux mentions in his introduction to these stories, he knew about O'Connor's lupus, but was unaware, as undoubtedly were other of O'Connor's friends, that it could not be controlled. O'Connor moved forward courageously during her final illness. "I have been thinking about this collection of my stories and what can be done to get it out with me sick," she wrote McKee on May 7, 1964. "I am definitely out of commission for the summer and maybe longer with this lupus. I have to stay mostly in bed. . . . If I were well there is a lot of rewriting and polishing I could do, but in my present state of health [the stories] are essentially all right the way they are." As she later wrote her agent, she signed the contracts and definitely wanted the title to be *Everything That Rises Must Converge*, provided Giroux concurred. She entered Piedmont Hospital in Atlanta on May 22, planning to deal with any problems McKee might have by phone from there. She decided later that she did not want "The Partridge Festival" included in the collection.[126] The stories as published in their original forms should serve as the base texts, she wrote, but she had found typewritten copies of "The Comforts of Home," "The Enduring Chill," "Revelation," and "The Lame Shall Enter First" and old galleys of "Everything That Rises Must Converge," should they prove useful to Giroux. O'Connor also mentioned to Giroux the possibility of including another story, whose title she did not give, but which she had been writing off and on for a number of years.

Giroux was most willing to comply with all of her requests:

Many thanks for your letter and for returning the contracts so promptly. I would be grateful for the typescript of "The Comforts of Home," "The Enduring Chill," "The Lame Shall Enter First," and "Revelation." I have the printed version of "Everything That Rises" and do not need your galleys. I agree that "The Partridge Festival" is not up to the others, though I like things about it, and I think you are right to exclude it. If the story you have been working on is ready, even after these are in galley proofs, I think you should put it in.[127]

Giroux subsequently sent McKee three signed copies of the contract, plus a check covering the first part of the advance. O'Connor reiterated that she wanted her unpublished story to be incorporated into the collection, even if it was added after the first galleys appeared.[128] On May 28, she hand-wrote a letter to Giroux, promising, "I've been in the hospital here since last Saturday but I hope to get out next week and I'll send you those manuscripts then. I hope the other story will work out." Uncharacteristically, she signed it with her full name. She wrote another letter to Giroux from Piedmont in early June, saying that she had been in the hospital for three weeks and had not been able to send him the typescripts of the stories. Thus she encouraged him to think about a spring 1965 publication date, since she anticipated that she would work better at home, especially as the blood transfusions seemed to help. O'Connor also wrote to Carver, discussing various stories and thanking her for her criticism of them.[129]

In mid-June she had a twenty-minute visit from Abbot More, Father Charles English, and Caroline Gordon, which must have touched her, especially the presence of a devoted mentor who never stopped sharing her views, for better or worse, about O'Connor's fiction.[130] Whatever had passed between them over the years now took on a different aura as

Gordon comforted O'Connor as best she could. Gordon wrote to Giroux, "She told me, with a grin, that the doctor had forbidden her to do any work but had said that 'it was all right to write a little fiction' so she was keeping a note-book under her pillow and trying to finish that last story, 'Parker's Back.' She did finish it and sent it to me. She had been 'letting me off the hook,' as she put it for the past few years, but this year she sent me two stories and I have thought that she did so because she realized that she didn't have long to live."[131] (When Sally Fitzgerald visited Gordon in Chiapas, Mexico, after O'Connor's death, she learned that Gordon had resented O'Connor's reluctance to accept her critiques.[132]) Other visitors included Carver, Sessions, and Robert Coles, M.D., later to become a Harvard professor and award-winning author, one of whose books focused on O'Connor.[133]

On June 23, 1964, Giroux wrote to O'Connor, thinking she was still in room 302 at the hospital; by that time, though, she had returned home, after spending one month there. "Incidentally, if there is now a chance of having a new story, we'd naturally prefer to wait for this. In other words, as long as we can send the manuscript to the printer before the end of September, books will be ready for publication in February."[134] With little to no energy, O'Connor had to keep communication to a minimum, something that did not escape Giroux's notice. She was pleased to learn that the story collection would be announced in the fall catalogue but probably published in the spring. Giroux was having difficulty locating the text of "Greenleaf" in the *Kenyon Review*, but he was sure the magazine would send him one soon. O'Connor was not sure whether to include the story "You Can't Be Poorer Than Dead" but was most willing to leave that decision up to Giroux; she did not want to add a story if it just looked like she was trying to fill out a volume. Likewise she was toying about including "Judgement Day," a story that dated from the mid-1940s that Carver had critiqued.[135] She was rearranging in her mind the stories for the volume, as she wrote to Giroux:

I have been home a week from the hospital and can work a few hours a day. I've completed one story which I think will do in place of "The Partridge Festival" but I want to keep it a few weeks longer and think about it before I send it.

There is considerable rewriting I want to do on the one called "The Enduring Chill," so you might wait to put that in galleys until I get the new version.

"Greenleaf" is in the 1957 O. Henry collection, also in a paper-back anthology edited by Arlin Turner and published by Rinehart, the title something about Southern Literature.

I am wondering what you would think about including "You Can't Be Any Poorer Than Dead," which is a version of the first chapter of *The Violent Bear It Away* and was published in *New World Writing*. It holds up well as a story.

I also hope to write another story that I have in mind ["Parker's Back"], so I think there will be at least nine or ten stories and they are fairly long most of them.

I guess you know that Archbishop Hallinan is not going to get to the 3rd session [of the Second Vatican Council]. He visited me in the hospital and I thought he looked very bad. He stays at St. Joseph's Hospital and can work a few hours a week. I understand he's writing a book on the council, but that is only hearsay; he didn't say so.[136]

Giroux replied, just over a week later,

I am certainly glad to hear that you are home from the hospital and that you are allowed to work at your writing. We now have all the tear-sheets of the stories in hand, except for "Greenleaf" which *Kenyon Review* is forwarding to us.

We shall certainly look forward to the revised version of "The Enduring Chill." As I am sure you intended, we shall have to hold up on the galleys until you are satisfied that the new story is ready. Another new story beyond the one to replace "The Partridge Festival" probably means it will be September before we have a complete script. (I don't see why "You Can't Be Any Poorer Than Dead" should not go in, but perhaps there ought to be a note about its relation to your last novel). If we keep to an early September deadline, spring publication is still possible.

I am enclosing a copy of our new catalogue which announces the book on page 25.

P. S. That is very sad news about Archbishop Hallinan. Since he is a Council Father, his book will have to wait until all the decrees have been published and the official secrecy ended. I would love to publish a book by him, but I hesitate to intrude at this point.[137]

Rallying to do the best she could with her final story, O'Connor sent Gordon, Hester, and Carver each a copy of "Parker's Back," seeking as she had done before the advice of trusted friends. Gordon replied by telegram, "Congratulations on having succeeded where the great Flaubert failed!" She listed, nevertheless, some mechanical details.[138] Even to the end, O'Connor's opinion of Gordon had not substantially changed: "She thinks every story must be built according to the pattern of the Roman arch and she would enlarge the beginning and the end, but I'm letting it lay," she wrote to Hester on July 2. "I did well to write it at all." O'Connor had decided to include just nine stories, she explained to Carver in mid-July, omitting "You Can't Be Poorer Than Dead." In particular, she wanted Carver's advice on "The Enduring Chill" because she did not like it all that much, but was afraid that any revisions would make it worse.

Sally Fitzgerald later shared her thoughts about O'Connor's final months and days, recalling,

> There is a sense of urgency throughout the last letters, but her mastery of herself was established by now. She never lost interest in her friends during the wearing year: her letters continued to pour out to them and, while she spoke often of her illness, her light tone was deceptive. Most of us didn't realize how sick she was, although in retrospect her letters tell us more than they did at the time. Mrs. O'Connor gallantly tried to keep the knowledge from Flannery herself, and perhaps Flannery was at the same time trying to keep it from her mother. In any case, she received Extreme Unction, now called the Sacrament of the Sick, at her own request, in July. She knew. The natural sorrow of separation she must have felt, and physical misery, too.[139]

O'Connor's last letter to Giroux, again handwritten, ends appropriately with an expression of gratitude: "Please excuse the note but I have been sick again and cannot type yet. Would you please send me the rest of your suggestions etc. and also the copy of the ms. that you have. I will have to put the corrections in it. I have made most of Mrs. Tate's corrections and the manuscript is very much better, I trust. Thanks a lot."[140] As is quite clear from O'Connor's literary efforts during the last few months of her life, she and Giroux were totally committed to the world of literature, or, more precisely, the creation and production of her highly imaginative fiction.

Since O'Connor seemed to accept the order of the stories that Giroux would finally choose, it is possible to say that she did not necessarily see a connection between one story and the next, leaving moot the question of whether the collection could also be considered a novel in some sense, like Faulkner's *Go Down, Moses* or Welty's *The Golden Apples*. Nor would it be overly wise to speculate about her novella in progress (with more than 375 pages of manuscript), seemingly based on her story "Why Do the Heathen Rage?" which was published in *Esquire* (July 1963). After her death on August 3, 1964, her mother arranged to have the funeral the next day, thus foreclosing the possibility of allowing her many friends and admirers to participate in this ceremony. She informed Giroux by telegram of her daughter's death.[141] Although Giroux did not attend O'Connor's funeral, at which Monsignor Joseph Cassidy of the Cathedral of Christ the King in Atlanta presided (Giroux told me he would have attended, had the burial been delayed a few days), he did participate in an August 7 memorial liturgy at Saint Patrick's Cathedral in New York.[142] No doubt he would have been pleased that the Cathedral of Saint John the Divine in Upper Manhattan created a niche for O'Connor in its American Poets Corner on November 3, 2014, with a quote from her 1953 letter to Elizabeth Hardwick and Robert Lowell describing her lupus: "I can, with one eye squinted, take it all as a blessing."

Giroux saw O'Connor's posthumous collection of stories through the press, respecting at every point O'Connor's wishes, as best he could determine them.[143] It is noteworthy that this book, in competition with works of fiction by E. L. Doctorow, Joyce Carol Oates, Cynthia Ozick, Walker Percy, and John Updike, received the National Book Award for fiction in 1972, the first time the award was given posthumously. Furthermore, Giroux had a pivotal role in counseling Sally Fitzgerald as she assembled and edited O'Connor's letters for *The Habit of Being*, winner of a National Book Critics Circle Award in 1979.[144] In October 1964, Giroux became a partner and the firm was renamed Farrar, Straus & Giroux. Fittingly, the first book to bear this imprint was *For the Union Dead*, by Robert Lowell, who had first brought O'Connor into Giroux's Harcourt, Brace office in early March 1949. It should be emphasized that O'Connor would never have been given an interview with Giroux without Lowell's explicit support. Knowing that Lindley and Kazin had not initially appreciated *Wise Blood*, Giroux did not change his opinion of O'Connor in the slightest, even making sure that her novel was reissued ten years after going out of print, not only to give her continued visibility as an important writer, but also to make sure that she could profit financially from her efforts, particularly at a time when her health was precarious. The friendship of O'Connor and Giroux had an unusual character to it, most poignantly seen in his desire to extricate her from being passed from one editor to the next at Harcourt, Brace. Giroux never wavered in his desire to publish O'Connor's four books of fiction, even when he became incensed that certain Harcourt, Brace officials had an anti-Catholic bias. His better instinct told him that no other editor at a major publishing firm understood O'Connor as well as he did. Giroux felt honored to be the recipient of O'Connor's handwritten hospital notes for her second collection of stories, which she, on her deathbed, so desperately wanted to finish. He assisted her in realizing a final dream, giving this book an authoritative stamp it would not otherwise have had. In his introduction to *The Complete Stories of Flannery O'Connor*, Giroux wrote that Merton had not exaggerated his estimate of O'Connor when he said she should not be compared with Hemingway, Porter, or Sartre, but rather with Sophocles.[145]

Giroux continued going to the office every day, year in and year out, steadily editing and attending meetings. He sometimes invited me to join him when he visited family and friends in and around New York City. We would meet for lunch at the Players Club on Gramercy Park or for dinner at the Century Club on Forty-Third Street. I remember with great fondness the conversations we had in his small office overlooking Union Square, as his colleagues and authors stopped by for one reason or another.[146] He relinquished his position as editor in chief in the spring of 1973 to assume the role of chairman of the board.

In 1994, Straus sold the firm to the German publishing group Verlagsgruppe Georg von Holtzbrinck, which had already purchased Henry Holt & Company and the journal *Scientific American*. Straus remained as president of the firm until his death on May 24, 2004. Jonathan Galassi, a recognized poet and accomplished translator who had served for ten years as poetry editor for the *Paris Review* (and studied under Robert Lowell and Elizabeth Bishop at Harvard), became an executive editor in 1986 and eventually editor in chief; he was succeeded in that post by John Glusman and Eric Chinski when he assumed the titles of publisher and president of the firm. Giroux grew old gracefully and gradually retired, and toward the end he had to use a cane to get around. With the fiftieth-anniversary Farrar, Straus & Giroux brochure in hand, which listed all of the books the firm published until February 1997, he ticked off in my presence the books he had edited and in a few cases coedited, though he did acknowledge the occasional assistance of junior editors. The total came to an impressive 480 books. As he looked at the list, he would pause over certain titles, smiling, recollecting the authors, and recounting in some cases the problems he faced in seeing their books through the press.

Toward the turn of the century, Robert Giroux and Charles Reilly, who remained inseparable and never hesitated about appearing in public as a couple, moved to Seabrook Village in Tinton Falls, New Jersey. Reilly had an extended family in the area, so both found the transition fairly easy. Alert until the very end, Bob died on September 5, 2008. I presided at the funeral liturgy, attended by his relatives and close friends, in Saint Elizabeth's Church in Avon-by-the-Sea. He was buried, as Charlie would be, in nearby Saint Margaret's Cemetery.

Theological Postscript

Flannery O'Connor's stories and novels deal not so much with make-believe as with make-to-believe. As a Jesuit priest with a background in American literature, I think I would be remiss not to conclude this book with some reflections on Flannery O'Connor and literature and theology. I do this not in an effort to foreclose discussion, but rather to open it up to newer dimensions, building on the demonstrated expertise of Susan Balée, Timothy J. Basselin, Mark Bosco, S.J., Robert Brinkmeyer, Gary Ciuba, Jordan Cofer, John Desmond, Paul Elie, Richard Giannone, Brad Gooch, Sarah Gordon, George A. Kilcourse Jr., Christina Bieber Lake, J. Ramsey Michaels, William Monroe, Farrell O'Gorman, Katherine Hemple Prown, Brian Abel Ragen, William Sessions, Ted Spivey, Susan Srigley, and Ralph C. Wood, among others.

From one perspective, O'Connor's fiction reveals characters who, though free, nevertheless experience human limitations; they can either accept themselves and their limitations or they can flee from the self-defeating dread in their lives. O'Connor boldly depicted religious situations in ways that Walker Percy, who certainly valued her repeated emphasis on the Incarnation and the Christian mystery / mysteries, simply preferred to do more obliquely. If a Catholic fiction writer incorporated explicitly religious themes into his or her fiction, Percy believed, readers' eyelids would begin to droop. "Fiction is the concrete expression of mystery," O'Connor stated forthrightly to the Savannah-Atlanta diocesan *Bulletin* editor Eileen Hall in March 1956, "mystery that is lived." While O'Connor began with this theological premise, she never-theless followed her characters once she had created them, interested in seeing where their fortunes and choices would lead them, rooted whether they knew it or not in a Christocentric world. "In the absence of this faith now, we govern by tenderness," she wrote in her introduction to *A Memoir of Mary Ann*. "It is tenderness which, long since cut off from the person of Christ, is wrapped in theory. When tenderness is detached from the source of tenderness, its logical outcome is terror. It ends in forced-labor camps and in the fumes of the gas chamber."[1] Father Smith, a dominant character in Percy's last novel *The Thanatos Syndrome*, understood well that a person who substitutes a sentimental ethos for a genuine commit-ment to Christ embraces the plausibility of a demonic lower choice. In effect, Percy wrote, clearly echoing O'Connor, "'Don't you know where tenderness leads?' Silence. 'To the gas chambers.'"[2]

For O'Connor, one of the tasks of the fiction writer was to achieve a sense of metonymy, of the whole found in a representative part, of rela-tionships that begin from the concrete here and now and spread out in some mysterious, transcendental fashion. In her essay "The Nature and Aim of Fiction," O'Connor wrote succinctly about her theory of litera-ture: "The kind of vision the fiction writer needs to have, or to develop, in order to increase the meaning of his story, is called the anagogical vision, and that is the kind of vision that is able to see different levels of reality in one image or one situation."[3] Avoiding the trap of trying to locate her fiction within some theoretical metaphysical discussion about the notion of reality, she states in her essay "On Her Own Work" that an anagogical vision offers some type of basis for finding language that re-jects unacceptable limits:

> I often ask myself what makes a story work, and what makes it hold up as a story, and I have decided that it is probably some action, some gesture of a character that is unlike any other in the story, one which indicates where the real heart of the story lies. This would have to be an action or a gesture which was both totally right and totally unex-pected; it would have to be one that was both in character and beyond character; it would have to suggest both the world and eternity. The action or gesture I'm talking about would have to be on the *ana-gogical level*, that is, the level which has to do with the Divine life and our participation in it. It would have to be a gesture that transcends

any neat allegory that might have been intended or any pat moral categories a reader could make. It would be a gesture which somehow made contact with mystery [emphasis mine].[4]

Thus her finest tales display an elusiveness within some framework of ambiguity (whether it be one of William Empson's seven types or not), which makes it impossible to reduce them to the sort of specific theological message that O'Connor would have eschewed. More than anyone else, I believe, Father William Lynch, a close friend of Caroline Gordon, Allen Tate, and Robert Fitzgerald, helped her in validating her particular literary direction. O'Connor reviewed two of his books for the Savannah-Atlanta diocesan *Bulletin: Christ and Apollo: The Dimensions of the Literary Imagination* (August 20, 1960) and *The Integrating Mind: An Exploration into Western Thought* (August 4, 1962).[5] Sallie TeSelle, an important theoretician of literature and the Christian life, has high praise for Father Lynch, writing, "Lynch's main contention is that Jesus Christ, understood as the God-man who entered fully into the complexity and limitation of human life, can be the model for the artistic imagination in its attempt to arrive 'somewhere' by going through the multifariousness of human limitation and temporality." She notes in particular that his thesis "insists on the humanity of Christ and, for this reason, permits and demands an art that investigates in all detail the muddiness and human, the dynamism and limitation, the thickness and ambiguity of finite and particularly human reality."[6] In developing his interpretation of the analogical imagination, not only in chapter six of *Christ and Apollo*, but also in his series of essays on "Theology and Imagination" in the journal *Thought*, which O'Connor likewise read and commented upon, Lynch brings together sameness and difference, stressing that the things of this world have their own reality, but also participate, as Kilcourse notes in a discussion of Lynch's thought, in the larger community of being.[7] For Lynch, as emphasized by Kilcourse, the analogical is "that habit of perception which sees that different levels of being are also somehow one and can therefore be *associated in the same image*, in the same and single act of perception."[8] As God became incarnate in Jesus—especially in the Gospel according to Saint John, where images of bread, light, a road, and the Good Shepherd, to cite but a few, point to the otherworldly—so too does the human imagination probe the finite, the particular, and the limited as a way of describing the mysteries of the infinite God. Thus

Catholic theology at once embraces the world and yet at times renounces it, but always sees it—even in its negative forms—as a participation in God's mysterious plan for his people, while seeking to go, as Gordon notes in *The Obedient Imagination*, from the specific to the horizon of the eternal moment:

> Most important, however, O'Connor found in Lynch's ideas a strong theological defense of the tenets of the New Criticism. After all, Lynch, who cites Allen Tate with frequency and respect, argues, with both Tate and Eliot, that the disassociated sensibility is the most crucial problem of the modern era. Most of Lynch's work was, in fact, devoted to reuniting that sensibility. Basing his assertions on an analogical model, Lynch places the text itself in the center of the spotlight, going so far as to end his book [*Christ and Apollo*] with a reiteration of the four levels of meaning—literal, allegorical, tropological or moral, and anagogical—common to medieval scriptural analysis.[9]

As O'Connor believed so firmly, the Incarnation is not a temporary blessing but a Christification of the world that renders the human sacrosanct—as depicted, for example, in the almost nude child Jesus in the Christmas crèche and the almost nude Christus on a crucifix above an altar. Finite and infinite realities coalesce, for Lynch, and thus there is no need to pull together what has never been separated. "The resurrection of Christ seems the high point in the law of nature," O'Connor wrote to Hester in September 1955, a loaded observation inferring that the resurrection of Jesus—like an earthly miracle—is a natural phenomenon, something within the laws of nature, an observation that coincides with Robert Fitzgerald's in his introduction to *Everything That Rises Must Converge*, about Ruby Turpin in "Revelation": "What the struggle requires of Mrs. Turpin is courage and humility, that is clear enough. Perhaps as a reward for these, her eyes are opened. And the ascent that she sees at the end, in an astonishment like the astonishment of the new dead, takes place against that field of stars."[10] For O'Connor, the mystery of God in every part of the universe undergirds the Christian imagination.

But more is at stake, I believe. The Manichean temptation for the human imagination, as Lynch explains, is "to win its freedom by seeking quick infinities through the rapid and clever manipulation of the finite" rather than passing through "all the rigors, density, limitations, and decisions of the actual."[11] In a telling fashion, O'Connor says that Lynch "describes the true nature of the literary imagination as found in a penetration of the finite and the limited. . . . In genuine tragedy and comedy, the definite is explored to its extremity and man is shown to be the limited creature he is, and it is at this point of greatest penetration of the limited that the artist finds insight. Much modern so-called tragedy avoids this penetration and makes a leap toward transcendence, resulting in an unearned and spacious [sic] resolution of the work."[12] Though O'Connor did not subscribe to the entirety of Lynch's thesis, she did agree with his general theory, since she realized its potential for explaining the Christic imagination, which she saw linked to the anagogical interpretation of Scripture as expressed in the Latin phrase *Littera gesta docet, quod credas allegoria, moralia qui agas, quo tendas anagogia* (The literal teaches events, allegory what you believe, the moral teaches what to do, the anagogical where you are headed). I feel sure that O'Connor would have altered or at least highly nuanced her views concerning the fourfold interpretation of Sacred Scripture, given not only the insights in Lucretia Yaghjian's fine article on O'Connor and Christology, but also the incredible hermeneutical developments in Scripture since her death, led in the United States by such eminent scholars as Raymond Brown, S.S., Joseph Fitzmyer, S.J., and Roland Murphy, O. Carm.[13] (It is interesting to note that Caroline Gordon, in an unpublished lecture at Saint Mary's College, Notre Dame, Indiana, given when she was writer in residence at Purdue University from 1963–1964, also discussed the fourfold sense of Scripture, particularly as related to Dante's poetry, stating that Dante structured the *Divine Comedy* using this method.)[14] O'Connor's assessment of Scripture reflects a Church that was just beginning to deepen its study of the Jewish Bible and the New Testament, as well as the language and categories appropriate for this type of study, much of it borrowed from German scholars. She would *not* have been aware of the dramatic impact it would have on the discussion and decrees of the Second Vatican Council. Her penchant for accepting a fourfold reading of Sacred Scripture is not without merit, however, because Catholicism, which accepts the Jewish Bible as part of its scriptural heritage, has always had layered relationships of one sort or another not only with Judaism but with other belief systems. Given the penchant for exploring highly developed hermeneutics, one would be hard put to find Scripture scholars today who embrace interpretations of Christian sacred texts based solely on medieval theological categories. Awakening to the importance of Sacred Scripture for most American Catholics, particularly in the vernacular, and concomitantly allowing access to cite and interpret such texts, occurred for the most part after O'Connor's death as part of the aggiornamento following the Second Vatican Council.

It is most curious that those who discuss O'Connor's views on theology and philosophy rarely mention that she was never formally trained in either discipline. This does not mean, of course, that she did not understand the books she read, but her knowledge came from these books and not from personal dialogue with experts in these fields. This is an important distinction because instruction by trained professionals and the resulting focused classroom discussions can assist one in gaining a larger view of the topic under discussion. In *Flannery O'Connor's Sacramental Art*, Srigley provides a fine caveat concerning the problematic relationship of theology and literature in O'Connor's work:

> Those who lack any interest in O'Connor's religious orientation assume that O'Connor's fiction can be interpreted and analyzed without the aid of the explicitly religious commentary found in her essays. Often what scholars find objectionable are religious interpretations of O'Connor's work that use her prose as a religious template to determine or finalize the meaning of her fiction. Certainly this is a reasonable objection. Statements of religious ideas should never be substituted for careful analysis and interpretation. On the one hand, using theological ideas as if they were formulas distorts the often subtle philosophical originality of O'Connor's religious thought in *Mystery and Manners*. On the other hand, those who radically separate her theological inquiry from her fictional landscapes refuse to acknowledge how profoundly the two are connected. . . . In my view, it seems quite possible to discover the inherent connection between O'Connor's theological and philosophical thought—as found in the essays and letters—and her fictional art.[15]

To talk about O'Connor's theology and the doctrines of the Roman Catholic Church, as most of her critics do with varying degrees of insight and depth, infers a history of the knowledge of specific doctrines and why and how they were formulated by Church councils, where opposing theo-

logical views, some of them highly nuanced, were given due consideration. Over the centuries, Church councils in Nicea (325), Constantinople
(381), Rome (382), Orange (529), and Trent (1545–1563), among others,
have been held to deal with issues about the nature of Jesus as Christ, the
trinitarian God, and the Church. To omit any acknowledgment of these
councils and the theologians who were instrumental in guiding the
Church in formulating its beliefs and religious practices is, in effect, to
reduce the history of the Church to a spiritual memo or blackboard message. One of O'Connor's major theological issues should not, for example,
be separated from the heated discussions by the bishops at Nicea: The
titles given to Jesus the Christ (Lord, Savior, Word, Son of God, Son of
Man, Messiah, Prophet, Priest) refer to relational categories of power,
function, and action. They do not, in and of themselves, define in an on-
tological way who Jesus the Christ *is*. As explained by John Courtney
Murray, S.J., one of the most distinguished American theologians during
O'Connor's lifetime, the dogmatic impact of Nicea was in using the
Greek word *homoousion* (consubstantial) to define that Jesus is begotten
out of the Father, that is, out of the substance of the Father: "It defined
what the Son is, in himself, and in his relation to the one God the
Father. The Son is from the Father in a singular, unshared way, begotten
as Son, not made as a creature. The Son is all that the Father is, except for
the Name of Father. This is what *homoousion* means. This is what the Son
is."[16] But the question for ordinary Christian Catholics, who accept the
certification of the Church's dogma as true, focuses on how they understand this dogma as proclaimed at Nicea. For the Scholastics, especially
Saint Thomas in dealing with the problem of God in questions 2–13 of
the first part of the *Summa Theologica*, this understanding is achieved
imperfectly and incompletely, often through the process of analogy, based
on a fundamental axiom: fides quaerens intellectum (faith seeking an understanding of itself). What Saint Thomas did, according to Father
Murray, was to transpose "the problem of God into a state of systematic
theological understanding."[17] Although human beings are made in the
image of God, they do not possess the consciousness of God, nor obviously are they God. But through analogy, a similarity between like features of two entities, as when one shows or argues or infers that one thing
or situation is similar to another in a certain respect, one can probe and
approach the mysterious Godhead. Thus, through analogy one enters

into the realms of similitude, comparison, likeness, resemblance, affinity, and most importantly for a Christian, participation.

Many of O'Connor's stories serve as traps for meditation, assisting readers to see and understand divine Mystery, to move toward an ever-receding horizon. In "A Temple of the Holy Ghost," to cite but one example, Benediction, a Catholic liturgical service, assumes a central part of the story, yet one would be hard pressed to find in a good deal of O'Connor criticism an explanation of Benediction and how God can be physically present to and among his people—even the freakish ones in a carnival sideshow, including a hermaphrodite—who are made in God's likeness, and how this devotion fits into the Church's liturgical tradition.[18] O'Connor's tendency is to depict a series of human incidents that indirectly, weirdly, obliquely show her readers, after some reflection and discernment on their part, a direction they might consider taking. She wanted to encourage the anti-institutional attitude of those who maintain "I'm spiritual but not religious" to open doors they knew existed but preferred not to pass through.

Though O'Connor showed no interest in the specific decrees of the First Vatican Council (1869–1870), she seemed willing to learn about the Church's complex process of updating and the change taking place in Rome during the latter years of her life. Raised in a Church that allows only six of its seven sacraments to women (women cannot be ordained priests), O'Connor developed a spirituality heavily informed by the theological discussions of the First Vatican Council, which was preceded by years of theological reflection, particularly concerning the sometimes unpopular notion of papal infallibility, commonly thought of as emanating from a sense of Roman triumphalism, and the less polemical belief in the Immaculate Conception of the Blessed Virgin Mary, both of which could and did at times have deleterious effects in promoting ecumenism, as O'Connor knew firsthand as a citizen of the Protestant South. Not surprisingly, her fiction never mentions either dogma. Out of this council came a mentality opposing what were called the errors of rationalism, materialism, and atheism—in short, the tenets of freethinking, uninformed by divine revelation, sometimes referred to as "Modernism." Rather, as a practicing Catholic in the widening wake of Vatican I, O'Connor believed God creates his creatures out of nothing, manifests his perfection to them, and leads them to their intended, freely chosen destination. In asserting the relationship between faith and reason, she believed, as did other Catholics of her day who followed the teaching of Saint Thomas Aquinas, that the full impact of the mysteries of faith could not be grasped by natural reason alone, though revealed, unassailable truth would never contradict the results of reasonable investigation. As a result every assertion is false, at least in a Thomistic framework, which contradicts the truth of an enlightened faith entrusted to the Church for protection and interpretation. In spite of reading the *Summa Theologica* about twenty minutes a day, just before going to bed, O'Connor was forthright about her knowledge of Saint Thomas: "I am a Thomist three times removed and live amongst many distinctions. (A Thomist three times removed is one who doesn't read Latin or St. Thomas but gets it by osmosis.)"[19] O'Connor's letters to Betty Hester in *The Habit of Being* show her absolute conviction in the dogmas of her Church. Miracles, which never seem to interest O'Connor, could confirm divine revelation. Unlike the dogmatic constitutions, declarations, and decrees of the Second Vatican Council, not in full force during O'Connor's lifetime, those of the First Vatican Council tended to be prescriptive rather than descriptive, based on what it considered to be assured, rock-solid, absolute certainty that could easily sniff out anything to the contrary.

Focused, concentrated, and forthright, O'Connor's statements about faith have a curious ahistorical character about them because they do not take into account the extended narrative accounts about Jesus the Christ in the New Testament or the sometimes controversial development of doctrine and Christology over the centuries. Why are there so few specific references in *Mystery and Manners*, the collection of her occasional prose, about the events of Jesus's life as mentioned by the four evangelists or by Saint Paul in his various letters? Yet Jordan Cofer has shown with tremendous insight that throughout O'Connor's work "there are significant biblical allusions which have been overlooked: more importantly, the methodology behind these allusions as a whole has been neglected. While it is necessary to acknowledge her biblical source material, it is critical to understand the impact it has had on her fiction. O'Connor's stories engage their biblical analogues in unusual, unexpected, and sometimes violent and grotesque manipulations, while conveying essentially the same message as their biblical counterparts. Theologically, her modus operandi was to argue many of the same points about grace that her biblical sources did, but to a modern-day audience."[20] Using various gospel pericopes and selected quotes from the letters of Saint Paul, Cofer provides a theological background for O'Connor's stories and novels. At times he shows how O'Connor parodies certain biblical figures and provides ironic reversals to these scriptural texts precisely to emphasize the theological import of her fiction, often subverting the reader's expectations. In doing so, however, Cofer has drawn attention to a larger theological and literary problematic, as expressed in his statement that O'Connor's stories convey "essentially the same message as their biblical counterparts." While it is most appropriate for Cofer to cite verses from Saint Paul's letter to the Galatians (4:13–15) about plucking out one's eyes, as does in fact Hazel Motes at the conclusion to *Wise Blood*, this particular Pauline letter, like all of Saint Paul's letters, as well as the gospel pericopes, has a much larger historical and theological context that cannot be captured in citing isolated phrases from the letter. Cofer has rendered an invaluable service to his readers in analyzing the scriptural background to O'Connor's fiction, but O'Connor never intended, nor could any creative writer ever manage, to embody the depth and scope of Catholic theology, as contained, for example, in the entire letter to the Galatians, into one of her short stories or novels. To infer that certain of O'Connor's stories or novels convey the same "message" as that contained in certain passages in Scripture fails to engage the larger context of the Scriptural passage in question. This said, Cofer has provided a detailed, nuanced theological interpretation of O'Connor's fiction.

O'Connor preferred to express her religious faith by relying on dogmatic concepts, such as sin, redemption, grace, and the sacraments, such as baptism, all within a context of the Christian mystery in its intensely dramatic sense. She had no intention of solving problems as if they were pieces in a Rubik's Cube. Throughout her entire life, O'Connor *heard* passages from the Jewish Bible and the New Testament read by priests at Mass in Latin, which might have been an obstacle to her entrance into the drama of Christ's life. But such generalities can be deceiving, I would be the first to admit, for the rituals and readings of Holy Week, including the performative power of the Stations of the Cross that vividly recall Jesus's Passion, are extraordinarily gripping. Still and all, the use of Latin in O'Connor's day provided a sense of awe for many faithful, not because they could necessarily understand Latin as a language (O'Connor had just one credit in high school Latin), but because it opened up and seemed to include a sense of the divine—and a way to be transported back to the days when Jesus walked the Holy Land, preaching his countercultural message. All of this is to say that O'Connor's discussion of theology, particularly its Thomistic formulations, reflects much of the thinking of her particular time and society.[21]

O'Connor became a consummate short story writer whose place in fiction is assured not only because of her theological bias, but also because she was ahead of her time. Out of the mainstream of writers of the 1940s and 1950s, she wrote in a postmodern mode, which refers to a radical shift in aesthetic and cultural sensibilities evident in art and literature after World War I. Modernism, often considered to include a range of artistic movements, such as symbolism and futurism, broke with so-called Victorian bourgeois morality, rejecting nineteenth-century optimism and opting instead for moral relativism. In literature, modernism is associated with the works of T. S. Eliot, James Joyce, Ezra Pound, Virginia Woolf, and William Butler Yeats. In their attempt to throw off the aesthetic burden of the realistic novel, these writers introduced a variety of literary tactics and devices, including the radical disruption of the linear flow of narrative, the frustration of conventional expectations of unity and coherence of plot and character, and the deployment of ironic and ambiguous juxtapositions that call into question the moral, theological, and philosophical meaning of literary action.[22] Several forms of modernist thought ground themselves in their own self-presence—without God and without a center. The pared-down, fragmentary, nonchronological poetic forms of Eliot and Pound revolutionized literature and, in turn, much of the American poetry and fiction of that time period. Faulkner's use of stream of consciousness in the Benjy section of *The Sound and the Fury* and Welty's use of myth as a structural principle in *The Golden Apples* challenged in their own ways traditional forms of representation. Perhaps because of its pervasive theological caste, O'Connor's fiction does not fit comfortably into a modernist ideology.

Postmodern movements in literature and theology attempt to challenge some modernist tenets. Thus, a fair number of postmodern literary theorists, rejoicing in intense irony and intellectual comedy, tended to deconstruct works of literature, arriving at books filled just with words arranged in certain, discernible patterns. But not all postmodern theorists are deconstructionists, especially not those who believe in God. As a postmodernist who kept her eyes and heart on a definite theological center, O'Connor resisted the temptation to depict her fictive world alinguistically and ahistorically, and astonishingly—at least to me—she resisted a prepackaged Thomistic theology, all-too-popularly imagined as a triangle with God at the top; bishops under Him; priests, nuns, and religious brothers under the bishops, and then the good, simple Catholic laity resting firmly at the bottom. Rather, in alignment with the thinking of the Second Vatican Council, a good number of her characters, people filled with marvelous foibles, are on a pilgrimage, holy or otherwise, and in need of conversion. O'Connor wrote about those whom the modern tradition too often repressed: the mystic, the prophetic, the marginalized— in short, she dealt with otherness, difference, transgression, excess— notions (some even might say buzzwords) so much part of contemporary critical parlance today. Her stories, as Alfred Kazin states in his *Bright Book of Life*, "remain in your mind as inflexible moral equations. The drama is made up of the short distance between the first intimations of conflict and the catastrophe."[23] O'Connor herself wrote in "A Fiction Writer and His Country" that a literary vocation "is a limiting factor which extends to the kind of material that the writer is able to apprehend imaginatively. The writer can choose what he writes about but he cannot choose what he is able to make live, and so far as he is concerned a living *deformed character* is acceptable and a dead whole one is not" (emphasis mine).[24] And this explains, in part, why she is so beloved by adult readers, who know about otherness, difference, transgression, and excess, but difficult for young adults who have yet to amass a critical number of potentially mortal weaknesses.

Sarah Gordon suggests that O'Connor might be partly responsible for pushing the critical argument about her works to become highly reiterative: "Can we be faulted if we ask just why it is that many commentators on O'Connor's works seem to sit outside or above the stories themselves as they weave their theories, especially theological ones, by which light we are enjoined to read everything? Because of her own public comments emphasizing the theological import of her fiction, is O'Connor herself inadvertently responsible for our spinning out theories that neatly cover, even disguise, the angularity and complexity of her vision?"[25] O'Connor's postmodern tendencies, seemingly old-fashioned, down-home, and local, nevertheless have a universal appeal, rooted in the polyvalent, unrestrictive sense of the Christian mystery she demanded in her own fiction.

For many, O'Connor's work can be conceived as an effort to recover the ideal of the Holy in an age in which both the meaning and reality of the concept have been obscured. She believed that the loss of the Holy involved for society a concomitant loss of depth and diminution of being. Therefore, as exemplified in "A Good Man Is Hard to Find," she felt the need to journey through the radically profane, not hesitating to look directly at evil in order to rediscover the good or pursue the demonic in order to arrive finally at the Holy. O'Connor never manipulates the destinies of her characters; they are free to choose their final dwelling place, whether it be heaven, purgatory (mentioned by Father Flynn in "The Displaced Person"), or hell. She constantly kept her focus on mystery and manners—the mystery of Christianity, sometimes radical Protestantism but more often traditional Catholicism, and the world of Southern manners. If Flannery O'Connor did not want her mule or wagon stalled on the same track when Faulkner's Dixie Limited came roaring down, something similar could be said about her tremendous strength as a fiction writer. Other writers with similar interests would be well advised to take alternate routes.

Introduction

1. *HB*, 80, 337; UL, FOC to JMC and George White, April 16, 1958, HBA; *HB*, 280.

2. DL sent his letter of reference to Henry Allen Moe, director of the John Simon Guggenheim Foundation, on November 28, 1955, HBA.

3. RG, introduction to FOC, *Complete Stories of Flannery O'Connor*, viii.

4. For a short discussion of Arbus and FOC, see Goodwin, *Modern American Grotesque*, 150–51.

5. Arbus, *Diane Arbus*, 3.

6. See Sontag, *On Photography*, 32–48.

7. UL, January 19, 1961, RGF.

8. Stephens, *Correspondence of Flannery O'Connor and the Brainard Cheneys*, 128.

9. See FOC's "Last Will and Testament," GC; also Moran, *Creating Flannery O'Connor*, 82, 115.

10. See RG, introduction to FOC, *Complete Stories of Flannery O'Connor*, ix.

11. See Souhami, *Gertrude and Alice*, 75.

12. UL, January 22, 1955, HBA.

13. A number of years before his death, RG donated many of his books, letters, and files to the Special Collections Room, Monroe Library, Loyola University, New Orleans. Some of his essays and talks have not been published, such as his talk upon accepting, on behalf of O'Connor, the National Book Award in 1972 for *Flannery O'Connor: The Complete Stories*, and his remarks in accepting the Thomas More Medal in Chicago, given by the Thomas More Association, for *Everything That Rises Must Converge*. Furthermore there exist a number of unpublished talks by RG on TM for which I served as sometime scribe and typist. Copies of these talks are in the files of PS.

14. See UL, RG to Mrs. Robert Lowell [Elizabeth Hardwick], January 22, 1957, NYPL.

15. See UL, RG to William Lynch, S.J., August 20, 1956, NYPL. Both RG and CC read at least one of Father Lynch's books in manuscript form (see William Lynch, S.J., to AT, June 15, 1958; also William Lynch, S.J., to AT, April 13 [no year], PU). The extensive correspondence of Father Lynch and AT is housed at PU.

16. See Ryan, "I Remember Mary Flannery," 50.

17. See the unpublished essay "My Memory of Mary Flannery O'Connor" by Nell Ann Summers Walters, EU.

18. *HB*, 56.

19. See the unpublished essay "Flannery, 1957" by Maryat Lee, NYPL.

20. Welty, "Place in Fiction," 128–29.

21. Hawkes, "Flannery O'Connor's Devil," 399.

22. See Cash, *Flannery O'Connor*, 259–97.

23. Once the Giroux family settled in New Jersey, after living for a while in Pennsylvania, Arthur Giroux, Robert's father, worked as a loom fixer before being promoted to plant superintendent in the Givernaud Silk Mill in Paterson, eighteen miles north of Jersey City. During a tour that RG once gave me of Jersey City, he pointed out, not with the greatest pride or affection, a number of places where his family had lived; he could count seven "homes" in all. About the time Robert was nine years old, his father stopped working in the Givernaud Mill; he never really understood the reason for this sudden change. Was his father fired or did he just quit, knowing that he had little future in this type of work? Young Robert deeply resented his father's behavior, particularly as he stayed at home most of the time, privately handicapping horses. When his granddaughter Roberta Rodriquez visited the Giroux family, she was fascinated by the pictures of horses and the racing charts Arthur had collected and taped to his wall. Though he took an occasional odd job working as a carpenter, he was clearly an embarrassment to his children. If anything, Robert was determined never to follow his father's example, knowing that some type of self-initiative was better than none.

24. See *HB*, 520, 13.

25. RG, "Education of an Editor," 11.

26. Welty, *The Optimist's Daughter*, 160.

27. See UL, RG to John Loudon, June 17, 1985, NYPL.

28. Blotner, "Did You See Him Plain?" 17–18, 22.

29. Although FOC had never heard of Faulkner before going to graduate school in Iowa, her story "Wildcat," written in Iowa, shows a decidedly Faulknerian influence. She later remembered reading *Sanctuary* and *The Sound and the Fury*, the first containing, as she acknowledges, Popeye, one of Faulkner's most demonic characters, and the second Quentin Compson, a Mississippian who commits suicide by jumping into the Charles River at the end of his first year at

Harvard—both of whom might have given her something to consider as she wrote about the Misfit in "A Good Man Is Hard to Find" and Bevel in "The River" (see *HB*, 221, 16, 63–64). One might also think that Enoch Emery's statement in *Wise Blood*, "Something's going to happen to me today" (*CW*, 78), is an allusion to Joe Christmas's phrase "Something is going to happen to me" in Faulkner's *Light in August* (*Faulkner: Novels: 1930–1935*, 475). "I keep clear of Faulkner," she wrote to Hester in March 1958, "so my own little boat won't get swamped." She later noted that she did not read Faulkner's fiction most likely because he made her feel that she, with her "one-cylinder syntax," should quit writing and just raise chickens (*HB*, 292). Her most famous quip about this Nobel Prize recipient occurs in her essay "Some Aspects of the Grotesque in Southern Fiction": "The presence alone of Faulkner in our midst makes a great difference in what the writer can and cannot permit himself to do. Nobody wants his mule and wagon stalled on the same track when the Dixie Limited is roaring down" (*MandM*, 45). See also Watson, "Escapes and Diversions, Whoring and Trash;" that issue of the *Flannery O'Connor Review* features essays comparing the fiction of FOC and Faulkner.

Chapter One

1. See RL, *Letters of Robert Lowell*, 115, 123.
2. See Ackroyd, *T. S. Eliot*, 287–89.
3. A copy of this photo is reproduced in Simpson, *Poets in Their Youth*, 172.
4. See RL, *Letters of Robert Lowell*, 3–4.
5. See *HB*, 36.
6. See RL, *Letters of Robert Lowell*, 110.
7. See RF, "Gold and Gloom in Ezra Pound," 138.
8. See RG, "Poet in the Asylum," 45; see also RG et al., "Celebration of Robert Lowell," 262.
9. UL, RG to JB, February 16, 1965, NYPL.
10. UL, FOC to EM, January 28, 1949, DU.
11. RL, *Letters of Robert Lowell*, 111.
12. In the early 1950s, EB met Maria Carlota ("Lota") Costallat de Macedo Soares, an architect and landscape designer, and lived with her in Petrópolis, fifty miles north of Rio de Janeiro. RG always considered EB one of his most distinguished authors, expending enormous time and energy in editing her poetry and letters. "I feel great remorse now . . . that I had allowed this friendship to dwindle just when she must have been aware she was dying," EB reminisced after FOC's death. "Something about her intimidated me a bit: perhaps natural awe before her toughness and courage; perhaps, although death is certain for all, hers seemed a little more certain than usual. She made no show of not living in a metropolis,

or of being a believer—she lived with Christian stoicism and wonderful wit and humor that put most of us to shame" (EB in Quinn, *Flannery O'Connor*, 717). See George S. Lensing, "Elizabeth Bishop and Flannery O'Connor."

13. RL, *Letters of Robert Lowell*, 699.

14. See letter dated "Thursday" [December 1948], PU.

15. RL first met JB in 1944 at Princeton through CG, and before long they became good friends. The Berrymans stayed with Lowell and Stafford for two weeks in Maine in the summer of 1946 (see JB, "Dream Songs," in *Collected Poems: 1937–1971*, 56, 171; see also RL, *Collected Prose*, 111; Simpson, *Poets in Their Youth*, 115–46; Mariani, *Dream Song*, 175–77; and Stafford's short story "Influx of Poets"). RL suggested in the summer of 1947, in a letter to Paul Engle, director of the Iowa Writers' Workshop, that JB replace him as a faculty member, noting that JB "is a wonderful person, a good poet and probably fifty times as good a teacher as I would have been" (RL, *Letters of Robert Lowell*, 64). RL accepted a post at the Workshop from February through May 1950, followed by a short summer stint at Kenyon College. In the fall of 1953 he taught at the Workshop, as did JB in the spring 1954 semester.

16. See *HB*, 39.

17. See Hulbert, *Interior Castle*, 192; see also Mariani, "'My Heavy Daughter,'" 4.

18. Kazin, *New York Jew*, 204; see also Kazin, *Writing Was Everything*, 123–25.

19. Kazin, *New York Jew*, 204; see UL, RG to FOC, December 13, 1955, RGF.

20. See Straus, *Paper Trail*, 50–60. RG last saw Stafford the day before she died on March 26, 1979.

21. Étienne Gilson, JM's contemporary, likewise a native Parisian, became director of studies for medieval philosophy at the École Pratique des Hautes Études in Paris. In 1926 he came to the United States for the first time, lecturing at Harvard and the University of Virginia before becoming in 1929 the cofounder of the Institute of Mediaeval Studies in Toronto, Canada, and in 1932 a professor at the Collège de France in Paris. Gilson particularly noted that medieval philosophy, under the influence of Christianity, opened up new ways of thinking, to such an extent that Christian revelation can serve as an indispensable aid to reason. Gilson, like some of his contemporaries, resisted synthesizing Thomism with philosophies not sympathetic with its spirit, such as the methodic doubt of Descartes, thus becoming a champion of a living, unadulterated Thomism. FOC's admiration for Gilson can be seen in her letter to Betty Hester (*HB*, 107) and in her review in the Savannah–Atlanta diocesan *Bulletin* (May 3, 1958) of his *Painting and Reality*.

22. See Gilson, *A Gilson Reader*, 101–2.

23. See *CW*, 951, 919.

24. RL, *Letters of Robert Lowell*, 452–53.

25. See *HB*, 242.

26. See UL, EB to RL, December 31, 1948, HU.

27. Hardwick, *Sleepless Nights*, 29–30.

28. RL, *Collected Poems*, 189.

29. RL, *Letters of Robert Lowell*, 226. For a fictional account of the FOC–RL relationship, see Carlene Bauer, *Frances and Bernard*.

30. See RL in Quinn, *Flannery O'Connor*, 59.

31. RL, *Letters of Robert Lowell*, 302.

32. See Daugherty, *Just One Catch*, 176, for a reference to EM as an editor at the *Atlantic Monthly*.

33. See UL, RG to FOC, December 13, 1955, RGF.

34. See UL, SF to RG, September 3, 1977, RGF.

35. UL, June 23, 1948, DU.

36. See UL, July 13, 1948, DU.

37. See UL, DU.

38. See UL, John Selby to EM, August 3, 1948, DU.

39. See UL, FOC to EM, September 3, 1948, DU.

40. Wray, "The Importance of Home to the Fiction of Flannery O'Connor," 104–5.

41. See UL, FOC to EM, September 18, 21, 1948, DU; see also *HB*, 7.

42. Born into a Jewish family in the Ukraine, Rahv immigrated to the United States in 1922, becoming known for his essays published in the *New Masses*, the *Nation*, and the *New Leader* and eventually cofounding the *Partisan Review*, a journal of literary and social thought that broke with the Soviet line in 1937 in the wake of the Moscow Trials. His reputation as an important member of the New York intelligentsia was confirmed by the publication of two well-received books, *The Discovery of Europe: The Story of the American Experience in the Old World* and *Fourteen Essays on Literary Themes*. FOC's "A Good Man Is Hard to Find" was first published in *The Avon Book of Modern Writing*, edited by William Phillips and Philip Rahv (New York: Avon, 1953), 186–99.

43. See Dunn and Driggers, eds., with Gordon, *Manuscripts of Flannery O'Connor*, xii.

44. See UL, FOC to EM, October 12, 23, 1948, DU; and November 8, 14, 24, 1948, DU.

45. UL, DU.

46. See UL, FOC to EM, February 3, 5, 1949, DU.

47. UL, February 16, 1949, DU.

48. DU; see partial version in *HB*, 9.

49. UL, February 18, 1949, DU.

50. See *HB*, 13.

51. See UL, EM to FOC, February 23, 1949, DU; see also UL, FOC to Miss Flack, February 23, 1949, DU.

52. UL, February 24, 1949, DU.

53. The novel went through three main stages: (1) By the time FOC had applied for the Rinehart Fellowship in Iowa, she had completed five chapters. (2) Selby said that he needed to see six chapters in order to make some evaluation of the novel for publication. Thus by early 1949, FOC had completed nine chapters plus an outline, both of which failed to impress Selby. (3) Between January 1949 and March 1951, she rewrote the novel from the beginning for RG (see Prown, *Revising Flannery O'Connor*, III–12). FOC rewrote much of her novel because she did not feel that the original chapters she had written were fit to show Selby. "For this reason, much of this [revised] version is substantially different from other *Wise Blood* typescripts in the files [in the Ina Dillard Russell Library at Georgia College], most of which pertain to the earlier twelve chapters" (Dunn and Driggers, with Gordon, *Manuscripts of Flannery O'Connor*, 69).

54. See Hamilton, *Robert Lowell: A Biography*, 145; see also RL, *Letters of Robert Lowell*, 115, 122; *HB*, 11; see also Price, *The Lives of Agnes Smedley*, 9, 403–4.

55. See Minutes of the Special Meeting of the Directors of Yaddo, 32 (copy at EU); see also Hamilton, *Robert Lowell*, 144, 484.

56. See Hamilton, *Robert Lowell*, 148–49; see also Mariani, *Lost Puritan*, 178–79; see also Simpson, *Poets in Their Youth*, 190–91.

57. See UL, PU.

58. See UL, RF to George Santayana, May 15, 1949, EU.

59. Simpson, *Poets in Their Youth*, 190.

60. See Florencourt, "Interview With Robert Giroux," 84.

61. Eileen Simpson gives Jean Stafford's account of RL's breakdown after his Yaddo stay, noting that RL went to a Benedictine monastery (not a Trappist one), most likely Portsmouth Abbey, Portsmouth, Rhode Island. See Simpson, *Poets in Their Youth*, 190–94.

62. See Hamilton, *Robert Lowell*, 150–51.

63. Vinh, ed., *Cleanth Brooks and Allen Tate: Collected Letters: 1933–76*, 148; see also Waldron, *Close Connections: Caroline Gordon and the Southern Renaissance*, 267.

64. See Doreski, *The Years of Our Friendship: Lowell and Tate*, 88–91.

65. Quoted in *HB*, 399.

66. For an extended analysis of AT's and CG's religious backgrounds, particularly as they concern FOC and WP, see O'Gorman, *Peculiar Crossroads: Flannery O'Connor, Walker Percy, and Catholic Vision in Post-war Southern Fiction*, 51–102.

67. See Mizener, *The Saddest Story: A Biography of Ford Madox Ford*, 439.

68. RL, "Visiting the Tates," 557.

69. Young and Sarcone, *Lytle-Tate Letters*, 108.

70. See RG, "Hard Years and 'Scary Days,'" 3.

71. See RL, *Collected Prose*, 22. After graduating from Vanderbilt in 1909, Ransom studied at Christ Church, Oxford, as a Rhodes scholar, and then re-

turned in 1914 to Vanderbilt to teach. He left in 1937 to join the faculty of Kenyon College. Curiously, there is no evidence from the FOC letters presently available that she ever read any of Ransom's poetry.

72. In her essay "Letter Watching," SF notes that CG loaned her letters from FOC to a graduate student who never returned them.

73. See *HB*, 255–56.

74. Twelve Southerners. *I'll Take My Stand: The South and the Agrarian Tradition*. New York: Harper & Brothers, 1930.

75. Prown, *Revising Flannery O'Connor*, 25.

76. See Haddox, "Contextualizing Flannery O'Connor," 173–74.

77. AT, "Miss Emily and the Bibliographer," 143.

78. See Dunaway, *Exiles and Fugitives*, 19.

79. See *HB*, 60.

80. AT did not remain faithful to CG (he reportedly had a number of affairs, one with Elizabeth Hardwick); they divorced in January 1946, then remarried that April in Professor Willard Thorp's study in Princeton, and then divorced again in April 1959. (Concerning AT's affair with Hardwick, see McAlexander, *Peter Taylor: A Writer's Life*, 93.)

81. See O'Hare, "Interview with Robert Giroux."

82. See RF, "Randall Jarrell: A Memoir," 132.

83. RL, *Letters of Robert Lowell*, 109.

84. See RG, "Flannery O'Connor," talk at the Walter Reade Theater, Lincoln Center, New York, April 30, 2001. Hereafter Walter Reade Theater.

85. See SF, "Flannery O'Connor: Patterns of Friendship," 417.

86. RF, introduction to FOC, *Everything That Rises Must Converge*, 12.

87. RF, introduction to FOC, *Everything That Rises Must Converge*, xii–xiii.

88. FOC, "The Writer and the Graduate School," 4.

89. See O'Hare, "Interview with Robert Giroux."

90. See Cash, *Flannery O'Connor*, 99; see also RL, *Letters of Robert Lowell*, 61.

91. See McAlexander, *Peter Taylor*, 98.

92. RG once made this list in my presence of authors whose works he had edited or helped to edit in some fashion, sometimes in translation, who were Nobel Prize laureates: Knut Hamsun (1920), Hermann Hesse (1946), TSE (1948), Pär Lagerkvist (1951), François Mauriac (1952), Juan Ramón Jiménez (1956), Salvatore Quasimodo (1959), Nelly Sachs (1966), Aleksandr Solzhenitsyn (1970), Pablo Neruda (1971), Issac Bashevis Singer (1978), Czeslaw Milosz (1980), Elias Canetti (1981), William Golding (1983), Wole Soyinka (1986), Joseph Brodsky (1987), Camilo José Cela (1989), Nadine Gordimer (1991), Derek Walcott (1992), and Seamus Heaney (1995). He also edited seven books that won the Pulitzer Prize: *77 Dream Songs* (1965) by John Berryman; *The Fixer* (1967) by Bernard Malamud; *The Collected Stories of Jean Stafford* (1970); *The Dolphin* (1974) by Robert Lowell; *Lamy of Santa Fe* (1976) by Paul Horgan; *The Morning of the Poem*

(1981) by James Schuyler; and *The Mambo Kings Play Songs of Love* (1990) by Oscar Hijuelos. In addition, he edited seventeen books that received the National Book Award.

93. For a fuller picture of the RG–TM relationship, see PS, *Letters of Robert Giroux and Thomas Merton*.

94. RG, introduction to FOC, *Complete Stories of Flannery O'Connor*, xiii.

Chapter Two

1. *HB*, 290–91.
2. McGill, "The Life You Write May Be Your Own," 32.
3. See Westling, "Flannery O'Connor's Mothers and Daughters," 510.
4. *MandM*, 84.
5. See DeLorme, "Alexander Semmes." For a comprehensive genealogy of the Semmes (Simms) family, see Harry Wright Newman, *The Maryland Semmes and Kindred Families* (Westminster, MD: Heritage Books, 2007).
6. For a discussion of FOC's ancestry, see SF, "Root and Branch: O'Connor of Georgia," and Flannery, "Genealogies of Select Flannerys in the U.S." Irish-born James Flannery married Margaret Dunn, who was born around 1746 in County Tipperary, Ireland, and died in 1794, most likely in Silvermines, County Tipperary. They had two sons, James and Michael. (Her husband outlived her and married Margaret Flannery in 1823 in Nenagh. They had two daughters, Anne and Mary, both born in Nenagh.) The elder son, James Flannery, was born in Nenagh, County Tipperary, and died at sea (after 1851). He married Hanna(h) Hogan after 1832 in Silvermines. They had twelve children: Patrick, Bridget, Catherine, James (John) (born in 1835 in Nenagh, County Tipperary), Hannah (or Honoria), William, Mary Anne, Mary, Ellen, Joseph, Michael, and Alice. The father of Cousin Katie, James (John) Flannery, came with his father and brothers from Ireland to South Carolina in 1851; in 1854, at age nineteen, he moved to Savannah and worked as a clerk and bookkeeper until the Civil War. During the war, he fought with Generals Johnston and Hood. When the war was over, he returned to Savannah and founded the Southern Bank of the State of Georgia. He was married in Savannah's cathedral in 1867 to the woman who would be Cousin Katie's mother, Mary Ellen Norton, the daughter of Patrick Norton and Honora Harty and the granddaughter of Patrick Harty of Locust Grove, died in August 1836. Mary Ellen Norton Flannery was born in Locust Grove and died in Savannah in 1899 (it was from her that Mary Flannery O'Connor received her baptismal name). They had six children: Mary Catherine, John (who died as an infant), Francis Xavier, another child called John, Henry, and Mary Victor. Captain Flannery died in Savannah on May 9, 1910. Mary

Catherine, born July 10, 1868, married Raphael Thomas Semmes in the Savannah Cathedral in 1891. Raphael Thomas Semmes was born July 27, 1857 in Canton, Mississippi, and died in Savannah on September 4, 1916.

7. See O'Gorman, *Peculiar Crossroads*, 24–26.

8. The paternal side of FOC's mother's family can be traced back to Irish-born Peter Cline from County Tipperary, who came to Georgia in 1843 and eventually taught Latin at the Richmond Academy in Augusta. Peter James Cline, the son of Peter and Bridget Cline, was born on September 22, 1845, in Augusta. At the deaths of his father and mother in 1848 and 1853 respectively, he became the ward of Miss Mary E. Cline, who sent him to school in Sharon and then, in 1861, to Saint Vincent's College in Pennsylvania. Soon after he started returning home in 1864, he ran out of money and thus took a job on the railroad in Nashville as a brakeman. He made his way to Augusta and then Atlanta. He published a biographical note in *Memoirs of Georgia* (1895), in which he tells of his life after the Civil War. In September 1870, he and a partner began a dry goods store in Milledgeville under the firm name of Cline & Quinn, which, after some difficult times, closed its doors. His efforts at raising full-blooded Jersey cattle, however, proved more successful, giving him an important standing in the community. He served as mayor of Milledgeville, a member of the board of trustees of the Middle Georgia Military and Agricultural College, and a director of a local bank. He married in succession two daughters of Hugh and Johannah Treanor: Kate and Margaret Ida. In all, Peter J. Cline was the father of sixteen children, including seven with Kate. FOC's mother, Regina Lucille, born in Milledgeville in 1896, was the seventh of the children born to Peter J. Cline and Margaret Ida Treanor Cline. After her primary school education, she was privileged enough to go to away to school at Mount Saint Joseph's Boarding and Day School for Girls in Augusta, where Mother Gabriel, a relative whom FOC once visited, served as the superior of the community (see *HB*, 142). See SF, "Root and Branch: O'Connor of Georgia," and Flannery, "Genealogies of Select Flannerys in the U.S."

9. For a portrait of FOC's father, see SF, "The Invisible Father," 15–16.

10. FOC's father and Private Steenhoek were in the same infantry unit and division. See Hartwell, "Pvt. Dick Steenhoek," for details about his wartime record, which would have paralleled that of FOC's father. Wartime data and quotes about the battles are taken from Private Steenhoek's journal.

11. See *CW*, 855.

12. See Sessions, "*Shenandoah* and the Advent of Flannery O'Connor," 237.

13. Katharine Ann Porter, Flannery O'Connor, et al., "Recent Southern Fiction: A Panel Discussion," in Rosemary M. Magee, ed., *Conversations with Flannery O'Connor* (Jackson: University Press of Mississippi, 1987), 70.

14. For an overview of FOC and her relationship to Milledgeville, see Sarah Gordon's "Milledgeville: The Perils of Place as a Text." For historical background

on FOC's story "A View of the Woods" and the dam on the Oconee River in Baldwin County, see Amason, "A View from the Woods: Preserving the Fortune of Andalusia," 149–56.

15. *MandM*, 127.

16. See *CW*, 850.

17. Gerard E. Sherry, "An Interview with Flannery O'Connor," in Magee, *Conversations with Flannery O'Connor*, 99.

18. See Fickett and Gilbert, *Flannery O'Connor: Images of Grace*, 38.

19. *HB*, 167–68; see *HB*, 166.

20. Kahane, "Re-vision of Rage," 447.

21. Kelly, "The World of Cartoons," 30.

22. Like many college students interested in literature, RG tried without great success to find his own literary voice while at Columbia. In July 1933 he sent off a film script to Fox Film Corporation on West Fifty-Sixth Street about a character named Robert who remembers the Armistice of World War I, goes to college in the East, and becomes a determined pacifist, seemingly insulting the memory of his father who had died in the war. Unfortunately, everyone he loves turns against him. After the script was turned down, *unread*, RG immediately wrote to D. A. Doran at Fox, explaining the significance of the story line. In short, he admitted, "It is a situation in which many a young man, including myself, has found himself." RG's prose, however, was reserved for campus publications. The December 1933 issue of the *Columbia Review* started off with another seemingly autobiographical story by RG about a thirteen-year-old eighth-grader leaving a local library. On his way home, he encounters a man he considers the Devil. Later, having escaped this unusual figure, he wonders if he should mention this in confession, but decides not to, sensing that he had done nothing wrong because he loved books. The April 1934 issue of the *Review* featured another RG short story, entitled "End of the World," for which he took first place in the contest sponsored jointly by the *Review* and Philolexion, a campus literary group. The next issue, for which RG served as an associate editor, contained his short essay on art and propaganda, prodding Communist sympathizers on campus to show their true colors—RG's way of ferreting out those who were naïvely smitten by revolutions. In point of fact, RG never involved himself in heavyhanded political discussions, something he had in common with FOC. By April of his senior year, the *Review*, at which RG served as coeditor, published four of JB's poems. These were heady, productive years for RG and JB. Professor Mark Van Doren's humanism influenced both RG, who later wrote without much critical fanfare *The Book Known as Q: A Consideration of Shakespeare's Sonnets*, and JB, whose posthumous *Berryman's Shakespeare* was edited with an introduction by John Haffenden.

23. UL, Paul Engle to RG, July 13, 1971, NYPL. RG, introduction to FOC, *Complete Stories of Flannery O'Connor*, vii. For a slightly different account of this

meeting by Engle, see Colman McCarthy, "The Servant of Literature in the Heart of Iowa: Paul Engle's Years of Bringing People Who Write to a Place Where People Farm," *Washington Post*, March 27, 1983.

24. *HB*, 187.

25. See Macauley in Quinn, *Flannery O'Connor*, 61–62.

26. RG, introduction to FOC, *Complete Stories of Flannery O'Connor*, vii–viii.

27. See Cash, *Flannery O'Connor*, 84.

28. TM to RG, April 29, 1965, in PS, *Letters of Robert Giroux and Thomas Merton*, 342.

29. See Prown, *Revising Flannery O'Connor*, 41.

30. UL, "Monday" [February 1950?], RGF.

31. See Gish, *Paul Horgan*, 16. See PH to John J. Quinn, S.J., April 25, 1969, saying he was FOC's teacher at Iowa (NYPL).

32. See Cash, *Flannery O'Connor*, 83; see also Lytle in Quinn, *Flannery O'Connor*, 33.

33. Prown, *Revising Flannery O'Connor*, 112.

34. AT in Quinn, *Flannery O'Connor*, 90.

35. See Warren in Quinn, *Flannery O'Connor*, 91.

36. "Wildcat" was published in the *North American Review* (Spring 1970) after FOC's death and subsequently in her *Complete Stories*. Another story, "The Coat," which was not part of her thesis, was first published by *Doubletake* (Summer 1996); it had been rejected around the time of her graduation by the *Southwest Review*, though when it was subsequently accepted by the *American Courier*, she refused permission to have it published then without payment. "The Turkey," renamed "The Capture," would appear in *Mademoiselle* (November 1948). "The Barber" was published in a student publication, *New Signatures* (1948), and then in the *Atlantic* (October 1970).

37. FOC, *Prayer Journal*, 10. Subsequent page numbers given in text.

38. Srigley, "'Far Away from God,'" 30.

39. See Macauley in Quinn, *Flannery O'Connor*, 34. In 1947–1948, poet Anthony Hecht attended the university and taught in the Writers' Workshop. He had served with Macauley in World War II, and because of war fatigue (what we now know as post-traumatic stress disorder), he left the academic world for a while to undergo psychoanalysis. There is no record that Hecht had any influence on O'Connor's fiction.

40. See *HB*, 117.

41. *CW*, 131.

42. FOC, "The Writer and the Graduate School," 4.

43. *MandM*, 81.

44. *MandM*, 75–76.

45. Gordon, *Obedient Imagination*, 85.

Chapter Three

1. See RG's unpublished autobiographical sketch, dated March 24, 1942, RGF.
2. Gilbert Godfrey and Robert Paul Smith (later known for his *Where Did You Go? Out. What Did You Do? Nothing* [1957]) were fellow students of JB and RG at Columbia.
3. UL, November 10, 1936, RGF.
4. Martin Feeney, "Robert Giroux '31," 8.
5. RG, "Education of an Editor," 12.
6. RG, Walter Reade Theater.
7. UL, January 2, 1942, RGF.
8. Both unpublished letters, n.d., RGF.
9. See Richard Behar, "Debt Topples," *Time* 135, no. 24 (June 11, 1990): 42.
10. See Martin Feeney, "Robert Giroux '31," 8–9.
11. See O'Hare, "Interview with Robert Giroux."
12. RG, introduction to *Complete Stories of Bernard Malamud*, ix.

Chapter Four

1. See Cash, *Flannery O'Connor*, 81.
2. RG, introduction to TM, *Seven Storey Mountain*, xvi.
3. Wilkes, "Interview with Robert Giroux," 25.
4. See SF's commentary in *HB*, 17.
5. UL, December 15, 1949, EU.
6. See UL, FOC to SF and RF, December 19, 1949, RGF.
7. See Wray, "Flannery O'Connor on the West Side," 71–78.
8. See UL, January 21, 1950, RGF.
9. See *HB*, 20; also Wray, "Flannery O'Connor on the West Side," 76.
10. See UL, FOC to EM, April 5, 1950, DU.
11. See UL, FOC to EM, May 30, 1950, DU.
12. *HB*, 21.
13. Wray, "The Importance of Home," 104.
14. UL, December 19, 1950, DU.
15. UL, n.d. [January 1951?], DU.
16. See *HB*, 22.
17. UL, EU.
18. See UL, RG to FOC, March 2, 1951, GC.
19. SF, "Flannery O'Connor: Patterns of Friendship," 425.
20. Folks, "Flannery O'Connor in Her Letters," 180.

21. McGill, "The Life You Write May Be Your Own," 37.

22. See *HB*, 317. MEC became well known for his translations of works by Erskine Caldwell, Truman Capote, John Dos Passos, William Faulkner, Shelby Foote, William Goyen, Ernest Hemingway, Reynolds Price, John Steinbeck, and William Styron. In the winter of 1989–1990, I went to see MEC at the Emile Roux Hospital in Limeil-Brévannes outside Paris. (We had talked several times before this particular meeting.) In conversing with him, I mentioned FOC. His eyes lit up as he talked about FOC's visit to Paris. Since FOC did not feel up to sightseeing when in Paris with her mother (she spent some quiet time with the Belgian novelist Gabrielle Rolin, who translated *Habit of Being* into French [*l'Habitude d'être*]), MEC gave Regina O'Connor and SF a tour of Paris. In his *Mémoires*, MEC mentions that William Goyen first mentioned FOC to him in 1958. MEC wrote of her, "Flannery était assez bonne psychologue pour savoir qu'il n'y a pas d'arme plus efficace que l'ironie, et que le ridicule tue plus radicalement que l'engin le plus meurtrier." [Flannery was a good enough psychologist to know that there is no more effective weapon than irony and that ridicule can kill more surely than any other device] (109). He was particularly attracted to FOC's character: "le courage dans l'adversité, une honnêteté sincère qui lui faisait haïr les imposteurs, nulle illusion sur la vraie nature d'une humanité qu'elle estimait à juste titre plus ridicule encore que méchante" [her courage in adversity, a sincere honesty that made her hate imposters, with no illusion about the true nature of humanity that she rightly considered more ridiculous than wicked] (118 [translation PS]). In early July 1958, FOC signed contracts for the German publication of *A Good Man Is Hard to Find*, but was a bit surprised that Claassen Verlag had decided to select only certain stories: "I'm curious to find out now which stories are not suitable for the German public. Didn't know I was quite *that* vicious" (*HB*, 289). The publishing house omitted "A Stroke of Good Fortune" and "A Temple of the Holy Ghost"—perhaps because the first dealt with a pregnancy and a fortune teller and the second a convent school and a hermaphrodite at a carnival show. Copies of twenty letters of FOC and MEC are at EU.

23. See MEC, "Lettres de Flannery O'Connor à M.E. Coindreau," 18, 19 (March 27, 1960, EU). Hereafter referred to as "Lettres."

24. See UL, MM to RG, May 7, 1951, GC.

25. UL, RG to FOC, May 10, 1951, GC.

26. See UL, RG to MM, June 1, 1951, GC.

27. UL, RG to FOC, June 7, 1951, GC. RG's "suggestions for revision" have not been located among FOC's papers.

28. SF, "A Master Class," 828; RF, introduction to FOC, *Everything That Rises Must Converge*, 15.

29. See SF, "A Master Class," 828–29.

30. UL, CG to RF, n.d., EU.

31. UL, June 9, 1951, RGF.

32. UL, June 26, 1951, RGF.

33. UL, "Wednesday" ["July 25, 1951," written in pencil on the letter], RGF.

34. See UL, August 3, 1951, GC.

35. See SF, "A Master Class," 830.

36. See UL, SF to FOC, "Feast of Stephen" [1950], EU.

37. Prown, *Revising Flannery O'Connor*, 96.

38. See Dunaway, *Exiles and Fugitives*, 83.

39. See SF, "A Master Class," 827.

40. See Prown, *Revising Flannery O'Connor*, 93.

41. See Makowsky, *Caroline Gordon*, 197; see also SF, "A Master Class," 829.

42. UL, FOC to SF and RF, September 20, 1951, EU.

43. Lytle, "Caroline Gordon and the Historic Image," 586.

44. UL, RG to FOC, November 30, 1951, GC.

45. Gordon, "Rebels and Revolutionaries," 43–44.

46. *HB*, 98.

47. UL, FOC to CG, February 6, 1953, EU.

48. See PS, *Walker Percy*, 160; see also Miss and PS "The Failure of *The Charterhouse*." During the Christmas holidays AT finished reading *The Charterhouse* in Minneapolis. He had not read CG's commentary and thus his reaction was not filtered through her critique. "It is a most impressive job, and I hope that you will be able to do the revisions necessary to round it out. I don't think there is anything fundamentally wrong with the book, but I do feel that there must be more work in detail" (quoted in PS, *Walker Percy*, 162). His comments dealt with the internal logic of the relationships within the novel rather than explicit techniques or points of grammar. AT tried to teach WP the value of action in a story; he did so to stress not description but the moral qualities of WP's characters.

49. UL, "The feast of St. Damasus," [December] 11, 1951, UNC.

50. Quoted in PS, *Walker Percy*, 163.

51. UL, RG to FOC, December 5, 1951, GC.

52. UL, RG to FOC, January 18, 1952, GC. Folders 149, 150, 151 of the Flannery O'Connor Collection at GC, which contain a late draft, galley proofs, and page proofs of *Wise Blood*, show no signs of editing or copyediting.

53. UL, January 10, 1952, HBA.

54. UL, February 6, 1952, HBA.

55. See *HB*, 31.

56. UL, February 8, 1952, HBA.

57. UL, February 11, 1952, HBA.

58. UL, February 13, 1952, HBA.

59. UL, RG to FOC, February 20, 1952, HBA.

60. UL, HBA.

61. In an internal memo dated 5/19/52 from "E. H." [E. Gerald Hopkins] to "D. L." [Denver Lindley], which RG reiterated in a letter to MM on the same

day, the reprint contract with New American Library for *Wise Blood* was carefully spelled out: "$4,000 guarantee payable as follows: $2,000 on signing agreement: $2,000 to be paid on NAL publication date: royalties of 1 cent [per word] to 150,000 copies; 1½ cents after, 1 cent on Canadian sales. New American Library shall publish no earlier than May 15, 1953, nor later than May 15, 1954, with the earliest possible date for publication to be specified by Harcourt, Brace in writing. Rights granted for 3 years from their publication date" (RGF).

62. UL, February 15, 1951, DU.

63. UL, RGF.

64. UL, April 5, 1952, HBA.

65. UL, RGF.

66. UL, May 7, 1952, HBA.

67. UL, April 11, 1952, HBA.

68. UL, April 14, 1952, HBA.

69. Unpublished memo, RGF.

70. UL, April 21, 1952, HBA.

71. Started in 1941 at the Cummington School of the Arts in Cummington, Massachusetts, under the aegis of Katherine Frazier, the press represents one of the tiny, hidden, Weltyesque undercurrents in O'Connor's life. The press initially featured creative work by its students, but it soon expanded to print books by established writers: AT's *Sonnets at Christmas*, *The Winter Sea*, and *The Hovering Fly and Other Essays*; R. P. Blackmur's *The Second World* and *The Good European*; Wallace Stevens's *Notes toward a Supreme Fiction* and *Esthétique du Mal*; RL's *Land of Unlikeness* (with an introduction by AT), and Robert Penn Warren's *Blackberry Winter*—all of which showed the distinctive style that became the cachet of the press. It would seem likely that Lowell, whom O'Connor had first met in 1947, had recommended that she apply for a "scholarship" to attend the six-week Cummington Summer Conference (see RL, *Letters of Robert Lowell*, 62).

72. See RL, *Letters of Robert Lowell*, 253.

73. Quoted in Sessions, "*Shenandoah* and the Advent of Flannery O'Connor," 231–32.

74. UL, July 25, 1952, HBA.

75. See RG, Walter Reade Theater.

Chapter Five

1. RF, introduction to FOC, *Everything That Rises Must Converge*, 16.

2. See UL, FOC to EM, July 16, 1952, DU.

3. UL, August 27, 1952, HBA.

4. UL, April 7, 1952, HBA.

5. See UL, RG to FOC, August 20, 1952; also UL, RF to FOC, "Sunday"; UL, RF to FOC, April 30 [1953]: all EU.

6. See *HB*, 46.

7. The story would be translated into French: "Sauver sa vie," *Profils* 14 (Winter 1956): 80–91.

8. See O'Hare, "Interview with Robert Giroux." See also Gooch, *Flannery: A Life of Flannery O'Connor* (New York: Little, Brown, 2009), 185.

9. UL, "Friday" [September 1953?], RGF; see *HB*, 62.

10. See RG to TM, May 1, 1953, in PS, *Letters of Robert Giroux and Thomas Merton*, 152.

11. See UL, RG to MM, March 5, 1954, HBA.

12. See UL, RG to FOC, April 2, 1954, GC.

13. See UL, FOC to CG, October 27, 1954, NYPL; also UL, FOC to RG, n.d., NYPL.

14. See UL, RG to FOC, December 29, 1954, HBA.

15. UL, January 2, 1955, RGF.

16. UL, January 5, 1955, HBA.

17. UL, January 10, 1955, HBA.

18. See UL, FOC to RG, January 15, 1955, HBA.

19. UL, February 26, 1955, HBA.

20. UL, February 19, 1955, NYPL.

21. UL, February 22, 1955, NYPL.

22. UL, March 1, 1955, NYPL.

23. UL, March 3, 1955, HBA.

24. UL, HBA.

25. UL, RG to FOC, March 16, 1955, HBA.

26. UL, March 23, 1955, HBA.

27. See UL, JMC to FOC, April 8, 1955, GC.

28. UL, RG to Frank Morley, March 25, 1955, RGF. Years later, Jovanovich wrote a gracious note thanking RG for the fine work he did editing *The Complete Stories of Flannery O'Connor* (UL, October 13, 1971, NYPL).

29. UL, March 31, 1955, RGF.

30. UL, March 27, 1955, RGF.

31. See UL, PH to JMC, n.d. [written from Roswell, NM], RGF.

32. See UL, RG to PH, July 29, 1955, RGF.

33. UL, April 2, 1955, RGF.

34. UL, BU. In a letter dated March 29, 1955, Naomi Burton informed JMC at HB that TM wanted to be released from his contract with this firm because he would like to continue having RG as his editor. The release was signed on April 4, 1955, RGF.

35. UL, April 21, 1955, RGF.

36. See Ian Parker, "Showboat: How a Legendary Publisher Handles Writers," *New Yorker* (April 8, 2002): 60.

37. The publishing houses Rinehart & Company and Farrar, Straus & Giroux have a direct historical relationship. Farrar & Rinehart was founded in June 1929 by John C. Farrar (vice president) and Stanley M. Rinehart (president), in partnership with Frederick R. Rinehart. In starting this firm, Farrar and the Rinehart brothers, sons of Mary Roberts Rinehart, left the massive Doubleday, Doran publishing house, the result of a merger between their employer, the George H. Doran Company, with Doubleday, Page & Company in 1927. In 1946, following Farrar's departure from Farrar & Rinehart, the firm took the name of Rinehart & Company until its 1960 merger with Henry Holt & Company and the John C. Winston Company to form Holt, Rinehart and Winston. When Farrar left his former company in 1946, he started this new venture with Roger Straus, which eventually became FS&G.

38. UL, April 21, 1955, RGF.

39. See UL, RF to RG, May 6, 1955, RGF.

40. UL, May 31, 1955, EU.

Chapter Six

1. See Michael Millgate, "Obituary: Catharine Carver," *London Independent* (November 14, 1997), www.independent.co.uk/news/obituaries/obituary -catharine-carver-1293892.html.

2. See UL, CC to RG, October 2, 1957, NYPL; also UL, CC to FOC, March 31, 1955, EU.

3. See Bellow, *Letters*, 161.

4. See O'Hare, "Interview with Robert Giroux."

5. See UL, FOC to CC, February 18, 1959, EU.

6. *HB*, 552.

7. See RG, Walter Reade Theater.

8. UL, June 10, 1966, NYPL.

9. UL, March 31, 1955, EU.

10. UL, RG to FOC, December 2, 1955; see UL, FOC to EM, April 12, 1958, both RGF; see *HB*, 280.

11. FOC supplied the following names, with appropriate addresses: John Ransom, Monroe Spears (*Sewanee Review*), John Palmer (*Yale Review*), Philip Rahv, J. F. Powers, Thomas Mabry, Paul Engle, Robie Macauley, Andrew Lytle, Randall Jarrell, Carl Hartman (*Epoch*, Cornell University), Robert Lowell, Ralph McGill (*Atlanta Constitution*), Arabel Porter, Peter Taylor, and Hansford Martin, a friend of Engle. Review copies were also sent to Anna C. Hunter, *Savannah Morning News*, Savannah, GA; Susan Myrick, *Macon Telegraph*, Macon, GA; Celestine Sibley, *Atlanta Journal and Constitution*, Atlanta, GA; Florence Moran, *The Union Recorder*, Milledgeville, GA.

12. RL, *Letters of Robert Lowell*, 253.

13. April 2, 1955, HBA; see partial version, *HB*, 76–77. On April 1, 1955, DL wrote to FOC, whom he had met once at HB's offices, indicating that RG had resigned (UL, GC). See also, UL, FOC to DL, April 3, 1955, GC.

14. SF, introduction to FOC, *Three by Flannery O'Connor*, xxii.

15. UL, April 6, 1955, HBA.

16. UL, DL to FOC, April 28, 1955, HBA.

17. See PS, "Tracing a Literary & Epistolary Relationship."

18. UL, DL to Eudora Welty, March 28, 1955, HBA.

19. See UL, CC to FOC, April 28, 1955, GC.

20. See UL, April 28, 1955, HBA.

21. RGF.

22. UL, EL to SF, November 13, 1979, EU.

23. Bosco, "Consenting to Love," 285.

24. See UL, EL to SF, November 13, 1979, EU, for his personal and detailed interpretation of "Good Country People."

25. UL, FOC to EL, April 29, 1956, EU.

26. Bosco, "Consenting to Love," 286.

27. For an account of EL's dating of FOC, see Bosco, "Erik Langkjaer: The One Flannery 'Used to Go With.'"

28. UL, FOC to EL, June 13, 1954, EU.

29. UL, Paul Engle to RG, July 13, 1971, NYPL.

30. UL, CC to FOC, May 16, 1955, HBA.

31. UL, May 18, 1955, HBA.

32. See UL, CC to FOC, May 20, 1955, HBA.

33. May 19, 1955, HBA.

34. UL, May 27, 1955, HBA.

35. *HB*, 121.

36. See FOC to SF and RF, June 10, 1955, EU; see partial version, *HB*, 85–86.

37. UL, RGF.

38. UL, June 8, 1955, RGF.

39. UL, HBA.

40. UL, June 10, 1955, RGF.

41. See UL, RG to TSE, 2, June 14, 1955, NYPL.

42. For information about books in FOC's library, see Arthur F. Kinney, *Flannery O'Connor's Library: Resources of Being* (Athens: University of Georgia Press, 1985).

43. UL, June 13, 1955, RGF.

44. UL, June 15, 1955, RGF.

45. See UL, June 23, 1955, BU.

46. See SF, "A Master Class," 55.

47. UL, HBA.

48. UL, June 16, 1955, RGF.

49. UL, June 17, 1955, DU.

50. UL, June 20, 1955, RGF.

51. UL, CC to FOC, July 1, 1955, HBA.

52. See UL, RG to Victor Gollancz, August 5, 1955, NYPL.

53. UL, July 13, 1955, DU.

54. UL, July 26, 1955, HBA.

55. UL, July 28, 1955, HBA.

56. UL, CC to FOC, August 4, 1955, HBA.

57. UL, CC to FOC, August 8, 1955, HBA.

58. UL, FOC to CC, August 10, 1955, HBA.

59. UL, FOC to CC, August 30, 1955, HBA.

60. See UL, CC to FOC, September 2, 1955, HBA.

61. UL, FOC to CC, August 29, 1955, DU.

62. UL, RGF.

63. See UL, September 5, 1955, HBA.

64. UL, September 8, 1955, HBA.

65. UL, FOC to RG, October 21, 1955, RGF. RG's letter of reference, sent to Henry Allen Moe on December 2, 1955, stated, "I consider Flannery O'Connor one of the two or three most accomplished writers of fiction on the American scene. Were she not to write another line, her present work has an assured place in our literary history. At the same time, because of her youth she is one of the most promising writers we have. She is also an original. I am proud to have published *Wise Blood*, her first book, at Harcourt, Brace and to have seen her book of stories *A Good Man Is Hard to Find* through the press of that publishing house. I heartily recommend her for a Fellowship" (RGF).

66. See *HB*, 101; also UL, FOC to EM, December 2, 1955, DU.

67. UL, September 26, 1955, HBA; see UL, FOC to EM, September 26, 1955, DU.

68. UL, September 30, 1955, HBA.

69. UL, CC to FOC, October 31, 1955, HBA.

70. See CC to FOC, November 18, 1955, GC.

71. UL, December 2, 1955, RGF.

72. Among the books RG edited for the winter / spring 1956 FS&C catalogue were *The Lamb*, by François Mauriac; *The Living Bread*, by TM; *Affairs of State: The Eisenhower Years*, by Richard Rovere; *Deliver Us From Evil: The Story of Viet Nam's Flight to Freedom*, by Thomas A. Dooley, M.D.; *A Walk on the Wild Side*, by Nelson Algren; *Sights and Spectacles*, by Mary McCarthy; and *The Ripening Seed*, by Colette.

73. UL, December 2, 1955, HBA.

74. December 9, 1955, RGF; see partial version, *HB*, 122.

75. UL, December 12, 1955; also UL, DL to FOC, December 20, 1955, both GC.

76. UL, December 13, 1955, RGF.

77. UL, December 16, 1955, GC.

78. UL, January 3, 1956, RGF.

79. UL, January 5, 1956, HBA.

80. See UL, January 8, 1956, HBA.

81. *HB*, 144.

82. See FOC, *The Presence of Grace and Other Book Reviews*, 3.

83. UL, January 6, 1956, RGF.

84. UL, January 13, 1956, HBA.

85. HBA. See partial version, *HB*, 129.

86. See UL, DL to FOC, January 20, 1956, HBA.

87. See Dunaway, *Exiles and Fugitives*, 57.

88. UL, FOC to DL, January 31, 1956, HBA.

89. Elie, *The Life You Save*, 240.

90. See UL, January 23, 1956, HBA.

91. UL, February 10, 1956, HBA.

92. UL, February 2, 1956, HBA.

93. UL, February 10, 1956, HBA.

94. HBA; see partial version, *HB*, 148.

95. See UL, DL to FOC, March 22, 1956, HBA.

96. See UL, FOC to DL, April 13, 1956; UL, DL to FOC, April 17, 1956, both HBA.

97. See UL, RG to RL, April 25, 1956, NYPL. A number of the books RG edited for the fall 1956 FS&C catalogue had religious themes: *A Report on the American Jesuits*, by John La Farge, S.J. (photographs by Margaret Bourke-White); *St. Ignatius of Loyola: The Pilgrim Years, 1491–1538*, by James Brodrick, S.J.; *The Life of Robert Southwell: Poet and Martyr*, by Christopher Devlin, S.J.; *Silence I Speak: The Story of Cardinal Mindzenty Today and of Hungary's "New Order,"* by George N. Shuster; and *Psychology and the Spirit*, by Gregory Zilboorg, M.D.

98. PH, RG, TSE, and Jean Stafford had lunch at the Carlton House restaurant in New York on June 4 (see PH, *Tracings*, 145). RG wrote TSE, "I've just finished reading the corrected galley proofs of *On Poetry and Poets*. I had read many of the essays individually, of course, and thought I knew them. Put together, they acquire new impact and meaning. It makes a magnificent book, and I am very happy that we are its American publishers" (UL, March 6, 1957, NYPL). RG went on to publish TSE's *The Elder Statesman* and *Knowledge and Experience in the Philosophy of F. H. Bradley*, in addition to two posthumous works, *To Criticize the Critic* and *Poems Written in Early Youth*.

99. UL, June 7, 1956, HBA.

100. UL, FOC to JMC, June 12, 1956, HBA.

101. UL, July 3, 1956, HBA.

102. See UL, FOC to JMC, July 14, 1956; also UL, JMC to FOC, July 25, 1956, both HBA.

103. See UL, EM to FOC, August 16, 1956, HBA; also UL, FOC to EM, February 25, 1956, DU.

104. UL, September 9, 1956, HBA; see *HB*, 175.

105. See UL, September 20, 1956, HBA; see *HB*, 181, 186.

106. See UL, October 11, 1956, HBA.

107. See UL, DL to FOC, October 25, 1956, HBA.

108. See UL, December 17, 1956, HBA.

109. Lillian Smith was one of the early and prominent white Southerners to denounce racial segregation, as revealed in her quasi-autobiographical work *Killers of the Dream*. Her popular novel *Strange Fruit*, named for a song made famous by Billie Holiday, portrayed an interracial love affair. From her home in Clayton she aggressively promoted values that were important to a growing number of social and political reformers, particularly Martin Luther King Jr., then addressing the yearlong bus boycott after Rosa Parks's arrest. Smith's manner of expressing her views on racial issues would have not endeared her at all to O'Connor, whose only consolation during this time was to read Madison Jones's *The Innocent*, sent to her by JMC. "It certainly is a fine book," she wrote to Lindley. "I seldom read novels through, particularly when they are that long, but I read all of that one. It's about as massive as the picture of the author on the back. I thought it was right all the way through. I thought it was absolutely fine. I hope Caroline [Gordon] has had time to read it" (quoted in a letter from FOC to DL, February 12, 1957, HBA). O'Connor took it upon herself to write a short note to Jones to try to console him on the disappointing reviews his novel received, a gesture he greatly appreciated. O'Connor would later highly praise Jones's *A Buried Land*, calling it "solid and sure and relentless." (See UL, DL to FOC, December 27, 1956, HBA; also *HB*, 123; UL, FOC to DL, February 12, 1957, HBA; UL, FOC to DL, March 6, 1957; also UL, DL to FOC, March 12, 1957, both HBA; UL, FOC to DL, July 13, 1963, EU.)

110. Featured in the fall 1957 and winter / spring 1958 FS&C catalogues were books that RG had edited, including *Soviet Russia in China*, by Chiang Kai-shek; *Coup de Grace*, by Marguerite Yourcenar; *A History of France*, by André Maurois; *Adenauer and the New Germany*, by Edgar Alexander; *Hercules, My Shipmate*, by Robert Graves; *Lines of Life*, by François Mauriac; *On Poetry and Poets*, by TSE; *The Disinherited Mind*, by Erich Heller; *Memoirs of a Revolutionist*, by Dwight Macdonald; *Roman Tales*, by Alberto Moravia; *The Selected Letters of D. H. Lawrence*, edited by Diana Trilling; *Thoughts in Solitude*, by TM; *Mitsou and Music Hall Sidelights*, by Colette; *The Sundial*, by Shirley Jackson; *The Antiphon*, by Djuna Barnes; and *A History of England*, by André Maurois.

111. UL, May 21, 1957, HBA.

112. See *HB*, 257, 259–62.

113. *CW*, 572.

114. See UL, FOC to DL, April 9, 1958, HBA.

115. See UL, DL to RG, May 26, 1958, NYPL.

116. UL, April 12, 1958, RGF.

117. See UL, JMC to FOC, April 14, 1958, HBA.

118. See UL, April 14, 1958, HBA.

119. See UL, Eudora Welty to Dan Wickenden, May 22, 1969, HBA; Dan Wickenden to Eudora Welty, May 27, 1969, HBA.

Chapter Seven

1. UL, RG to FOC, April 15, 1958, RGF.

2. UL, April 16, 1958, HBA.

3. UL, April 17, 1958, RGF.

4. See UL, RG to FOC, April 18, 1958, RGF.

5. UL, JMC to FOC, April 18, 1958, HBA.

6. UL, April 20, 1958, HBA.

7. See PH, *Tracings*, 146–51.

8. See UL, TSE to RG, March 31, 1958; UL, TSE to RG, April 10, 1958; UL, TSE to RG, May 29, 1958; UL, TSE to RG, June 4, 1958: all NYPL.

9. See UL, FOC to SF and RF, "Tuesday" [1958], EU.

10. UL, FOC to EB, June 1, 1958, VC.

11. See MEC, "Lettres," 15 (FOC to MEC, December 4, 1958, EU).

12. See UL, May 17, 1958, HBA.

13. UL, August 14, 1958, RGF. Among the nineteen books RG edited for the summer / fall 1958 FS&C catalogue were *Satan in Goray*, by Isaac Bashevis Singer; *The Last Year of Thomas Mann*, by Erika Mann; *Words Are Stones*, by Carlo Levi; *An American Amen*, by John La Farge, S.J.; *Engaged in Writing*, by Stephen Spender; *Claudine in Paris*, by Colette; and *T. S. Eliot: A Symposium for His Seventieth Birthday*, edited by Neville Braybrooke. RG had also started editing books for the winter / spring 1959 FS&C catalogue, including *The Secular Journal of Thomas Merton*, by TM; *Chaim Weismann*, by Isaiah Berlin; *Rome Eternal*, by Paul Horgan; *Life Studies*, by RL; *The Elder Statesman*, by TSE; *A History of Spain*, by Max Livermore; *Israel's Odyssey*, by Abraham Mayer Heller; and *General Sherman's Son*, by Joseph T. Durkin, S.J. From winter of 1959 to the spring of 1962, he edited 160 books, of which two—Malamud's *The Magic Barrel* (one of FOC's favorite books), and RL's *Life Studies*—would win the National Book Award, while another author, Salvatore Quasimodo, would receive the Nobel Prize in Literature in 1959.

14. Mounier, *Personalism*, 49.

15. See Kirk, *Critical Companion*, 134; see May, "The Violent Bear It Away: The Meaning of the Title," 83–86.

16. See UL, Valerie Eliot to RG, November 2, 1958, NYPL.

17. See MEC, "Lettres," 17.

18. UL, April 10, 1959, RGF. Among the twenty-one books RG edited for the summer / fall 1959 FS&C catalogue were *The Tender Shoot and Other Stories*,

by Colette; *The Frozen Revolution, Poland: A Study in Communist Decay*, by Frank Gibney; *Questions of Precedence*, by François Mauriac; *Malcolm*, by James Purdy; *Station Wagon in Spain*, by Frances Parkinson Keyes; *The Private Life of Mr. Pepys*, by John Harold Wilson, and *Memoirs of Hecate County*, by Edmund Wilson.

19. See O'Hare, "Interview with Robert Giroux."

20. See RG, Walter Reade Theater.

21. O'Hare, "Interview with Robert Giroux."

22. See RG, introduction to FOC, *Complete Stories of Flannery O'Connor*, xiv–xv.

23. For a slight variation of this incident, see O'Hare, "Interview with Robert Giroux."

24. See UL, RG to Frank Morley, September 20, 1958, NYPL.

25. UL, April 11, 1995, archives of Roberta Rodriquez Gilmor.

26. See UL, May 11, 1959, RGF.

27. UL, May 31, 1959, RGF.

28. UL, July 7, 1959, NYPL (on microfilm).

29. UL, FOC to RG, July 17, 1959, RGF.

30. UL, July 22, 1959, RGF. RG and PH were close friends. One of the first works RG edited after he left Harcourt, Brace was PH's *The Saintmaker's Christmas Eve*. PH had come to RG's new firm in mid-April 1955 through his literary agent Virginia Rice. With the exception of Robert Penn Warren, few of those FOC knew at Iowa could equal PH's productivity or peer recognition. On June 9, 1956, FOC reviewed for the Savannah-Atlanta diocesan *Bulletin* PH's book *Three Novelettes*, which she believed had a calm classical quality about them. In 1990, RG and I drove up together to Middletown, Connecticut, and had dinner with PH, who had been a fellow at Wesleyan University's Center for Advanced Studies for a number of terms, beginning in 1959, and then served as its director from 1962 to 1967. Before FOC's death in 1964, RG edited the following books by PH: *Give Me Possession* (FOC reviewed this in the *Bulletin* [October 12, 1957]), *Rome Eternal*, *A Distant Trumpet*, *Citizen of New Salem*, *Mountain Standard Time*, *Conquistadors in North American History*, and *Things as They Are*. After FOC's death, RG edited fourteen more of PH's books.

31. UL, July 27, 1959, RGF.

32. See UL, FOC to EB, August 2, 1959, VC.

33. UL, RGF.

34. UL, August 6, 1959, RGF.

35. UL, FOC to RG, September 20, 1959, RGF; see UL, RG to FOC, September 17, 1959, RGF.

36. UL, September 24, 1959, RGF.

37. See UL, FOC to EM, August 27, 1956, EU.

38. UL, September 25, 1959, RGF; see UL, FOC to EM, April 2, 1956; June 2, 1956; November 14, 29, 1956; July 13, 1957, all DU.

39. UL, RG to FOC, October 5, 1959, RGF.

40. UL, October 6, 1959, RGF.

41. UL, October 6, 1959, RGF.

42. See UL, October 8, 1959, RGF.

43. See UL, FOC to RG, October 18, 1959, RGF.

44. See MEC, "Lettres," 17 (FOC to MEC, November 1, 1959, EU).

45. UL, RG to FOC, October 26, 1959, RGF.

46. UL, October 31, 1959, RGF. FOC's corrections are as follows:

> p. 91 His eyes widened and an inner door in them opened in preparation for some inevitable vision.
>
> p. 104 The boy continued to study the machine. His uncle's face might have been only an appendage to it.
>
> p. 110 Rayber smiled. Then he laughed. "All such people have in life," he said, "is the conviction they'll rise again."
>
> p. 122 He stopped with a shock of disappointment. The place was only a bakery.
>
> p. 131 He stared back at her. Her eyes remained on his face for a moment. A deep shock went through him. He was certain that the child had looked directly into his heart and seen his pity.
>
> p. 132 and this time her eyes moved directly to Rayber's face in the window and he knew they sought it.
>
> p. 134 She was moving in his direction, the people in front of her forgotten.
>
> p. 135 He wanted nothing but to get back home and sink into his own bed whether the boy returned or not.
>
> p. 145 He seemed to be drawn toward the child in the water but to be pulling back,
>
> p. 154 His shoes were not run-down but he might have slept in his seersucker suit every night.
>
> p. 155 He seemed to see the little boy and nothing else,
>
> p. 191 Without warning its meaning pierced Rayber and he felt
>
> p. 198 He seemed poised there waiting to make a momentous move
>
> p. 208 got to

In addition, FOC sent RG two more pages of corrections, citing page and line numbers (NYPL).

47. See the unpublished FS&C internal memorandum, dated November 30, 1959, NYPL.

48. See UL, RG to TSE, August 12, 1959; UL, TSE to RG, September 9, 1959; UL, RG to TSE, September 11, 1959: all NYPL.

49. UL, November 3, 1959, RGF. Father D'Arcy's book contains several passages concerning the theology of Pierre Teilhard de Chardin, S.J.

50. UL, November 10, 1959, RGF.

51. UL, November 20, 1959, RGF.

52. UL, November 22, 1959, RGF.

53. UL, RG to FOC, November 25, 1959, RGF.

54. UL, FOC to RG, November 29, 1959, RGF; see UL, FOC to RG, December 2, 1959, RGF.

55. UL, RG to FOC, December 3, 1959, RGF.

56. It is just as well that FOC had only a beginner's knowledge of French. In his introduction to this translation, MEC, who was at Princeton when he wrote it, focuses on an assortment of preachers and religious writers—Billy Sunday, Billy Graham, Mary Baker Eddy, Aimee Semple McPherson, J. Wilbur Chapman, and the Reverend Whitfield in Faulkner's *As I Lay Dying*. The introduction as a whole is not exactly pertinent to the text. FOC read MEC's introduction, but as she noted in a letter to him, she could only "get the gist" of what he had written. From my perspective this introduction seemed quite tangential to the plot of the novel, though it reflected, as MEC mentioned in an interview, his own interest in American evangelists, a religious phenomenon unknown in France at that time (MEC, "Lettres," 18; see Gresset, "Interview with Maurice-Edgar Coindreau," 3).

57. UL, FOC to RG, January 5, 1960, RGF.

58. UL, RG to FOC, January 7, 1960, RGF. FOC requested that RG send copies of the novel to forty-eight friends and critics, NYPL.

59. UL, FOC to RG, January 9, 1960, RGF.

60. UL, January 22, 1960, RGF.

61. See UL, FOC to RG, January 18, 1960, RGF.

62. See UL, FOC to RG, January 30, 1960, RGF.

63. *HB*, 372. Unfortunately, RL's letter to FOC, which prompted her response to him, is not among FOC's published letters nor is it reproduced in *Letters of Robert Lowell*.

64. UL, RGF.

65. See UL, February 10, 1960, RGF.

66. UL, February 29, 1960, RGF.

67. See UL, FOC to Maryat Lee, March 23, 1960, NYPL (on microfilm); also UL, FOC to RG, March 12, 1960, NYPL.

68. UL, January 28, 1960, RGF and EU.

69. UL, June 2, 1960, RGF. In mid-July, RG and Charles Reilly headed for a six-week vacation to Europe, RG's first time abroad in five years. They dined with the Eliots at their Kensington Court Gardens home on July 16 before heading for the Continent (see UL, RG to TSE, February 5, 1960; UL, RG to TSE, March 18, 1960; UL, RG to TSE, May 23, 1960; UL, RG to TSE, June 24, 1960, all NYPL; UL, RG to TM, July 13, 1960, BU).

70. See *HB*, 417. JM wrote to MEC in January 1966, after reading in French *The Violent Bear It Away*, "C'est un très beau livre, d'une magnifique violence. . . . Il me semble que les critiques le comprennent mal. Elle détestait ces prophètes

sauvages, oui, sans doute, mais ils la fascinaient" (It is a striking book, with a magnificent violence about it. . . . It seems to me that critics have not understood it. She hated these wild prophets, yes, without doubt, but they nevertheless fascinated her) (MEC, *Mémoires*, 109–10, translation PS).

71. See MEC, "Lettres," 20 (FOC to MEC, July 18, 1960, EU).

72. December 8, 1960, RGF; see partial version with variations, *HB*, 421–22.

73. UL, January 19, 1961, RGF.

74. See O'Hare, "Interview with Robert Giroux."

75. UL, December 17, 1962, VC.

76. UL, February 3, 1961, RGF.

77. UL, February 6, 1961, RGF.

78. UL, FOC to RG, February 12, 1961, RGF.

79. UL, RG to FOC, February 14, 1961, RGF.

80. See UL, February 20, 1961, RGF.

81. See UL, FOC to RG, March 15, 1961, RGF.

82. See UL, RG to FOC, March 24, 1961, RGF.

83. UL, FOC to RG, March 26, 1961, RGF.

84. See UL, EM to RG, March 31, 1961, RGF; also UL, RG to FOC, April 5, 12, 1961, RGF.

85. April 14, 1961, in PS, *Letters of Robert Giroux and Thomas Merton*, 266.

86. UL, RG to FOC, April 12, 1961, RGF.

87. UL, April 17, 1961, RGF.

88. UL, RG to FOC, April 21, 1961, RGF.

89. See UL, EM to RG, May 2, 1961, HBA.

90. UL, FOC to RG, August 17, 1961, RGF.

91. See UL, RG to FOC, June 30, 1961, RGF.

92. See UL, RG to FOC, July 7, 1961, RGF.

93. See UL, WP to SF, September 14, 1978, EU, in which WP mentions one other letter he received from FOC, but I could not locate it; see also PS, *Walker Percy*, 230–31; *HB*, 501; Lawson and Kramer, *Conversations with Walker Percy*, 232.

94. See UL, WP to Phinizy Spalding, June 7, 1965, EU.

95. UL, April 18, 1979, EU.

96. See UL, October 11, 1961, RGF.

97. UL, October 14, 1961, RGF.

98. See UL, December 3, 7, 1961, RGF.

99. See RG to TM, November 20, 1961, in PS, *Letters of Robert Giroux and Thomas Merton*, 276. See UL, RG to FOC, December 8, 1961, RGF. In an unpublished memorandum, dated January 24, 1962, RG indicated that he had talked to Victor Weybright at the New American Library, who wished to bring out a new paperback edition of *Wise Blood*, plus another work, as a "jumbo" Signet Book, around mid-1963, at a possible retail price of 75 cents. In addition, RG thought that FS&C might do their own paperback edition of *Wise Blood* in early 1963. All

of this would be discussed during an editorial meeting. "I have received a letter dated February 21st from Julian Muller," EM wrote to RG. "It refers to their reverting on March 23, 1961, to Flannery O'Connor all publishing rights in *Wise Blood* with the exception of the reprint rights. Their agreement with New American Library for these rights has been terminated and Harcourt is formally notifying us that they are reverting these rights to Flannery" (UL, February 27, 1962, RGF). RG wrote to FOC, curiously without having consulted her in advance, about a decision he had made with McKee: "I have just been speaking to Elizabeth McKee about the inclusion of *Wise Blood* in the Philip Rahv anthology of eight American short novels. Rahv presented his collection as so unusual, and with such a distinguished group of contributors (only two of whom—you and William Styron—are living writers), that we felt we should grant permission. Their advance was $500. Elizabeth has forwarded the book to you and I hope you agree that we made the right decision" (UL, May 21, 1963, RGF). FOC subsequently said she was pleased to be included in the Rahv anthology (see UL, FOC to RG, May 23, 1963, RGF).

100. See UL, RG to FOC, December 8, 1961, RGF.

101. UL, RG to TSE, August 21, 1961; see UL, RG to TSE and Valerie Eliot, January 10, 1962; UL, RG to TSE, February 23, 1962: all NYPL.

102. UL, RGF.

103. UL, FOC to RG, April 23, 1962, RGF.

104. UL, FOC to RG, May 16, 1962, RGF; see RG to FOC, May 11, 1962, RGF.

105. See UL, RG to FOC, May 22, 1962, RGF.

106. See UL, June 22, 1962, RGF.

107. See UL, RG to FOC, June 27, 1962, RGF; also UL, FOC to RG, June 29, 1962, RGF; UL, CC to RG, July 26, 1962, NYPL.

108. UL, RG to FOC, November 2, 1962, RGF. It could be that the anthology *Modern Catholic Thinkers: An Anthology*, edited by A. Robert Caponigri (London: Burns & Oates, 1960) is the one to which RG referred. RG communicated regularly with his friend Thomas Burns. In addition, this anthology, simultaneously published in 1960 by Harper & Brothers in New York, contains an essay by Pierre Teilhard de Chardin, S.J., entitled "The Divinization of Activities" (190–99), which is a translation of part of his *Le Milieu divin*. This article discusses, among other topics, the notion of convergence, although nowhere in the article are words in French used. It should be noted that RG does not say that he possesses or has seen this anthology, but just that he has heard that it exists.

109. UL, FOC to RG, November 5, 1962, RGF.

110. Kreyling, "A Good Monk is Hard to Find," 13. See Westarp, *Precision and Depth*, 81–87. Personal note: During the three years I studied philosophy as a Jesuit seminarian (1961–1964), we were not allowed to read the works of Teilhard

de Chardin without special permission from the seminary rector. Eventually this restriction was lifted.

111. Pope Francis, *Laudato Si'*, section 236 (May 24, 2015), http://w2.vatican .va/content/francesco/en/encyclicals/documents/papa-francesco_20150524 _enciclica-laudato-si.html.

112. In a 1960 letter to Youree Watson, S.J., O'Connor called Teilhard de Chardin "the great Christian prophet of this century" (May "Blue-Bleak Embers," 341).

113. See *HB*, 334; Straus, *Paper Trail*, 153–60.

114. See UL, FOC to RG, September 27, 1963, NYPL.

115. See *HB*, 554.

116. UL, CG to FOC, January 8, 1964, EU.

117. *HB*, 563–64.

118. UL, RG to FOC, January 27, 1964, RGF.

119. UL, FOC to RG, February 1, 1964, NYPL.

120. UL, RGF. George and Dollie Long read the book and formally gave their consent for its publication on January 24, 1961 (NYPL).

121. At the end of November 1963, the Eliots arrived in New York by plane so that TSE could discuss a cooperative arrangement between Wesleyan University Press in Connecticut and Faber & Faber. At Wesleyan, they had lunch with RG and PH at PH's house on campus. At year's end, after four weeks in New York, the Eliots flew to Nassau for their winter vacation. RG and Charles Reilly flew to Nassau on March 7, 1964, to be with the Eliots. (See UL, RG to TSE, March 1, 1963; UL, RG to TSE, August 2, 1963; UL, TSE to RG, August 23, 1963; UL, TSE to RG, September 27, 1963; UL, RG to TSE, October 18, 1963; UL, TSE to RG, October 25, 1963; UL, TSE to RG, November 5, 1963; UL, RG to John Kelly, March 6, 1964, all NYPL; see also PH, *Tracings*, 153).

122. UL, RG to FOC, March 24, 1964, RGF.

123. MEC, "Lettres," 22 (FOC to MEC, May 12, 1964, EU).

124. See UL, FOC to EM, May 7, 1964, RGF.

125. UL, May 18, 1964, RGF.

126. See FOC to EM, May 21, 1964, RGF; see partial version, *HB*, 580.

127. UL, RG to FOC, May 25, 1964, RGF.

128. See UL, RG to EM, May 25, 1964, RGF.

129. See UL, FOC to CC, May 21, 1964, June 17, 1964; June 27, 1964; July 15 [1964], all EU.

130. See *HB*, 584; also Gordon, "Heresy in Dixie," 265–66.

131. UL, CG to RG, September 12, 1964, RGF.

132. See O'Hare, "Interview with Robert Giroux."

133. See UL, CC to RG, February 23, 1965, EU.

134. UL, RGF.

135. See UL, CC to FOC, "Sunday, July 12 (or so)," EU; also Westarp, 53–62.

136. UL, June 28, 1964, RGF; see partial version, *HB*, 589.

137. UL, RG to FOC, July 7, 1964, RGF.

138. Gordon, "Heresy in Dixie," 266.

139. UL, SF to RG, October 11, 1977, RGF; see *HB*, 560.

140. UL, July 19 [1964], RGF.

141. See UL, August 3, 1964, NYPL.

142. See UL, RG to Regina O'Connor, August 7, 1964, NYPL.

143. For an analysis of RG's role in editing *The Complete Stories of Flannery O'Connor*, see Moran, *Creating Flannery O'Connor*, 95–108.

144. For an analysis of RG's role in editing *Habit of Being*, see Moran, *Creating Flannery O'Connor*, 110–26.

145. RG, introduction to FOC, *Complete Stories of Flannery O'Connor*, xv; see also TM, "Flannery O'Connor: A Prose Elegy," 49–53.

146. I accompanied RG when he received the 1987 Alexander Hamilton Award at Columbia University, the 1988 Campion Award at Regis High School, the 1988 Elmer Holmes Bobst Award at New York University, the 1989 Unity and Freedom Medal from the Asociación Pro Unidad Latinoamericana at the Metropolitan Club in New York, the 1989 Mayor's Award at Gracie Mansion in New York City, and the 2002 Award for Distinguished Service to the Arts from the American Academy of Arts and Letters, as well as honorary doctorates from Seton Hall University and Saint Peter's College.

Theological Postscript

1. *MandM*, 227.

2. Percy, *Thanatos Syndrome*, 361.

3. *MandM*, 72.

4. *MandM*, 111.

5. See FOC, *Presence of Grace*, 74, 94.

6. TeSelle, *Literature and the Christian Life*, 41, 43.

7. See *HB*, 132; see also Kilcourse, *Flannery O'Connor's Religious Imagination*, 114.

8. Kilcourse, *Flannery O'Connor's Religious Imagination*, 114.

9. Sarah Gordon, *Obedient Imagination*, 142.

10. Fitzgerald, introduction to FOC, *Everything That Rises Must Converge*, xxxiv.

11. Lynch, "Theology and Imagination II," 545.

12. FOC, *Presence of Grace*, 94.

13. See FOC, "The Nature and Aim of Fiction," *MandM*, 72–73; also FOC, "On Her Own Work," *MandM*, 111.

14. PU.

15. Srigley, *Flannery O'Connor's Sacramental Art*, 11.

16. Murray, *Problem of God*, 45.

17. Murray, *Problem of God*, 67–68.

18. In her article on "A Temple of the Holy Ghost," Denise T. Askin initially considers the reader an outsider to the Catholic theology of this story: "Further, the story is filled with pre-Vatican II Catholic 'insider' references and allusions," she writes. "Benediction; the monstrance; St. Scholastica, the brilliant sister of St. Benedict; St. Perpetua, the beautiful martyr in the arena with wild animals (who also had a prophetic vision of a kind of androgyny); St. Thomas, the 'dumb-ox' Scholastic; the Stations of the Cross; the legendary medieval miracle of the bloody host; and the Latin office of Corpus Christi. In this story, a vintage nun tells her charges how to handle fresh boys; the child's convent-school cousins sing the *Tantum Ergo* in Latin; and the protagonist herself winds up in the convent chapel kneeling next to a nun and recognizing that she is in the 'presence of God.' . . . Moving from the protagonist's childish derision to her transcendent epiphany, the story traces the child's initiation into sacramental vision and O'Connor's vocation as a Catholic comedic artist" (557).

19. See *HB*, 93, 438–39. I am grateful to Helen R. Andretta for sending me a copy of her essay "A Thomist's Letters to 'A'," presented at the American Literature Association's Conference, May 30, 1998, in San Diego, California.

20. Jordan Cofer, *The Gospel According to Flannery O'Connor: Examining the Role of the Bible in Flannery O'Connor's Fiction*, 3.

21. See Gooch's informative essay "Thirteenth-Century Lady."

22. See Barth, "Literature of Replenishment," 68. See also Joseph Feeney, "Can a Worldview Be Healed?" 12–16.

23. Kazin, *Bright Book of Life*, 58.

24. *MandM*, 27.

25. Sarah Gordon, *Obedient Imagination*, 214–15.

Ackroyd, Peter. *T. S. Eliot*. London: Hamish Hamilton, 1986.

Amason, Craig. "A View from the Woods: Preserving the Fortune of Andalusia." In *Ragione, Fiction e Fede: Convegno Internazionale su Flannery O'Connor*, edited by Enrique Fuster and John Wauck. 149–56. Rome, Italy: EDUSC (Pontificia Università della Santa Croce), 2011.

Arbus, Diane. *Diane Arbus: An Aperture Monograph*. Millerton, NY: Aperture, 1972.

Askin, Denise T. "Carnival in the 'Temple': Flannery O'Connor's Dialogic Parable of Artistic Vocation." *Christianity and Literature* 56, no. 4 (2007): 555–72.

Balée, Susan. *Flannery O'Connor: Literary Prophet of the South*. New York: Chelsea House, 1994.

Barth, John. "The Literature of Replenishment." *Atlantic* 245, no. 1 (1980): 65–71.

Basselin, Timothy J. *Flannery O'Connor: Writing a Theology of Disabled Humanity*. Waco, TX: Baylor University Press, 2013.

Bauer, Carlene. *Frances and Bernard*. New York: Houghton Mifflin Harcourt, 2013.

Bednar, G. C. "From Emptiness to Hunger: Lonergan, Lynch, and Conversion in the Works of Flannery O'Connor." *Renascence* 68, no. 3 (Summer 2016): 195–209.

Bellow, Saul. *Letters*. Edited by Benjamin Taylor. New York: Viking, 2010.

Berryman, John. *77 Dream Songs*. New York: Farrar, Straus & Giroux, 1964.

———. *Collected Poems: 1937–1971*. Edited by Charles Thornbury. New York: Farrar, Straus & Giroux, 1989.

———. *His Toy, His Dream, His Rest: 308 Dream Songs*. New York: Farrar, Straus & Giroux, 1968.

———. *Homage to Mistress Bradstreet*. New York: Farrar, Straus & Giroux, 1956.

Blotner, Joseph. "Did You See Him Plain?" In *Fifty Years of Yoknapatawpha: Faulkner and Yoknapatawpha, 1979*, edited by Doreen Fowler and Ann J. Abadie, 3–22. Jackson: University Press of Mississippi, 1980.

———. "The Sources of Faulkner's Genius." In *Fifty Years of Yoknapatawpha: Faulkner and Yoknapatawpha, 1979*, 248–70.

———. "William Faulkner: Life and Art." In *Faulkner and Women: Faulkner and Yoknapatawpha, 1985*, edited by Doreen Fowler and Ann J. Abadie, 3–20. Jackson: University Press of Mississippi, 1986.

Bosco, Mark, S.J. "Consenting to Love: Autobiographical Roots of 'Good Country People.'" *Southern Review* 41, no. 2 (2005): 283–95.

———. "Erik Langkjaer: The One Flannery 'Used to Go With.'" *Flannery O'Connor Review* 5 (2007): 44–55.

Bosco, Mark, S.J., and Brent Little, eds. *Revelation and Convergence: Flannery O'Connor and the Catholic Intellectual Tradition.* Washington, DC: Catholic University of America Press, 2017.

Brooks, Cleanth and Robert Penn Warren. *Understanding Fiction.* New York: Appleton-Century-Crofts, 1943.

———. *Understanding Poetry.* New York: Appleton-Century-Crofts, 1938.

Cash, Jean. *Flannery O'Connor: A Life.* Knoxville: University of Tennessee Press, 2002.

———. "O'Connor in the Iowa Writers' Workshop." *Flannery O'Connor Bulletin* 24 (1995–96): 67–75.

Ciuba, Gary M. *Desire, Violence and Divinity in Modern Southern Fiction: Katherine Anne Porter, Flannery O'Connor, Cormac McCarthy, Walker Percy.* Baton Rouge: Louisiana State University Press, 2007.

Cofer, Jordan. *The Gospel According to Flannery O'Connor: Examining the Role of the Bible in Flannery O'Connor's Fiction.* New York: Bloomsbury Academic, 2014.

Coindreau, Maurice-Edgar. Introduction to *La Sagesse dans le sang*, by Flannery O'Connor, translated by Maurice-Edgar Coindreau, vii–xxiii. Paris: Gallimard, 1959.

———. "Lettres de Flannery O'Connor à M. E. Coindreau." *Delta* 2 (Université de Montpellier, France: Mars 1976): 13–25.

———. *Mémoires d'un traducteur.* Interviews with Christian Guidicelli. Paris: Gallimard, 1974.

Daugherty, Tracy. *Just One Catch: A Biography of Joseph Heller.* New York: St. Martin's Press, 2011.

DeLorme, Rita H. "Alexander Semmes, Civil War surgeon and Catholic Priest, moved from battlefield to mission field." *Southern Cross* (Diocese of Savannah, GA: April 8, 2004): 3.

Desmond, John. *Risen Sons: Flannery O'Connor's Vision of History.* Athens: University of Georgia Press, 1987.

Doreski, William. *The Years of Our Friendship: Lowell and Tate.* Jackson: University Press of Mississippi, 1990.

Dunaway, John M., ed. *Exiles and Fugitives: The Letters of Jacques and Raïssa Maritain, Allen Tate, and Caroline Gordon.* Baton Rouge: Louisiana State University Press, 1992.

Dunn, Robert J., and Stephen G. Driggers, eds., with Sarah Gordon. *Manuscripts of Flannery O'Connor at Georgia College.* Athens: University of Georgia Press, 1989.

Edmondson, Henry T., III. *Return to Good and Evil: Flannery O'Connor's Response to Nihilism.* Lanham, MD: Lexington Books, 2005.

Elie, Paul. *The Life You Save May Be Your Own: An American Pilgrimage.* New York: Farrar, Straus & Giroux, 2003.

Eliot, T. S. *The Complete Poems and Plays.* New York: Harcourt, Brace, 1952.

Engle, Paul. *American Song: A Book of Poems.* Garden City, NY: Doubleday, 1934.

———. *Worn Earth.* New Haven: Yale University Press, 1932.

Faulkner, William. *Faulkner: Novels: 1930–1935.* Edited by Joseph Blotner and Noel Polk. New York: Library of America, 1985.

Feeney, Joseph, S.J. "Can a Worldview be Healed? Students and Postmodernism." *America* 177, no. 15 (November 15, 1977): 12–16.

Feeney, Martin, S.J. "Robert Giroux '31: A Great American Editor." *Regis Alumni News* 50 (New York: Regis High School, 1985): 8–9.

Fickett, Harold, and Douglas R. Gilbert. *Flannery O'Connor: Images of Grace.* Grand Rapids, MI: William B. Eerdmans, 1986.

Fitzgerald, Robert. "Flannery O'Connor: A Memoir." In *The Third Kind of Knowledge: Memoirs and Selected Writings of Robert Fitzgerald,* edited by Penelope Laurans Fitzgerald, 105–24. New York: New Directions, 1993.

———. "Gold and Gloom in Ezra Pound." In *Third Kind of Knowledge,* 138–45.

———. Introduction to *Everything That Rises Must Converge,* by Flannery O'Connor, 5–30. New York: Farrar, Straus & Giroux, 1965.

———. "Randall Jarrell: A Memoir." In *Third Kind of Knowledge,* 131–34.

Fitzgerald, Sally. "Flannery O'Connor: Patterns of Friendship, Patterns of Love." *Georgia Review* 52, no. 3 (1998): 407–25.

———. Introduction to *Three by Flannery O'Connor,* vii–xxxiv. New York: Signet, 1983.

———. "The Invisible Father." *Christianity & Literature* 47, no. 1 (1997): 5–18.

———. "Letter Watching." *Columns* (Georgia College & State University) 24 (1979): 4–7.

———. "A Master Class: From the Correspondence of Caroline Gordon and Flannery O'Connor." *Georgia Review* 33, no. 4 (1979): 827–46.

———. "Rooms with a View." *Katallagete* 8, no. 1 (1982): 4–11.

———. "Root and Branch: O'Connor of Georgia." *Georgia Historical Review* 64, no. 4 (1980): 377–87.

Flannery, Colleen D. "Genealogies of Select Flannerys in the U.S.: James Flannery and Margaret Dunn: Dolla, Silvermines, Nenagh, County Tipperary to Savannah, Georgia." Flannerys of Baltimore. 2002. http://www.angelfire.com/md3/flannery_bmore/captflannery_maryellennorton.htm.

Florencourt, Frances. "Interview with Robert Giroux." In *At Home with Flannery O'Connor: An Oral History*, edited by Marshall Bruce Gentry and Craig Amason, 83–90. Milledgeville, GA: The Flannery O'Connor-Andalusia Foundation, 2012.

Fodor, Sarah J. "Marketing Flannery O'Connor: Institutional Politics and Literary Evaluation." In *Flannery O'Connor: New Perspectives*, edited by Sarah P. Rath and Mary Neff Shaw, 12–37. Athens: University of Georgia Press, 1966.

Folks, Jeffrey J. "Flannery O'Connor in Her Letters: 'A Refugee from Deep Thought.'" *Modern Age* 47, no. 2 (2005): 176–80.

Friedman, Melvin J., and Lewis A. Lawson. *The Added Dimension: The Art and Mind of Flannery O'Connor*. New York: Fordham University Press, 1966.

Gentry, Marshall Bruce. *Flannery O'Connor's Religion of the Grotesque*. Jackson: University Press of Mississippi, 1986.

Getz, Lorine. *Flannery O'Connor: Her Life, Library and Book Reviews*. New York: Edwin Mellen Press, 1980.

Gilson, Étienne. *A Gilson Reader*. New York: Image Books, 1957.

Giroux, Robert. *The Book Known as Q: A Consideration of Shakespeare's Sonnets*. New York: Atheneum, 1982.

———. "The Education of an Editor: The 1981 R. R. Bowker Memorial Lecture." New York: R. R. Bowker Company, 1982.

———. "Flannery O'Connor." Talk at the Walter Reade Theater, Lincoln Center, New York, April 30, 2001. Private files of PS.

———. "Hard Years and 'Scary Days': Remembering Jean Stafford." *New York Times Book Review* 89 (June 10, 1984): 3, 28–29.

———. Introduction to *Complete Stories of Bernard Malamud*, by Bernard Malamud, ix–xv. New York: Farrar, Straus & Giroux, 1997.

———. Introduction to *Complete Stories of Flannery O'Connor*, by Flannery O'Connor, vii–xvii. New York: Farrar, Straus & Giroux, 1971.

———. Introduction to *The Seven Storey Mountain*, by Thomas Merton, O.C.S.O., xi–xvii. New York: Harcourt, Brace, 1988.

———. "The Poet in the Asylum." *Atlantic* 262, no. 2 (1988): 40–41, 44–45.

———. "Rescue at Truk." *Collier's* 113, no. 20 (May 13, 1944): 18–19, 80–81.

Giroux, Robert, Charles McKinley, Robert Dana, and Saskia Hamilton. "Celebration of Robert Lowell." *Kenyon Review* 22, no. 1 (2000): 255–74.

Gish, Robert. *Paul Horgan*. Boston: Twayne, 1983.

Gooch, Brad. *Flannery: A Life of Flannery O'Connor*. New York: Little, Brown, 2009.

———. "Thirteenth-Century Lady." *Flannery O'Connor Review* 5 (2007): 23–34.

Goodwin, James. *Modern American Grotesque: Literature and Photography.* Columbus: Ohio State University Press, 2009.

Gordon, Caroline. "Heresy in Dixie." *Sewanee Review* 76, no. 2 (1968): 263–97.

———. *The Malefactors.* New York: Harcourt, Brace, 1956.

———. "Rebels and Revolutionaries: The New American Scene." *Flannery O'Connor Bulletin* 3 (1974): 40–56.

Gordon, Caroline, and Allen Tate, eds. *The House of Fiction: An Anthology of the Short Story with Commentary.* New York: Charles Scribner's Sons, 1950.

Gordon, Sarah. *Flannery O'Connor: The Obedient Imagination.* Athens: University of Georgia Press, 2000.

———. "Milledgeville: The Perils of Place as a Text." *Flannery O'Connor Bulletin* 20 (1991): 73–87.

Greene, Helen. "Mary Flannery O'Connor: One Teacher's Happy Memory." *Flannery O'Connor Bulletin* 19 (1990): 44–48.

Gresset, Michel. "Interview with Maurice-Edgar Coindreau." *Delta* 2 (Université de Montpellier, France: March 1976): 3–11.

Haddox, Thomas F. "Contextualizing Flannery O'Connor: Allen Tate, Caroline Gordon, and the Catholic Turn in Southern Literature." *Southern Quarterly* 38, no. 1 (1999): 173–90.

Hamilton, Ian. *Robert Lowell: A Biography.* New York: Random House, 1982.

Hardwick, Elizabeth. *Sleepless Nights.* New York: Random House, 1979.

Hartwell, Joe. "Pvt. Dick Steenhoek: Company K Runner, 325th Infantry, 82nd Division: WWI 1917–1919." *Remembering the Sounds of My Grandfather's Footsteps.* November 23, 2005. http://freepages.military.rootsweb.ancestry.com/~cacunithistories/Pvt_Steenhoek.html.

Hawkes, John. "Flannery O'Connor's Devil." *Sewanee Review* 70, no. 3 (1962): 395–407.

Hawkins, Peter. *The Language of Grace: Flannery O'Connor, Walker Percy, and Iris Murdoch.* New York: Seabury Classics, 2004.

Horgan, Paul. *Tracings.* New York: Farrar, Straus & Giroux, 1993.

Hulbert, Ann. *The Interior Castle: The Art and Life of Jean Stafford.* New York: Knopf, 1992.

Kahane, Claire. "The Re-vision of Rage: Flannery O'Connor and Me." *Massachusetts Review* 46, no. 3 (2005): 439–61.

Kane, John F. *Building the Human City: William F. Lynch's Ignatian Spirituality for Public Life.* Eugene, OR: Pickwick Publications, 2016.

Kazin, Alfred. *Bright Book of Life: American Novelists from Hemingway to Mailer.* Boston: Little, Brown, 1973.

———. *New York Jew.* New York: Knopf, 1978.

———. *On Native Grounds.* New York: Reynal & Hitchcock, 1942.

———. *Writing Was Everything.* Cambridge, MA: Harvard University Press, 1995.

Kelly, Gerald. "The World of Cartoons and Their Importance to O'Connor's Fiction." In *Flannery O'Connor's Radical Reality*, edited by Jan Nordby Gretlund and Karl-Heinz Westarp, 26–41. Columbia: University of South Carolina Press, 2006.

Kilcourse, George A., Jr. *Flannery O'Connor's Religious Imagination: A World with Everything Off Balance*. Mahwah, NJ: Paulist Press, 2001.

Kirk, Connie Ann. *Critical Companion to Flannery O'Connor*. New York: Facts on File, 2008.

Kreyling, Michael. "A Good Monk is Hard to Find." In *Flannery O'Connor's Radical Reality*, edited by Jan Nordby Gretlund and Karl-Heinz Westarp, 1–17. Columbia: University of South Carolina Press, 2006.

Lake, Christiana Bieber. *The Incarnational Art of Flannery O'Connor*. Macon, GA: Mercer University Press, 2005.

Lawson, Lewis A., and Victor A. Kramer, eds. *Conversations with Walker Percy*. Jackson: University Press of Mississippi, 1985.

Lensing, George S. "Elizabeth Bishop and Flannery O'Connor." In *Elizabeth Bishop in the 21st Century: Reading the New Editions*, edited by Angus Cleghorn, Bethany Hicok, and Thomas Travisano, 186–203. Charlottesville: University of Virginia Press, 2012.

Lowell, Robert. *Collected Poems*. Edited by Frank Bidart and David Gewanter. New York: Farrar, Straus & Giroux, 2003.

———. *Collected Prose*. Edited by Robert Giroux. New York: Farrar Straus & Giroux, 1987.

———. *Letters of Robert Lowell*. Edited by Saskia Hamilton. New York: Farrar, Straus & Giroux, 2005.

———. "Visiting the Tates." *Sewanee Review* 67, no. 4 (1959): 557–59.

Lynch, William, S.J. *Christ and Apollo: The Dimensions of the Literary Imagination*. New York: Sheed & Ward, 1960.

———. *The Integrating Mind: An Exploration into Western Thought*. New York: Sheed & Ward, 1962.

———. "Theology and Imagination." *Thought* 29, no. 112 (1954): 61–86; "Theology and Imagination II: The Evocative Symbol." *Thought* 29, no. 115 (1954–55): 529–54; "Theology and Imagination III: The Problem of Comedy." *Thought* 30, no. 116 (1955): 18–36; "The Imagination and the Finite." *Thought* 33, no. 129 (1958): 205–28.

Lytle, Andrew. "Caroline Gordon and the Historic Image." *Sewanee Review* 57, no. 4 (1949): 560–86.

Magee, Rosemary M., ed. *Conversations with Flannery O'Connor*. Jackson: University Press of Mississippi, 1987.

Makowsky, Veronica A. *Caroline Gordon: A Biography*. New York: Oxford University Press, 1989.

Mariani, Paul. *Dream Song: The Life of John Berryman*. New York: William Morrow and Company, 1990.

———. *Lost Puritan: A Life of Robert Lowell*. New York: W. W. Norton, 1996.

———. "'My Heavy Daughter': John Berryman and the Making of 'The Dream Songs.'" *Kenyon Review* 10, no. 3 (1988): 1–30.

Maritain, Jacques. *Art and Scholasticism with Other Essays*. London: Sheed & Ward, 1930.

May, John R. "The Violent Bear It Away: The Meaning of the Title." *Flannery O'Connor Bulletin* 2 (1973): 83–86.

———, ed. "Blue-Bleak Embers: The Letters of Flannery O'Connor and Youree Watson." *New Orleans Review* 6, no. 4 (1979): 336–56.

McAlexander, Hubert. *Peter Taylor: A Writer's Life*. Baton Rouge: Louisiana State University Press, 2001.

McCullen, Joanne Halleran, and Jon Parish Peede, eds. *Inside the Church of Flannery O'Connor: Sacrament, Sacramental, and the Sacred in Her Fiction*. Macon, GA: Mercer University Press, 2007.

McGill, Robert. "The Life You Write May Be Your Own: Epistolary Autobiography and the Reluctant Resurrection of Flannery O'Connor." *Southern Literary Journal* 36, no. 2 (2004): 31–46.

Merton, Thomas, O.C.S.O. "Flannery O'Connor: A Prose Elegy." *Jubilee* 12, no. 7 (1964): 49–53.

———. *The Seven Storey Mountain*. New York: Harcourt, Brace, 1948.

Michaels, J. Ramsey. *Passing by the Dragon: The Biblical Tales of Flannery O'Connor*. Eugene, OR: Cascade Books, 2013.

Miss, Stephen, and Patrick Samway, S.J. "The Failure of *The Charterhouse*: Foote, Gordon, and Tate and the Literary Apprenticeship of Walker Percy." *Literature and Belief* 16, no. 2 (1997): 51–84.

Mizener, Arthur. *The Saddest Story: A Biography of Ford Madox Ford*. London: Bodley Head, 1971.

Moran, Daniel. *Creating Flannery O'Connor: Her Critics, Her Publishers, Her Readers*. Athens: University of Georgia Press, 2016.

Mounier, Emmanuel. *Personalism*. Translated by Philip Mairet. New York: Grove Press, 1952.

Murray, John Courtney, S.J. *The Problem of God*. New Haven: Yale University Press, 1964.

O'Connor, Flannery. *Collected Works* (*Wise Blood, A Good Man is Hard to Find, The Violent Bear It Away, Everything That Rises Must Converge, Stories and Occasional Prose, Letters*). Edited by Sally Fitzgerald. New York: Library of America, 1988.

———. "Fiction is a Subject with a History—It Should be Taught That Way." *Collected Works of Flannery O'Connor*, 849–52.

———. *The Habit of Being: Letters of Flannery O'Connor*. Edited by Sally Fitzgerald. New York: Farrar, Straus & Giroux, 1979.

———. Introduction to *A Memoir of Mary Ann*, by the Dominican Nuns Who Took Care of Her, 3–21. New York: Farrar, Straus & Cudahy, 1961.

————. "The King of the Birds" (originally titled "Living with a Peacock"). *Holiday* 30, no. 52 (1961): 52, 110–12, 114.

————. *Mystery and Manners: Occasional Prose.* Edited by Sally and Robert Fitzgerald. New York: Farrar, Straus & Cudahy, 1969.

————. *A Prayer Journal.* Edited by William A. Sessions. New York: Farrar, Straus & Giroux, 2013.

————. *The Presence of Grace and Other Book Reviews.* Compiled by Leo J. Zuber; edited by Carter W. Martin. Athens: University of Georgia Press, 1983.

————. *La Sagesse dans le sang.* Translated by Maurice-Edgar Coindreau. Paris: Gallimard, 1959.

————. *Three by Flannery O'Connor.* Edited by Sally Fitzgerald. New York: Signet, 1983.

————. *Wise Blood.* 2nd ed. with author note. New York: Farrar, Straus & Cudahy, 1962. First published 1952 by Harcourt, Brace.

————. "The Writer and the Graduate School." *Alumnae Journal: Georgia State College for Women* 13 (June 1948): 4.

O'Gorman, Farrell. *Peculiar Crossroads: Flannery O'Connor, Walker Percy, and Catholic Vision in Postwar Southern Fiction.* Baton Rouge: Louisiana State University Press, 2004.

O'Hare, Christopher. "Interview with Robert Giroux." Unpublished transcript, 2000. RGF.

Percy, Walker. *The Charterhouse.* Walker Percy Collection. Louis Round Wilson Library. University of North Carolina at Chapel Hill (Unpublished novel).

————. *The Thanatos Syndrome.* New York: Farrar, Straus & Giroux, 1987.

Plimpton, George. "Robert Giroux: The Art of Publishing III." *Paris Review* 42, no. 155 (2000): 161–91.

Price, Ruth. *The Lives of Agnes Smedley.* New York: Oxford University Press, 2005.

Prown, Katherine Hemple. *Revising Flannery O'Connor: Southern Literary Culture and the Problem of Female Authorship.* Charlottesville: University of Virginia Press, 2001.

Quinn, John J., S.J., ed. *Flannery O'Connor: A Memorial.* Scranton, PA: University of Scranton Press, 1995. See also *Esprit* 8, no. 1 (University of Scranton, Winter 1964): 12–49, for guest tributes.

Ragen, Brian. *A Wreck on the Road to Damascus: Innocence, Guilt, and Conversion in Flannery O'Connor.* Chicago: Loyola University Press, 1989.

Ryan, Elizabeth Shreve. "I Remember Mary Flannery." *Flannery O'Connor Bulletin* 19 (1990): 49–52.

Samway, Patrick, S.J. "Jesuit Influence in the Life and Works of Flannery O'Connor." Lecture at the 2004 Hopkins Literary Festival, Monasterevin, Ireland. www.gerardmanleyhopkins.org/lectures_2004/jesuit_influence.html.

————, ed. *The Letters of Robert Giroux and Thomas Merton*. Notre Dame, IN: University of Notre Dame Press, 2015.

————. "Review of Flannery O'Connor's *A Prayer Journal*." *Flannery O'Connor Review* 12 (2014): 117–19.

————. "Toward Discerning How Flannery O'Connor's Fiction Can Be Considered 'Roman Catholic.'" In *Flannery O'Connor's Radical Reality*, edited by Jan Nordby Gretlund and Karl-Heinz Westarp, 162–75. Columbia: University of South Carolina Press, 2006.

————. "Tracing a Literary & Epistolary Relationship: Eudora Welty and Her Editor, Robert Giroux." *Eudora Welty Review* 8 (Spring 2016): 37–76.

————. *Walker Percy: A Life*. New York: Farrar, Straus & Giroux, 1997.

Schwartz, Lawrence. "Launching Flannery O'Connor: The Rockefeller Foundation and a Literary Reputation." *Mississippi Quarterly* 68, no. 1–2 (Winter–Spring 2015): 213–34.

Scott, R. Neil, and Irwin H. Streight, eds. *Flannery O'Connor: The Contemporary Reviews*. Cambridge: Cambridge University Press, 2009.

Sessions, William A. "*Shenandoah* and the Advent of Flannery O'Connor." *Shenandoah: A Tribute to Flannery O'Connor* 60, no. 1–2 (2010): 229–41.

Simpson, Eileen. *Poets in Their Youth: A Memoir*. New York: Random House, 1982.

Sontag, Susan. *On Photography*. New York: Farrar, Straus & Giroux, 1977.

Souhami, Diana. *Gertrude and Alice*. London: Pandora, 1991.

Srigley, Susan. "'Far Away From God': Flannery O'Connor's Struggles with a Demanding Faith." *America* 213, no. 1 (July 6–13, 2015): 28–30.

————. *Flannery O'Connor's Sacramental Art*. Notre Dame, IN: University of Notre Dame Press, 2004.

Stafford, Jean. "Influx of Poets." *New Yorker* 54, no. 38 (November 6, 1978): 43–52, 55–56, 58, 60.

Stephens, Ralph C., ed. *The Correspondence of Flannery O'Connor and the Brainard Cheneys*. Jackson: University Press of Mississippi, 1986.

Straus, Dorothea. *The Paper Trail: A Recollection of Writers*. Wakefield, RI: Moyer Bell, 1997.

Tate, Allen. *Collected Poems: 1919–1976*. New York: Farrar, Straus & Giroux, 1977.

————. "Miss Emily and the Bibliographer." In *Essays of Four Decades*, by Allen Tate, 141–54. Chicago: Swallow Press, 1968.

Teilhard de Chardin, Pierre, S.J. *The Divine Milieu: An Essay on the Inner Life*. Translated by Bernard Wall. New York: Harper & Brothers, 1959.

————. *The Phenomenon of Man*. Translated by Bernard Wall. New York: Harper & Brothers, 1959.

TeSelle, Sallie McFague. *Literature and the Christian Life*. New Haven, CT: Yale University Press, 1966.

Vinh, Alphonse, ed. *Cleanth Brooks and Allen Tate: Collected Letters: 1933–76*. Columbia: University of Missouri Press, 1998.

Waldron, Ann. *Close Connections: Caroline Gordon and the Southern Renaissance.* New York: Putnam, 1987.

Warren, Austin and René Wellek. *Theory of Literature.* New York: Harcourt, Brace & World, 1949.

Watkins, Steven R. *Flannery O'Connor and Teilhard de Chardin: A Journey Together Towards Hope and Understanding About Life.* New York: Peter Lang, 2009.

Watson, Jay. "Escapes and Diversions, Whoring and Trash: Two Case Studies in Aesthetics, Psychology, and Economics of the Twentieth-Century American Short Story." *Flannery O'Connor Review* 8 (2010): 5–21.

Welty, Eudora. *The Optimist's Daughter.* New York: Random House, 1972.

———. "Place in Fiction." In *The Eye of the Story,* by Eudora Welty, 116–33. New York: Random House, 1978.

Westarp, Karl-Heinz. *Precision and Depth in Flannery O'Connor's Stories.* Aarhus, Denmark: Aarhus University Press, 2002.

Westling, Louise. "Flannery O'Connor's Mothers and Daughters." *Twentieth-Century Literature* 24, no. 4 (1978): 510–22.

Whitt, Margaret Early. *Understanding Flannery O'Connor.* Columbia: University of South Carolina Press, 2004.

Wilkes, Paul. "Interview with Robert Giroux." In *Merton by Those Who Knew Him Best,* edited by Paul Wilkes, 15–27. New York: Harper & Row, 1984.

Wood, Ralph C. *Flannery O'Connor and the Christ-Haunted South.* Grand Rapids, MI: William B. Eerdmans, 2004.

Wray, Virginia. "Flannery O'Connor on the West Side: Dr. Lyman Fulton's Recollections of a Short Acquaintance: Interview with Virginia Wray." *English Language Notes* 39, no. 1 (2001): 71–78.

———. "The Importance of Home to the Fiction of Flannery O'Connor." *Renascence* 47, no. 2 (1995): 103–15.

Yaghjian, Lucretia B. "Flannery O'Connor's Use of Symbol, Roger Haight's Christology, and the Religious Writer." *Theological Studies* 63, no. 2 (2002): 268–301.

Young, Daniel Thomas, and Elizabeth Sarcone, eds. *Lytle-Tate Letters: The Correspondence of Andrew Lytle and Allen Tate.* Jackson: University Press of Mississippi, 1987.

"Good Country People" (O'Connor),
136–39, 150–51, 163
"Good Man Is Hard to Find, A"
(O'Connor), 251, 254n29
Good Man Is Hard to Find, A
(O'Connor)
  British rights to, 179
  Carver's role in, 150, 155, 156, 169
  composition of, 138–39
  contract for, 134–35, 155–61, 163–64
  German publication of, 265n22
  Giroux as editor of, 147–48
  order of stories in, 136–38
  reviews of, 2, 161, 169, 269n11
  sales of, 162, 168
  television rights, 180
  writing of, 133
Gordon, Caroline (CG)
  background of, 43
  conversion to Catholicism, 109
  critical attention of, 115–16
  critique of *Wise Blood*, 42–43, 106–7,
    112–14, 121
  on the fourfold sense of Scripture,
    243
  friendship with O'Connor, 102,
    259n72
  "How Not to Write Short Stories,"
    116
  impact on O'Connor's career,
    42–43, 71–72
  The Malefactors, 174, 176–77
  marriage to Tate, 43, 44, 45–46,
    259n80
  mentorship of O'Connor, 23,
    108–11, 227–28
  Penhally, 44
  "Rebels and Revolutionaries," 114
  relationship with Giroux, 46
  relationship with Lowell, 41–42,
    45–46
  relationship with Stafford, 45–46

  review of *Wise Blood*, 124
  The Strange Children, 127
  visits with O'Connor, 232–33
  visit to Milledgeville, 203
Gordon, Sarah, 75, 83, 250
Goyen, William, 121
Great Depression, 7, 61–62
Greene, Helen, 27, 150
"Greenleaf" (O'Connor), 42, 178, 231,
  233–34
Gresset, Michel, 192
Guggenheim Fellowship, 2, 35, 96,
  109, 147, 168

Habit of Being, The (O'Connor), 8, 48,
  236, 247
Hall, Eileen, 239–40
Harcourt, Alfred, 87, 141
Harcourt, Brace
  bias against Catholic Church, 140,
    237
  and *The Catcher in the Rye*, 91–92
  Giroux as editor in chief, 89–93
  Giroux as junior editor, 86–88
  Giroux's resignation from, 91,
    139–41
  A Good Man Is Hard to Find con-
    tract, 155–61, 163–64
  under Jovanovich, 90–93, 140
  Lindley's resignation from, 2,
    182–83
  literary focus of, 2
  and Malamud, 92–93
  O'Connor's decision to stay with,
    175
  O'Connor's departure from, 186–88
  O'Connor's initial interest in, 36,
    37
  and *The Seven Storey Mountain*,
    89–90
  and Thomas Merton, 89–90,
    268n34

PATRICK SAMWAY, S.J., professor emeritus of English at St. Joseph's University in Philadelphia, is the author or editor/co-editor of thirteen books, including *The Letters of Robert Giroux and Thomas Merton* (University of Notre Dame Press, 2015) and *Walker Percy: A Life*, selected by the *New York Times Book Review* as one of the notable books of 1997.

CPSIA information can be obtained
at www.ICGtesting.com
Printed in the USA
LVOW11*0748030518

575825LV00005B/37/P

9 780268 103095